Penguin Special S265
The Politics of Harold Wilson

KU-769-787

Paul Foot was born in Haifa, Palestine, in 1937. He had his early education in Jamaica, but later went to Shrewsbury and then University College, Oxford, where he was Editor of *Isis* and President of the Union. After Oxford he went to Glasgow for three years as a feature writer on the *Scottish Daily Record*. He became an active trade unionist in the National Union of Journalists and was a delegate to the Glasgow Trades Council for two years.

After six months working for the *Sun*, Paul Foot wrote for the Mandrake column of the *Sunday Telegraph*. He now works on *Private Eye*, for which he writes the 'Footnotes'. He is the author of the Penguin Special *Immigration and Race in British Politics*, published in 1965. Paul Foot is married and has two children.

Paul Foot

The Politics of Harold Wilson

Penguin Books

Penguin Books Ltd, Harmondsworth, Middlesex, England
Penguin Books Australia Ltd, Ringwood, Victoria, Australia

First published 1968
Copyright © Paul Foot, 1968

Made and printed in Great Britain by
Hunt Barnard & Co. Ltd, Aylesbury
Set in Monotype Times

This book is sold subject to the condition that
it shall not, by way of trade or otherwise, be lent,
re-sold, hired out, or otherwise circulated without
the publisher's prior consent in any form of
binding or cover other than that in which it is
published and without a similar condition
including this condition being imposed on the
subsequent purchaser

Contents

Acknowledgement

For permission to quote from Hansard,
the author would like to thank Her Majesty's
Stationery Office.

Introduction

The shock of full employment and apparently permanent economic growth anaesthetized political journalism in the 1950s. In Britain, America and Germany the new prosperity produced conservative Governments and liberal, impotent Oppositions. Eisenhower, Adenauer, Churchill and Macmillan presided in grandfatherly bonhomie over conservative affluence, while political reporters, journalists and theorists wrestled with old weapons of analysis. (In Britain, hardly a political book of any significance was written. The only exceptions were John Strachey's *Contemporary Capitalism* and Anthony Crosland's *The Future of Socialism*.) Issues were still important in politics but which issues and with what emphasis was not clear. Political correspondents and authors became drugged by the atmosphere of affluence and were aroused only, briefly, by the last despairing act of British imperialism – at Suez.

The first faint faltering in the post-war economic growth in Britain – the recessions of 1956 and 1957 – produced stirrings of radicalism in political journalists and thinkers. Demands for 'change' were expressed very much in the 'thrusting' language of advertising which, by 1957 and 1958, had entered the homes of most British people through the medium of television. Dynamic personalities on the television screen presented what most people knew to be a pack of lies but what seemed attractive because of its urgent presentation. Similarly, in politics. Politicians, political journalists and commentators throughout the Western world began to proclaim a 'new radicalism' in advertising terms. The demands gathered pace and vehemence as the 1950s came to an end. Old socialist 'dogmas' and conservative reaction were systematically replaced by the 'throbbing' rhetoric of 'change'.

These demands and this rhetoric first penetrated the public consciousness in the campaign, which started in the autumn of 1959, of John F. Kennedy for the Presidency of the United States. The professors and journalists who rallied to Kennedy portrayed his challenge, from the outset, as a challenge of dynamism against sluggishness; of change against decay. The change was defined mainly in nationalist terms – the need to 'make America greater'. Yet it maintained a grip on the imagination, if not of the American people, at least of her political journalists.

The story of the 1960 Kennedy campaign has been told in minutest detail by Theodore H. White, in his book *The Making of the President, 1960* (Athenaeum, 1961; Cape, 1962), whose hard-back edition sold 200,000 copies in America, and whose impact in Britain was no less great.

Theodore White understood better than most the central feature of American Presidential elections, that they are conflicts, not of issues, but of organizations and personalities. The enthusiasm which American elections excite is almost wholly organizational. The structure of the two main Parties, loose confederations bound together by old allegiances, many of them irrelevant by modern political criteria, is so organized that the selection of the two candidates and the election campaign between them is based entirely on organization, on public relations and on personalities.

As White admits of the 1960 campaign:

Rarely in American history has there been a political campaign that discussed issues less or clarified them less (*Making of the President, 1960*, p. 291).

Of the opening season of the Kennedy campaign, White says:

At this moment they [the Kennedy campaign organization] were interested not in what they could do with the power of America, but how it might be seized: *a completely different problem* [my italics] (ibid., p. 28).

How to write a 'narrative history of American politics in action' without writing about politics: this was Theodore White's problem. And he solved it with a journalistic technique which became the prototype of political journalism in the English language for several years.

The first essential of the technique is the portrayal of the leading personalities in larger-than-life images, with the use of liberally dispensed adjectives and superlatives. Thus, in White's book, almost all of Kennedy's aides are 'brilliant', 'indefatigable', 'hulking', 'prolific'. The praise for Kennedy himself knows no bounds, and topples again and again into hero-worship:

Kennedy loped into the cottage **with** his light, dancing step, as young and lithe as springtime, and called a greeting to those who stood in his way. (ibid., p. 171).

He let his mind travel an ungoverned span of thoughts which came and went as his mind flicked across the country. It was the range, the extent, the depth and detail of information and observation, that dazzled, then overwhelmed the listener (ibid., p. 144).

These giants of intellect, humour and oratory moved in a rarefied world, where every detail of their habits, characteristics and preferences were faithfully chronicled by their roving Boswell. Theodore White perfected the technique which *Time* magazine had started before the war of 'setting the scene' for great events. The two most important scene-setting subjects are food and the weather:

In March, as the primary approached, Wisconsin still lay beneath its snow. The snow stretched in a crystal carpet all across the hills as the plane flew west from New York, a white blanket across the slopes of the Appalachians, embroidered by the black and leafless trees; the snow covered the gray ice of the frozen lakes, just beginning to show the seams and cracks of coming thaw; the snow covered Wisconsin.

It had, in short, been snowing. But wait:

Under the snow it is impossible to tell poor farm from rich farm, for snow forces farmers to shelter automobiles and equipment indoors; the snow gives a white uniformity to the landscape, to dairy farm and corn farm, to German-American and Polish-American homestead, to Anglo stock, to Scandinavian stock, to Catholic and Protestant (ibid., pp. 82, 83).

Against such lurid backcloths, the drama unfolds, and the audience soon discovers that the heroes, the god-like creatures with steps like springtime, eat and sleep like ordinary people. Kennedy, for instance, liked soup.

The stewardess brought him a steaming bowl of hot tomato soup; with complete relish he stirred in a thick gob of sour cream and supped. At almost any moment of afternoon and evening on the road, soup is the favourite Kennedy dish – almost any kind of soup; chicken soup, tomato soup, bean soup and . . . his favourite New England clam chowder (ibid., p. 145).

The soup theme crops up again and again, as do the most detailed descriptions of the Kennedy breakfast (see pp. 168, 172, 252 and 253). No detail is too irrelevant to include in this exhilarating chronicle: for, however banal, each detail proved that the journalist himself was actually *there*. He too moved with the gods and he could bring any literate American right into the Kennedy compound at Hyannisport or the cabin of the Kennedy campaign plane as it travelled from cheering crowd to cheering crowd, over the white snow, the blue sea, the green valleys or whatever.

Perhaps the best example of White's political journalism is his chapter on the television debates between the two Presidential candidates. Throughout the chapter White does not mention a political issue, and admits that the television debates between the candidates were about personalities, not politics. What mattered above all was the make-up used by the candidates, and the colour of the backdrop:

The Vice-President, to begin with, suffers from a handicap that is serious only on television – his is a light, naturally transparent skin. . . . On television, the camera on Nixon is usually held away from him, for in close-up his transparent skin shows the tiniest hair growing in the skin follicles beneath the surface, even after he has just shaved. And for the night of the first debate, CBS, understandably zealous, had equipped its cameras with brand-new tubes for the most perfect projection that could only be harmful to the Vice-President. (In the later debates Nixon was persuaded to wear theatrical make-up to repair the ravage TV's electronic tube made of his countenance; but for this first debate he wore only 'Lazy Shave') (ibid., p. 289).

The patchwork quilt of irrelevancy, sycophancy and personalization is stitched together by the organizational excitement of the contest. This gives the same thrill as the Western Novel or the Great Sport Series; it is the fight between Goodies and Baddies; Cowboys and Indians; Rovers against Rangers. And, the right man, *our* team, wins.

But, object the Theodore White fans, this is good journalism.

This is what *does* happen in American politics, and this is therefore how it ought to be portrayed. On the contrary, however, there is nothing objective about White's journalism. The nature of his style and language shows how irretrievably he is trapped by the glamour of his subject. White's book ventures only very briefly into a discussion of real political issues, but, where it does, he betrays the patronizing elitism of the Kennedy clan. When discussing West Virginia, for instance, he tells us that the Negroes are 'treated with respect and good manners' (p. 100), and tells us how his candidate, 'fresh from a brief rest at Montego Bay, Jamaica, could scarcely bring himself to believe that human beings were forced to eat and live on these cans of dry relief rations'. At the end of the book, assessing 'crowd response', he talks angrily of crowds in places like the Congo, who 'forced their way into decisions that were none of their business, and thus warped reason and order'. Politics, after all, should be left to the politicians, while the crowds cheer in meaningless adoration.

The political journalist's most valuable weapon is his scepticism; his ability to measure the words, promises and hypocrisy of public life against the reality. White's book, like the political journalism which it unleashed in Britain and America, has no scepticism. It is adulatory and sycophantic. Far from reporting accurately, it conjures controversy out of conformity; involvement out of psephology; change out of decay; integrity out of corruption; excitement out of banality; originality out of cliché; radicalism out of sentimentality; toughness out of anti-Communism; and politics out of public relations.

By the time Theodore White settled down to write *The Making of the President, 1964*, the technique was almost useless. The rhetoric of Kennedy's New Frontier had to be balanced with the reality: Kennedy's refusal to 'move too fast' on civil rights; his inauguration of America's heavy military commitment in Vietnam (especially the formation of the 'efficient' and brutal Special Forces); his invasion of the Bay of Pigs. Johnson's defeat of Goldwater in 1964, portrayed once more by White as a victory of Good over Evil, was immediately followed by the wholesale acceptance of Goldwater policies in Vietnam, the Caribbean and Latin America. By 1968, as yet another Presidential contest looms, the facts of American politics are outpacing the frantic electioneering of the candidates. Before long, real issues will have to be faced and answered.

Nevertheless, in 1961, even before White's book was published in the autumn, the myth of the New Frontier had crossed the Atlantic. In the *Observer* of 19 and 26 March 1961, for instance, Michael Davie wrote two long articles, entitled 'Washington on the Move', making full use of the 'change' rhetoric and 'larger than life' personalities which had inspired the Kennedy campaign. 'Change', 'dynamism' and 'the New Frontier' were rapidly absorbed into British politics. Mr Anthony Crosland, for instance, in *Encounter*, and in his book *The Conservative Enemy*, demanded an end to 'old-style' politics, both of Left and Right, and called for a dynamic 'revolution'. In the summer of 1962, White's book was published in Britain. In the same summer, *Anatomy of Britain* by Anthony Sampson followed White's example by raising mediocrities and public relations bureaucrats to almost ethereal prominence. On the *Observer*, Sampson concentrated on the Daylight column, which experimented in the new form of 'blow by blow', chunky journalism which White had perfected. Daylight's classic adventures into 'digging' stories dealt with the Cuba crisis, in November 1962, and the sterling crisis of November 1964.[1]

Similarly, the *Sunday Times*, on the day that Harold Wilson became leader of the Labour Party, started its more serious and more successful Insight column. The battle for the Tory leadership after the resignation of Harold Macmillan the following autumn was appropriately entitled 'The Making of a Prime Minister'. The 'supporters' of each contender, Hogg, Home, Butler and Maudling, 'fought it out' in the corridors of Blackpool hotels just as the crusaders for Johnson, Kennedy, Symington and Stevenson had fought in Los Angeles in 1960. The 1964 General Election was reported in the Theodore White tradition, with the accent on irrelevant detail. By the time Edward Heath replaced

1. The latter opened, ominously: 'Nine days ago a dark cloud growing on the financial horizon started to mushroom at frightening speed . . . ', and continued in like vein, including the memorable sentence, 'On Monday, 16 November, white-tied Wilson delivered reassuring words about keeping the pound "riding high", speaking in a hot-bed of City gents and turtle soup – the Guildhall.' This quotation, and many others of equal richness, have already been included in Christopher Booker's magnum opus, *The Neophiliacs*, to be published shortly.

Sir Alec Douglas Home in July 1965, Insight had returned to the breakfasts – and the weather:

> At 8.27 on Friday morning he [Sir Alec] stepped off the night sleeper in Berwick to drive the fourteen miles to his beloved Hirsel. But there was no respite for him there. At 9.30 on Sunday morning, the newspapers arrived: the *Sunday Times*, the *Sunday Telegraph*, the *Sunday Express*, the *Sunday Post*. Mulling over them, among the remains of a porridge-and-eggs breakfast, Sir Alec reached the turning point. . . .
>
> That afternoon, though, he ambled again into the gardens to be alone, wandering about cutting roses. By the time the weather changed, his mind seemed made up.
>
> He came briskly into the drawing room and started re-writing his speeches (*Sunday Times*, 25 July 1965).[1]

Yet if the *Sunday Times* and the *Observer* were ideal receptacles for the dynamic journalism of Theodore White, the techniques of the Kennedy Mafia were not wholly applicable to British politics, nor to the British Labour Party. For, unlike the Democratic Party in America, the British Labour Party was founded on class lines, with a clear purpose of assisting the cause of working-class people through Parliamentary endeavour. Elections had been fought, won and lost, not on 'dynamic' rhetoric or even on growth, but on issues: on plans for 'fair shares', for nationalizing certain industries, for improving welfare services, for redistributing wealth. The boyish enthusiasm of a millionaire Senator might appeal to the suburbs of Michigan and win approval in Democratic caucuses, but Kennedy tactics were not immediately appealing to the sturdy rank and file of the British Labour Party.

Yet the Labour leadership, particularly Harold Wilson, watched the Kennedy election of 1960 with considerable interest. The Kennedy style was both attractive and victorious. Pundit after pundit had informed the Labour Party leadership that it had lost the General Election of 1959 because its policies and 'image' were 'out of date'. Hugh Gaitskell's answer to this problem was to seek to change the Party's policies; Wilson's to seek to change its image. When Wilson became leader of the Party in 1963, he set to work playing down the traditional emphases of British Labour –

1. The *Sunday Times* Insight column soon broke away from the 'smoke-filled rooms' style of reporting to deal more seriously and with much greater effect with genuine political issues.

on equality, on welfare, on fighting issues rather than personalities – and introduced the Kennedy rhetoric of 'dynamism and change'. His speeches at the Scarborough Labour Party Conference in 1963 and at Birmingham on 19 January 1964 established this rhetoric as the new language of British Labour. The switch delighted no one more than the journalists and the communicators, whom Wilson cultivated as carefully as Kennedy had done. Unanimously, and totally without scepticism, they helped to build up the image of a new, dynamic Labour leadership bursting to get Britain 'on the move'.

The journalists and commentators were followed by authors. In the spring and summer of 1964 three biographies of Harold Wilson were written. The fullest of these was by a right-wing Conservative MP, Dudley Smith, who lost his seat in the 1964 election, and won another one in a by-election in 1968 (*Harold Wilson: A Critical Biography*, Hale, 1964). Although Smith had a considerable regard for his subject, his political upbringing and approach made it almost impossible for him to understand or appreciate the role of Harold Wilson in the Labour Party. Dudley Smith's obvious antagonism to Aneurin Bevan and his obsession with Parliamentary procedure and geography ('he sat on the third row under the gangway') further distorted his dry account.

Dudley Smith ends his book by writing: 'Few know much about Wilson the man' – a gap which was quickly filled by two more biographers. Leslie Smith, a BBC producer, had personal access to Wilson, and much of what he writes about Wilson's youth is Wilson's own story (*Harold Wilson: The Authentic Portrait*, Hodder, 1964). Half Leslie Smith's book deals with the period before Wilson entered Parliament, in which time almost every incident, however apparently irrelevant, is faithfully retailed. Here is the clean young Methodist Yorkshireman, quelling a nasty little outbreak of homosexuality at school; leading Scout patrols; competing with his Oxford room-mate over the number of hours work put in each day; saving money to help his unemployed father; and engaging in a delightful and successful love-affair with a clergyman's daughter. Once Wilson enters Parliament, Leslie Smith's exhilarating narrative falters, if only through his determination to prove that every political act and decision of Harold Wilson between 1945 and 1964 was inspired by Boy-Scout selflessness. According to Leslie Smith, Wilson was right to resign with Bevan in 1951; right to take Bevan's place in the Shadow Cabinet in 1954 when the latter resigned; right to oppose Bevan in the Labour leadership contest in 1955–6; right to support Gaitskell in 1956, oppose him in 1960 and support him again in 1962.

If Leslie Smith's happy fantasy strains the imagination from time to time, it is thin gruel compared with the powerful concoction of Gerard Noel, a rich Catholic aristocrat, who fought Argyll for the Liberals in 1959 (*Harold Wilson and the New Britain*, Gollancz, 1964). Mr Noel is the editor of *Pentagram, Man and his Quest*, a journal which deals with the more bizarre aspects of psychoanalysis, and strays from time to time into the realms of black magic. In a recent editorial, Mr Noel quotes Jung on the 'widespread interest in all sorts of psychic phenomena as manifested in the growth of spiritualism, astrology, theosophy and so forth' (*Pentagram*, Candlemas 1967, p. 2).

The connexion between aristocratic Catholic spiritualism and Harold Wilson may not be immediately obvious, but Mr Noel quickly clarifies the matter. His chapter headings betray the hushed wonder which he holds for the personality and politics of Harold Wilson: 'The Wilsons of Rievaulx'; 'Trumpet Voluntary at Ormskirk'; 'The Spider of Park Lane'; 'The Walnut Panelling'. One passage succinctly summarizes the style and significance of Mr Noel's book. It describes the scene at Scarborough in 1963 as Wilson prepared to make his famous 'technology' speech:

Moving to the back of the hall, it was possible to take a mental 'snap' of the darkened scene of expectant faces and then, turning quickly round, of the floodlit galaxy of packed celebrities the other side of the floodlights. Delighted and impatient delegates were almost laconic compared to the scribes at the Press table. Photographers at the Speaker's feet and more reporters in the gallery stirred hungrily. One or two nursed notable hangovers not yet blown away by the North Sea air. Some wielded fountain pens already loaded with admiration; others, no doubt, yearned for goose quills dipped in venom to do full justice to their finer feelings. Blunt, north-country pencils jostled with those sharpened to razor point by the keenest wits in Fleet Street. . . .

It was impossible not to think immediately of Daniel Defoe, so strangely similar to Harold Wilson in so totally dissimilar an epoch. Defoe, the enlightened non-conformist, realist and man of the people, trading expert and acute observer of events, was one of the first to recognize and hail the long era of prosperity that lay ahead. Would the creator of Robinson Crusoe and Moll Flanders in his role of political satirist have compared Labour's opponents in 1964 to a desert island or a thieves' kitchen? . . .

Theodore White himself could not have raised the temperature so climactically nor have 'set the scene' with such vivid irrelevance. Admirers of Mr Noel's prose style were delighted when, shortly before the 1966 election, Mr Noel produced a second work, entitled *The New Britain and Harold Wilson: An Interim Report*, published by Noel himself, which, if anything, was even more spiritualist than its predecessor.

During the 1964 General Election, Harold Wilson was pursued, White-style, by two journalists on the *Sunday Times*, Anthony Howard and Richard West, who wrote a book in the classic White tradition, properly entitled *The Making of the Prime Minister* (Cape, 1965). Howard and West are both sceptics, hardened by many years in journalism and ruthlessly critical of the excesses of public relations. Yet so influenced were they by Theodore White that they portrayed the Labour Party's old guard as a band of hardy warriors storming the British New Frontier. The actors on the British political stage suddenly became larger than life. There was Herbert Bowden, 'respected and knowledgeable Chief Whip' (p. 11); George Brown, 'a man of great intellectual force' (p. 14); 'the volatile and brilliant Richard Crossman' (p. 16); 'Crosland himself, brilliant, dashing and debonair' (p. 17); 'a ruminative, reliable, cautious figure like Patrick Gordon Walker' (p. 18); the Labour Party staff under 'massive, impassive Len Williams' (p. 235) were almost all 'able and intelligent', as indeed were all the journalists who followed Wilson in the campaign. These were the Sorensens, the Schlesingers, the O'Donnells, the Baileys gathered round the court of the Great Kennedy himself, Harold Wilson, who becomes 'a statesman of maturity and even of humility' (p. 32).

The other crucial aspect of White's style, the 'setting of the scene' with irrelevant, extraneous information, was also mastered by Howard and West. Not a detail escaped their ruthless attention. After the votes for the Labour leadership election had been counted, they remained for some time in 'the ballot box – a large cardboard contraption with a slit on the top' (p. 28). Then there was the famous story of the HP sauce bottle, with our hero remembering every one of the French words written on it. Theodore White had been able to rely on the organizational intensity of American elections to carry his readers over his anecdotes. Howard and West, however, were frustrated by the lack of the same organizational intensity in British elections, and, as a result, their anecdotes took hold of what little narrative there was to tell, and destroyed it.

Wilson's victory in 1964, and the actions of his Government following it, inspired one of his greatest admirers, the political correspondent of the *Sunday Mirror*, Anthony Shrimsley, to immortalize *The First Hundred Days of Harold Wilson* (Weidenfeld and Nicolson, 1965). Shrimsley, too, is a master of detail, notably irrelevant detail (p. 30):

His [Wilson's] day, which had started with the morning papers, got into its stride at about 9.45 a.m. when he settled in his chair at the centre of the Cabinet table. At his right hand was the solitary telephone. Pens and pencils lay neatly arranged before him at the edge of his blotter. A tin of Gold Block tobacco would rest on the table, and next to it a small panel of buttons with which he could summon secretaries and messengers. There was a study but he never used it. He preferred to sit here, at the controls of his powerhouse, the twenty-two empty seats at the Cabinet table a constant reminder of the web of Government of which he was the centre.

In the energetic formation of Harold Wilson's first Government, nothing escaped the hawk eye of Mirrorman Shrimsley. Writing about the setting-up of the Department of Economic Affairs, Shrimsley told his readers, unforgettably (p. 50):

By mid-January, 3,000 items were requisitioned by the furnishing and office equipment department of the DEA. The inventory included: chairs 790; tables 207; desks, writing 180; desks, typing 80; cupboards 147; carpets 94; bookcases 65; wastepaper baskets 242; pictures and maps 54; mirrors 22; filing cabinets 90.

To Anthony Shrimsley, as to Leslie Smith, Anthony Howard, Richard West, Gerard Noel and Ernest Kay (a friend of Harold Wilson's whose biography *Pragmatic Premier* was published by Leslie Frewin in February 1967 and contains some interesting information about Mr Kay's family), Harold Wilson could do little wrong. He was the Great Campaigner, the representative of change, the new broom which would sweep the cobwebs out of British Government and British boardrooms. His political future was, it seemed, from reading this huge complex of praise, assured.

John F. Kennedy and his brother Robert were assassinated before their promises and rhetoric were nullified by events. Harold Wilson, however, has not been assassinated, and the Wilson myth, so ably and repetitively propagated, has been cruelly shattered. The reasons for this cannot be found in any of the books mentioned above, for the reasons have nothing to do with Wilson's personality, his ability in organizing election campaigns, his tactical sense, his humour, his intelligence, his academic ability, his memory or his liking (or otherwise) for HP sauce. The reasons have to do with politics; a subject which is rarely mentioned by the biographers of Harold Wilson.

*

The idea for this book grew out of a long discussion with Tony Godwin, then editorial director of Penguins, in June 1966, in the middle of the seamen's strike of that month which inspired the first grass roots Labour disillusion with Wilson's Government. The idea then was to write a polemical essay on the nature of the politics which Harold Wilson represented. Then, in quick succession, came the July measures, the application for entry into the Common Market, and the *Tiger* meeting. Labour's disillusionment grew into despair and the essay grew into an attempted analysis, not merely of Harold Wilson, but of the development and decline of socialist theory over the last thirty years. I must therefore apologize for the failure to refer at, I think, any stage to food or to the weather; to the Boy Scouts; to bare-foot schooldays; to the Scilly Isles; to the Huddersfield Town football team of 1927; to fish and chips *with* vinegar; to HP sauce, to Gold Block tobacco or to the number of wastepaper baskets in the Department of Economic Affairs.

Inevitably, I imagine, this book will be characterized as a personal attack on Wilson, in the sense that an alternative Premier is clearly visible who will lead Britain to socialism. I will be asked: If not Wilson, who else? The question is as irrelevant as it is unanswerable. For the damage done to the British Labour movement since 1964 has not been the personal work of Harold Wilson; nor has it been due to tactical errors in his leadership or approach. It has been due to the politics which he represented, and which are shared, with only marginal differences, by the entire Labour Cabinet and most Labour MPs. No new leader can pull the Labour Party out of its present difficulties. Nor, in present circumstances, will any of the available leader-alternatives pull Britain any nearer socialism. What is required is not a new leadership but a new socialist politics, with roots deep down in the Labour rank and file.

I am grateful to a very large number of people who have helped me considerably over the past two years. I mention only some of them: Mr R. B. McCallum, Master of Pembroke College, Oxford; Mrs Margaret Cole; Mr Raymond Walton, QC, whose memory of his Liberal days at Oxford thirty-three years ago is prodigious; Lord Byers; Sir William Lawther and Sir James Bowman, former President and Vice-President of the National Union of Miners; Mr Ian Mikardo, MP; Mr Tom Driberg, MP; Miss Jo Richardson; Mr Christopher Booker; Mr David Cox, Senior Tutor at University College, Oxford; Mr John Junor, editor of the *Sunday Express*; Mr George Elvin, general secretary of the ACTT; Mr Christopher Mott; and, particularly, Sir Michael Balcon, who guided me patiently through the problems of the post-war British film industry.

My special thanks are due to Nicholas Deakin, of the Institute of Race Relations, and Anne Darnborough of Anti-Apartheid, who read Chapter 8, and made valuable suggestions and corrections; to Andrzej Krassowski of the Overseas Development Institute, who did the same for Chapter 9; and to Peter Jay, Economics Editor of *The Times*, who read and corrected many errors in Chapters 5 and 6 with indefatigable patience and cheerfulness in the full knowledge that he would almost certainly disagree with every conclusion reached. The stern criticism of Nigel Harris, editor of *International Socialism*, corrected several theoretical deviations in the last chapter.

Perhaps the greatest practical problem I faced – in common with many others in a similar predicament – was the lack of a public cuttings library – or even a comprehensive cuttings library available to freelance journalists by subscription. We are at the mercy of newspaper librarians. For the first year of writing this book, I was lucky to have regular access to the cuttings of the *Daily Telegraph*. Since then, I have been courteously received by the librarians at the *Sun*, the *Sunday Times* and the *Financial Times*, to all of whom I am very grateful. Throughout the last two years I have been a persistent, irritating visitor to the library of the Oxford Union, and owe much of the research to the patience of the librarian, Mr Walters.

Most of this book was written in the house of my uncle and aunt, Michael and Jill Foot, who provided me with essential isolation from my, as yet, unpolitical children. The views and criticisms in Chapter 10, must, in the light of this, lay claim to being the greatest abuse of hospitality on record. Should these views have been omitted in deference to a respected and hospitable uncle? I hope and calculate that their suppression would do greater injury to his libertarian spirit than their inclusion will offend him.

Chapter 1
Young Liberal: 1916–45

Harold was regularly aroused by another experience – the camp fire ceremony, and its accompanying incantations. This ceremony, dating back to the Red Indian days, was frequently held in his Group. In summer it took place out of doors round a real fire, but at other times it was held indoors round a mock fire made by an apprentice electrician belonging to the Group. . . . The boys sat on their haunches and clustered round the fire. The leader walked over to it, intoning: 'Brothers, I light the Council fire to burn.' Everyone then chanted: 'Burn, fire, burn.' The leader would then say: 'Let it burn up all hatred.' 'Burn, fire, burn,' chanted the chorus. 'Let it burn up all greed,' the leader added, with the chorus again chanting its endorsement of 'Burn, fire, burn.' And so on with injustice, blasphemy, greed, intolerance and all other evils consigned to the flames (Leslie Smith, *Harold Wilson: The Authentic Portrait*, p. 31).

For us, May Day is representative of the traditional Merrie England of bygone days, before this country was transformed by capitalism, the factory system and the growth of large towns, when the craftsman and the farmer joined in the celebration of spring. . . . We are entitled to express our confidence that soon we shall be beginning our great programme to re-establish Merrie England and a better Britain for all our people . . . the day now dawning will mark the end of a long winter of persecution and terror and the beginning of a glorious summer of victory (May Day message to the constituents of Ormskirk from Harold Wilson, Prospective Parliamentary Labour Candidate, *Ormskirk Advertiser*, 3 May 1945).

At the start of the Easter (Hilary) term of 1935, the Oxford University Liberal Club had two active members. The Club had failed to make any headway with the freshmen who had come up to Oxford the previous term. The Labour Club, on the other hand, had almost doubled its membership. The latter's success was due in the main to the increasing popularity and relevance of Marxist views. On 7 November 1934, for instance, the Oxford Union passed by a majority of more than fifty votes a motion that the class struggle was the only effective means of dispensing with capitalism. When Clement Attlee spoke at the Labour Club, he was howled down as a revisionist. In response, the Conservative Association gained strength and coherence. Everywhere, except in the Liberal Club, political consciousness among the undergraduates was on the increase. Even the weekly paper *Isis* had contrived to shake off the summer torpor of its former editor, Jo Grimond, and apply itself to the problems of one and a half million unemployed at home and the triumph of Fascism in Italy, Germany and Austria.

Oxford Liberalism – never a powerful force – had been demoralized first by the secession of the 'Simonites' – or National Liberals – who fought the 1931 election on a Macdonald–Baldwin platform, and by the Ottawa agreements on Empire protection which had driven the Liberals out of the National Government.

The Liberal Club might well have foundered altogether had it not been for an energetic freshman at Christ Church called Frank Byers. Byers approached a second-year Liberal called J. A. Brown, and the two undergraduates, with the President, T. D. F. Griffiths, embarked on a rescue operation. 'We did it mainly,' says Byers today, 'on sherry.' And capitalizing on their sherry successes, Byers and Griffiths organized an Oxford Liberal Club dinner at the end of the Hilary term, on Friday, 1 March 1935. The guest speaker, procured with the help of Frank Byers' considerable connexions in the Liberal hierarchy, was Sir Herbert Samuel.

Much of the cost of the dinner, which was attended by 150 people and gave the Oxford Liberal Club a new lease of life, had been borne by the Eighty Club. The Eighty Club had been formed in 1880 to encourage support among Liberals for Mr William Gladstone, who was threatening once again to take power. It grew rapidly into perhaps the most influential inner-party caucus in British political history. In the Liberal heyday before the First World War it had a membership of 800, and Liberal politicians often chose an Eighty Club dinner to make important statements of policy. The majority of the Club's membership came from outside the House of Commons, and therefore provided a useful link between the Parliamentary Party and the leaders of the Liberal rank and file. Election to the Eighty Club was considered one of the highest Liberal honours.

Between the wars the Club lost much of its influence and

prestige, but it remained a body of some force in Liberal politics. Its organizers concentrated their attention on the universities. University Liberal Clubs were encouraged to book speakers through the Eighty Club, which paid the necessary expenses. It also paid the fares and hotel bills of university Liberals who were prepared to canvass in the constituencies during vacations.

The collapse of university Liberalism, particularly at Oxford, in the academic year 1934–5, dismayed the committee of the Eighty Club, who were delighted to assist in the organization of the Oxford dinner. The Eighty Club used the dinner as a springboard for a big recruiting drive for membership among Oxford Liberals. In 1935 the Eighty Club committee admitted six members from the Oxford University Liberal Club: Miss Honor Balfour, who had been President of the Club the previous year; Frank Byers; James Brown and Raymond Walton, both of whom became President not only of the Liberal Club but also of the Oxford Union; at their committee meeting on 26 March 1935 the Eighty Club admitted two recently elected committee members of the Oxford Liberal Club: A. L. Lamaison, Exeter, who later became President of the Club, and J. H. Wilson, Jesus, who did not.

This rush of members from Oxford provoked the diehards on the Eighty Club Committee to complain that 'any Tom Dick or Harry can get into the Eighty Club nowadays'. These complaints were bitterly refuted. Not only were the new members doing all in their power to revive Liberalism at Oxford, but each applicant had been interviewed and had impressed both his interviewers and his colleagues in the Liberal Club as being devoted to the Liberal cause. The committee was left in little doubt that Honor Balfour, Frank Byers, Jimmy Brown, Raymond Walton, A. L. Lamaison and J. H. Wilson would prove of permanent value to the Liberal Party.[1]

Certainly there can have been little serious cause for concern about J. H. Wilson, who was then known to his Liberal colleagues as 'James' or 'Jimmy'. Wilson's upbringing had been rich in Liberal influence. In the summer of 1928, seven years before he joined the Eighty Club, Wilson had travelled with his parents on a

1. The prediction was very nearly right. Miss Balfour, Byers, Brown, Walton and Lamaison remained keen and effective Liberals for more than thirty years.

holiday tour of Scotland. In Stirling, he had stood under the statue of John Campbell Bannerman, while his father sang the Liberal leader's praises, and explained why he had switched allegiance from Liberal to Labour.

In the Colne Valley, where the Wilson family lived, the Liberal cause had slumped and the best chance of keeping the Tory candidate out was by voting Labour. Indeed the Labour candidate, Philip Snowden, had been elected in three consecutive general elections in 1922, 1923 and 1924 with majorities each time of less than 2,500, and each time opposed by a Liberal, as well as a Conservative. In these circumstances, a vote for the Liberal, J. H. Wilson's father explained, was likely to let the Tory in.

This lesson in anti-Conservative pragmatism appears to have made a deep impression on the young J. H. Wilson, whose interest in politics had been aroused the previous year on a visit, with his mother, to stay with his Uncle Harold (Seddon) in Western Australia. All Wilson's biographers have underlined the importance of this trip.[1]

Harold Seddon, who had had such a great impact on his young nephew, had reached the climax of a turbulent political career. Largely for health reasons, he had emigrated to Australia at the age of twenty, and had settled in the Kalgoorlie goldfields in West Australia. He joined the staff of the West Australia Government railways as an electrical engineer, and, like most working people in that part of the world at that time, became a supporter and member of the Australia Labour Party. Before long he represented his union, the Engineering Union, at national union and labour conferences, and, shortly before the First World War, became a member of the Australia Labour Party's district council.

In 1916, however, the Australia Labour Party split on the issue

1. 'It was a memorable voyage and it made a deep impression on Harold' (Noel, p. 23): 'The trip to Australia made a lasting impression on Harold Wilson' (Kay, p. 17); 'It was an exceptional experience for a young boy and the trip greatly widened his horizons' (Leslie Smith, p. 26); Dudley Smith tells us that Harold Wilson's meeting with Uncle Harold, who was a member of the Western Australian Legislative Council, 'was his first encounter with a live politician and he savoured the experience with the relish one might expect' (p. 17). Ernest Kay goes even further: 'It was on the journey home that he (Harold) remarked to his mother: "I am going to be a Member of Parliament when I grow up. I am going to be a Prime Minister" ' (p. 17).

of conscription. The politics and mechanics of the split resembled in almost every detail the split in the British Labour Party in 1931. The Labour Prime Minister, W. M. Hughes, returned from a European trip determined to shovel more Australian troops into the European slaughter. Australian Labour, however, would have none of it, and Hughes and his colleagues were warned by the Party and the majority of the Labour Cabinet that any attempt to enforce conscription would lose him the support of the Labour Party. Hughes was undeterred, and ordered a referendum on conscription. By a small majority, the electorate voted against it. Yet Hughes insisted on a general call-up. Accordingly, the Labour Party withdrew its support and Hughes was forced to form a National Government, with a small band of his former colleagues, and the 'discriminating' support of the Australian Liberal Party, which was and is the main anti-Labour force in Australian politics. Only a tiny segment of the Labour Party sided with Hughes and split from the majority to form the 'National Labour Party' – among them Harold Seddon, who became his State's secretary of the National Labour Party. In 1917, he contested Kalgoorlie as a Nationalist candidate, losing heavily to Labour. The Nationalist Party by this time consisted almost entirely of the Liberal Party and the National Labour Party, both of which had dissolved.

Harold Seddon was appointed to the Legislative Council of Western Australia in 1922, during one of that state's brief periods of anti-Labour rule. Western Australia was Labour from 1924 to 1930 and from 1933 to 1947, during all of which time the Labour majority in the House of Representatives had to cope with obstructive tactics from the appointed Legislative Council. Harold Seddon became an ardent supporter of Robert Menzies' United Australia Party in the 1930s, which reverted to its original title of Liberal Party in 1945. When the Liberals stormed back to power after the war, Harold Seddon was appointed President of the Legislative Council in Western Australia, and, accordingly, in 1951, received a knighthood.

To the two Liberal influences on the teenage Harold Wilson – John Campbell Bannerman and Harold Seddon – must be added a third – William Ewart Gladstone. In his studies at school – at Royds Hall Grammar School in Huddersfield and the Wirral

Grammar School, Cheshire – he had developed a great admiration for Gladstone, and the admiration and interest straddled his first term's study of history and his later studies of Modern Greats. An essay on the state of the railways won him the Gladstone prize in 1935, and many of his holidays in Cheshire were spent at the library in Hawarden, which is rich in Gladstonian material.

Nothing, in short, was more natural than that J. H. Wilson should join the Oxford University Liberal Club, accept nomination for the Eighty Club, and, in so far as his studies allowed him, work for the Liberal cause at Oxford. Such decisions were entirely consistent with his upbringing and attitudes. Yet, for some reason, the authorities have sought other explanations for Wilson's Oxford Liberalism, and, in so doing, have played havoc with the facts. The official view is unanimous:

Strangely enough, one of the few clubs he did join was the Liberal Club, for he was still at this time a stalwart Gladstonian. A year or so later, however, he transferred to the Labour Club (Noel, p. 34).

Towards the end of his second year he joined the Liberal Club. He had first carefully enquired about its membership and outlook, and felt satisfied that its aims were genuinely progressive: almost semi-socialist in fact. With the intention of converting it wholly to socialism he actively participated in its affairs, and even became an officer of the Club. But as time went on, he realized his original hopes were futile; so he ceased to take any further part in its affairs (Leslie Smith, p. 72).

. . . he suspected that the Labour Club was under Communist influence. Eventually he joined the Liberal Club instead and served on its committee for a time hoping, no doubt, to convert the faithfuls to Socialism (Dudley Smith, p. 22).

He did, however, at the beginning of his time at Oxford, join the University Liberal Club and eventually became its Treasurer. At this time he was still a supporter of Gladstonian Liberalism. It was not until his second year as an Oxford undergraduate that he resigned from the Liberal Club and joined the Labour Club (Kay, p. 19).

And, finally, from the source itself:

When, as I saw it, all these public school Marxists, many of them Communists, most of them knowing absolutely nothing of the conditions in which we in the North were living or had been brought up, I reacted so strongly against it that I felt the Oxford Labour Club wasn't for the likes of me and for a short time I joined the Liberal Club, hoping vainly to convert them to my ideas of radical socialism. That didn't last long. I soon saw there was no hope of that. But certainly I never had any common cause with the public school Marxist (Harold Wilson, BBC interview, *Listener*, 29 October 1964).

The facts, however, are as follows. As we have seen, Wilson joined the Eighty Club in March 1935 – at the end of his second term at Oxford. He must, therefore, have joined the Liberal Club, as Kay says, 'at the beginning of his time at Oxford'. At the end of his second term, also, he was elected to the Liberal Club Committee, where he served for his third term. At the end of his third term (summer, 1935) he was elected Treasurer of the Club. He remained Treasurer, under Frank Byers' presidency, *for the whole of his second year* – in the winter (Michaelmas) term, 1935, the Easter (Hilary) term, 1936, and the summer (Trinity) term, 1936. There is some dispute as to whether or not he then stood for President against the secretary, Raymond Walton. Frank (now Lord) Byers writes to me: 'I am pretty sure he (Wilson) stood for President,' although Walton, whose memory is prodigious, remembers no contest. At any rate, the *Oxford Guardian* – a Liberal undergraduate weekly which started in October 1936 – records that J. H. Wilson, ex-Treasurer, remained on the Liberal Club Committee for the whole of his final year.

Nor was Wilson a casual member of the Club. The job of Treasurer, which he held for a year, required regular attendance at committee meetings and scrupulousness with figures. R. B. McCallum, Wilson's tutor in politics, and Senior Treasurer of the Liberal Club throughout this period, cannot recall anything but the highest efficiency with the Club accounts during this period. And McCallum was particularly sensitive to any inefficiency, having been forced, at the end of 1934, to organize a 'whip-round' among graduate Liberals to pay off the Club's substantial debts.

Moreover, Wilson attended two vacation conferences of the Union of University Liberal students – one held in Liverpool, from 9 April to 11 April 1935, and the other in Manchester, from 8 January to 10 January 1936.[1]

Although both conferences were near his Cheshire home, Wilson

1. At the latter, a speech of Wilson's cautioning moderation on a motion criticizing the League of Nations was reported in the *Manchester Guardian*, 11 January 1936.

would hardly have attended them as a mere dilettante. Certainly he was regarded as one of the leading undergraduate Liberals of the time. As late as January 1938, after Wilson had taken his Finals, a keen Oxford Liberal, Derek Tasker, wrote to Frank Byers suggesting a book on Oxford Liberalism, with chapters from contemporary Oxford Liberals. Tasker's draft of the book suggested a chapter on unemployment and the depressed areas by J. H. Wilson. Unhappily for posterity, Derek Tasker, who is now Canon Residentiary at Southwark Cathedral, cannot even remember writing the letter, let alone whether he ever approached J. H. Wilson to write the chapter. What matters is that, even at that stage, J. H. Wilson was regarded by undergraduate Liberals as a leading Oxford Liberal, and one who specialized in economics and unemployment.

Wilson's own assertion, faithfully peddled by his biographers, that his political role in the Liberal Club was to convert its members to 'radical socialism' is greeted by Oxford Liberals of the time with a mixture of amusement and derision. Frank Byers, for instance, writes to me (21 December 1967):

It was towards the end of my period or even just after it that Harold Wilson became Treasurer. He was very efficient at this, but I cannot remember his taking any strong political line at any time and certainly I had no indication that he was likely to join Labour, and this was at a time when Michael Foot and others were very vocal about the differences between Liberal and Labour, even though some of them had gone down by then. . . . Certainly I remember being very friendly with Harold at this time and there was nothing political which separated us as far as I know. I was absolutely staggered to discover in 1945 that although I had been elected as a Liberal he had been elected as a Socialist.

Raymond Walton, who was President of the Liberal Club in the first term of Wilson's last year, describes the view that Wilson was a hidden socialist, seeking to convert unsuspecting Liberals as 'absolute bunk'. 'I don't remember ever hearing him propose anything political of any kind', he says. 'Rick' Allison, a later President of the Club, now headmaster of Greenmoor College, remembers Wilson as 'a Keynesian – like all of us then. There were very few of the old *laissez-faire* Liberals. Wilson was very much a Keynesian, but no further Left than that'.

In the light of all this it is difficult to accept the assertion of Dudley Smith that Wilson 'took the formal step of joining the Labour Party at the age of nineteen' (that is between March 1935 and March 1936). If Dudley Smith is right (and there is no indication *which* constituency Labour Party Wilson allegedly joined), Harold Wilson must have been the only Labour Party member in history who joined while Treasurer of the Oxford University Liberal Club and a member of the Eighty Club.

The truth almost certainly is that Harold Wilson's politics while he was an undergraduate were Liberal politics, and that he joined the Liberal Club quite naturally because its views most suited his own. R. B. MacCallum, now Master of Pembroke College, who taught Wilson in politics during the latter's last two years as an undergraduate, cannot remember any political bias in his brilliant pupil. 'I think,' he writes to me, 'I could have told that he was not a Tory. That is all.' McCallum remembers two main aspects of his teaching of Wilson, both of which clearly stuck:

I do remember harping on a favourite theme, the moral force (I suppose it would now be called charismatic) of Campbell-Bannerman as a leader which gave him loyalty and influence that neither of his greater successors could quite enjoy.

I probably drew his attention to the case for specialist committees in the House of Commons. I usually did this with a reference to Lloyd George in the Committee on House of Commons Procedure, 1931. I also warned my pupils against the cant notion that specialist committees were an evil French device and responsible for instability in French politics. I asked them to think of the US Congress, the Swedish Riksdag and many other legislatures and to get rid of the French bogey. Unfortunately, I do not remember discussing this with Wilson though it is almost inconceivable that I did not. What is important is that, if I did, I did not get the standard reaction that I usually got from committed Labour Party students which was a violent hostility to select committees as obstacles in the beneficent process of a strong socialist Government with a strong majority churning out endless reforms to which a committee would be a nuisance and a danger . . . [1]

The moral force of Campbell-Bannerman, the grandeur of Gladstone, the electoral weakness of the Labour Party, even after 1935, the Marxism of the Labour Club, which changed its rules to

1. Letter to the author, 19 April 1967.

absorb the Communist October Club in December 1935, the facts of Parliamentary life as taught by Mr McCallum – all these combined to maintain Harold Wilson's Liberal allegiances.

Eric Sharpe, one of Wilson's closest friends at Oxford, thinks that Wilson's political activity at Oxford complemented his work, both in economic and political history. There is a lot of evidence for this. In his second year he entered an essay for the Cecil Peace Prize on the private manufacture of armaments, which 'was written more in the form of a declaratory sermon than a serious study and brought him no success' (Leslie Smith, p. 71). One of the two resolutions moved by the Oxford University Liberal Club at the UULS Conference in January 1936 took note of the 'dangers inherent in a system of private manufacture of armaments and munitions' and called on the Government 'to work wholeheartedly for the complete abolition of private enterprise in this field'. The motion was ably supported by the Liberal Club Treasurer, J. H. Wilson. Similarly, the only other position held by Wilson in a university club was secretary of the non-partisan Political and Economic Society – a post which he was offered in return for his regular attendances at Society meetings addressed by distinguished academic figures on subjects which were covered by the Modern Greats syllabus.

Raymond Walton takes the view that Wilson's main ambition at Oxford was to get a first-class degree. 'He was clearly on the make,' says Walton, 'but he hadn't yet decided quite where he wanted to go.' Though he was keen on politics, and could hardly suppress his childhood political ambitions, he forced himself to concentrate, particularly in his last year, on his academic work.

The Oxford School of Politics, Philosophy and Economics is based on two unalterable principles: first, everything written about politics and philosophy by Karl Marx (1818–83) is out of date and dangerously biased, while everything written by John Stuart Mill (1806–73) is modern, vigorous and untainted by bias; secondly, everything written about economics by Karl Marx (1818–83) is out of date and dangerously biased, while everything written by Alfred Marshall (1842-1924) is modern, vigorous and untainted by bias.[1] Wilson could cheerfully throw away *Das Kapital*

1. Anthony Crosland, for instance, a classic alumnus of Oxford P P.E. describes him as 'the great Marshall' in *The Future of Socialism* (Cape, p. 353).

after reading two pages without any fear of losing ground in his Finals. He could soak himself in Marshall, Mill, Gladstone, Disraeli, Canning, Palmerston and the other heroes of Oxford Radicalism. The mean, sentimental, elitist liberalism fostered by the Oxford P.P.E. school exactly fitted Wilson's political attitudes.[1]

Encouraged by these influences, Harold Wilson remained a Liberal all his three years as an undergraduate. What changed in his post-graduate years was not his politics nor his attitudes, but the external political atmosphere at Oxford. The Labour collapse of 1931 had led to a polarization in Oxford political theory. Socialists at the universities were obliged, if only by Labour's Parliamentary impotence, to re-think socialist theory and socialist objectives. In this atmosphere, the Oxford Labour Club moved decisively to the Left, following the authoritarian Marxism of Sir Stafford Cripps, and reading the more diluted analyses of Harold Laski, G. D. H. Cole and particularly of R. H. Tawney. Those young Liberals who abandoned the Liberal Party for socialism did so not so much for reasons of political power, or even because they objected to old-fashioned *laissez-faire* Liberalism, which the Liberal Party had long since abandoned, but more because they rejected the Keynesian model of managed capitalism.

The Liberal Party was the first officially to adopt Keynesian policies, with their *Yellow Book* policy statement on which they fought the 1929 elections, polling 5 million votes. Keynesianism, far from being the prerogative of Labour, was first espoused by the Liberal Party, and those young Liberals who joined the Labour Party in the 1930s had been converted away from Keynesianism, to the case for public ownership and the transformation of capitalist society. Men like Michael Foot and A. J. Irvine, both prominent undergraduate Liberals, joined the Labour Party not because Labour offered more chance of legislating reforms, but because Labour, for them, was a Party which would transform and abolish capitalist society.

The transformation and abolition of capitalism, however, had no attraction for Harold Wilson. As long as Labour, in the shape of the Labour Club, represented such anathema, he remained a

1. Philosophy presented greater problems. And Wilson overcame them by prodigious means. He made a digest of Kant's *Critique of Pure Reason*, then made a digest of the digest and learnt the final draft off by heart.

Liberal. Ironically the situation was changed by the increasing support in Oxford Labour circles for the Popular Front.

To the right-wing leaders of the Labour Party the Popular Front represented a menace from the Left – a vote-losing spectre of Communism. Yet the demand for a Popular Front had the additional and in the long run more crucial effect of blurring theoretical distinctions on the Left and, in the universities, of opening Labour doors to anyone of vaguely 'radical' thought who was opposed to Fascism in Europe and unemployment at home.

Ironically, too, the most tenacious socialist ever known at Oxford, G. D. H. Cole, was responsible for the first major moves to broaden the socialist front. Cole was a Russophile, and supported the fusion of the Communist Party with the Labour Party. But he spread his net in other directions, not excluding the university Liberals.

A. W. Wood, President of the Oxford University Liberal Club (and later of the Union), wrote an article for *Isis* on 2 June 1937 entitled 'Liberalism in Oxford', holding out rosy prospects for the growth of university Liberalism:

> A section of the Labour Party, led by G. D. H. Cole, is now realizing that immediate Liberal reforms are more important in the immediate future than a formula about the nationalisation of the means of production, distribution and exchange.

This statement was firmly based. On 9 November, the previous year, Cole had written an article for the Liberal *Oxford Guardian* entitled 'A People's Front'. Support for the Front, argued Cole, should be based on five points:

1. Maintenance of peace and the checking of Fascist aggression through the League of Nations.
2. An increase in home consumption.
3. The abandonment of the Means Test.
4. The enlargement of civil liberty.
5. Public control over arms manufacture, utilities, and all industries essential to improving the standard of life.

In the same issue an editorial, no doubt written by the energetic Mr Wood, trumpeted:

> Ninety per cent of the Labour Party are now Liberals. . . .
> So great has been the swing to the Right of the Labour Party under

right-wing dominance during the last few years that it seems possible that in any Liberal Labour alliance the Liberals would provide the radical element. . . .

This, we take it, is why Mr Cole, the sincerity of whose belief in socialism no one could question, puts forward in his article five specific practical aims for a Popular Front in which the first four are planks of the Liberal platform and only the fifth and last has any specific connection with socialism (*Oxford Guardian*, 9 November 1936).

The jibe was a fair one. The 'five points' were extraordinarily mild. Even the fifth spoke only of 'public control' – not of public ownership. And the second – the call for 'increased consumption' – was a statement of Keynesianism which had wide support in the Liberal Party and in the Conservative Party. Indeed, there was nothing in the five points which would have excluded young Tories who were campaigning against the appeasement of Fascism in Europe and for ending unemployment at home. Men like Edward Heath, who started to make headway in the union shortly after Harold Wilson passed his Finals, and Harold Macmillan were, on the basis of Cole's five points, candidates for the Popular Front. G. D. H. Cole, who, only a few terms earlier, had been campaigning in uncompromising terms for a restatement of Marxist principles and a more relentless application to the class struggle, had opened the theoretical door to all manner of class collaborators and pragmatists.

This change in the political scene at Oxford was observed by Harold Wilson, who, in the summer of 1937, had achieved one of the best Firsts of his generation, and, after winning the Webb Medley Senior Scholarship in economics, had become a don at New College. G. D. H. Cole had been one of the judges of the Webb Medley Junior Prize, which was won by Wilson in 1936, and had watched Wilson's progress with some interest. When Sir William Beveridge, the Master of University College, where Cole taught economics and politics, wanted a research assistant for his work on unemployment, Cole suggested Wilson, and Wilson duly became a Junior Research Fellow at University College in 1938.

In his two years at University College, Wilson spent most of his time working for Beveridge in a feverish effort to complete a massive work on unemployment and the trade cycle. He visited a large number of unemployment exchanges in the South of

England, comparing statistics and compiling an exhaustive study of the trade cycle from the end of feudalism. His connexion with Cole cannot therefore have been as close as he and his biographers have suggested. He assisted Cole with teaching economics. But the political connexion between the two men was always slight. Wilson had not attended the 'Cole Group' for undergraduate discussions while he was a Liberal undergraduate, and, equally, he did not – in the memory of almost all the attenders at that time who are still alive – attend the 'pink lunches' which Cole held in University colleges on Thursdays for left-wing dons. By that time, the 'pink lunches' concerned themselves almost exclusively with foreign affairs, with the Spanish civil war, the dominance of Fascism in central Europe and so on, and Wilson, on his own testimony, was far more concerned with economic questions:

With regard to the Spanish civil war, we all felt strongly about it at that time, politically. I was at Oxford for the greater part of it. We felt strongly particularly about the Hitlerite aggression, the Munich period, and all the rest of it, though I think I would be right in saying that most of my passionate feelings at the time were in terms of unemployment and home affairs, rather than foreign affairs (BBC interview, *Listener*, 29 October 1964).

Throughout his time at Oxford, Harold Wilson accepted the Keynesian analysis of and solutions for the economic crisis. G. D. H. Cole, on the other hand, thought differently. As G. D. N. Worswick has put it:

In the later thirties Cole was looking outwards, to the Spanish War and the rise of Fascism in Europe, but it was partly, I suspect, because he was out of line with the mainstream of academic economics. To his way of thinking, the enthusiasm for Keynes' *General Theory of Employment, Interest and Money* was quite excessive: all Keynes was doing was to re-state what Hobson had said some years before. In any case the whole business was only tinkering: the structure of capitalism had developed cracks far deeper and wider than could be papered over with mere changes in monetary and budgetary practice. As for business behaviour, he thought the orthodox methods of analysis, with their diagrams and semi-mathematical techniques, altogether too narrow and fiddling to be of use in understanding the harsh realities of modern capitalism.[1]

1. 'Cole and Oxford' by G. D. N. Worswick, from *Essays in Labour History*, edited by Asa Briggs and John Saville (Macmillan, 1960).

These 'orthodox methods of analysis' with their diagrams and semi-mathematical techniques were typified by the work at the end of the 1930s of Sir William Beveridge and Harold Wilson, whom Beveridge described as 'the ablest research assistant I ever had'.

Unhappily, the bulk of this work was never published. In his two years as a research fellow, Wilson published only one article in academic and post-graduate journals – a dry affair entitled 'Industrial Activity in the Eighteenth Century', which consisted almost entirely of diagrams. The only glimmer of social theory came in a footnote, which quoted Defoe:

The demand abates, the price sinks, the poor spinners and workfolk are dismissed to starve. But the cause is not in the trade, but in the work-men, not in the manufacture, but in the manufacturers; the quantity of goods made are too many for the consumption, and the market is perhaps glutted for a year or more to come; and thus, and not otherwise, the commerce is abated (*Economica*, New Series, Vol. 7, May 1940, p. 150).

Further detail of Wilson's work during this period is given by Sir William Beveridge in his book *Full Employment in a Free Society*. In particular, Beveridge refers to 'new facts' uncovered by Wilson on the prices of primary products, notably of raw cotton, and the effect on the trade cycle of the uncontrolled price changes of primary products (pp. 304–5):

It is difficult to avoid the conclusion that an important and hitherto almost wholly neglected element in the causation of the trade cycle is the relation between primary producers and the industrial users of their products: that a fundamental cause of the trouble has been the condi-tions under which primary production has been carried on, making its volume singularly irresponsive to changes in price, and therefore un-manageable in an unplanned market economy.

If there is any substance in the suggestions made here – and the main facts cannot be denied – one of the inner secrets of the trade cycle is to be found, not in bankers' parlours or the boardrooms of industries, but on the prairies and plantations, in the mines and oil wells. The new sign-post points clearly to the need for joint action by many nations to bring order into the production and marketing of primary commodities

This mixture of mathematics and piety was a typical Keynesian brew. Keynes himself had written an article entitled 'The Policy of

Government Storage of Foodstuffs and Raw Materials' in which he pointed out that the average annual price range of the four major primary commodities throughout the 1930s had been 67 per cent. 'An orderly programme of output,' opined Lord Keynes, 'either of the raw materials or of their manufactured products, is scarcely possible in such conditions' (*Economic Journal*, September 1938, p. 451).

The careful demands of the Keynes–Beveridge school for more order and common sense in the capitalist system had appealed to intelligent Liberals long before they became the official economic doctrine of the Labour Party.

The older socialist theoreticians like Cole and Laski, brought up on more revolutionary conceptions of abolishing capitalism and replacing it with an entirely new order, viewed with some dismay the mass conversion of young Fabian academics to the 'new Keynesianism'. Yet, in a sense, it was accepted by default of argument. The socialist imagination was, at that time, almost wholly preoccupied with the perilous political situation in Europe and the struggle in Spain.

It seems unlikely that G. D. H. Cole was impressed or even interested in the political attitudes of his young assistant at University College. Nevertheless, Cole did have a great admiration for Wilson's ability to absorb information and to concentrate his energies. Mrs Margaret Cole writes to me (20 April 1967) that her husband 'had a high opinion of him [Wilson] as a worker and an economist'. Moreover, as the possibility of a Labour victory emerged with Labour Ministers joining the Churchill Coalition Government in 1940, Cole forced himself to examine the practical problems of a Labour Government in Parliament. On more than one occasion he would collect a group of Labour dons together, appoint a 'Minister' of a Department and instruct the Minister to present the next meeting with a Bill for the socialization of the coal industry, or for increasing welfare benefits or for some similar reformist legislation. He also produced a series of practical pamphlets indicating how a Labour Government could overcome the problem of converting capitalist society by stages.[1] Much of

1. See *The Machinery of Socialist Planning*, G. D. H. Cole (Hogarth Press, 1938), which sought to instruct 'the next Socialist Government' how best 'not only to pass legislation which will meet at once the most pressing griev-

this went against the grain for Cole, who had, ever since his great works on Guild Socialism in the 1920s, maintained an extra-Parliamentary approach to politics, concentrating on conferences, on trade unions and on workers' education rather than on the mechanics of Parliament. In spite of repeated requests, he had refused to stand for Parliament except once, and then on condition that he was not elected. Yet Harold Wilson remembers Cole most for this brief and uncharacteristic essay into 'pragmatism'. When Cole died in 1959, Harold Wilson, acting out of that personal loyalty which is perhaps his most attractive characteristic, wrote an addendum to Cole's official biography in *The Times*:

> The Cole Group, with its membership drawn from every college in Oxford, was, over thirty years, undoubtedly Oxford's biggest contribution to the education and inspiration of successive generations of Oxford-trained socialists. The fact that its work and discussion were so solidly grounded in the hard realities of economic and social affairs, rather than theory, has made it a strong formative influence on so many of the leading figures in the modern Labour movement (*Times*, 26 January 1959).

During his period at University College, Wilson broke off his formal links with the Liberal Party[1] and leaned, without any great commitment or enthusiasm, towards the 'Keynesian socialism' which was then fashionable among Labour intellectuals. On one or two occasions, he tells us, he even became irritated by Beveridge's excessive pragmatism. 'I'd realized,' Wilson told Kenneth Harris of the *Observer* in July 1963, 'that Beveridge hadn't grasped the fact that unemployment on the scale and of the kind he was dealing with was a built-in factor of the pre-Keynesian economy – not an unfortunate accident, frictional or anything like that, but positively built in.' Without officially joining the Fabian Society, he agreed informally to help Cole with some of his work for the New Fabian Research Bureau. Robert Shackleton, then a third-year undergraduate Liberal, remembers attending a study group on Federal Union organized by Beveridge, which was held in Wilson's rooms at University College with Wilson as secretary. Mr Shackleton writes to me (16 January 1968):

ances of the people, but also to lay secure foundations for a socialist economic system' (p. 9).

1. He resigned from the Eighty Club, for instance, in February 1938.

I certainly regarded him as a socialist then (probably a right-wing socialist), and knew nothing of his Liberal past.[1]

Wilson's politics throughout his time as a don, as when he was an undergraduate, always took second place to academic work. Very few of the people who knew him well at that time thought that he was in the least bit interested or concerned as a politician. David Cox, now Senior Tutor at University College, was then a young history don, an exact contemporary of Wilson's who followed him each dining night into hall and sat next to him. Cox cannot remember a single political discussion with Wilson, nor the slightest indication that Wilson would become a politician. He too records his astonishment at hearing the news, in 1944, that Wilson was to stand for Parliament.

The influence and patronage of Beveridge stayed with Wilson during the first two war years, when he was drafted into the civil service. After a brief spell at the Ministry of Supply, he moved to the Cabinet Secretariat, on Beveridge's recommendation, and, when Beveridge became chairman of the manpower advisory committee, Wilson became its secretary. Finally, Beveridge, who at this stage was growing closer to the Government, became an Under-Secretary at the Ministry of Labour, and at once appointed his protégé to be head of the Manpower, Statistics and Intelligence Branch. His stay in that exalted position was cut short, largely through Beveridge's increasing irritability and the personal differences between Beveridge and the Minister of Labour, Ernest Bevin. In the summer of 1941, Beveridge left the Ministry and Wilson chose to move to the Mines Department of the Board of Trade in a relatively junior capacity.

The decision, however, was a shrewd one, for coal assumed greater and greater importance as the war effort increased. Wilson's ability as a statistician was stretched to the limit by the complicated differentials in shifts per day and wages per shift in the coal mines.

In the early summer of 1942, he was appointed secretary of the

1. Mr Shackleton, who later became Librarian at the Bodleian, also writes: 'My only clear recollection of Wilson in those days is that in his rooms at Univ. he had a very large bookcase and very few books (a frequent enough situation with young dons); but in his bookcase the only prominent work was a lavishly-bound edition, in several volumes, of the works of Disraeli!'

Greene Committee on miners' wages, which sat for most of the rest of that year. In his work for that committee, Wilson met the leaders of the Miners' Federation (which became the National Union of Mineworkers in 1944). William Lawther, who was President of the Federation, James Bowman, Vice President, and Arthur Horner, General Secretary, remember Wilson as a sympathetic and efficient secretary of the Committee. 'He did a tremendously good job, and he got us the national minimum wage, which had been suggested by the Liberal Government in 1912 but was never given us,' says Lawther. 'We used to meet Wilson a lot at the time – he was writing something for the Fabians on the coal industry and we helped him with it.' Bowman recalls how well Wilson got on with the miners' leaders, and how sympathetic he was to their claim. 'He talked Left at that time,' says Horner. Yet the man who probably dealt most with Wilson on the Greene Committee was Sidney Ford, then the union's chief administrative officer. Ford believes that Wilson's influence was at least partly responsible for the granting of the minimum wage, and, more importantly, of the stabilization of wages, negotiated nationally, not, as before the war, dependent on the profitability of each individual mine. 'This stabilization,' says Ford, 'was crucial to the miners then, and Wilson was always in favour of it. I doubt whether we would have got as much out of the Committee and the Ministry were it not for Wilson.'

Sir Sidney Ford remembers too that there was no obvious political bias in Wilson's attitudes and approach to the problems. 'He always looked at the facts, and made his judgements accordingly. He didn't have that immediate bias towards the miners which you found in most socialists at that time. If you'd asked me at the time, honestly, I'd have said he was a Liberal.'

While the Greene Committee was meeting, coal was taken away from the Board of Trade and put under a separate Ministry of Fuel and Power, with Major Gwilym Lloyd George as Minister, and Wilson as Director of Statistics. Lloyd George and Wilson worked closely together and Wilson's work on coal statistics is regarded throughout the civil service as one of the most brilliant statistical achievements in civil service history. At about this time, however, Wilson's determination and ambition as a politician, which had been part of him ever since the days as a boy when he paraded the streets of Huddersfield silently mouthing his first speech as the town's MP, hardened, and he decided on a political career. No doubt his meeting the miners' leaders confirmed his view that the strength of the trade unions was far greater than anything which could be found in the Liberal Party, and also, although none of the miners' leaders at the time recalls him making any visits to pits to meet and talk to the miners, inspired him with some sympathy for the miners' cause. In October 1943, on the recommendation of the Chairman, G. D. H. Cole, the Fabian Executive Committee co-opted Harold Wilson, and he at once agreed to write a pamphlet advocating the nationalization of the coal industry.[1] Even more significant, perhaps, were the regular brains trusts organized in the Ministry of Fuel to raise the morale and consciousness of its staff. At regular intervals the Minister and his Under-Secretaries would gather in a large room in the Ministry together with a selected panel to answer questions from assembled Ministry personnel. The questions were never very controversial (capital punishment, euthanasia and so on), but the occasions gave Harold Wilson a chance to take part, side by side with a Minister of the Crown, in public debate.

There were also the unmistakable signs of a Labour revival. By-election after by-election, though not contested officially by Labour, signified the anti-Conservative mood. Nor was there any serious sign that the Liberals would achieve a dramatic electoral recovery. In December 1943 Wilson's name was proposed to Transport House as a potential Parliamentary candidate by John Parker, general secretary of the Fabian Society, and Tom Smith, Parliamentary Secretary at Wilson's Ministry.

Wilson's reaction to this move was, according to his biographer Leslie Smith, to seek advice from William Beveridge. Beveridge had by now recovered from his row with Bevin and was seriously considering joining the Labour Party. Discussions were arranged with Morrison and Attlee, at which Beveridge, eager for political power, demanded some eminence in the Labour Party as his prize for joining it. These demands were eventually turned down. In some dudgeon, Beveridge retired to the haven of the Liberals and was

---

1. Wilson joined the Fabian Society at the same time as he joined the executive.

elected as Liberal MP for Berwick in 1944, where he was beaten in 1945.

Nevertheless, at the time when he was consulted by his young admirer, the Liberal Beveridge had come to the same conclusions as his protégé about the political reality: namely that the proper place for all Keynesians who sought political power was the Labour Party. Beveridge warmly recommended Wilson to accept the proposition, and look for a good nomination, advice which was gratefully received and loyally followed.

On 9 September 1944, therefore, after some horse-trading between constituencies, Wilson was selected as Labour candidate for Ormskirk in Lancashire, from a short list of four (the other three were a farmer, a ticket collector and a trade-union organizer). The *Ormskirk Advertiser* pronounced solemnly, without citing evidence:

He has the reputation of being a forceful and impressive speaker and is regarded as one of the up-and-coming young men of the Labour Party, being one of the Left wing, but far from an extremist (9 September 1944).

This view did not reflect that of Wilson's colleagues and friends. Mounting a bus in Whitehall in 1944 he met Edward Jackson, an exact contemporary of Wilson's at Oxford, who, like Wilson, had entered the Civil Service as a statistician during the war. 'I'm standing for Parliament,' Jackson remembers Wilson saying brightly. 'Really?' said Jackson, who was a keen socialist. 'For which party?'

The *Daily Telegraph* noted Wilson's resignation from the Civil Service with the comment:

At 28, Mr Wilson is looked on by socialists as a coming President of the Board of Trade or Chancellor of the Exchequer (14 October 1944).

Such thoughts, Wilson assured his colleagues at University College, Oxford, where he and his wife returned in the autumn of 1944, were quite absurd. In 1944 the College had hastily passed a rule that no Member of Parliament could hold a position in the College – a rule inspired by the decision of Sir William Beveridge, then Master of University College, to stand for Parliament. Some dons expressed their irritation that Wilson, after resigning prematurely from the civil service, should come back to college 'to fill in time' before going to Parliament. Wilson hastily reassured the sceptics that Ormskirk was a hopeless seat, represented by a highly respected non-Party candidate, Commander Stephen King-Hall, and not at all the sort of constituency which would be represented by a socialist. He was duly appointed Domestic Bursar of the college and wrote a long detailed account of College Finances, eschewing political comment:

Present prices are controlled, and for four years have been kept from rising further by Treasury subsidies to the extent of about £220m. per annum. Whether these subsidies and a system of price control will be in force in 1947, is a question impossible to answer, raising as it does all kinds of political issues into which the present writer does not feel competent to stray.[1]

Much of his time at University College was spent finishing his work on the coal industry, which was too long to be published by the Fabians and was therefore published as a book by a young, up-and-coming publisher called George Weidenfeld. The book was called *New Deal for Coal*, and is probably the best book which Harold Wilson ever wrote.

New Deal for Coal showed that, to some extent at any rate, Wilson's sojourns with the miners' leaders had driven him off the political fence. The first chapter gives a thorough account of the waste, the inhumanity and the incompetence of the mine owners between the wars. In later chapters – perhaps the best part of the book – Wilson attacked the wartime system of 'Dual Control' and the Conservative plans for State-sponsored amalgamation of the pits:

The owners' attitude throughout the war was the starvation philosophy that output can never be adequate nor the industry put on a sound economic basis except where wages are on or below subsistence level. As a philosophy for a democratic community, this is damnable, and as a rule of action completely out of place in conditions of full

1. To this modest statement, Wilson added a footnote: 'This sentence was written on 25 July 1945. Shortly after that date the political situation clarified somewhat and it now appears reasonable to assume that food prices will be controlled and subsidized as long as shortage remains, and that profiteering and inordinate price increases due to the shortage will be prevented.'

employment. The owners were willing to endanger not only the future of their industry but also the safety of the state by clinging to this philosophy. . . .

And, on state amalgamations (with how many lessons for the future!):

If the state came in as the principal provider of finance it would need to be represented on the board of every borrowing company to ensure that the money was being wisely spent in a way which would promote efficiency. Apart from the difficulties which would be found in the state nominee and the private directors (particularly such private directors as exist in coal) working together, there is the impossibility of appointing so many state nominees. Clearly the state could come into the financial picture only in a radically-reorganized industry.

Wilson's suggestions for the nationalized industry, were, in the event, very closely followed by the Labour Government. A National Coal Board of eleven members ('including at least one miner'), plus National Joint Coal Councils, plus Regional Joint Councils, plus pit councils. Except on the Board itself, Wilson made no provision for the actual representation of miners on the Councils, and his blueprint remained, as the Coal Board actually became, essentially elitist. This elitist essence made nonsense of his hope that

the old and frequently heard phrase 'the two sides of industry' would die, and the Councils proposed would be indicative of the kind of partnership of the various types of state employees in the industry, rather than, as at present, a carefully-balanced representation of the two sides of the class struggle.

Yet the bulk of the argument for nationalization in *New Deal for Coal* was that private ownership was 'not capable of carrying through the technical reorganization of the industry which is required'. Capital accumulated during the coal boom of 1923 was 'spent in riotous living when it should have been spent in a vigorous and urgent programme of modernization, mechanization and new development'. The mining boardrooms, wrote Wilson, were dominated by the principle of 'third-generation control'. Of the seventy women mining directors, forty-two bore the same name as male directors. 'The vast proportion of colliery directors are "amateurs" in the worst sense of the word.' The final paragraph in the book adequately summed up Harold Wilson's priorities in the argument for coal nationalization:

> Just as nationalization will not of itself solve the problem of industrial relations, but is an essential condition of such a solution, so also, in the technical sphere, nationalization will do no more than create the conditions in which the skill and experience of mining engineers and miners will have full scope. Nationalization will call for forbearance and a sense of responsibility, for leadership and a willingness to fight the bitterness of the past. But the reward of success will be not only the preservation and prosperity of the British coal industry but the achievement of proving that, freed from the present handicaps, it can again lead the world. More important still, it will show not only that socialism and efficiency are compatible but also that socialism, properly applied, is the only means to full efficiency.

Much of *New Deal for Coal* deals with the importance of 'stability for the miner', and the book is inspired to some considerable extent by the plight of the miners throughout the twentieth century.[1]

Yet the solutions in *New Deal for Coal* were posed as solutions for the coal industry without any reference to the situation outside. The nationalization of coal was proposed by Wilson, not as part of a general socialist plan or offensive, but as the best solution to the industry's immediate problems. As such, of course, there was nothing socialist about the proposals. Lord Sankey's Commission in 1919, composed not by any means of socialists, had called for public ownership of the mines, and the Union of Uni-

1. All his life, until he became Prime Minister in 1964, Wilson championed the miners' cause. At the stormy Labour Party Conference of 1960 he chose to sum up the debate on Labour's Fuel Policy, and closed with the words: 'Comrades, the mineworkers have always stood at our side even in the darkest days, so let us show by passing this resolution, that we are standing by them now' (1960 Conference Report, p. 207).

More specifically he championed the coal industry against oil: 'Three years ago we called for a national fuel policy, for a figure that the Government would honour for the size of the industry. 200 million tons was mentioned as a figure for the national indigenous coal industry to work to. This would have meant controlling fuel oil imports and controlling other things as well, but the Government insisted on what they called freedom of choice – by which they meant, of course, a refusal to touch the profits of the oil companies' (House of Commons, 7 November 1961).

versity Liberal students in 1938 had upheld a motion for the nationalization of coal. These demands had been made on the assumption that the British economy would remain essentially capitalist, and that public ownership of coal would enhance British capitalism. Harold Wilson's book overlooked the issue: was the public ownership of coal to take place against a capitalist background or against a socialist one?

Nevertheless, Wilson's well-argued little book established his reputation in the Labour hierarchy and delighted the miners' leaders. One of his most successful election meetings in the 1945 campaign was held at the mining village of Skelmersdale, at which the guest speakers were William Lawther and James Bowman, President and Vice-President of the miners' union. Lawther and Bowman had made a special visit to Lancashire to speak for the young man who had served them so well during the war and who had argued their case so expertly in *New Deal for Coal*.

In the nine months between his selection for Ormskirk and the General Election of 1945, Harold Wilson devoted a great deal of time to the Constituency – a vast rambling area of Lancashire based on the towns of Croxteth (population 30,000), Ormskirk (13,000), Maghull (6,500), Formby (5,800), and the villages of Skelmersdale, Aughton, Rainford, Tarleton and Aintree. His speeches in all these places during that period were based almost exclusively on the hope and idealism experienced by Labour Party supporters throughout the country, and on an unequivocal defence of working people against their employers, as represented by the Tories:

By becoming one of the great parties of State, the Labour Party is becoming respectable and is losing the fervour and enthusiasm of the early days. I hope we will get back to that driving power which played such a great part in the birth of the party (Adoption meeting, *Ormskirk Advertiser*, 5 October 1944).

The trade unions are vested interests, for they stand for the vast mass of the people in this country. They stand for the needs and interests of the common people against a limited number who want to make a profit and run the economic system in favour of themselves, and not in the interests of the people of this country (Speech at Ormskirk, *Ormskirk Advertiser*, 18 January 1945).

Not until a great many industries have passed into the hands of

Government ownership and control will there be prosperity and the kind of country we all want to see (14 October 1944).

These speeches contained only a hint of the professionalism and technology-obsession of Wilson's later years. In his first speech at Ormskirk he told his supporters that 'the Government is made up far too much of tired old men . . . during the war there was a great industrial and technical revolution. Great changes have taken place in science, radio, electricity. . . . We are living in a totally different world.'

For the rest, he devoted his speeches to promises of social reform, to attacking (though not always unequivocally) the idea of a coalition Government and to the promise of a new dawn:

I am at the outset of my political career, and I look forward to seeing the socialist Commonwealth, and not only the socialist commonwealth in this country but to an international movement which will make the world a happier place to live in (Adoption meeting, *Ormskirk Advertiser*, 21 June 1945).

As he moved around his constituency, Wilson soon realized that his chances of victory were higher than even he had believed. In the event, he was elected with a majority of more than 7,000 over the Conservative, with Commander King-Hall bottom of the poll. The victory sustained his enthusiasm for a few months longer: 'We are,' he told a meeting at Maghull in December, 'moving forward towards establishing a system of socialism in which production should be for the good of the many and not for the profit of the few. We intend to move forward without consideration of class or profits to a world in which poverty and insecurity will be abolished.'

Harold Wilson had a name for this new world. In a speech on National Savings immediately after his election, he proclaimed:

The people of this country have a great chance of investing in the New Britain. Those who invest their money will be shareholders in the New Britain (4 October 1945).

And, the following May Day, he managed to break off his concentration on the brick shortage to appeal to a meeting at Ashurst Beacon for the 'loyalty of the Labour movement'. He urged:

We need that loyalty, and we have a right to demand that loyalty, for this is a fight for the New Britain.

The most disloyal socialist at the meeting can hardly have guessed how long that fight was to last.

Chapter 2
Consensus, Crisis and Resignation: 1945–51

No Minister in this Administration has had such an easy time as
the President of the Board of Trade. That is largely because there
is a clash between the President of the Board of Trade and the
Government. On the one hand, the Government are trying to pull
the industries of the country to pieces, while, on the other hand, the
President is doing a rather weak and methodical best to pull them
together. There are very few things on which we have to speak
harshly to him because we feel that, in a Government opposed to the
main means by which the country earns its livelihood, he is doing
his best (Mr William Shepherd, Conservative MP for Bucklow,
House of Commons, 1 July 1948).

In all my long association with the House of Commons, I have
never known a President of the Board of Trade with a greater technical grasp of his subject, more verve, more foresight and greater
courage. And that goes for his Tory predecessors (Sir Patrick
Hannon, Conservative MP for Birmingham, Moseley, since 1921,
and leading industrialist, House of Commons, 13 July 1949).

Mr Harold Wilson is a good man (Editorial in the *Daily Express*
20 August 1949).

Throughout the 1930s, Sir Stafford Cripps, founder of the Socialist
League, urged his followers to ensure themselves against 'another
1931'. The collapse of the 1929–31 Labour Government and the
resulting chaos and disillusionment in the Labour Movement was
due, said Cripps, to the obsession of the Government with the
forms and traditions of Parliament. He wrote:

If we are to witness a change in the economic and social structure of the
country, such as we believe to be essential to prosperity, it is clear that
such a change can never be brought about under the existing Parliamentary forms. . . . One factor in the change is of vital importance. A
change so fundamental cannot take place unless the Government of the
country is assured of the support of those who hold the economic, as
distinct from the political power. We must face the fact that those who

at present hold the economic power will refuse their support to any Labour Government. The idea that if the Labour Party is gentle and well-behaved, it will persuade the capitalists to hand over their economic power to the Government is quite fantastic (*Daily Herald*, 12 April 1933).

And again:

Continuity of policy, even in fundamentals, can find no place in a socialist programme. It is this complete severance with all traditional theories of Government, this determination to seize power from the ruling class and transfer it to the people as a whole, that differentiates the present political struggle from all those that have gone before.

It was theory of this kind which led Cripps to advocate the immediate enactment of Emergency Powers by a new Labour Government, restricting the movement of capital and the power of the press, and abolishing the House of Lords. Under these powers, he argued, the Labour Government could proceed with the nationalization of British industry free from the threat of striking capital.

There was not, apparently, a great deal of discussion about these central issues among the leaders of the newly elected Labour Government of 1945. Sir Stafford Cripps himself, the new President of the Board of Trade, seems to have forgotten completely about the 'continuity problem'.

Let Us Face the Future, Labour's manifesto for the 1945 campaign, promised a 'tremendous overhaul' for the nation, which would be accomplished by the conventional, if untried, Fabian tactics of 'drastic policies of replanning', progressive taxation, partial nationalization and 'a firm, constructive hand on our whole productive machinery'. Business, explained the manifesto, which was 'not yet ripe' for nationalization would be 'left to get on with their useful work' and Labour's National Plan would give 'an appropriate place to constructive enterprise and free endeavour'.

Continuity of Parliamentary form was the principle which guided Mr Clement Attlee as he constructed the first majority Labour Government in history. Not one new Ministry was created. The Ministers of Fuel (Emmanuel Shinwell), Education (Ellen Wilkinson) and Health (Aneurin Bevan) were brought into the Cabinet, but otherwise the exact size and shape of Government was borrowed from the Conservative 'caretaker' Government formed by Winston Churchill the previous May.

Having settled the 'continuity problem' by conforming with Tory practice, Attlee looked about him for young men to fill the lesser Government jobs. The new and vast Parliamentary Labour Party consisted in the main of youthful idealists and worthy trade unionists (not to mention a handful of unashamed Marxists and fellow-travellers) – few of whom had any administrative experience. Continuity of Parliamentary and civil service procedure, and co-partnership with private enterprise – the twin rocks upon which Labour policy was founded – prevented the appointment of idealists or ideologues to the great offices of state. Yet, once the senior posts were filled, there were very few Labour MPs with the necessary administrative experience, technical competence and lack of ideology.

Accordingly, Hugh Dalton, Labour's new Chancellor and arch-patron, convened a dinner for 'young victors' (the phrase 'young eagles' was not yet fashionable) to which were invited the brightest and safest brains on the Labour back-benches. Dalton's favourites at the dinner were Hugh Gaitskell, whom he had known for several years, and Harold Wilson, whom on Gaitskell's advice he had appointed Secretary to the Greene Commission on miners' wages three years earlier. At that time Dalton regarded Wilson as even more able than Gaitskell, and recommended accordingly.

Leslie Smith tells us that when Attlee rang up Wilson in Oxford and offered him a post in the Government as Parliamentary Under-Secretary of the Ministry of Works, his exact words were: 'I want you to be Parliamentary Secretary at the Ministry of Works. This is a planning job.' A planning job, that is, as opposed to a job which could conceivably be regarded as policy-making, or which required theoretical ideas. Any doubts Wilson may have had about the wisdom of accepting office without even a day's back-bench experience (he had, apparently, told Dalton, that 'it would be quite wrong to put a newcomer into such a position') were quickly dispelled by Attlee's offer, which was gratefully accepted.

The innumerable administrative problems involved in the transition from a war to a peace economy required the total absorption of the new Labour Ministers, and the more junior the

Minister the more complicated the detail. Very quickly, the vision of a Merrie England and a socialist Commonwealth which had fired Harold Wilson in the election campaign was lost in bureaucracy. In a remarkable confession to his electors only a year after he had taken office Wilson admitted:

I often feel in the day to day struggle with so many problems that we are further even from the socialist commonwealth on which our eyes were fixed a year ago. It is only when we can get away from our struggle that we can see how far we have moved, and realize that the road we have been treading is the right road (Speech at Church House, Ormskirk, *Ormskirk Advertiser*, 10 October 1946).

Like many others of his colleagues, Wilson found it more and more difficult to 'get away from our struggle and see how far we have moved'. The tenuous links with socialist theory, most of them forged by G. D. H. Cole, were very quickly broken. In an essay on Cole, G. D. N. Worswick has written:

The 1945 Parliamentary Labour Party contained not only a number of professional economists many of whom had indeed learnt much from Cole, but also men who had during the war acquired first hand experience of Government in the wartime civil service. . . . Then, too, though Cole himself was the most ardent advocate of the view that the practical measures needed to cope with the reconstruction of the British economy in a war-torn world were the same as those which would hasten the transformation of the economy into a fully socialist one, this consideration was by no means so obvious to others. Cole found himself increasingly out of sympathy with Labour leaders pre-occupied with the balance of payments, production and efficiency to the neglect of socialist ideals. . . . He was out of sympathy with the 'technocratic' tendencies among Labour leaders and intellectuals and felt the need to withdraw completely from current questions.

On the rare occasions when Clement Attlee, who had relied on Cole's theoretical dynamic in the twenties and thirties, agreed to see his former mentor, he would almost always crack the same joke: 'Give me a pair of starry eyes, Douglas, and I will do what you say.' This bovine, arrogant approach forced Cole into political isolation from the Labour Government. Wilson, together with Gaitskell and other former Cole disciples, dropped out of Cole's life.

Very soon, however, Harold Wilson found a new hero and a new guide. In March 1947 he was appointed Parliamentary Secretary for Overseas Trade at the Board of Trade. There for the first time he came into close contact with Sir Stafford Cripps, the President. No other British politician, not even Disraeli, had a greater influence on Wilson than Sir Stafford Cripps. At almost every stage in Wilson's political career, whatever the occasion, he has found it difficult not to reach for his Hansard to quote from his former chief.

Until the age of forty, Cripps had devoted himself to the Bar and the Church of England. He then became a cautious Minister in Ramsay Macdonald's 1929 Government. After the split with Macdonald in 1931, Cripps veered violently leftwards, founded the Socialist League on a programme of working-class power and, later in the 1930s, supported the Popular Front of Communists and Socialists against Fascism in Europe. His attack on the mine-owners at the public inquiry into the pit disaster at Gresford in 1935 won him widespread respect in the Labour and trade-union movement.

Cripps's politics were not based on deep theoretical study. He read the minimum necessary to grasp the rudiments of his case, and relied on his considerable ability as a propagandist and lawyer. Throughout the period, he closed his eyes to the monstrosities committed by Stalin in the name of socialism and communism, and stoically defended Soviet society and Soviet practice.

In five years of war, all this theory vanished, as suddenly as it had taken root. In its place, Cripps revived his interest in Christianity and patriotism. As a patriot and Christian (though still technically expelled from the Labour Party) he accepted a post in the Churchill Government, which he held until the end of the war. By then, all talk about working-class power, Emergency Powers and striking capital had dried up. Instead, Sir Stafford could tell the workers of Belfast:

We must create within our industries, especially the older ones, a conscious team spirit between directors, management and workers for progress and development (*Belfast Newsletter*, 21 August 1944).

And in July 1944, he gave a sermon in St Stephen's Church, Walbrook:

We have been thrilled and stimulated by the great technical advances that mankind has made during our generation. . . . On the material side we have excelled, but not on the moral side. The value in this situation of the teachings of Christ is incalculable (7 July 1944, quoted in Colin Cooke, *Life of Richard Stafford Cripps*, Hodder, 1957).

With these new values firmly entrenched, Cripps set to work at the Board of Trade. Almost at once, he became the most conventional of the Labour administrators, working prodigiously hard at the administrative problems of export and production. When, in 1947, he became Chancellor of the Exchequer in place of Hugh Dalton, the Opposition, the City of London and the entire ruling class which Cripps had savaged ten years previously sighed with relief, and watched with approval as Cripps ended Dalton's 'cheap money' policy, and set about conventional Conservative remedies to the recurring balance of payments crises.

This post-war Cripps was a hero to the young Harold Wilson, who had so despised the 'public-school Marxists' whom Cripps had represented in the 1930s. Cripps's aloof command of detail, his scientific education and knowledge, his administrative genius, his belief in bureaucracy, his patriotism, his Christianity and even his vegetarianism combined to make what Harold Wilson regarded as the perfect politician. Through the grim years of Opposition in the 1950s and the even grimmer years of power in the mid-1960s, Wilson referred publicly and privately to a speech made by Cripps while Wilson was still his junior, and which the young Minister regarded as the high peak of political oratory. It was made in the House of Commons in a State of the Nation debate on 7 August 1947; and it dealt with 'the kernel of the whole problem – how we are to produce more':

Our failure or success will depend in the last resort upon the spirit of our people. The quality of effort that is needed in the next few years is not such that it can be evoked by mere material considerations or by intensification of self-interest or competitive self-seeking. Employers, staffs, technicians and workers alike must be fairly rewarded. . . . There must be no sense of injustice and no favouritism or privilege except as the reward for an honest contribution to the needs of the nation. . . . We must bring home to our people the seriousness of the country's economic plight, and the future problems that we face. We must convince them of their power to overcome all difficulties by common effort. We must draw out from our people that courage and determination which have always been the hallmarks of the British character. We can offer no immediate prospects of relief. The struggle of production, the balance of payments, is as tough a proposition as any that this country has ever faced, and there is no easy way out. Production, and production alone, can find us relief in our immediate situation. It is not part of the British character to resign ourselves to such difficulties or to fail to take the measures, however hard, to overcome them. It has been truly said that by our faith we can move mountains. It is by our faith in ourselves, in our country, in the free democratic traditions for which the people of this country have for centuries fought and battled and for which they must fight again as willing' on the economic front as upon the oceans, the land and in the air – it is by our faith in the deep spiritual values that we acknowledge in our Christian faith, that we shall be enabled and inspired to move the present mountains of our difficulties and to emerge into that new and fertile plain of prosperity which we shall travel in happiness only as a result of our own efforts and our own vision.

If there is such a thing as a political text this mixture of asceticism, bombast and chauvinism was, and is, Harold Wilson's. The belief that the economic and political problems of mankind can be solved by faith in God, patriotic exhortation and hard work was as crucial to Wilson's political and theoretical development as was his contempt for everything which Sir Stafford Cripps had said before the war.

The Board of Trade in 1947 was the leading production department, and at that time dealt with all industries which were not allotted to other Ministries (as were coal, gas, electricity to Fuel and Power; iron, steel, metals, vehicles, engineering and explosives to Supply). It dealt also with prices, insurances, distribution of industry, overseas trade, census of production, enemy property and the enormous range of controls over industry which had been inherited from Churchill's wartime administration.

It is, therefore, the department of state with the greatest and most complicated detail. Harold Wilson once said that his greatest deficiency is his obsession with detail, and to anyone with an obsession for detail the Board of Trade is at once a paradise and a death-trap. Paradise, because it provides every conceivable outlet for administrative flair; death-trap because it distracts its chiefs from the wider implications of what they are doing.

Harold Wilson cannot have been long at the Board of Trade

before realizing that any talk of 'seizing power from the ruling class and transferring it to the people as a whole' belonged to fantasy. Never before or since has the Board of Trade been so dominated by businessmen. The principal industrial adviser was Sir William Palmer, chairman of the British Rayon Federation. G. R. White, the Board's leather controller, was an official of the United Tanners' Federation. Its match controller worked for Bryant and May, Britain's biggest match company, and his office was conveniently situated on the firm's premises. Sir Ralph Reed, chairman of the big paper company of the same name, was the Board of Trade Paper Controller. The shoe controller, Major F. J. Strattom, was a director of Dolcis; the controllers for hosiery, furniture, tobacco, and 'molasses and industrial alcohol' were all leading trade-association officials; the Cotton Control was staffed almost exclusively from the Boards of Lancashire cotton firms, while the Timber Control, the biggest of all, was run entirely by the industry.[1]

Firms were encouraged by the Government to appoint associations to speak for the entire industry, and the increase in power of the trade association – which later provided so much ammunition for industry's assault on the Government – was originally inspired by the Government. Several crucial activities of the Board of Trade were actually administered by trade associations.

The control of newsprint, for instance, which caused the President a lot of anxiety and hostile press criticism, was administered by the Newsprint Rationing Committee – a body specially set up by the trade. Most of this machinery was inherited from the Conservatives, yet Harold Wilson was delighted with it, and, in his four years at the Board of Trade, bolstered up the system of control by still further appointments of prominent businessmen to positions of power and influence.

The businessmen who offered themselves to the Board of Trade and other Government departments for Government jobs were not, on the whole, drawn from the politically motivated ranks of old-guard Tory industrialists. The new men had read their Keynes, and had come to the conclusion that large-scale unemployment

1. See Rogow and Shore, *The Labour Government and British Industry 1945–1951*, Blackwell, 1955 – a book so crucial to this period of Wilson's life that I have shamelessly plagiarized it.

was not necessarily a by-product of capitalism. More importantly, they had accurately gauged the political mood of the country which was impatient of pre-war Tory ideology. As students of Labour politics, they understood the essentially reformist nature of the Party, and the abhorrence with which its leaders regarded revolution. They knew, too, that unemployment in men and plant means comparatively low profits, and that the capitalist system works best for everyone, including employers, when industry and labour are fully employed. They saw the Labour Government, with its ability to placate the unions, as a stabilizer of a dangerous political situation and a promoter of a properly subsidized, thriving capitalism, with its unprofitable substructure administered by the state. There was, in their view, no serious danger to private capital. Quite the reverse. As one 'Tory radical', Angus Maude, declared in Parliament soon after his Party had won the 1951 election: 'Since the war ended it has been easier to make higher profits without being really efficient than probably at any period in my lifetime.'

Such men, maintaining an implicit and dedicated faith in the private enterprise system, were only too keen to serve the new Labour Government and its Ministers. Before long they were working splendidly together, and had even managed to persuade the old-guard industrialists to hold their fire.

When still at the Ministry of Works, after six months' hectic administration, Wilson could reassure the House of Commons about the 'feeling that the operation of monopolies and trade associations might be impeding the national effort for increased production'. 'Up to the present, at any rate,' he said, 'we have not had anything like the amount of trouble from such organizations as I expected. We have had virtually no trouble at all' (Hansard, 25 March 1946).

And again, a month later, after attending a conference of industrialists in Manchester to discuss the brick shortage, he could say: 'We found the spirit of the conference highly cooperative and believe the region will play its part.'

Wilson was deeply impressed by the spirit of cooperation among so many progressive industrialists. More and more, he shed his initial suspicions about them and relied upon them for advice and decisions. It was during his two years as an Under-Secretary and his first two years at the Board of Trade that Wilson worked out his attitude to industry and the national economy.

His first principle was that 'the solution in the long term to Britain's problems can come *only* by the development of efficiency in British industry and in British exports' (House of Commons, 24 March 1947). Again and again, he stressed all-party agreement on this proposition:

There are many things in this country which divide us in the political sense, but in the national effort to increase exports we are united (*Daily Telegraph*, 9 May 1950).

Any disagreement on their paramount need to increase exports was, for Wilson, unthinkable. Yet if he had read the former speeches and writings of his Cabinet colleague and friend, Aneurin Bevan, he would have discovered a jarring note of controversy on the export issue. Bevan summed up his opposition to export obsession in his brilliant pamphlet, written shortly before the end of the war, *Why Not Trust the Tories?*

Before the war exports represented about one fifth of our total production. We were doing our best to lift that percentage to a still higher figure. At the same time as we were trying to persuade people in other parts of the world to buy increased quantities of goods from us, millions of our own people were going short of these same goods. Now all trade is an act of exchange. Nevertheless, by some twist of the Tory mind, it is good trade to persuade someone in a remote part of the world to buy our goods, but ruinous to allow the same goods to be consumed by our own people.

We are told now by some people who ought to know better that we shall need to increase our exports after the war by fifty per cent. Why? Because we are told we have used our foreign investments to pay for arms to fight Hitler. Now who bought the foreign shares we had to sell? In the main it was the USA. Yet a short time ago the Chairman of the American Chamber of Trade informed us that when the war is over, America is going to embark on a great trade drive to increase her exports. Just like us, in fact. So we are setting out on a drive for exports because we have lost our foreign investments, and the nation that bought our foreign investments is going to do the same thing. You see, the loss of our foreign investments has not very much to do with it. The truth is that our manufacturers try to sell their goods to people in other lands mainly because our own people are too poor to buy the goods themselves.

At the same time that American Tories are pushing their products on the world markets, millions of American workers are going short of many things they badly need. In competition with them British Tories will try to send goods abroad that you yourself would buy if you could. *Expanding exports are the will o' the wisp private enterprise is compelled to pursue by underpaying its own workers and thus limiting its own home market.*

There is no virtue in exports in themselves, just as there is no merit in digging holes and filling them up again merely in order to get work. We require to export only what is necessary to buy what we need from abroad. The commonsense way is to produce all we can and then sell what we must. The Tory puts it the other way about. He gives first claim to exports and not to home consumption. In short, he pays more attention to the twenty per cent we spend abroad than to the eighty per cent we produce and consume at home.

In the debate on the Beveridge Report in June 1944, another future Labour Minister, Emmanuel Shinwell, declared:

The hon. and gallant member for Bolton [Sir E. Cadogan] has emphasised our alleged reliance on exports. I am sure the hon. member for Pudsey and Otley would agree and the hon. and gallant gentleman would agree that increased exports are demanded. There never was a greater fallacy uttered in this or any other Assembly.

In the same debate Jim Griffiths summed up the deep dissatisfaction even among middle-of-the-road Labour thinkers with the doctrine of the export-obsessed:

I am increasingly appalled in this House to hear everybody talk as though at the end of the war there will be a struggle for exports and we shall have much competition. With whom are we going to compete? Over there across the Channel, Americans and British are fighting alongside each other and dying together. Are we going to compete at the end of the war with people who are our allies in war? Are we sending out our message to the world that although we can collaborate to win a war, we cannot collaborate in order to achieve the well-being of the people of the world? I say that at the end of the war, we should end another war: the competition for the markets of the world.

Such arguments have long since been annihilated by the epidemic of export-obsession which has struck down all modern leading politicians. But at that time, most Labour thinkers of Right and Left were determined not to enter the export rat-race with the enthusiasm of pre-war Tory Governments. Harold Wilson, however, was not embarrassed or influenced by these 'ideological' arguments. From the moment he entered the Board of Trade as Overseas Secretary in March 1946, he threw himself into the export drive with a nationalist zeal which astonished and delighted the Opposition and the *Daily Express*.

Almost every speech of the President of the Board of Trade from September 1947 to 1951 impressed upon his audience the importance of exports. The Export Credits Guarantees Department – a Tory creation, whose purpose was to insure exporters against potential loss – was refurbished more than once with further hundreds of millions of pounds in two Acts of Parliament. By Wilson's own edict, steel was allocated to the motor industry on the basis that a certain percentage would be exported, and in many other areas of industry the Board of Trade pursued the principle which Bevan had so ruthlessly attacked: 'that it is good trade to persuade someone in a remote part of the world to buy our goods, but ruinous to allow the same goods to be consumed by our own people'. Purchase tax and physical controls were kept on as late as 1949, not, Wilson declared, to provide for poorer people, but to ensure that vital goods were not sold at home. Wilson himself admitted that clothes rationing, for instance, had the salutary effect of diverting many textile products away from the home market.

Jim Griffiths' idealistic hopes that men who had fought together in the war might unite afterwards to stop the trade war were comprehensively dashed. To the new Labour Government and President of the Board of Trade, no competition mattered more than competition with America. The young President called on his countrymen to work harder to close the Dollar Gap. He himself set up the Dollar Exports Board, inevitably presided over by one of the country's biggest businessmen, C. D. McCarthy, an oil and shipping magnate. As late as 1949 Wilson was referring to 'the problem which dominates all others – the problem of exports to North America' and was proudly telling the Commons of his detailed plans to divide the American market into four segments. 'A small number of enterprising merchant firms,' he explained, 'and merchant bankers have, after a careful study of the market, set up regional selling organizations. The North American export drive is our *first national task* in 1949' (House of Commons, 11 April 1949).

Wilson backed up his call for more and more exports with language which was unashamedly capitalistic and chauvinist. Free competition was his main slogan.

We want to remove import restrictions, imposed for balance of payments reasons. We want to see import restrictions which are imposed for less respectable reasons such as protection of home industries, banned as an instrument of national policy (Speech to the Institute of Bankers, 16 August 1949).

And a new phrase, borrowed from the flag-wagging romances of his favourite historian, Arthur Bryant, was introduced into his Ministerial vocabulary – the 'merchant venturer'.

Many other industries, instead of pursuing maximum efficiency, instead of taking their merchant venturer spirit into the markets of the world, went in for the apparently easier and safer, but ultimately more disastrous policy of the restriction of supply, price fixing, feather bedding and reliance on a safe, protected home market (House of Commons, 12 April 1948).

I hope that at the conference I mentioned earlier, and which is to take place immediately after Easter, we shall see the merchant venturer spirit of 1949 spring to life [1](House of Commons, 11 April 1949).

There is a great deal of evidence that men like Bevan and the younger, more 'ideological' members of the Parliamentary Labour Party swallowed this doctrine with some distaste. If they were convinced at all of the need for export hysteria, they saw it as a necessary condition for national and economic survival, made inevitable by American protectionism. What distinguished Wilson from these doubters was his immediate, unconditional support for exports for exports' sake. With his enthusiasm for exports went an admiration for private enterprise. That private enterprise was good for the Labour Government and *vice versa* Wilson was seldom in any doubt. He learnt a great deal about the

1. In his first major speech in the campaign which put him in Downing Street – in Birmingham on 19 January 1964 – Wilson called for a return to 'brashness and saltiness, and political irreverence, our energy, determination and merchant adventuring spirit'. Anthony Howard and Richard West in their book *The Making of the Prime Minister* refer to this last phrase as 'oddly imperialistic'. Imperialistic, perhaps, but certainly not odd.

nation's affairs from his discussions with small groups of what he regarded as 'progressive businessmen', which he chose and convened himself. In May 1949, he announced that a 'small group in the City would be available to give advice to the Government on financial and banking matters' (the leader of the group was Charles Hambro, the 'progressive' banker).

With the advice of such men ringing in his ears, Wilson championed the cause of private enterprise in the Commons, in the country and even in his constituency. The success of the export drive, he told the Commons in September 1948, was 'the really important achievement' of both Government and industry in the post-war period. He went on:

> Those sections of industry which still remain under private enterprise are doing a whole lot better under a socialist Government than they ever did under a Tory Government. What the present Government has done for private enterprise is to provide markets for their output by maintaining full employment and the purchasing power of the worker at a high level (17 September 1948).

And, in a speech at Ormskirk in his constituency a few months later:

> There are some people who delight in playing down our efforts to further the export drive. These people have said that the Labour Government would be the end of the small trader but the fact that these traders are much more prosperous under the socialists gives the lie direct. It has been proved that private enterprise can function under a Labour Government (*Ormskirk Advertiser*, 9 December 1948).

In the largest control operated by the Board of Trade – Timber Control – Wilson revelled in the cooperation he offered and received from the big timber merchants. 'In the case of timber,' he told the Commons on 20 April 1950, 'as in many more, it took a socialist Minister to make free enterprise free and enterprising.'

Such Cobdenite enthusiasm for the free market irritated his supporters and bemused the Opposition. In a speech on economic affairs on 11 April 1949, Wilson was interrupted in full flood by a genuinely confused Tory:

WILSON: Private enterprise has produced on a vastly greater scale under this Socialist Government than it ever did when we had a Tory

Government. Of course the production and export achievement of 1948 and 1949 are a tribute to private enterprise. . . .

SIR WILLIAM DARLING (Edinburgh South): Is it the view of the Rt Hon. gentleman that the more socialism there is in this country, the more successful private enterprise will be?

WILSON: On the limited experience of the last few years, that is certainly so.

The new conviction, by now rooted in the young administrator, that socialism and free enterprise were synonymous and advantageous to one another led him, perhaps logically, to the view that the freer the enterprise the more socialist the socialism. Thus he embarked with enthusiasm on two major measures to smash the chains of state interference on private enterprise.

The first was the famous 'bonfire of controls' in November 1948 (announced on Guy Fawkes Day to show that the young President took an interest in public relations). Restrictions requiring roughly 200,000 licences on more than 60 industrial commodities and a wide range of 'necessary goods' (especially household goods) were removed or relaxed. Another bonfire was lit five months later, involving nearly a million licences, and the quota system, limiting firms as to quantity of goods produced and sold, was almost completely removed. The process was continued in 1950 with the abolition of petrol rationing, price control, steel licensing (except sheet and tinplate) and the extension of Open General Licensing to Marshall Aid countries.

Most of these controls were bureaucratic excesses, remnants of wartime necessity unrelated to each other, let alone to a general national plan.

Yet, although they were abolished they were not replaced. No phoenix of a national plan rose from the ashes of the burned wartime licences. Winston Churchill's controls were replaced by the free market. By the end of 1948, the Labour Government in general and Harold Wilson in particular had abandoned all pretence at economic planning. In its place they substituted the law of the market place. As A. A. Rogow has written in his admirable little book:

The Labour Government seemed far more interested in removing controls than in improving or extending control techniques. . . . In 1948–50, when the economy appeared to be gaining both internal and external balance, there was a substantial shift away from planning in the direction of a free market system.

When Harold Wilson was interrupted by the rubber merchant, Walter Fletcher, the Tory Member for Bury, he replied crossly: 'The Hon. Member always pressed for rubber to be returned to a free market, and it has been' (House of Commons, 14 July 1949). This process corresponded precisely with the views and theories of the young President of the Board of Trade.

What Wilson had called 'the limited experience of the last few years' had taught him one further lesson, namely that public ownership, or nationalization, was not a matter of principle or faith, but a weapon to be used to help private enterprise on its booming way.

The role of the state was not to break down class privilege and wealth, but on the contrary to lubricate the awkward machinery of the market. Power and transport, for instance, could not be provided for the export industries if coal and the railways remained under private ownership and control. Wilson's favourite quotation during his four years in office was that of Lord McGowan, chairman of Imperial Chemical Industries, one of the most powerful and wealthy capitalists in the land, who had told a meeting of industrialists that without coal nationalization the nation would be getting a million tons of coal less every week, with appalling consequences for private industry, notably for chemicals. 'Leading businessmen,' Wilson trumpeted with pride at a meeting at Burscough in his constituency, 'admit that had it not been for the improved output since nationalization there would have been no basis for private enterprise to work on' (*Ormskirk Advertiser*, 31 March 1949).

'Nationalization,' said Wilson, summing up his attitude at a Christian meeting during the 1950 election campaign, 'as it affects each industry must be considered individually. Each industry must be considered on its merits' (*Prescot and Huyton Reporter*, 10 February 1950).

Nationalization by Board became increasingly unpopular – not merely because the technical details were complicated, but also because it was not entirely successful in its stated aim, to assist British private industry in its export drive, in increasing productivity and efficiency and producing more. Harold Wilson, when in power, was always sceptical about wholesale nationalization, but he believed wholeheartedly in less drastic Statist manoeuvres worked out originally by his hero, Sir Stafford Cripps.

Of these the most prominent were the Development Councils. Shortly before Wilson took over at the Board of Trade, his predecessor sponsored the Industrial Organization and Development Act 1947, which gave powers to the Government to establish Development Councils in suitable British industries. The Councils consisted of industrialists, trade unionists and independent members whose votes could swing the balance.

The powers of the Development Councils were negligible. They could levy compulsorily from industry; collect statistics by compulsory order and keep a register; and initiate training and research schemes to promote greater efficiency. The work of the Council depended entirely on the cooperation of the industry concerned. Even when the Council initiated schemes it was still open to firms to ignore them.

Harold Wilson supported the Development Councils with almost embarrassing enthusiasm. Before long, the Councils had become the foundation of Government policy towards private industry. Wilson made every effort to persuade the various industries to form a Council, assuring them that nothing but the good of the industry and free enterprise was at stake. Announcing the formation of a Development Council for the Potteries industry in September 1948 he declared:

There was never any intention in any part of this House in passing this act to operate half-way houses towards nationalization. . . . The establishment of a Development Council in that [the cotton] industry in no way weakens the poistion of the trade association on either side of the industry.

On the specific question of the Potteries Development Council, Wilson went out of his way to reassure the employers:

We revised the draft order in certain particulars on lines which I hoped would make it more acceptable to the manufacturers (House of Commons, 14 September 1948).

Yet in spite of all these pleas and bribes the potteries employers coolly rejected the proposals for a Development Council. Indeed, the whole Development Council effort was a miserable failure. Only four Councils were set up – in cotton, jewellery, furniture and clothing – and in five other major sets of industries, the Government received a polite but firm brush-off. The Jewellery Development Councils were abolished soon after the Labour Government was voted out of office and none of the others made the slightest impact upon the relevant industry's development. The Development Councils failed to provide a boost to research and efficiency and to establish a new partnership between state and industry. They were hardly worth the many hundreds of hours the young President of the Board of Trade had wasted in the unsuccessful attempt to persuade private enterprise to make itself more enterprising without any real threat to its privacy.

Nothing more clearly portrays Wilson's attitude to private industry and to state interference than his Monopolies Act of 1948 – perhaps the biggest and most important piece of legislation to come out of the Board of Trade while Wilson was in office.

Anyone who believed in the value of free enterprise and competition as much as Harold Wilson did in his years as President of the Board of Trade was horrified by 'the restrictive practices' which arose from time to time to frustrate the smooth workings of the markets. Wilson complained bitterly about 'the feather bed of restrictive practices on both sides of industry' – most notably, as far as the Monopolies Bill was concerned, the fixing of manufacturers' prices. 'There has grown up,' said Wilson on the second Reading of his Monopolies Bill,

a host of restrictive arrangements in British industry which have had the effect of frustrating and destroying the operation of that free enterprise which I think some sentimentalists fondly imagined characterized British industry. . . . Competition is the public's natural safeguard in any industry which continues on the basis of private enterprise, and the attitude of mind that I have just described is a denial of everything which goes with private enterprise (House of Commons, 22 April 1948).

Yet Government fury at price-fixing had to be tempered by still more important considerations. At the outset, Wilson had admitted that the 'test of the effect of a restriction on the public interest is this: does it make the task of selling British goods in world markets easier or more difficult?'

In other words, although monopoly was wrong, it was even more wrong to enforce free competition against the interests of Britain's export industry. Harold Wilson was one of the first modern politicians to understand that monopoly or merger provides facilities for investment which do not obtain under the old competitive system.

Monopoly legislation therefore presented the post-war Labour Government with a cruel problem. On the one hand the ideological case for stamping out cartels and price-fixing was obvious to all. On the other, the importance of *not* curtailing the centralization in industry of technological know-how and development was crucial to Britain's survival as an industrial power. The dilemma was stated most lucidly by the President of the Board of Trade, Harold Wilson, in his third-reading speech on the Monopolies Bill:

There is one thing on which we are all agreed and that is the danger to our economic life, not from any racketeering or any search for excessive profits, but from the inertia and feather-bedding which some firms may possibly be guilty of under the protection of price-fixing arrangements. . . . We cannot afford that sort of thing on one side of industry or another. The measures we have taken in this Bill will be applied very much toward weeding out lack of enterprise connected with monopolistic conditions and restrictive practices because that is demanding attention.

So far, so good. But there were difficulties:

We have not provided powers to bust a trust or bust a monopoly as is done for instance in Transatlantic legislation. Units in many industries are getting larger and larger, because this is necessary for technical purposes. They may be efficient. It may be true that in many industries the existence of a large number of small units would be highly inefficient on technical grounds. Therefore we should not seek to bust a trust, merely because it is large, merely because it is responsible for one-third or even one hundred per cent of the production of goods in this country (House of Commons, 29 June 1948).

In other words, price-fixing arrangements are bad, but in some cases firms owning 100 per cent of production (and therefore, by definition, fixing prices) may be efficient. In which case, price-fixing arrangements are not bad.

The result of this dilemma was the crucifixion of the Monopolies Bill. The Monopolies Commission was not set up for almost a year after the Bill became law, and by the time the Labour Government left office the Commission had submitted two reports (on dental and rain-water goods) and was investigating four others. The two reports made no impact of any kind on the two industries concerned and the chairman of the Dental Manufacturing Company told his shareholders that 'the provisions of the Dental Monopolies Order will not in any way vary or restrict your Company's trading' (quoted in Rogow and Shore, p. 97). When it came to ending price-fixing, Harold Wilson's Monopolies and Restrictive Practices Act was worse than useless. Its sponsor's predilection for efficiency, investment and technology took preference over the promise in Labour's manifesto of 'public supervision over monopolies and cartels'.

But perhaps the most striking illustration of Harold Wilson's attitude towards industry and monopoly was his reaction to the recurring crises in British films. During his period at the Board of Trade the problems of British films took up more of his time and more of his Parliamentary speeches than any other single issue. Throughout the 1940s films provided the only mass entertainment. In 1945 – the heyday of the British film industry – nearly 5,000 cinemas catered every week for more than 20,000,000 people. More than half the adult population visited the cinema every week and the standard and frequency of films was a national issue as it has never been before or since.

By the time Harold Wilson came into the Labour Government, British films were dominated in every department by one man: the Yorkshire miller, J. Arthur Rank. Rank had learnt about monopoly in the milling trade. But a milling monopoly was not enough to satisfy his Methodist conscience or his business appetite, and, in 1939, he joined the board of one of the country's biggest cinema owners, Odeon Cinemas. Very soon he was chairman of Odeon, and in October 1941, he bought a majority shareholding in Gaumont British, the biggest cinema chain in the land. In four years Rank had become the controller of two of the three biggest circuits, incorporating 650 cinemas and selling more than a fifth of all the seats in Britain. This interest spilled over into distribution and production. Rank owned and controlled General Film Distributors Ltd, Eagle–Lion and United World Pictures, which distributed all the films made in his studios. He owned and controlled film studios at Denham, Pinewood, Highbury, Islington and Shepherds Bush – rather more than 70 per cent of all the studio space available in the country; his production companies included Two Cities, Independent Producers, Individual Pictures, Cineguild and Gainsborough Pictures. The only film company which rivalled the Rank organization in size and profitability was Associated British Picture Corporation, with a circuit of 450 cinemas, and studios, distribution companies and production companies to match. These two companies with their three circuits controlled more than half the crucial 'first-run' cinemas, and 200 of London's 300 'first-run' cinemas.

The two companies, and particularly Rank, exercised almost complete control over the production of films in Britain. No film could make money unless it was shown on the major circuits. And even if a film was accepted by the circuits, the booking arrangements could be – and often were – fixed against the interests of the production company not owned by Rank or ABC. The standard joke among the more satirical independent producers was that any film of theirs booked by Rank would be shown in 'Wakes Week' in Warrington, 'Fairs Fortnight' in Glasgow and the week after Christmas everywhere else. Even the competition between Rank and ABC was illusory. The two giants made certain that neither suffered too much from the other's policy.

Towards the end of the war, in spite of this increasing monopoly, British films enjoyed their best period in their history. The flow of film from companies like Two Cities (*Henry V*, *The Way Ahead*, *In Which We Serve*, *Brief Encounter* and *Way to the Stars*), Ealing Studios (*The Foreman Went to France*, *Nine Men*, *Convoy*, *San Demetrio London*, *Next of Kin*), Crown Film Unit, Charter, Gainsborough, and British National, and the emergence of directors like David Lean, Laurence Olivier, Carol Reed, Frank Launder and Sidney Gilliatt, provided for a brief period a basis for a real recovery of the British film industry. To a great extent, this was a sign of the times: of a new creative idealism among British film artists which, in the days before television, fulfilled itself exclusively in the cinema. The new idealism was born out of contempt for the political and cultural sterility of the inter-war years and the hope for a new socialist era. Rank, in this period, played the benevolent despot. Good British films were making good money (the dividend paid out to shareholders of the Odeon Cinemas, for instance, was increased from 10 per cent in 1942, when Rank took over, to 25 per cent in 1945 – a 150 per cent increase).

The Methodist miller was greatly moved by the spirit of patriotism which consumed the nation, and he lashed out funds to the production companies as they required it. David Lean used to refer to Rank, behind his back, as 'the golden goose'. More publicly he praised the Rank policy of not interfering in film-making and producing (see article in Penguin Film Review, No. 4, October 1947).

Filippo del Giudice, the driving force behind Two Cities, was particularly successful in squeezing capital from the golden goose in those halycon years. And Rank himself could tell the Methodist Recorder: 'If I could relate to you some of my various adventures and experiences in the larger film world, you would not only be astonished, but it would, I think, be as plain to you as it is to me that I was being led by God.'

Unhappily, however, the flow of golden eggs from the golden goose could not last for ever and soon after the war J. Arthur Rank, patriotic patron, was replaced once more by J. Arthur Rank, Yorkshire miller. The Rank organization managing director – the hard-headed accountant John Davis – immediately set about 'cleaning up' the Rank Organization and making sure that the British film industry was run on the lines which he best understood – those of the box office.[1]

The threat to the independence of British producers and production companies came chiefly from America. Britain represented by far the biggest market for the American film companies, and any earnings in Britain almost always represented clear profits for

1. Occasionally, Davis, who was never wrong about money, was wrong about films. Coming out of Pinewood Studios after seeing one of Michael Powell's films, Davis is reported to have said: 'I would never have allowed this film to be shown, if Rank hadn't insisted on it. It's a loser from the start.' The film was The Red Shoes, which made hundreds of thousands of pounds for many years.

American films which had covered their costs in America. The price was set deliberately low to beat home competition. American 'B' films were sometimes priced as low as £10,000 each, which, for a man like Davis, represented manna from heaven. If the films were drivel, and if their booking on a main circuit shut out an excellent home-made documentary, that was either bad luck or the law of the market.

Even in the late war years, American domination of British films and film-making increased. American earnings from films shown in Britain rose from £4.8 m. in 1940 to £15.6 m. in 1944, to £70 m. in 1947. By 1945 – the best year in British film history – 80 per cent of the films shown in Britain were made in America. Were it not for the Quota Act of 1927 and its subsequent amendments, which forced the British distribution companies and cinema circuits to show a percentage of British-made films, the entire industry would have been swallowed by Hollywood. J. Arthur Rank's patriotism, like his Methodism, was always kept strictly within the limits of the dividend percentage. And his Organization accelerated the process of buying cheap, buying American and concentrating home production on ugly colossals (like *Caesar and Cleopatra*). The colossals took a long time to make, and kept down the production level of British films, but they could sometimes make handsome profits in the American market.

Peter Forster, in his essay on the film industry in the compendium *Age of Austerity*,[1] writes: 'Rank stood massively, almost monolithically for British films.' In fact, Rank never scrupled to engage in economic deals which clearly compromised the British film industry. He held vast shareholdings in the American companies, 20th Century–Fox, Universal, and Selznick International. Films from these companies, bought on the cheap, got regular preference in the Rank circuits. Similarly, Warner Brothers' 37 per cent shareholding in the Associated British Picture Corporation gave Warner's films a guaranteed showing on the ABC circuit. The very existence of the monopoly forced independently made British films out in place of cheaply made American ones. Not only the film technicians' union (the Association of Cinematographic Technicians) but most Labour MPs who studied the

1. *Age of Austerity*, edited by Michael Sissons and Philip French (Penguin Books, 1963).

question and most independent-minded people in the film industry agreed that the duopoly of the circuits restricted independent film production not only by denying independent films access to the cinemas but also by encouraging the showing of cheap, third-rate American films.

All these problems relating to films came under the aegis of the Board of Trade, by history and tradition the most bureaucratic and least sensitive of Government departments. At the Board of Trade administrative competence takes precedence over artistic sensitivity, and, even in the idealistic post-war years, the new Labour Ministers at the Board had little in common with the world of the film director. Nevertheless, the entire Labour leadership was very quickly seduced by the glamorous atmosphere of the cinema world. Sir Stafford Cripps, the ascetic vegetarian, and his wife were regular guests at the luxurious luncheons thrown at Grosvenor House by Filippo Del Giudice. At Del Giudice's country villa, after a gay dinner, the guests, liberally sprinkled with glamorous starlets, would retire to 'Del's' private cinema where the guest of honour, usually a Labour Cabinet Minister, would select a film. The more irreverent guests dreaded the visits of Ernest Bevin, Foreign Secretary, who with his wife would invariably select the most banal film available.

Like his mentor, Cripps, Harold Wilson greatly enjoyed the atmosphere of the film world, even though his taste in films was hardly more sophisticated than Ernest Bevin's. He told the Commons:

We are getting tired of some of the gangster, sadistic and psychological films of which we have seen so many – of diseased minds, schizophrenia, amnesia and diseases which occupy so much of our screen time. I should like to see more films which genuinely show our way of life, and I am not aware that amnesia and schizophrenia are stock parts of our social life[1] (House of Commons, 17 June 1948).

Also like Cripps, Wilson applied himself to mastering the problems of the industry, which, by the time he took over at the

1. What Wilson liked was something more simple: 'I have no doubt that I sing and whistle almost in my sleep most of the hits in *Oklahoma* and *Annie Get Your Gun*, but there are many British tunes which I would like to see exploited just as much,' he told a dinner of the Performing Rights Society (*Evening Standard*, 15 July 1948).

74 The Politics of Harold Wilson

Board of Trade in October 1947, had reached unimaginable proportions. Two months previously, Hugh Dalton, Chancellor of the Exchequer, in a desperate attempt to help close the dollar gap, had imposed a duty of 75 per cent on the value of imported films. The tax, it was hoped, would save Britain about £57 m. of the £70 m. which American films were making in this country.

The Motion Picture Association of America reacted with startling solidarity by announcing the following day that no further American films would be allowed into Britain while the *ad valorem* duty obtained. The strike was immediately effective and utterly crippling. The British public was furious at missing the vast majority of new films, and old American films still in the country were repeated *ad nauseam*, thus increasing the dollar drain. As Wilson put it, 'we were actually paying not 17 but 50 million dollars for the privilege of seeing *Hellzapoppin*' for the third time and *Ben Hur* for the twenty-third' (speech to ACCT, 11 April 1948).

The patriotic Rank was furious. With the boycott of American films, the greater part of his revenue disappeared. His reliance on American films had left his production companies hopelessly short of funds to fill the gap which followed the embargo. In November 1947, Rank announced plans for forty-seven new feature films. But simultaneously he and his associates brought heavy pressure upon the Government to remove the *ad valorem* duty.

Harold Wilson took office in the middle of the American film companies' embargo. It was clear from the outset, particularly after Dalton's fall from grace, that the Government would have to grovel to the Americans, and Wilson soon found himself closeted with Eric Johnston, tough negotiator for the American film interests, working out the extent of the British withdrawal.

The final agreement was announced on 11 March 1948. The 75 per cent duty was withdrawn. The Americans were allowed to take £17 m. out of the country and leave the rest of their film earnings in the country, most of which, clearly, would be invested in films and film production. The agreement was sharply attacked from Right and Left as a surrender to Hollywood, but there was little else which Wilson could do. In the face of a solid embargo of the American film companies, an increase in the overall dollar drain and the opposition of J. Arthur Rank he was powerless.

Speaking at the annual conference of the Association of Cinematograph and Allied Technicians the following month, Wilson defended the agreement, and called for an all-out effort to produce more British films. He would assist further home production, he promised, by raising the compulsory quota for British films.

As far as the quota is concerned, I have given a repeated assurance, and I repeat it now, that the quota will be fixed at such a level as to provide a full outlet for the whole production of British films of satisfactory quality, and that we contemplate a rising quota over the ten-year period of the new Act, keeping step with the progressive increase we hope to see in the production of British films.

In line with this pledge, Wilson raised the quota of mandatory British feature films from 30 per cent (under the 1927 Act) to 45 per cent: a startling increase which infuriated the American motion-picture industry. More interestingly, it infuriated J. Arthur Rank and his dynamic managing director, who resented the loss of revenue from the cheap American films almost as much as they disliked the prospect of increasing their film production at home. Rank and Davis set up a howl of protest, complaining that the talent was not available to make the necessary 45 per cent of British films, although, as the late war years had shown and the outbreak of television in the early fifties would show, the available talent depended very much on the atmosphere and opportunities provided by the industry. Rank then abandoned his promised programme for forty-seven feature films and concentrated still further on the colossal spectacular which, he hoped, would recoup some cash in the American market. The consequent collapse of British film production forced Wilson to welsh on his pledge of 'a rising quota over the ten-year period'. By 30 March 1949, he was asking the Commons to approve the Cinematograph Films (Quotas) Amendment Order, which reduced the quota of first feature British films from 45 per cent to 40 per cent. Exactly a year later he again reduced the quota – to 30 per cent, the figure with which he had started: the entire policy of building a springboard for British films and gradually increasing the quota as production increased had been sabotaged by the Rank/ABC duopoly, without a single effective gesture from the Board of Trade.

For at least eighteen months before that, however, the duopoly, and especially Rank, had come under fire from many quarters – from the more progressive (and the best) production companies, from a growing group of Labour MPs, many of them recruited by Sir Michael Balcon, and from the cinema workers' and technicians' union. All these people had argued for the public ownership of one of the three big cinema circuits to be run in competition with Rank and ABC, and to give priority and encouragement to British film production, particularly the independent producers. The demand for a public third circuit had been shirked immediately after the war. In an impressive ACTT pamphlet issued in May 1946, the film producer Ralph Bond argued for a National Film Finance Corporation and a nationalized distribution company, but held back from advocating a fully nationalized third circuit. 'Nationalization,' he opined, 'does not appear to be practical politics for the time being.' By mid-1948, however, Bond, his union and almost everyone who wanted the future of independent British film production to be assured were convinced that a third circuit was the only permanent answer. Their minds had been made up by the intransigence and philistinism of the men in charge of the duopoly, who had hamstrung the independent producer, deliberately kept down British film production, and, as a consequence, had driven much of their talent out of the country. A leaflet, distributed by the ACTT in 1949, insisted:

> The crisis in the British film industry worsens. Many film studios are closed; fewer films are being made; thousands of film technicians and workers are denied the chance of using their skill. . . . As private enterprise has failed, the State should step in and take the necessary action.
> The powers of the big circuits should be curtailed by the setting up of a state-owned circuit and cinemas administered by a public corporation. This circuit would give the public a better range of entertainment. . . .

The more the argument was put, the more unanswerable it became. Past history had shown that the more independent film production was encouraged, the more ability and creative instinct was let off the box-office leash, the greater the success of British films.

While the duopoly had deliberately kept production down, a public corporation could insure indefinite film production in this country, and would almost certainly compete with the big companies. Yet the campaign for a public third circuit was not as powerful as it might have been. The left-wing Labour MPs could not decide whether or not to argue for wholesale nationalization. And Sir Michael Balcon remembers with some regret that he fought almost exclusively for the monopolies to pay more attention to the independent producers, rather than for a State circuit to compete with the monopolies. Sir Michael now thinks that more would have been accomplished if he and those who agreed with him had fought more on the political front for a National Film Circuit.

Harold Wilson understood these arguments, and the numerous delegations which argued with him for a third circuit got the distinct impression that he agreed with them. In the event, however, he proposed, in mid-1948, a National Film Finance Corporation, with a capital of £5 m. to encourage and promote independent British film producers. The NFFC was granted a further £1 m. in 1950.

Together with the NFFC, Wilson proposed further measures to help the independent producers, notably an amendment to the Film Act of the previous year, whereby each of the big circuits were instructed to show at least six films per year from independent producers, the films to be recommended by the Films Council. A further order denied the circuits the right to amalgamate.

The NFFC was received with considerable relief in the cinema industry, and its annual reports since then show that, without its funds, the British film industry would have been much poorer. Film after film, which would never have seen the screen but for the financial backing of the NFFC, achieved considerable successes at the box office; *The Third Man* and *Seven Days to Noon* were two conspicious examples. Yet weaknesses of the NFFC were immediately apparent. First, it opened the door to Government patronage for individual production firms and distribution companies. Wilson was from the outset charmed and impressed by Alexander Korda, whose British Lion Company received massive grants from the NFFC, some of them wasted. Secondly, more importantly, the NFFC did not remove or even influence the duopoly. If Mr Forster, in *Age of Austerity*, is right that the purpose of the NFFC was 'to counterbalance Rank', the scheme was a miserable failure. Rank and ABC retained almost total control of the film industry. Indeed the success of the NFFC-backed films disproved the Rank propaganda about lack of talent in British films and strengthened the case for wider and more powerful state interference in the industry.

Despite the NFFC, Rank and ABC tightened their grip on the British film industry in every year following Harold Wilson's measures. His amendment insisting on six Council-sponsored films was simply ignored by the duopoly, and those few films which were shown under the amendment were effectively stifled. Wilson's provision that the three circuits should remain independent was also broken, this time by a Conservative Government. In a letter to John Davis on 5 September 1958, the President of the Board of Trade, Frederick Erroll, gave the Government's permission to break the commitment entered into under Wilson's Presidency, effectively to dismantle the Gaumont Circuit. The effect of this permission was further to increase the power of the duopoly, and the influence of the American companies. The quota system, which previously had demanded 30 per cent of British films in *three* circuits, now demanded 30 per cent British films from *two* circuits, thus further weakening the independent British film industry. George Elvin, then, as now, general secretary of the ACTT, recalls that 'almost every attempt by Wilson to get an assurance or a pledge out of the big boys, or to restrict them in some way, has failed'.

Still shirking a decision on a third public circuit, Wilson set up a committee on Distribution and Exhibition (under Lord Portal, and, after his death, Sir Arnold Plant). The Plant Committee recommended some relatively radical measures for assisting the producers at the distributors' expense. Wilson approved most of the recommendations but did not act upon any of them. Instead, he agreed to an increase in the price of cinema seats, half of which would be paid through the British Film Production Fund to the producers. The Fund doled out the money on application, and was heavily biased in favour of the representatives of the big companies. Thus under what became known as the 'Eady Plan' (after Sir Wilfred Eady, the chief films officer at the Board of Trade) the film magnates doled out money to the producers of their choice. Entertainments tax was lowered, and a consensus between the duopoly and Harold Wilson was arrived at, from which the British film industry has never recovered.

George Elvin says that his members all over Britain and of different political complexions have a 'soft spot for Harold Wilson. He gave us the National Film Finance Corporation, which has saved what's left of British films.' And Wilson's Tory biographer concludes: 'He helped to put the industry on a sound post-war footing from which it flourished until overtaken by the expanding television competition of the 'fifties' (Dudley Smith, p. 77).

Certainly, the NFFC has helped, and certainly a Conservative Government would never have set it up (though the Conservatives in Opposition did not oppose it). Yet the real truth about Harold Wilson's stewardship over the British film industry is that he missed a real and vital opportunity to establish a base upon which talent among British film directors, producers and technicians could thrive without having to cross the Atlantic. The opportunity was missed because of Wilson's and his Government's doctrinaire antagonism to the expropriation of profitable interests. The 'third circuit' would have entailed the expropriation (though no doubt with lavish compensation) of half Rank's empire. That was what Wilson and his Government feared. In its place he proposed every conceivable method of restricting and controlling private enterprise by assurance and remedial legislation. Instead of embarking on a bold operation which would without any doubt have strengthened the production of creative and successful British films, Harold Wilson opted for a shoddy mixture of statist interference and patronage. Since then the duopoly, in some relief, has shrugged off the statist interference, extended the area of patronage and continued relentlessly to wreck the independent British film industry.

According to the political philosophy forged by Harold Wilson and his colleagues in the first few halcyon years of Labour Government private enterprise had to provide the main dynamic for economic development. The state, therefore, far from hampering or threatening private enterprise, became its chief assistant, centralizing information and statistics, improving research, assisting the efficient, nationalizing the unprofitable. Wilson had told a Tory MP that this sort of socialism was good for private enterprise 'on the limited experience of the past few years', and indeed the first few years of Labour Government were marked by considerable cooperation from private enterprise. In 1945, the capitalist system was in some disarray. Elections in Britain and in France had proved that the political situation was potentially revolutionary. The war had cost British capital much of its reserves. Before the war the 'nation' could survive on the fat of interest from overseas investments. Many of these investments had been sold to buy arms. Business cooperation with the Government was essential, not only because a deliberate course of obstruction could lead to revolution, but also because only the state and 'a national approach' could win back the assets lost in the war.

Most intelligent industrialists were delighted with the 'moderation' of Labour Ministers in the early years, and for a considerable period Harold Wilson at the Board of Trade achieved a 'consensus' between Labour and Tory Parties, employers and labour. His admirers still imagine him in those years as a battling crusader carving out a hunk of the socialist commonwealth against the bitter resistance of wealth and privilege. Ernest Kay tells us, for instance, that 'he got through a whole series of Parliamentary Bills in the face of powerful opposition'. In fact, not one of the Parliamentary Bills pushed through the House of Commons by Wilson was opposed by the Tories or the Liberals. Two separate Export Guarantees Bills, the American Aid and European Provisions Bill, the Patents and Designs Bill, the Distribution of Industry Bill, the Cinematograph Film (Special Loans) Bill, the Monopolies Bill and the Development of Inventions Bill were not only supported in the lobbies by the Tories but in many cases openly welcomed by their front bench spokesmen. The speeches of Oliver Lyttleton (later Lord Chandos), William Shepherd, Sir David Maxwell Fyfe (later Lord Kilmuir) and other leading Tory statesmen on Board of Trade matters are littered with kind and comradely phrases for the good work which the Rt Hon. Member for Ormskirk was doing at the Board of Trade. The consensus was working, and Wilson revelled in it. More and more of his speeches contained references to the 'need to keep this matter free from merely party controversy'. In a speech on economic affairs in January 1949, Wilson outlined his Party's ill-fated four-year 'National Plan', which he called a 'national document'. 'The Plan,' he said, 'is not a Party plan. It should be adopted by all parties' (House of Commons, 28 January 1949).

The precise moment when the consensus between industry and the Labour Government was broken is difficult to gauge. The first major showdown took place between the Iron and Steel Federation and the Government over the decision, first announced in the spring of 1948 and finally passed through Parliament in the summer of 1949, to nationalize steel. In the face of the obstructionist techniques of the steel manufacturers (not to mention the Conservatives in both houses), the final Bill was too weak and too late. The success of their colleagues in steel inspired employers and industrialists in other sectors. From April 1949, all pretence at cooperation was dropped and the Government were fought by industry and commerce on almost every one of their proposals.

To some extent, too, the Conservatives and industrialists were assisted in their campaigns by the fact that the Labour Party had reached the crossroads. The nationalization of basic industries and much of the promised welfare measures (the National Health Service and the Industrial Injury Act) had been accomplished. The alternative for the Labour Government was either to continue nationalizing and introduce further welfare reforms or to stop legislating altogether. They chose, in the event, to *announce* that they were proceeding with a radical programme, to abandon many of their controls and rely on what they had already done.

A Labour Party Statement of 1949, for instance, spoke of definite plans for the nationalization of life assurance, meat, water, cement, sugar and minerals. None of these measures were carried out or even put into draft legislation. Yet the effect of the announcement was to unleash a stream of propaganda in favour of private enterprise and against the Government. It was led by Lord Lyle (of Tate and Lyle), Mr Cube and Richard Dimbleby, and, on their success, the chorus was joined by almost all the members of the Federation of British Industries. The Tories leapt on the bandwagon and harried the Government relentlessly.

Even Harold Wilson at the Board of Trade, who did not approve of wholesale nationalization, was engulfed in this tide of opposition. In a very short time the carefully woven fabric of the consensus was torn to shreds in front of his eyes. Even the civil servants who had helped him build bridges of confidence to industry rounded on him. C. H. Kitchen, who had been the London Regional Director of the Ministry of Works when Harold Wilson was Parliamentary Under-Secretary, wrote an article in the *Financial Times* (whose editor, Brendan Bracken, nursed a particular personal dislike of Wilson) arguing that Labour's building controls should be simplified (*Financial Times*, 13 December 1951). And the Chairman of the Cotton Board, whom Wilson himself had praised in the House of Commons as a 'distinguished industrialist', made a speech during the election campaign of 1951 in which he argued that the Government's attempts at 'regulation in the play of consumer demand, price and quality are inconsistent with the situation in which our industry is called upon to export more than a quarter of its products to free commercial markets overseas'.

Even the most harmless product of the consensus – the Development Council – was cruelly savaged by the Opposition and private industry. The orders setting up development councils in cotton (March 1948), furniture (November 1948) and jewellery (December, 1948) had been accepted and welcomed by the Conservatives. Yet when Wilson presented an order for a Clothing Development Council in November 1949, the Tories, for the first and last time in the four years of his Presidency, divided the House against him. They argued that the clothing employers' associations, representing some 25 per cent of employers and manufacturers in the industry, were opposed to the Council. When Wilson tried to press the matter and establish the Council without their consent, the employers fought him in the courts. When the Council was finally set up, most of them refused to serve on it. Later, after the nightmare was over, Wilson admitted:

I was more than a little surprised at the sudden hostility which blew up. A hostility which in some way became infectious, covered a number of industries which had previously accepted or supported the idea and now turned against it. I do not think that this was dissociated from the special meeting called by the Federation of British Industries for the purpose of concerting the attitude of various employers' organizations to the Development Councils (House of Commons, 16 December 1952).

The FBI had indeed met, on a number of occasions, to plan their concerted opposition to the Government, and not only on the question of the Development Councils. As far as the FBI was concerned, the Labour Government had reached the point of maximum reform. Further taxation, further nationalization, further welfare measures might, cautioned the Federation's economic experts, upset the delicate balance of class power. The Government had to be attacked simultaneously on all possible fronts with the full armoury of private industry. A consensus, they argued, though useful in periods of crisis like 1931 and 1945, can never be permanent between those who possess power and wealth and their potential dispossessors.

The negative and obstructionist attitude of industry shocked Wilson into a sullen and almost silent truculence. He took refuge from political decisions by retreating into the Board's administrative labyrinth, soaking himself in detail and avoiding the conflict with industrialists which he had worked so hard to abolish. From the spring of 1949 Wilson's speeches lacked the messianic fervour with which he had proclaimed the 'new cooperation' between private enterprise and Government in a fully employed society.

The spring of 1949, in fact, was a watershed for the Labour Government, not only in their relations with industry. 1948 had been, by the narrow standards of export levels and balance of payments successes, a triumph. The slump, which biblical Marxists had been predicting with increasing desperation, had not materialized, nor looked like materializing. Then, very suddenly, in the early spring of 1949 the American economy began to show unmistakeable signs of recession. The effect on the sterling–dollar gap was catastrophic. In the first months the dollar deficit was £239 m., compared with £170 m. forecast in the year's *Economic Survey*. Once again the words 'financial crisis' reappeared to haunt Labour's economic Ministers.

The American administration responded quite cheerfully to the desperate complaints from Britain about the closure of the dollar gap by recommending devaluation of the pound. Mr Snyder, Truman's local bank manager who had been promoted rather rapidly to the Secretaryship of the United States Treasury, hinted publicly that Britain should solve her problems with a change of parity. In early July he visited Britain only to be asked politely but firmly by Sir Stafford Cripps and his economic advisers to keep his mouth shut, which, to everyone's astonishment, he did. The official communiqué after the talks stated baldly and falsely: 'No suggestion was made that sterling be devalued.' In the two-day Commons debate on the economic situation, on 14 and 18 July, Cripps clung desperately to the hope that the gap would close itself. The only practical measure he proposed was a £100 m. cut in American imports. Harold Wilson followed faithfully in similar optimism, hardly touching on devaluation except to remind the House that 'the sterling area is the greatest multilateral trading centre in the world at this time'.

At that time almost all the Government Ministers followed Cripps in rejecting devaluation. Sir Stafford himself had expressed his own opposition in the House of Commons and privately rejected the opinion of his two main economic advisers – Edwin Plowden, chief planning officer and chairman of the Economic Planning Board, and Robert Hall, director of the economic section of the Cabinet office, who took the view that devaluation was inevitable. Yet even then some Ministers were dubious. Hugh Gaitskell, Minister of Fuel, for instance, rejected the 'chin up in a crisis' approach of Wilson and Cripps. In a speech at Porthcawl on 4 July he had spoken of 'a moment of supreme crisis for the Government'.

These doubts were confirmed at the first-ever Commonwealth Finance Ministers' Conference, which opened in London on 13 July. A particularly impressive speech was made by the young finance Minister for Southern Rhodesia, Sir Edgar Whitehead, who argued that all that country's vast natural resources and wealth would suffer grave damage unless the imbalance between British and American prices was rectified. Whitehead showed with a long list of prices that the price discrepancy was often as high as thirty per cent.

Sir Stafford Cripps found it difficult to absorb the argument. He was tired, and weakened by a spinal infection and digestive trouble. The following Monday (18 July), Attlee announced in the House of Commons that Cripps was going for a six weeks' rest cure to Zurich, and that he himself would be 'overlord' of economic affairs, over a group of four Ministers – Harold Wilson, Hugh Gaitskell, Douglas Jay and Glenvil Hall, respectively Economic and Financial Secretaries to the Treasury. (Hall played no part in the crisis, largely owing to an illness which confined him to hospital.)

During that week, as the sterling crisis worsened, Gaitskell and Jay, almost simultaneously, became convinced of the case for devaluation. They approached Wilson, who indicated agreement with them and arranged a formal meeting attended by officials and advisers, the most influencial of whom were Sir Edward (later Lord) Bridges, Permanent Secretary to the Treasury,who had been Secretary to the Cabinet from 1938 to 1946, and Sir Henry Wilson Smith, Second Secretary to the Treasury. Gaitskell outlined the arguments for devaluation, and Sir Edward was suitably outraged. It was, he said, quite impractical to make such a decision at that stage, with the Chancellor in Switzerland, and Parliament about to adjourn for the summer recess.

Harold Wilson, summing up as the senior Minister, dealt not so much with the arguments for or against devaluation, but agreeing basically with Sir Henry that the time was not opportune. Gaitskell and Jay later met Wilson privately and after a long discussion again elicited from him some support for devaluation.

Thus reinforced, Gaitskell and Jay demanded a high-level meeting with the Prime Minister, Clement Attlee and the Lord President of the Council, Herbert Morrison. Once again, Gaitskell outlined the devaluation arguments, once again Sir Edward Bridges 'outlined the difficulties', and once again Wilson found himself in agreement with Sir Edward. Attlee was as non-committal as ever. The economic situation deteriorated daily. A dock strike in London and Liverpool and the refusal of American importers to pay for goods until the last possible deadline combined to convince Gaitskell and Jay that a decision to devalue had to be reached before the end of the Parliamentary session, and the following week – the last before the recess – they demanded a further meeting with the Prime Minister and the leading officials. By this time, it was clear to Attlee, Morrison, Wilson and most of the officials that devaluation was inevitable, and the discussion turned not so much on whether to devalue but when and by how much. One of the chief difficulties was the position of Sir Stafford Cripps, who had left instructions that no state papers of any kind should be sent to him at Zurich, but whose assent to devaluation was clearly crucial. Wilson then told the meeting that he, by chance, had arranged a holiday in Switzerland, and asked if he could call on his former chief to convey the views of the Prime Minister, and other economic Ministers, and to persuade Cripps that devaluation was inevitable. The proposal was brusquely rejected by Attlee and Morrison. Instead, a letter, written by Jay in the Treasury on Saturday, 30 July, agreed by Gaitskell and signed by Attlee the following day at Chequers, was personally taken to Zurich by C. M. P. (Max) Brown, the Principal Private Secretary to the President of the Board of Trade. Cripps received the letter and grudgingly initialled his agreement to the devaluation. In conditions of total secrecy the devaluation operation was worked out – largely by Sir Edward Playfair, one of the most 'positively vetted' mandarins in the Treasury hierarchy.

In the event Wilson *did* pay a private, personal visit to Cripps in Switzerland on the afternoon of 6 August. Dudley Smith indicates that Cripps's opposition to devaluation 'was obviously shaken by the powerful line his one-time protégé had taken'. In fact Cripps's opinion of Wilson deteriorated from that moment.

When Cripps, only partially recovered, and Ernest Bevin left early in September for a conference with the Finance Ministers of Canada and the United States, the devaluation details were complete. A harassed Mr Snyder received the news with considerable relief. And the British Cabinet was presented with a *fait accompli* some days later, on the afternoon of 18 September – only a few hours before Cripps broadcast the news to the nation.

A rather different account of Harold Wilson's role in the devaluation crisis by a number of curiously similar press reports several weeks later, and all Wilson's biographers, indicate that Wilson was in favour of devaluation from the start of the crisis. All propound the myth that Attlee 'appointed Wilson as his emissary' to the ailing Cripps in Switzerland (Dudley Smith, p. 104; Leslie Smith, p. 150; Kay, p. 50). In fact, Wilson did not make up his mind until the feeling among the economic Ministers was unanimous for devaluation, and his attempt to be appointed 'emissary' to Cripps was specifically sabotaged by Attlee and Morrison. Wilson's speech in the big Commons debate on devaluation, for which the Commons were recalled on 27 September, dealt only briefly with the arguments for the change in the exchange rate, and concentrated instead on scathing references to 'the attacks' made by foreigners on sterling and the good name of Britain.

In the eyes of the Big Four – Attlee, Morrison, Cripps and Bevin – Wilson's role in the devaluation crisis had not enhanced his reputation. From that moment his meteoric rise was slowed, while Gaitskell's stock rose.

Hugh Gaitskell came into the Cabinet as Minister of State at the Treasury shortly after the 1950 election. Wilson watched appalled as Gaitskell persuaded the ailing Cripps that the cost of the social services was too high, and forced through a Bill allowing for the imposition of health prescription charges. When Bevan, the Minister of Health, violently attacked the proposals, Wilson intervened on his side, and, according to one biographer, took much pleasure in mediating between Cripps and Bevan, over Gaitskell's head, for the indefinite postponement of health charges. This mediation did little to help him. When, in October, Cripps finally resigned as Chancellor, Wilson was again by-passed. Gaitskell's promotion to Chancellor was specifically recommended by Dalton and Cripps, both of whom had supported Wilson in earlier years. It was the worst moment of Wilson's political career up to that time, and his support for Bevan in the Cabinet grew in every subsequent month.

That support was far from ideological. In the 1950 election campaign (when he had won his new seat at Huyton with a diminutive majority), Wilson had stuck firmly to his moderate views. One of his supporting speakers, Sir Frank Soskice, himself a moderate, had described Wilson's election address as an 'understatement rather than an overstatement' (*Prescot and Huyton Reporter*, 27 January 1950). His election speeches were painstakingly mild, harping on familiar themes like success in exports and cooperation with private enterprise. His one venture into unorthodoxy, at a St Helens Fabian Society dinner presided over by Sir Hartley Shawcross, had been to advocate 'more powers' for his beloved Development Councils 'in order that they may guide and lead industries to maximum efficiency and to the fulfilment of national objectives' (*Financial Times*, 20 January 1950).

In Parliament and in speeches in the country after the election, Wilson continued to assert that the main purpose of public enterprise was to lubricate competition and increase efficiency in private industry. His Parliamentary activities reflected the general impasse of the Labour Government, harried by the Tories and holding on to an overall majority of six. Only two major measures were proposed by the Board of Trade that year – the Distribution of Industry Bill and the establishment of the National Film Finance Corporation, both, inevitably, welcomed by the Tories. Yet, with each attempt at appeasement, private industry and the Tories howled all the more angrily. The President of the Board of Trade, the department most easily associated with controls and bureaucracy, became the Opposition's favourite target. As the guest of honour at a dinner of the Institute of Production Engineers in October 1950, Wilson embarked on a placatory speech on the theme that 'private enterprise has done a lot better under this Government than any other'. Before long, he was shouted down by the worthy gentlemen, one of whom called out 'Rot' as Wilson started each sentence. Sir Leonard Lord, chairman of Austin Motors, voiced the horsey propaganda of the old-style Tory industrialist, let off the Central Office leash for election purposes, when he announced that 'we have been cajoled, bullied, bludgeoned and bribed by this Government, by the Board of Trade and by Mr Harold Wilson'. The National Chamber of Trade called for Wilson's dismissal. And the *Financial Times* opined that 'Mr Wilson is a pedestrian Parliamentarian who speaks too fast and whose early preferment has not endeared him throughout his Party. Deprived of administrative opportunity, Mr Wilson's star would be reduced to a faint flicker in the political firmament' (19 February 1950). Each new assault filled the young President, who had done so much to please his assailants, with further confusion, frustration and disgruntlement.

Even his successes in the export field were vanishing before his eyes. From early in 1947, the holders of sterling at home and abroad had launched a series of speculative offensives on sterling, which had effectively cancelled out all the economic progress the Government had made, and had consigned their National Plan to the Treasury wastepaper basket. In 1948, the rapid export advances had been obliterated by a slump in world prices and the consequent loss in revenue for the sterling area. So now, in late 1950, the 'record' exports of £200 m. announced in October were quickly offset by the Korean war and the American stockpiling of raw materials. The anarchy and unpredictable behaviour of international capital made the Labour Government look like blunderers and the Tory Party and press were keen to promote Harold Wilson to the undeserved post of Blunderer-in-Chief.

Two clashes with his colleagues early in 1951 exhausted Harold Wilson's patience. The first was an attempt to extend and improve his favourite 'utility' clothing scheme by maintaining selective controls on clothing and persuading housewives to purchase more of the utility product. The Cabinet, nervous of any mention of controls, voted the scheme out. Secondly, in March 1951, Wilson decided unilaterally to challenge the Tory practice of keeping senior Ministers up late in the night with 'prayers' against minor Government orders for delegated legislation. On 19 March Wilson abruptly broke off talks with some thirty powerful trade associations who were negotiating for permission to increase maximum prices. The trade associations were told that the President would not be available while the Conservatives in the House continued their delaying tactics.

Unknown to Wilson, his superiors in the Government, notably Chuter Ede, the Home Secretary, and Herbert Morrison, the Leader of the House, were already negotiating with the Tories for an agreement on Parliamentary time-wasting. Wilson's action served to postpone settlement, irritate the Government and allow the Tories further to castigate the Government. Ironically, Wilson's first and only decision unilaterally to launch an offensive on private industry and their representatives brought him disaster – from his political colleagues. Ede and Morrison were furious, and insisted in the Cabinet and Parliamentary Party, where Wilson's action had much support, that the negotiations should continue pending discussions with the Opposition about 'prayers'. Wilson held out for a fortnight, and then capitulated. But the resentment against both Ede and Morrison for making him a public laughing stock never died. In the fierce policy battles which continued to divide the Labour Cabinet, Harold Wilson began to take an increasingly oppositionist and 'Bevanite' approach to the Conservative policies of the Labour leadership.

Of these, the most important was the proposed 'tough' budget, against the background of a worsening balance of payments position and shortage of raw materials. Hugh Gaitskell, the new Chancellor, firmly backed by Morrison, who was Deputy Prime Minister while Attlee was in hospital with a stomach illness, had decided to take a stand on the issue of health charges. He had noticed with some anger the previous year that Bevan and Wilson had dissuaded Cripps from imposing health charges, and was determined that no such manoeuvre should succeed again.

On 10 April 1951, Gaitskell submitted his Budget to the Commons, proposing 50 per cent charges for false teeth and spectacles, and Aneurin Bevan walked out of the Chamber. That evening Bevan and Wilson visited Attlee in St Mary's Hospital, Paddington, and the two emerged smiling. A compromise seemed inevitable, especially when, on the following day, Bevan made a speech to the Parliamentary Labour Party attacking the charges, but according to the press, denying that he would resign. On 17 April, however, the Cabinet met, and, after a furious discussion, agreed to introduce the necessary legislation to enact the charges earlier than planned – on Monday, 24 April. Bevan and Wilson almost certainly made their decision to resign on the following Thursday night (the 19th) when a small group of Bevan's supporters met at midnight in the House to be informed of the pending resignations. That evening, the left-wing weekly *Tribune*, on whose editorial board sat Jennie Lee, Bevan's wife, carried a violent attack on the Budget and the charges. Ernest Kay reveals that his wife and Mrs Wilson were having coffee on the Friday morning (the 20th) when Mary Wilson revealed to Mrs Kay that Bevan would resign the following morning and that Wilson and Freeman would follow him on the Monday. Accordingly Bevan's resignation was reported exclusively in the *Wolverhampton Express and Star*, on which Ernest Kay was employed, that Friday afternoon. Bevan resigned on the Saturday, and his letter of resignation was published on the Monday. Wilson followed suit, after seeing Attlee on the Sunday evening. For the first time since entering Parliament five and a half years previously, Harold Wilson became a back-bencher.

Wilson's role in the resignation had been the subject of two conflicting views. First, that he was keen to resign early in the controversy, and, according to one report, 'was more insistent on drastic action than Mr Bevan and has been urging his colleague

to resign, promising that he too would leave the Government'
(Guy Eden in the *Daily Express*, 11 April 1951). Almost all
Wilson's biographers insist that Bevan tried to dissuade Wilson
from joining him in resigning, but that Wilson insisted. Dudley
Smith tells us that 'it was understood in some quarters that after
Gaitskell began his Budget speech, Wilson visited some of his
closest advisers at the Board of Trade, told them he was leaving
shortly and shook hands in farewell' (Dudley Smith, p. 120).

The contrary view was taken by John Junor, political leader-
writer of the *Daily Express*, who later became editor of the
Sunday Express and a personal friend of Wilson. On Monday,
23 April, Junor's front page article on Bevan's resignation
reflected on Wilson's predicament:

> He is a young man and he sees quite clearly that in the right-wing of
> the socialist Party there is no room for him to expand. For Mr Gaitskell,
> who resembles Mr Wilson in so many respects, is there taking up all the
> room.

Two days later (25 April), again on the front page and under
the heading 'Did He Fall or Was He Pushed?', Junor dealt at
greater length with Wilson's motives. Unlike any other political
journalist at the time, Junor directed himself to the question: why
was Wilson's letter of resignation not published? Seldom before or
since has a Cabinet Minister resigned without outlining his
reasons in a published letter. Wilson wrote such a letter, but, on
agreement with Attlee, the letter was not published.

> Wilson's opponents [wrote Junor] believe that Mr Wilson did not
> want the correspondence published for the good reason that it would
> show Mr Wilson as not wanting to resign at all. That, in fact, he was
> pushed out by Mr Herbert Morrison, Deputy Prime Minister and
> Foreign Secretary. The men who take this view argue that when Mr
> Wilson first began to push the Bevan barrow, he did not realize where
> Bevan was heading. He never dreamed that Mr Bevan would go as far
> as resignation on the issue of Health Service charges. He expected
> stormy scenes. But no more than that. The last thing he wanted to do was
> to endanger the Government. So when Mr Bevan's resignation became
> an immediate possibility, Mr Wilson found himself in a situation which
> he had never expected. He thereupon took all possible steps to bring
> about a compromise whereby he and Mr Bevan would stay in the Party.

But Mr Morrison was in no mood for compromise. Either Mr Wilson completely toed the line or Mr Wilson got out. Mr Wilson resented the Foreign Secretary's attitude. And, according to this theory, he showed his resentment in the letter he wrote to Mr Attlee. For it was a protesting, as well as a resigning, letter. It took the view that the schism in the socialist Party need never have happened if Mr Attlee had not been so sick and Mr Morrison had not been in charge. If this interpretation of Mr Wilson's actions is correct, it is understandable that his correspondence has not been published. For no martyr would wish it to be said of him that, until the last moment, he was prepared to pawn his crown for a compromise.

Junor's source for this article was Tom Cook, then Under-Secretary for the Colonies, whom Junor had known since they had fought on opposing platforms (Junor as a Liberal) in Dundee. Cook had for some years been Wilson's Parliamentary Private Secretary, and his close personal friend. So great was Cook's personal loyalty to Wilson that he had himself offered his resignation, only to be patronized by Morrison into submission.

But perhaps the best support for Junor's theory came from Wilson himself. In his resignation speech in the House, widely acclaimed throughout the Tory press as 'much more impressive' than Bevan's the day before, Wilson included a section, which was not quoted in the press at the time or in biographies since:

I have tried in every way open to me to find some means of avoiding the situation which has now come upon us. I should have thought that even after my Rt Hon. Friend's [Gaitskell's] Budget speech, it would have been possible to re-examine the financial basis of our national accounts in the light of the changed rearmament position, and then after that to come to a decision on their implication for a further distribution of the burden. I should have thought that it would be possible to examine even the current expenditure that is now going on rearmament.

I should have thought again that the Bill, if it must be proceeded with, could have been delayed in operation until these examinations, which will in any case be necessary, are complete. I should have thought that the apprehensions of my hon. friends could have been partially allayed by a provision in the Bill that this was a temporary measure, strictly limited in time. *But these efforts to provide an acceptable solution foundered on the determination to proceed with the Bill with all haste and no compromise.*

I should have thought that there was no need for urgency in pressing on with this legislation, and that the whole matter could be left until my Rt. Hon. Friend returned, and we could have had a full examination of the defence programme carried out under his authority (House of Commons, 24 April 1951).

There were, as far as Wilson was concerned, five possible compromises, all of which, he implied, would have convinced him not to resign. First, there could have been an inquiry into future accounts; second, an inquiry into current accounts; third, a temporary delay in the Bill; fourth, a provision that the Bill was temporarily strictly limited in time; and fifth, a delay until Attlee came out of hospital.

Bevan's speech the day before had carried few references to compromise. It was a furious, tempestuous, in some parts almost lyrical affair, with attacks on 'the anarchy of American capitalism', a demand to 'take economic planning away from the Treasury', and a sharp jibe at the 'added misfortune of having an economist as the Chancellor of the Exchequer himself'. It was the speech of a man whose principles had been sold by his friends. Wilson, on the other hand, did not mention the anarchy of American capitalism nor did he attack the Treasury or the Chancellor of the Exchequer. What really annoyed Wilson about the situation was the fact that Herbert Morrison had refused all concessions and compromise. Bevan was wholly opposed to a breach in the health service, while Wilson was prepared to tolerate such a breach provided it could be 'strictly limited in time'.

As Wilson also inferred in his speech, his tactics had succeeded the previous year, when the Cabinet accepted his compromise on health charges, included the possibility of such charges in the Finance Bill but, after some delay, shelved the actual legislation for the charges.

In 1951, however, Morrison flatly and rudely refused to contemplate any of Wilson's proposals. His statement in his autobiography that 'I certainly did my best to avoid any resignations' is a lie of truly Morrisonian proportions.

The compromises suggested by Wilson himself in his resignation speech, and, no doubt in stronger and more personal terms, in his unpublished letter of resignation, made it clear that, although he was opposed to health charges, he did not think the charges in themselves constituted a resigning issue. Wilson resigned not so much because the health charges were imposed, but because his

efforts to reach a compromise were rebuffed. The shoddy treatment he received from Morrison came on top of a long list of
similar insults and failures: Gaitskell's leap-frogging over him
into the Treasury; Ede's deliberate snub over the trade associations and 'prayers'; the shelving of his utility scheme and the
refusal to include clothing subsidies in the Budget. All these,
taken together with Morrison's rudeness and Gaitskell's arrogance, must have strengthened Wilson's resolve to get out and
watch his former colleagues try to cope with their already hopeless
predicament.

The real reasons for Aneurin Bevan's resignation were never in
serious doubt. A few weeks before the Budget he had told a meeting in Bermondsey that he 'would never be a member of a Government which makes charges on the National Health Service for
the patient'. That, for Bevan, was the central issue. Certainly, he
disagreed with Government policy on a number of other crucial
issues, and many times in the previous six months had been
tempted to resign. The blatant and provocative interference in his
treasured Health Service was the final blow.

Yet Bevan's letter to Attlee read strangely in the light of these
undoubted priorities. He listed his reasons for resigning in the
following order:

1. The Budget failed to apportion the burden of rearmament
costs fairly.

2. Military expenditure, both current and planned, was too
high.

3. Military expenditure was to be met by allowing prices to
rise and thus cutting personal consumption.

4. The health services charges made a breach in the social
services.

Attlee was surprised at Bevan's letter. 'I notice,' he wrote in
reply, 'that you have extended the area of disagreement with your
colleagues a long way beyond the specific matter to which, as I
understood, you had taken exception. I had certainly gathered that
if the proposal for imposing charges on dentures and spectacles
had been dropped, you would have been satisfied.'

Attlee had a case. For, on the first visit to St Mary's Hospital,
Bevan had concentrated almost exclusively on the health charges,
as he had done publicly and privately beforehand. Why then,

when it came to outlining the reasons for resigning, did he, in Attlee's words, 'extend the area of disagreement'?

The answer, almost certainly, lay in the tactical brain and persuasive powers of Harold Wilson. Wilson insisted from the outset that their resignation should not be 'just a matter of teeth and spectacles'. The teeth and spectacles issue, he argued, should be relegated to the bottom of the list of reasons. At the top should be the excessive arms estimates and the refusal to bolster rising prices with subsidies. Bevan agreed, and, accordingly, his resignation speech stressed the points about armaments, expenditure and prices.

Yet even in the much broader issue of arms expenditure there was a marked contrast between Bevan's and Wilson's approach. Bevan's resignation speech indicated his general discontent over many months with the level of the rearmament proposals, and the system of priorities which put armaments before welfare. Wilson, on the other hand, stuck closely to a purely technical theme – that the three-year estimates for arms expenditure of £4,700 m. were beyond the nation's resources.

Wilson's conviction that the arms programme was impractical certainly represented a dramatic conversion. For many months previously, as President of the Board of Trade, he had campaigned for recognition of the rearmament problem, and for building up resources to rearm.

On the 10 December 1950, he had told his constituents at Huyton:

Let those who profess to be united with us in their resistance to aggression recognize that this resistance involves high costs and great sacrifices for the people of this country. Let them recognize the real truth: that the high cost of living is the high cost of peace (*Daily Telegraph*, 11 December 1950).

And at Page Moss, a few days later, he glimpsed a silver lining in the Korean clouds:

The defence programme will be a further benefit to the area. While we all regret that world developments should force us to turn so high a proportion of our national resources to defence needs, we are determined to see that so far as possible and without in any way affecting the speed or effectiveness of our defence programme, we shall so direct it as to aid our economic and social policy of bringing work to the workers (*Prescot and Huyton Reporter*, 15 December 1950).

All his speeches at that time underlined the need for increased production to meet the rearmament programme. The £4,700 m. defence budget, which, according to his later speeches, was the main reason for his resignation, was announced first in January 1951. It inspired Wilson to still further exhortations to his countrymen:

We face the certainty of sacrifices in terms of higher living costs and shortages of many things, of harder work with less reward to our standard of living (Lewisham, 9 February 1951).

If the Tory Party knew of the need for an increased rearmament programme six or twelve months ago, why did it take up this false promise of 300,000 houses a year? (Patchway, nr Bristol, 11 February 1951).

Above all else, there is the importance of maintaining our defence programme (Oxford, 16 February 1951).

Our own rearmament programme is placing an additional strain on available supplies, but I think that the hon. gentleman misrepresented the Chancellor of the Exchequer in the quotation of his speech. *The real problem is not the additional rearmament*, but world shortage of supplies of materials (House of Commons, 2 March 1951).

We have had to turn our attention to the *great task of defence*, not with the view of strength or military power, but to prevent a third world war (*Prescot and Huyton Reporter*, 18 March 1951).

On 16 April, the Monday of the week in which he resigned, Wilson made an important speech in the Commons on economic affairs. He wound up with a peroration of Churchillian tone and purpose:

In the interests of the common defence production of all our partners in NATO, current defence production and other essential uses should have priority not only over the building up but over the maintenance of stockpiles. . . .

World events have forced us to embark on a rearmament programme, costly in money terms and also in real terms though not costly if it secures for us the peace which is beyond all price and beyond all measurement of economic cost. . . .

Explaining that in war the national effort had been concentrated on military production, and in peace-time on exports, Wilson concluded:

Now we have to do both, defence production and exports. In many ways, therefore, this presents to British trade and industry, to management and workers alike, a greater task, a greater challenge even than they faced in wartime and the post-war years. But the great record of production in war and peace, as recorded in the Economic Survey, has given us some assurance that in meeting this challenge this country will not fail (House of Commons, 16 April 1951).

Wilson heard of Bevan's final decision to resign on the evening of Friday, 20 April, from a phone call received in Great Yarmouth shortly before making a speech there. In the full knowledge therefore that he would be resigning, allegedly on the rearmament issue, within a day or two, Wilson coolly went back to the meeting hall there to urge the audience to greater production efforts 'to meet the vital needs of our increased rearmament programme' (*Daily Telegraph*, 21 April 1951).

Government policy on rearmament did not change between January and April 1951. The figures for the massive arms programme remained the same through the four months. There was certainly no major Cabinet policy decision on rearmament in the fourth week of April, or indeed in any of the preceding weeks.

The key issue which forced the resignations in April 1951 was an issue of principle – the health charges. Harold Wilson's resignation was couched in the language of technocracy – a straightforward assessment of what was economically possible and what was not. Thus, as Wilson no doubt intended, the simple issue of the health-service charges became blurred. It was not only Attlee who noticed that the original disagreement on the health-service question had been 'extended'. Woodrow Wyatt, a young Labour back-bencher with Bevanite sympathies, summed up the puzzlement of many of his colleagues when he said, in a speech on the introduction of the Health Service charges, that 'Bevan and his friends did not think of the reasons for their resignation before resigning'.

Perhaps the last word on the resignations should come from Harold Wilson himself. In an interview with Kenneth Harris of the *Observer* shortly after his election as leader of the Labour Party in 1963, Wilson was asked the real reasons for the 1951 resignation. He replied:

Although I supported a big increase in defence expenditure, I felt that the £4,700 m. programme was physically beyond our capacity, and would cause a breakdown, producing in the end less defence production, not more. *It was a practical problem. Nye saw it more as an issue of principle* (*Observer*, 8 July 1963).

Whatever the real motivation which drove Wilson out of the Government in April 1951, no one can doubt that the decision, in terms of his future political career, did him nothing but good. Until that time, in the eyes of the average Labour Party worker, Wilson was a right-wing economist, at best an efficient administrator, at worst a collaborator with capitalism. Even Herbert Morrison, one of the most uncompromising reactionaries in the history of the Labour movement, opined that

When Wilson was President of the Board of Trade, I found him moderate in his views, too moderate for my liking. His anti-monopolies Act was something of a compromise, and therefore not too effective, and he appeared to get inordinate pleasure from his bonfire of economic controls. In the main he was right but I consider that, in v.ew of the economic situation at the time, he overdid it. At that time he would certainly not be classed as left-wing (*Autobiography*, p. 325).

In his election campaign in Huyton in 1950, the main speakers were Bessie Braddock, James MacColl, Christopher Shawcross and Sir Frank Soskice: eminently respectable Fabians drawn from the extreme right-wing of the Parliamentary Party. Eighteen months later another election campaign in Huyton was set alight by Aneurin Bevan and Barbara Castle. Such was the extent of Harold Wilson's conversion.

The month after his resignation, Wilson accepted the post of economic adviser to Montague Meyer's timber firm – the salary for which, it was reported, easily made up the difference between a back-bencher's salary and a Minister's. Wilson's acceptance of the Meyer job shocked Bevan, who had had no prior knowledge of it, and who, for the first time, became a little wary of his young lieutenant.

Harold Wilson's resignation from the 1950–51 Labour Government disguised his political attitudes for the previous six years in a cloak of left-wing principle. The best-known fact about Harold Wilson's role in the 1945–51 Labour Government is that he resigned from it. In fact, Wilson played as important a part as any other Labour Minister in the least-publicized but most important achievements of the post-war Labour Government: its establishment of capitalism on a full-employment basis, and its use of the state to nationalize unprofitable 'substructure' and to promote industrial research and technology. For the construction of this 'New Britain' three distinct qualities had been essential: a genuine faith in the dynamic of capitalist competition; an interest in, if not an obsession with, technological development and industrial efficiency; and a contempt for political theory, particularly socialist theory. All these qualities Harold Wilson had in abundance in 1951. His resignation brought him into contact for the first time with ideas which, for all their incoherence, were founded on socialist theory. It was an uneasy encounter and it was not to last long.

Chapter 3
The Mantle of Nye: 1951-4

I would like to say at the outset that I think the people of Huyton should be exceedingly proud to have a man like Harold Wilson to represent them in the House of Commons. I have formed a great admiration for Mr Wilson's ability, honesty and courage. When he was appointed President of the Board of Trade I felt very proud that the Labour Party is still able to produce men like Harold Wilson. We need men like him (Aneurin Bevan, speech at Huyton, 21 July 1951).

He [Harold Wilson] wished to be able to state publicly that he only accepted [a post in the Shadow Cabinet] with Bevan's full approval. Crossman went to Bevan to seek this approval. But Bevan replied that he would regard it as an act of personal disloyalty to himself if Wilson accepted. 'So you regard Harold as expendable?' said Crossman. 'Yes, and you too,' Bevan replied (Hugh Dalton, *High Tide and After*: *Memoirs, 1945–60*, pp. 408-9 referring to an incident in April, 1954).

In the spring of 1947 a group of Labour back-benchers published a pamphlet called *Keep Left*, calling on the Government to maintain the socialist momentum and keep Labour on the path which it had taken in 1945. The group then met in the House of Commons every week to discuss broad political issues and day-to-day Parliamentary business. Under the Labour Government, attendance at group meetings was never more than twenty, and usually considerably less, though the group commanded considerable support in the rank and file of the constituency parties.

The Keep Left group meeting on the 17 April 1951 was particularly badly attended. The chairman, Harold Davies, had sent his apologies. Those present were Richard Crossman, Michael Foot, Marcus Lipton, Ian Mikardo and George Wigg. Regular attenders who were not present included Sir Richard Acland, Barbara Castle, Ian Horobin, Tom Williams, Fenner Brockway and Leslie Hale. The meeting discussed the impending crisis in the Labour Party and a paper on the subject by Richard Crossman

which predicted the resignation of Aneurin Bevan and a deep split
in the movement. The chief concern of the group was the future of
Aneurin Bevan, whose politics and attitudes corresponded closely
with those of the group. Bevan, as Minister of Health and of
Labour had, of course, never attended group meetings, but there
was little doubt in most of the members' minds that, if he resigned,
he would become its champion.

Even at that late moment there was little or no mention of
Harold Wilson. Crossman's paper, for instance, though rich in
references to 'Nye', does not mention Wilson. When Wilson
resigned with Bevan, he was enthusiastically welcomed by the
Keep Left group, and became a regular attender. Before long he
was unanimously elected the group's chairman.

The group grew hugely in the months following Bevan's resignation. The meetings in the House of Commons on Tuesday
afternoons were well attended, often by more than fifty MPs, and,
particularly after the 1951 election, there was a high level of
debate and discussion. Meetings were not restricted to MPs and
were regularly attended by three prominent economists from the
universities, G. D. N. Worswick, Thomas Balogh and Dudley
Seers. Balogh and Seers enriched the group with a flow of papers
on economic and overseas affairs which were carefully studied and
discussed. Many of the MPs also wrote papers, whose list over the
short period in which the group was allowed to meet makes
impressive reading: 'Memorandum of the Economic Position of
the Gold Coast', by Richard Acland and Dudley Seers (February
1951); 'The British Aircraft Industry', by John Freeman (January
1952); 'Notes on the Budget', by Dudley Seers (April 1952); 'The
Progress of the Colombo Plan', by Richard Crossman (April
1952); 'The Puzzle of the British Position', by Thomas Balogh
(July 1952); 'Across the Channel', by Ian Mikardo (December
1952); 'German Rearmament', by Barbara Castle and Ellis Smith
(July 1952). Most of these papers dealt with the practical problems
and issues of the day, rather than general theory.

The group also carried on prodigious propaganda work outside
Parliament. A massive apparatus of *Tribune* Brains Trusts, held at
the rate of four or five a week, and supplemented by numerous
week-end schools, reached into almost every constituency in the
land. In the 1951 election the group organized a roster of their own

speakers to speak for each other, particularly in marginal constituencies.

The popularity of the group with the Labour rank and file, symbolized by the success of the *Tribune* pamphlet of 1951, by Bevan and Wilson, which sold more than 100,000 copies, was too much for a worried and bankrupt Labour leadership. Accordingly, when fifty-seven of the group members voted against the Tory defence policy against the orders of the Labour Whips (the official policy was to abstain) the group was banned from meeting by the Parliamentary Party, under threat of expulsion from the Party. None of its members protested more bitterly than Harold Wilson.

The hard core of the 'Bevanites' (as they became known in the press, though Bevan himself was not a regular attender of the group's House of Commons meetings) continued to meet every Tuesday for a buffet lunch in Richard Crossman's home in Vincent Square. It consisted, in the main, of Bevan himself, his wife (Jennie Lee), Richard Crossman, Ian Mikardo, Michael Foot, Barbara Castle, Anthony Greenwood, Tom Driberg, J. P. W. Mallalieu, Thomas Balogh and John Freeman. Harold Wilson, of course, was also a regular guest.

Wilson's two years as chairman of the 'Bevanite' group are remembered by his former colleagues mainly for his careful chairmanship and a wry humour. Jo Richardson, the secretary of the group, recalls meeting Wilson half an hour before every group meeting to discuss with him the chief points on the agenda. He was, she remembers, 'most meticulous about all the details, and a very good chairman, but I can't remember him taking any distinctive line. He always went along with group decisions, and voted with us in the Parliamentary Party meetings.'

Inquiries from other Bevanites of the time elicit the same blank response. Tom Driberg can remember 'nothing about him. I'm sorry – but he didn't seem to do much except smoke his pipe.' Thomas Balogh at the time was particularly suspicious of Wilson, and referred scathingly on more than one occasion to the 'bonfire of controls'. Ian Mikardo recalls a 'faint feeling of dissatisfaction about him – even at the time. I always saw him as an empiricist – more interested in the technical problems than the broad issues.'

Harold Wilson's political activity at the time was not confined to the Bevanite group. During the same period he rose quickly up the ladder of the Fabian Society executive, which he had left, necessarily, when he joined the Government in 1945. Soon after his resignation, he was again co-opted on to the executive, but in the four years following he stood for election, coming third in the ballot in 1952 and 1953, second in 1955 and becoming chairman of the executive in 1955–6. For the following two years he was elected top of the committee, after which, owing to pressure of work as Shadow Chancellor, he dropped out of the Society altogether. In the year of his chairmanship he came into close contact with the young Fabian Society assistant secretary, Gerald Kaufman, whose efficiency and administrative ability greatly impressed him.

The Fabian Society in the late 1940s had, as in the past, represented a broad cross-section of Labour thinkers and intellectuals. It was by no means a closed shop for the right-wing. Ian Mikardo, one of the most committed signatories of the *Keep Left* pamphlet, was elected Treasurer of the Fabian Society in 1947 – a post which he held until 1950. Richard Crossman and Thomas Balogh were regularly on the executive in the early 1950s. After 1951, however, the Fabian leadership merged closely with that of the Party, and, largely under the influence of Hugh Gaitskell, its discussions and elections became increasingly sectarian. In 1954, Ian Mikardo left the executive in protest against the co-option of favoured candidates on to the Fabian executive, and against the refusal of the Society to accept a rule ending co-option altogether. After that, the Society became almost exclusively the province of what later became known as 'Gaitskellites' (with the single and doubtful exception of Harold Wilson, who became chairman in the year after Mikardo had stormed out of the Society).[1]

Despite Wilson's excellent electoral record in the Society, he wrote very little for it, and certainly produced no original work. In 1957, he wrote his one and only Fabian pamphlet – a dry account of economic policies of the different Governments since the war.

Though his progress in the Fabian Society went almost unnoticed, the press were quick to single Harold Wilson out as the

1. Hugh Gaitskell, Kenneth Younger, John Diamond, Roy Jenkins, Anthony Crosland, Denis Healey, Shirley Williams, Arthur Skeffington, William Rodgers, Austen Albu and Gerry Mitchison were regularly elected on to the Executive Committee, and the Society's politics and pamphlets reflected very much the views of the Labour leadership and right wing.

least Bevanite of the Bevanites. The first sign was his rapid re-appearance on the Labour front bench. Though not elected on to the 'Shadow Cabinet' (or Administrative Committee), Wilson was soon leading for the Opposition on Board of Trade matters in the manner, not of a resigning rebel, but of a former Minister. When the Opposition tabled a list of three hundred amendments to the first Tory Budget in April 1952, the *Daily Telegraph* commented (30 April 1952):

The name of Mr Harold Wilson, former President of the Board of Trade, comes after that of Mr Gaitskell, former Chancellor of the Exchequer, on many amendments. It is further evidence of a reconcilia-tion between the socialist front bench and Mr Wilson, who resigned from the last Government in sympathy with Mr Bevan.

The reconciliation was well-earned. A month earlier, Wilson had travelled to Wigan to make a statement on Party loyalty:

If there were another free and even secret ballot for a party leader with each person free to choose from a complete list of the Parliamentary Labour Party, my vote would go to Clement Attlee (*Daily Telegraph*, 10 March 1952).

Most Bevanites felt otherwise. In their view, the best possible leader of the Party was Aneurin Bevan. This gratuitous statement of support for the ageing Attlee, at a juncture when the pressure on the Bevanites from the official leadership was gathering strength, seemed to many, at worst a brush-off, at best an insurance policy. Small wonder that the keen ear of the *Daily Telegraph*'s corres-pondent Peterborough picked up 'reports of a slight estrangement between Mr Wilson and the Bevanites'. Or that a Tory MP, John Hare, later Lord Blakenham, could comment that 'whatever the outcome of the struggle for power within the Labour Party, Mr Wilson will be able to claim he backed the winner.' (*Daily Tele-graph*, 11 March 1952). When Wilson's *Tribune* pamphlet, 'In Place of Dollars', was published in September 1952, the *Manchester Guardian* opened its first leader:

The latest Bevanite pamphlet is a rather different thing from the first. Indeed, if Mr Harold Wilson is to be taken as guide, the whole Bevanite movement has changed its character. That, however, would be too much to assume. Mr Wilson has always been the most sensible of the group and the surprising thing is that he ever strayed into it.

On more than one occasion Wilson himself found his association with the Bevanites embarrassing to the point of distress. At
one big Bevanite meeting shortly before the 1951 election, Wilson,
to the astonishment of the crowd and the visiting speakers,
insisted that 'the audience stood and the National Anthem was
sung' (*Prescot and Huyton Reporter*, 28 September 1951). And a
few months later, at a *Tribune* Brains Trust held at Huyton, a
questioner asked the panel what they thought of the monarchy.
The panel – consisting of Ian Mikardo, Harold Davies, Leslie
Hale and Tom Williams – replied with a mixture of republican
fervour and light-hearted banter. Suddenly, the chairman, Harold
Wilson, announced in some heat:

Not only do I support the principle of a monarch in this country, but I
believe it essential to democracy as we know it. It is the link binding the
Commonwealth (*Prescot and Huyton Reporter*, 29 February 1952).

Despite such deviations, however, the Bevanites held Wilson in
high regard.

On 21 July 1951, shortly after the resignations, Aneurin Bevan
travelled to Huyton for a packed public meeting.

I would like to say at the outset [he said], that I think the people of
Huyton should be exceedingly proud to have a man like Harold Wilson
to represent them in the House of Commons. I have formed a great
admiration of Mr Wilson's ability, honesty and courage. When he was
appointed President of the Board of Trade I felt very proud that the
Labour Party is still able to produce men like Harold Wilson. We need
men like him.

Barbara Castle, an intractable Bevanite, was a regular visitor to
Huyton, where her praise for Harold Wilson knew no bounds.
'He is a man who was a hero to his PPS,' she told an election meet-
ing in October 1951, and two years later at a Huyton Labour
Party gala she burst out:

I am sure all of us look forward to the day when this great, bright
young prodigy is once again back on the front bench of a Labour
Government, putting real socialism into practice.

The 'real socialism' of Harold Wilson consisted in the main of
five demands.
First, a cut in the Gaitskell/Shinwell rearmament programme.

Wilson's repeated attacks on the level of the arms programme, though inevitably, and especially at Young Socialist Conferences, couched in idealistic slogans about turning swords into plough-shares, were based on technical economic arguments and the need above all to keep Britain's defence strong:

> I accept the need for rearmament, and am prepared to accept the sacrifices an effective defence programme entails. But I believe that if the rearmament programme is too big, the nation will not get more tanks, planes, guns and ships. It will get less (Huyton, 5 May 1951).
>
> We are overloading our economy to danger point. We could not only avoid disrupting the economy, but we should find that the actual effective production of essential munitions was higher than if we kept on straining at an unrealistic programme (Huyton, 9 March 1952).
>
> We are not opposed to rearmament. I myself am strongly in support of an effective defence programme (Wigan, 9 March 1952).
>
> A recasting of our arms programme would result not so much in a diversification of resources from guns to butter, but in the increased production we need (*Tribune*, 10 October 1952).
>
> The Atlantic arms programme has dealt a blow at the re-equipment and modernization of our industries (*Tribune*, 12 December 1952).

Joan Mitchell, in her analysis of the politics of 1951 (*Crisis in Britain*, Secker and Warburg, 1951), deals at length with Wilson's speech on economic affairs in the House of Commons on 26 July 1951, which she regarded as the most lucid criticism of the Labour Government from its own back benches.

> There is very little really, in the analytical part of Mr Wilson's speech, with which the Chancellor and his advisers would not have agreed, or indeed had not themselves said. . . . His analysis of Britain's own economic difficulties did not differ in any important respect from the Government's own. Criticism of the policy then pursued by the United States Government was by no means confined to Bevanite Labour opinion. Many journals and commentators, not all of them of any political attachment at all, were expressing similar apprehensions at the time.

The most widely held Bevanite view was that armaments should be cut down to allow more expenditure on social services, welfare and consumption. Wilson, on the other hand, was concerned lest the programme overstrain the economy, undercut the country's defences and delay 'the re-equipment and modernization of our industries'. As Joan Mitchell commented, these views were not restricted to Bevanites. The Tory *Economist* had been proclaiming them for years, and indeed the first converts to Wilson's view of the rearmament programme were the new Conservative Ministers.

One of the first acts of Sir Winston Churchill's Conservative administration after their election in 1951 was to scale down the ambitious arms programme of Hugh Gaitskell and Emmanuel Shinwell. In his July speech on economic affairs, Wilson had stated that 'we could not carry out both the increased armament programme and our export programme at the same time'. Almost exactly a year later, Lord Swinton, spokesman for the Tory Government on defence matters, told the House of Lords:

Exports are even more vital today than defence, because our capacity to defend ourselves depends on our capacity to trade effectively (House of Lords, 8 July 1952).

Harold Wilson, writing in *Tribune* in December 1952, triumphantly quoted Sir Winston Churchill:

It is on a satisfactory development of our economic position and particularly our balance of payments that the maintenance of our future defence effort must depend.

'These words,' wrote Wilson, 'might have been taken direct from the resignation speeches of Aneurin Bevan and myself.'

The second aspect of Harold Wilson's politics which appealed to the Bevanites was his declared faith in public ownership. While a member of the Government, Harold Wilson had avoided any commitment to nationalization, except in those unprofitable 'structural' industries which Labour had already nationalized. Out of the Government, he became more committed and more specific. In his speech to the Labour Party Conference in 1953, replying for the Executive to an economic debate, he warned:

I hope Conference will not forget that, however important finance may be, manipulation of the financial system can never be a substitute for socialist policies in trade and industry. We have to remember that taxation and monetary policies can never be a substitute for the policy of public ownership which we have been discussing (Labour Party Conference Report, 1953, p. 187).

This was a direct challenge to his colleagues in the Fabian Society, who were already arguing that taxation, properly used, was a better weapon than nationalization. Hugh Gaitskell, who spoke almost immediately before Wilson, had told the Margate conference:

We shall certainly get a far bigger contribution to the ideals of socialism and a classless society by further instalments of death duties than by nationalizing one or two industries (ibid, p. 186).

Although Wilson did not tell the conference what industries he would nationalize, he left them in no doubt that he disagreed with Gaitskell and the more conventional Fabians on the nationalization issue. And those delegates who had been following his progress since the previous year's Conference at Morecambe could hardly doubt his credentials on nationalization. In a speech on 30 November 1952, at Malden, Wilson, emphasizing that he was speaking from a personal point of view, said:

The Labour Party will have to treat as a matter of urgency those nationalization projects which could make the biggest contribution to economic recovery.

He then outlined his nationalization list which included land, chemicals and fertilizers, heavy engineering, aircraft, textile machinery, machine tools and insurance. On chemicals, he asked:

Why is consideration always limited to heavy chemicals and not for instance to the Unilever monopoly, which affected both consumer goods here and vast trading interests in Africa?

And on the heavy engineering industries:

If they do not expand, our recovery will be imperilled: if they do, to meet a demand largely created by Government action, is there not a case for the economic surplus thus created to come to the community? Moreover, heavy engineering and shipbuilding, are, together with steel and chemicals, among the basic armament industries; opinion in the Labour movement has always been against the basic armaments industries existing for private profit.

The speech ended with a let-out, that 'there might be strong arguments against nationalization in some of these cases', but it created a storm. The *Daily Telegraph* (1 December 1952) branded it as 'a determined effort to assert socialist fundamentalism'.

Harold Wilson disagreed. At that time he was writing regularly on politics for *Reynolds News*, the Co-operative Sunday newspaper, and, a few weeks later, replying to the critics, he wrote:

All the economic measures to be considered should be subject to this acid test: will they be relevant to the need for increased production and exports, for reducing our dependence on dollar materials, and for the great programme of developing the Commonwealth and other areas of the globe? In a recent speech at Malden, speaking purely in a private capacity, I suggested some of the industries which might be considered for nationalization, not on any doctrinaire or ideological grounds, but as measures essential to our economic solvency. . . . the urgent task for the Movement in 1953 is to decide what measures of public ownership will make the biggest contribution to national solvency and international independence.

The central theme of the Labour Party policy document *Challenge to Britain*, Wilson explained, was the need 'to make British industry more efficient and more economic'. While in speeches to the Party rank and file, in articles in *Tribune* and in the Bevanite pamphlets *One Way Only*, *Going our Way* and *Quo Vadis*, Wilson emphasized the importance of a wide extension of public ownership, in the Commons he argued that State interference was only justifiable where it helped exports or increased industrial efficiency. There was nothing essentially contradictory about this approach, nor could Wilson be accused of deceiving his Labour audience. Only very seldom did he resort to socialist arguments for public enterprise. Almost always he argued for it in terms of capitalist success.

While Bevan and most of his colleagues saw public ownership as a means of redistributing wealth and power, and advancing towards a New Order, Wilson spoke and argued for it in terms of 'national solvency', 're-equipment of our industries', 'industrial efficiency' and 'maintaining the volume of investment'. These were the guiding principles of Wilson's policy, and there was therefore nothing contradictory in arguing in one place for public ownership, in another for private ownership.

During his Bevanite period, Harold Wilson confirmed what he had suspected in the last few months of his Presidency of the Board of Trade – that unadulterated private enterprise could not and would not provide the basis for capitalist success in Britain.

Private enterprise required to be guided, instructed, even bullied by the State if the national economy was to prosper. The guidance and instruction might take the form of outright nationalization, development councils, planning councils, joint industrial boards, prices and incomes boards, or anything similar, but all these could conveniently be lumped together under the heading 'public enterprise'.

Harold Wilson was advocating a system of national state capitalism in which business efficiency and investment problems became increasingly the prerogative of the state, and in which the competitive dynamic of capitalism was transferred from inter-firm competition to inter-state competition. The rhetorical difference between the two forms of competition is crucial, particularly for Labour politicians. Few Labour candidates would urge workers in one British firm to work harder in order to beat another British firm in the same industry. Yet inter-state competition can be justified in the glamorous phraseology of patriotism. Particularly in the post-war years, when patriotic appeals were still associated with anti-Fascism, appeals on the basis of 'the needs of Britain' or of 'making Britain great' worked wonders with Labour audiences.

Yet the *real* difference between the two systems, particularly as it affects the vast majority of Labour supporters, is negligible. One system is controlled by men of inherited wealth and elitist education, the other by technocrats and civil servants. Both systems are based on class distinctions, on a low priority for welfare facilities and a tendency to monopoly and bureaucracy. Most of the Bevanites envisaged an entirely different society, classless and democratic. But the distinction between socialism and state capitalism was not clear to them. Advocacy of public ownership was sufficient qualification for joining the Bevanites.

It was, no doubt, Wilson's conversion to state capitalism which led him to perhaps his most strongly held conviction during the Bevanite period – that Britain should trade more extensively with Russia and China. His work with Montague Meyer took him on more than one occasion to Russia, where he spoke to Molotov, and to China, where he interviewed Chou En Lai.

Wilson had never been a Communist. He had always been bored by Marxism, and he regarded the Communist Party as an anti-

British nuisance. He was never one of the left-wing Labour MPs who received unsolicited compliments from Communist front organizations and newspapers, and the Communists, to their credit, despite Wilson's lip-service to the Left in this period, never took him for more than a conventional Labour politician. Yet Wilson's political antagonism to the revolutionary implications of Communism conflicted sharply with his admiration for Russia's economic achievement. Wilson saw more clearly than any other leading Labour Party politician at the time that it was both possible and logical to divorce Russia's economic achievements from her revolutionary socialist background. He saw that Russia's economic success arose from her ability so to regulate her economy that investment got the highest priority. Decisions about investment and technology can, in the Russian economy, be taken without fear of obstruction from unrestricted bargaining between trade unions and management, pressure for welfare services, factory legislation and so on. The economist in Harold Wilson greatly envied the ability to make crucial economic decisions without such hindrance. Thus his attitude to Russia was one of disapproval of her political institutions and admiration for her economic system.

This contradiction was expressed again and again in his speeches and writings during the Bevanite period. No single issue was given more emphasis than the need to trade more with the East, with Russia and with China. Peaceful co-existence with the East was, for Wilson, crucial, and he warned his countrymen to take note of the fantastic economic achievements of the Russian system:

One fact the West cannot ignore is Russia's spectacular increase in production and productive capacity. We have devoted so many of our resources to countering her military power that we are in danger of ignoring her industrial power. Despite the tremendous burdens she has shouldered, we shall ignore the economic implications of her growing industrial potential at our peril (Speech at Prescot, *Daily Telegraph*, 28 September 1953).

The Bevanites and the Labour Left, were then, as now, hypnotized by the spectacle of what they regard as socialism, or at least a bastard socialism, in the East. The survival of a statified economy, with state-owned industries and state-owned agriculture, has always been held in high regard by the Labour Left, many of whose supporters at that time saw the Russian issue as the touchstone of Left and Right in Labour politics. The Left was pro-Russia. The Right was anti-Russia. Thus Harold Wilson's cautious campaigning for more trade with the East and his admiration of the 'efficiency' of a fully stratified economy earned him many admirers on the Labour Left without committing him to socialist theory or socialist policies.

The fourth aspect of Harold Wilson's politics which endeared him to the Labour Left was his advocacy of 'utility' remedies to deal with the inevitable Tory slump. Wilson seized every opportunity to warn the nation of the impending crisis:

Slump conditions are spreading slowly across the country aided by the financial policy of the Government and we are facing dollar crisis and unemployment at the same time. The crisis when it finally comes will not therefore be a repetition of 1947 and 1949. It will be another 1931 (Speech at Coventry, *Times*, 7 June, 1952).

What we are facing is not merely another 1947 or 1949; it is another 1931 (*Reynolds News*, 27 July 1952).

It is another 1931, with foreign exchange difficulties on the one hand and heavy unemployment on the other (House of Commons, 29 July 1952).

I must warn the Conference that we may be called upon to take control in conditions of a major financial crisis comparable with that of 1931 That is what we are heading for now, despite the complacency of the Tories and their boasting about the phoney temporary recovery going on (Labour Party Conference Report, 1953, p. 187).

In this atmosphere Wilson called for increased subsidies on food, controls on prices and 'utility' schemes. Only by ensuring 'fair shares' – and by working hard – could the impending crisis be avoided. Otherwise, forecast the most brilliant Oxford economist of his generation, the economy would collapse in another 1931.

Slump hysteria of this kind was highly fashionable at that time among Labour supporters who believed that the post-war Labour Government had *created* full employment. They reckoned that a Tory Government, necessarily, would revert to pre-war slump conditions and a permanent 'pool of unemployment'. In the event, precisely the reverse happened. British capitalism entered its most successful period of all time, during which both full employment and the Welfare State were rigorously maintained. Full employment, it became clear, was not the creation of one Party or another, but of external economic conditions over which neither had any control.

Strangely enough, Harold Wilson came closer than all Labour politicians, even John Strachey, to understanding and analysing the real cause of post-war full employment.

In an article in *Tribune* entitled 'Peace Need Not Mean a Slump' on 24 April, 1953, Wilson wrote:

> There is no doubt that the world capitalist system is faced with some very hard thinking. Since 1945, the need to replace war damage, and then, as this was failing, the Cold War and the rise of the Joe Stalin industry kept Western economies at more or less full stretch. If our Western economies require a war to keep them employed, then the only sane course is to declare war now not on Communism or some temporal power but on mankind's ancient enemies, poverty, hunger, illiteracy and disease.

And, a few months later:

> World capitalism has known prosperity only in time of war, of preparation for war or in the sellers' market which follows a war. Full employment has been maintained not so much by the Korean war as by the Cold War, and it is the future of the Cold War that will determine the timing and intensity of the slump (*Reynolds News*, 2 August 1953).

This analysis, however, did not deter Wilson from crying 'Slump' with his comrades in the Bevanite Group and in the Parliamentary Party leadership. The conception, so dramatically vindicated by events, that capitalism was safe from pre-war conditions as long as the big industrial countries spent half their investible surplus upon armaments would, had it caught on in the Labour Movement, have given rise to relevant, if not revolutionary, policies. As it was, Wilson's isolated references to the 'permanent arms economy' were ignored, even by their author. In practice, on the hustings and in the Commons, Wilson continued to call for more austerity, more 'utility' goods and more sacrifice at a time when the foundations of the Cold War Affluent Society were being laid. In this total misapprehension of what was happening in the world economy he was not alone. The entire Bevanite group, and indeed most of the more conventional Parliamentary Party leaders, subscribed to the view that the Tories could never maintain full employment, which Labour had 'created'.

Finally, Wilson joined the Bevanite group in their fight on the two major foreign affairs issues at that time: the rearmament of Germany and American foreign policy in the Far and Middle East. Wilson's attitude while in power towards the rearmament of Germany had never been clear. Six weeks before his resignation, for instance, he had told a sceptical meeting of the United Hebrew Congregation:

The rearming of Germany is not for the purpose of war, but to prevent it (*Times*, 5 March 1951).

Two and half years later he was unconditionally opposed to German rearmament:

The reason for the move in Trieste is that American policy is being dictated by the necessity of having Germany rearmed, which the Labour Party is against. The Americans have held the pistol to the head of France on the issue, and now they have offered Trieste to Italy as a dirty bribe for their support (Meeting at Huyton, 7 November 1953, *Prescot and Huyton Reporter*, 13 November 1953).

And, at another constituency meeting, two months later:

I am sure no one here wants Germany rearmed, nor does France, nor does Russia. I do not think the Germans do either, apart from some neo-Nazis who are creeping back to power (ibid., 24 January 1954).

The following month, the Parliamentary Labour Party (including several Labour peers) voted for rearmament by 113 votes to 104. Wilson moved a compromise amendment postponing the decision until after the Geneva conference, 'in the interests of Party unity', which was defeated by two votes. The following month, he left the front benches, where he had been leading for Labour on financial matters, and spoke in support of the 'substantial minority in the Party who opposed German rearmament'. Most of his speech was about Party unity.

Formal unity without a right sense of directon has been the prerogative not of statesmen but of Gadarene swine throughout the ages (House of Commons, 25 February 1954).

Yet on the issue of rearmament itself, Wilson's speech was mild and conciliatory, complaining merely that the rearmament negotiations had not been tough enough. After thus dipping his toe into controversy, he retired quickly to the safe ground of East–West Trade and peaceful co-existence.

In March, he spoke again to his constituency on the subject, underlining the importance of controversy in the Party – a familiar theme of Wilson's during his brief periods of disagreement with the Party leadership.

We do not apologize for holding different views in the Party, because it is vital that in a matter of such importance, no view is silenced. As I told the Tories in the House, unity can be a bad thing if it is not unity travelling in the right direction (Speech at Huyton, 7 March, *Prescot and Huyton Reporter*, 12 March 1954).

A motion approving German rearmament was carried by the Labour Party Conference in 1954, again by a tiny majority, and after some switching of votes by the Amalgamated Society of Woodworkers. Wilson, a member of the Executive and the Shadow Cabinet, did not speak at the 1954 Conference. He told an *Observer* interviewer nine years later:

At the Party Conference, German rearmament was carried again by the narrowest of margins. We accepted the majority decision. *I never spoke against German rearmament again.* You've got to have a sense of responsibility to the whole.

Wilson's 'sense of responsibility' had replaced his former conviction that 'on a matter of such importance, no view should be silenced'.

Throughout his Bevanite period Harold Wilson maintained a steady assault on American foreign policy, particularly in South East Asia (see Chapter 6, pp. 199–205). The encirclement of China with puppet states bound together in a military alliance greatly disturbed the Labour Left, not least Aneurin Bevan, who argued passionately that the Labour Party should publicly oppose the formation of the South East Asia Treaty Organisation. Gaitskell and Morrison rallied the anti-Communists in the Shadow Cabinet and Bevan was defeated. At once, he resigned from the Shadow Cabinet.

The Party rules laid down that any vacancy in the Shadow Cabinet (or Parliamentary Committee, as it was called) had to be filled automatically by the unsuccessful candidate in the Shadow Cabinet elections who had received the highest votes. In this case, 'the next man on the list' for Bevan's vacancy was Harold Wilson.

Bevan resigned on 15 April 1954 and in the *Evening Standard* that evening Wilson was quoted as saying: 'I entirely agree with the policy of Mr Bevan in his statement last night.' The formal invitation to take Bevan's place on the Parliamentary Committee reached Wilson on 23 April. The *Daily Telegraph* opined: 'Harold Wilson will probably decline automatic succession to the vacancy.'

Not so. The following day, Wilson, in a letter to the secretary of the Parliamentary Party, agreed to fill the vacancy:

I am in entire agreement, as the Party knows, with Aneurin Bevan on the policy issues involved – on the dangers not only of Mr Dulles' policies in South East Asia, but also of German Rearmament. Nevertheless, what matters in the last resort is the unity and strength of the Party. I have given a great deal of anxious thought to this question in the last ten days, and have not lacked advice. My conclusion is that, in the Party's interests, it is impossible for me to refuse co-option.

This decision, to all intents and purposes, finished the friendly relationship between Harold Wilson and Aneurin Bevan, and Wilson's association with the Bevanites. In a long discussion in the House of Commons with his former friend, Wilson tried to get Bevan's sanction for his decision but was bitterly and contemptuously rebuffed. His statement in the *Daily Express* that 'Nye and I are the best of friends' was neither confirmed nor denied by Bevan, but Wilson's decision met with almost unanimous hostility at the Bevanite meeting in Crossman's house in Vincent Square on the Tuesday after Bevan's resignation. The issue was raised by Crossman, who argued that Wilson should accept the Shadow Cabinet post. Wilson agreed. Everyone else, however, attacked Crossman's suggestion in no uncertain terms and Wilson and his host were left in a minority of two.

In his book on the Labour Party in the 1950s, *The Road to Brighton Pier*, the journalist Leslie Hunter has recorded (p. 79):

Wilson's presence in the Shadow Cabinet demonstrated that it was possible for Right and Left to work together in something like mutual tolerance, if not agreement. . . . But from now on Wilson and Crossman were slowly to diverge from the rest. They had set foot on the main Brighton road.

Many of Bevan's closest colleagues in Parliament were as angry
as their leader over what they regarded as Wilson's betrayal. A. J.
Irvine, the Bevanite Member for Liverpool, Edge Hill, cancelled
an engagement to speak to the Huyton Fabian Society at Roby, in
Wilson's constituency, and issued a statement to the Press.

Mr Wilson's letter seems to imply that Mr Bevan, in resigning from
the Committee, has disregarded these considerations of party unity and
strength. I have the strongest dislike for a statement capable of this
interpretation, and I know that great numbers of the rank and file of
the Labour Party will share my feelings (*Daily Telegraph*, 30 April 1954).

In a special interview with the political correspondent of the
Liverpool Daily Post, under the heading 'NO TRUE BEVANITE',
Mr Irvine spelled out what he meant:

I believe that, on the whole, in public life it is always best to say
clearly and honestly what you believe. As I think Mr Wilson has made a
serious mistake by joining the Parliamentary Committee and has disappointed many of us who were associated with him, that opinion has to
be expressed.

The *Post*'s political correspondent went on:

Mr Irvine's statements are in part designed to counteract any impression that the Bevanites still have a representative on the front bench.
Apparently he no longer regards Mr Wilson as a true supporter of Mr
Bevan. He told me last night 'You are either for or against a man'. He
does not believe there is any hope of patching up the differences on these
issues. Mr Irvine is not alone in the one-time Bevan group in strongly
condemning what they regard as Mr Wilson's desertion of Mr Bevan....
He is supported by Jennie Lee, Mr Ian Mikardo, Mr Tom Driberg, Mr
Geoffrey Bing, Mr Douglas Baird, Mr Harold Davies and Mr Michael
Foot (*Liverpool Daily Post*, 30 April 1954).

The following month, Mr Cecil Poole, the member for Birmingham, Perry Barr, issued a statement to his local papers about the
episode, adding the comment:

Opportunism never pays dividends in the long run (*Birmingham Post*,
20 May 1954).

Wilson greatly resented this criticism and increased his attacks
on American foreign policy in an attempt to maintain his Bevanite

associations. Asked on a television Press Conference by Malcolm Muggeridge (7 May 1954) whether he was still a Bevanite, Wilson replied:

> The question is not quite so simple as it sounds. Certainly I have not changed any of my ideas about politics.

In fact, as he knew well, Harold Wilson had abandoned the Bevanites, taking with him his trusted supporter, Richard Crossman. In an interview eighteen months later, Mr Hugh Gaitskell, then a leading contender for the Labour leadership, stated 'the only Bevanites I would have in a Government would be Dick Crossman, Harold Wilson and Barbara Castle'.

Yet, if it irritated a group of Bevanite Members of Parliament, Wilson's action in taking Bevan's place in the Shadow Cabinet in no way damaged his position with the Party rank and file. Bevan predicted that Wilson's joining the Shadow Cabinet would lose him his seat on the National Executive. But Wilson knew more of the machinations of internal party politics. At the 1954 Conference, at which, tactfully, Wilson did not speak, he was elected top of the Constituency section. He occupied one of the top four places in that section every succeeding year, until 1963, when he was elected leader of the Party.

Wilson's 1951 resignation was enough to convince the Party rank and file that he was a man of the Left. But though the Party rank and file liked a militant, and were suspicious of dedicated revisionists like Hugh Gaitskell, they preferred their militants 'safe'. Only men with the impeccable record of a Bevan could combine continued attacks on the leadership with the support of the rank and file. Lesser men, if they wanted to stay on the Executive, had to demonstrate that their socialist principles were tempered by 'loyalty to the Party leadership'. This is one reason why Wilson and Crossman always got bigger votes for the executive than the more faithful Bevanites, Mikardo and Driberg. The mantle of Nye was, for the moment at any rate, no longer necessary for Harold Wilson's continued progress on the National Executive and in the Parliamentary Party. It could safely be cast aside, revealing a more genuine and contented Harold Wilson, setting out on the high road to respectability and power.

Chapter 4
The Collapse into Technology: 1954–64

Given a Labour victory, the test is this: will there be, twelve
months from now, a narrowing of the gap between rich and poor,
quite apart from any general upward movement there may be as a
result of increased national production? The answer is, quite
simply, that there will. This has been the central theme of both our
election speeches and the party's television programmes (Harold
Wilson, *New Statesman*, 3 October 1959).

The fundamental inspiration of *Signposts for the Sixties* and the
statement which followed is the need to make Britain up-to-date,
dynamic, vigorous and capable of playing her full part in world
affairs. . . . We begin from the need to strengthen Britain's economy,
to secure a steady and purposive expansion in industrial
production (Harold Wilson, *New York Times*, 11 September 1963).

Aneurin Bevan ascribed Labour's loss of the 1955 election to the
bankruptcy of Labour Party policy and the failure of the leadership to analyse or attack the central features of Tory policy. The
Party leaders, on the other hand, blamed the election result mainly
on poor Party administration and organization. Subsequently the
National Executive decided to appoint a 'high-powered' sub-
committee to investigate Party organization, and recommend
measures to improve it. The chairman of the Committee, in his
new role as Party unifier, was Harold Wilson.

Wilson's report was submitted shortly before the 1955 Party
Conference, and caused such a furore among top Party bureaucrats, notably Morgan Phillips, the General Secretary, that it was
withheld and altered in several tactful ways before its publication
on 5 October. Labour's electoral machine, pontificated the Report
in familiar language, was 'at the penny-farthing stage in the jet-
propelled era, and, at that, is getting rusty and deteriorating with
age'. A long list of innovations, most of them administrative, many
of them petty, none of them political, was suggested to help the
Party entice or bully their supporters to the polls.

Though the Report was generally well received by the Party

leaders, and to some extent even acted upon, it infuriated Aneurin
Bevan. In a speech at a *Tribune* meeting in Manchester in February
1956 which was widely regarded as one of the most brilliant
platform performances of his career, Bevan savaged the report and
its author.

It was unlikely, he said, that the Party would achieve the spirit
of 1945 by ensuring that 'the right buttons are on the right desks
and that bells have to ring'. In a reference to the 'penny-farthing'
metaphor, Bevan declared himself 'not sure whether we want the
car to go faster if it is going over a precipice'. There were, he went
on, far too many decisions taken at the top of the movement without reference to the rank and file. The democratic arteries of the
Party were being stiffened by bureaucracy. Though he only
mentioned Wilson once by name, he left his audience in no doubt
that he was referring not merely to the new leader of the Party,
Hugh Gaitskell, whom he had attacked on so many occasions in
the past, but Gaitskell's new lieutenant and confidant, Harold
Wilson.

By this time, Wilson was firmly entrenched in the Labour
leadership. As early as August 1955, Walter Terry of the *Daily
Mail* took the view that 'close colleagues of both Mr Gaitskell and
Mr Wilson are convinced the two have reached agreement on
tactics'. And Crossbencher of the *Sunday Express*, reporting the
Tribune meeting at the Labour Party Conference in October,
described Wilson as 'the only Gaitskellite on the platform'
(*Sunday Express*, 16 October 1955).

Harold Wilson had lost no time in re-establishing contact with
his friends and colleagues of the old, pre-Bevanite days. Sam
Watson, for instance, the leader of the Durham miners, had
broken with Wilson over the 1951 resignations, even though
Watson had sided with Bevan in the early debates about nationalization. On 25 March 1955, Watson wrote to Wilson:

Whatever policy issues may have divided us (and I do not think they
have ever gone beyond policy) our past friendship and the fruitful talks
we have had in the past, suggest to me that you and I occupy rather key
positions in what must be a real, united effort to pull the party together
and clear up some of the difficulties which have been overshadowing all
our activities. I well remember the talks we had in Durham (I think it
was on the 11th of September 1952) and although we went on till mid-

night, I think the discussion remained unfinished – we had inevitably spent more time with the past than the future.

Leslie Smith recounts a long conversation between Gaitskell and Wilson in Gaitskell's car as the 1955 Labour Party Conference broke up. Wilson, apparently, explained that in his view Gaitskell had made mistakes, but was still 'the only possible leader'. 'I'll back you for it wholeheartedly,' he went on, according to his biographer, 'so long as you stop trying to force every issue, by always trying to get a majority decision on everything that crops up. If you'll really try to work with the *whole* party and take a unifying not a divisive view of your responsibilities, you can count on my complete support when Attlee goes, and on my continuing loyalty' (Leslie Smith, p. 174). Gaitskell, according to Smith, 'was very pleased'.

Whether or not the exact words of this conversation were as flattering as Mr Smith makes out (which is unlikely), Wilson certainly did do a deal with Gaitskell during that period, and, no doubt, in the course of it expressed his apprehensions about Gaitskell's instinctive dislike of compromise. A week later Gaitskell and Wilson met again privately in St Ermins Hotel to 'draft proposals on the structure of new committees and generally to streamline Party policy' (*Daily Telegraph*, 27 October 1955). In the elections for the Party leadership the following month, Wilson lobbied for Gaitskell and voted for him (against Bevan and Morrison). On 14 February 1956, only a week after Bevan's outburst in Manchester, Wilson was appointed Shadow Chancellor of the Exchequer and soon afterwards chairman of the Party's organization sub-committee.

Nothing could go wrong for Harold Wilson, Shadow Chancellor. As the Tory Government grappled with unaccustomed economic recession in 1956 and again in 1957, Wilson developed a lively, knockabout speaking style which, though grossly overwritten in the press, astonished some of his adversaries of former years. Lord Chandos, who as Oliver Lyttleton was Wilson's main adversary when the latter was President of the Board of Trade, writes to me on 23 May 1967:

It is curious that, during my time in the House, Wilson's speeches erred on the dull side, and he avoided fireworks. Almost suddenly, as it appeared to me, he decided to make use of his powers of wit and ridicule, and from having rather bored the House, he very soon found himself entertaining them with all kinds of epigrams and quirks. He might almost have been described as a successor to Oliver Stanley in these respects.

The press reported after each Budget speech that the 'shafts struck home', but they also pointed out that the wit never exceeded Parliamentary propriety, and no one enjoyed Wilson's attacks more than his opponents.

Nevertheless his Bevanite past and his renown as 'scourge of the Tories' in Parliament kept him in the ascendancy in both key sections of the Labour Movement – the Constituency Parties, and the Parliamentary Party. In the voting for the National Executive in 1956, 1957 and 1958 he came, respectively, first, first and fourth while for the Parliamentary Committee (or Shadow Cabinet) he came first, second and first. No other Labour politician of the time achieved similar ascendancy in both sections during the same period. Only after he had finally sunk his differences with the Party leadership was even Bevan so simultaneously popular in both fields. Of the others, only James Callaghan bridged the gap between the relative militancy of the rank and file and the leadership-neurosis of the Parliamentary Party, and Callaghan was never sure of a place on the Executive. T. F. Lindsay of the *Daily Telegraph* could report with some accuracy on 2 March 1959 that

If Mr Bevan has gone into eclipse, Mr Harold Wilson shines the brighter by contrast.

All this was a bit much for Gaitskell, who had never been popular in the constituency parties, and had never trusted Wilson though he had praised him in the most forthright terms at the 1958 Party Conference. By 1959, Gaitskell, according to a number of reports, was considering moving Wilson from the Shadow Chancellorship and replacing him with the prince of loyalists, Patrick Gordon Walker. Wilson, however, was well protected from such manoeuvres by his popularity in all sections of the movement.

Then suddenly, as Wilson's position seemed unassailable, it was undermined by his age-old enemy: controversy.

To Wilson's intense irritation and dismay, Gaitskell reacted to the 1959 Election defeat by insisting on an irrevocable showdown with and purge of those elements in the Party which were 'spoiling its image' with the floating voter. These image-spoilers were identified for Hugh Gaitskell either by their enthusiasm for nationalization or by their desire for Britain unilaterally to renounce nuclear weapons.

The first argument developed around Clause 4 of the Labour Party Constitution, written by Sidney Webb in 1918 – the only clause in the Constitution which defined the political aims of the Party. The clause, which was re-printed on every Labour Party membership card, proclaims the aim:

> to secure for the workers by hand or by brain the full fruits of their industry and the most equitable distribution thereof that may be possible, on the basis of the common ownership of the means of production, distribution and exchange and the best obtainable system of popular administration and control of each industry and service.

Gaitskell argued, in the wake of the 1959 defeat, that the Party in all its policy statements since the war had effectively abandoned this aim; that nationalization as a general economic principle was 'no longer relevant' and that therefore, both to be honest and to win the votes of the non-socialist middle class, the constitution should be re-written to omit the offending clause. Gaitskell lost this battle, largely because the big trade-union leaders found to their embarrassment that some similar sentiment was written into *their* constitutions, and they did not relish a confrontation with their rank and file. Yet what must have irritated Gaitskell, perhaps even more than the political defeat he suffered on this issue, was the opposition he encountered from some of those closest to him: notably his Shadow Chancellor, Harold Wilson.

Harold Wilson has never made a public policy statement in his life which remotely resembles Clause 4. He does not believe, and has never believed, in 'the common ownership of the means of production, distribution and exchange' still less in 'the best available system of popular administration and control of each industry and service'. His attitude to public ownership has been consistently bureaucratic, and he has always seen well-managed public ownership and control as a minority shareholder in, not as an alternative to, private enterprise. This attitude was reinforced during his 'Gaitskellite' period as Shadow Chancellor of the Exchequer. In a speech at Widnes, shortly after the 1955 General Election, he made his attitude quite clear.

The speech concentrated on the chemical industry. Labour's declared policy in its election manifesto was to take 'appropriate sections' of that industry into public ownership. Explaining this policy, Wilson said:

Labour does not say the [chemicals] industry is inefficiently managed, though when monopoly rules it is often difficult to measure efficiency.

Certainly profits are no test. What we do say is that the concentration of monopoly power, either through interlocking public ownership or price rings, means that only public ownership can protect the community.

But there is a stronger argument than this. In this second half of the twentieth century, the chemical industry is as important a source of raw materials as steel itself. It is not only a citadel of economic power. . . .

How shall we do it? By taking over the shares of some of the principal companies. What we shall do is to substitute the state for the absentee and by now meaningless control of the shareholders.

The structure of the companies is likely to continue to be what it would have been in private ownership. Technicians and research workers, management and workers will be free to get on with their job – free from the incubus of financial interests at present controlling them.

How will it affect the position of the workers? Some firms, helped by their monopoly position, have looked after their workers well. We shall safeguard under public ownership the rights those workers have won from private industry.

Almost a year after Harold Wilson made that speech, Anthony Crosland, a young Fabian intellectual, published the book which was to be the bible of the 'revisionists' in the Labour Party – *The Future of Socialism*. One of the central arguments in Crosland's book was that state ownership – legal title – was becoming more and more irrelevant to industrial strategy and economic policy. What mattered, he argued, was state *control*. As long as the state had a say in the control of industry, the question of ownership could be decided empirically – in some cases it was desirable, in others not – and it was certainly not a matter of principle. Wilson had always accepted this thesis. The state, he argued, should decide the general direction of industrial and economic policy in order to make industry more efficient and more competitive. Given that aim, it was axiomatic that 'the structure of the companies is likely to continue to be what it would have been under private ownership'. The Webb Constitution argued for common ownership 'to secure for the workers the full fruits of their industry', while Wilson believed that the state must guide British capitalism through the storms of international capitalist competition. Both these clearly contradictory attitudes could be lumped together under the heading 'public ownership'.

The 'Crosland view' on nationalization was incorporated into the controversial Labour Party policy statement of 1957, *Industry and Society*, which Harold Wilson helped to write. The statement promised the nationalization of steel and road haulage and the state buying of shares in any industry which was 'failing the nation'. The document produced an outcry from the Labour Left. At the 1957 Labour Party Conference at Brighton, Jim Campbell, left-wing General Secretary of the National Union of Railwaymen, moved a resolution referring *Industry and Society* back to the Executive. Campbell described the document as a 'clumsy conception of the consolidation of capitalism', and deplored 'the present tendency to deviate from accepted socialist principles'.

Though Campbell's was the only big union to support the reference back (the Transport and General Workers, under their new leader, Frank Cousins, voted loyally with the Executive) his resolution commanded wide support in the constituency parties and mustered nearly one and a half million votes. Yet the majority for the document was enormous, and the delegates responded warmly to the two executive speeches supporting it, from Harold Wilson, moving, and Hugh Gaitskell, winding up.

Wilson protested that the document did not propose 'a substitute for traditional forms of nationalization'. He promised, 'When we say "extend public ownership in any industry", we mean "take over, nationalize".' Nor was it a problem that only two industries were scheduled for nationalization. 'After all, we cannot judge which industries will be most relevant to the problems we are facing, until we take over the responsibilities of Government and know what the circumstances are at that time.' An exactly similar line of argument was pursued by Gaitskell at the end of the debate.

The proposals in *Industry and Society* were reproduced in the

1958 policy statement *The Future Labour Offers You*, which, in terms of public ownership, represented a considerable retreat from the 1955 Election Manifesto.

On public ownership, from 1956 until the 1959 election, Harold Wilson was in complete agreement with the Labour leadership, and their intellectual inspiration, Anthony Crosland. Even more explicitly, he agreed with the leadership in the other main controversy – about nuclear weapons.

The decision to make the British independent nuclear deterrent had been taken by the Attlee Government – of which Harold Wilson was a member. That same Government, under the influence of another of Wilson's heroes, Ernest Bevin, had aligned Britain with the Western powers in the Cold War and had signed the North Atlantic Treaty, binding America, Britain and Western Europe in military unity against the East. With all of this, Wilson was in total agreement.

On 30 April 1954, only a day after Wilson had taken Bevan's place in the Shadow Cabinet, the House of Commons voted on a private members' motion complaining about the continued manufacture of nuclear weapons. The vote was 'free', though the Labour Party leadership made their disapproval clear. Nevertheless, a number of Labour members did vote for the motion, including three of the Whips, Arthur Royle, John Taylor and Kenneth Robinson. Wilson's name, however, did not appear in the division lists. And the following month, when about fifty Labour MPs, including Bevan, refused to vote for the official Opposition amendment to another H-bomb debate, Wilson loyally supported the official amendment. His loyalty to the Executive was neatly summarized by the Shadow Chancellor himself, when he answered the *Evening Standard*'s questions about his personal attitudes to the 'unilateralist' issue:

> They leave finances to me, and I leave foreign affairs and the H-bomb to Bevan and Gaitskell. I have always spoken in favour of the NEC policy about the bomb, and I shall continue to do so (*Evening Standard*, 10 July 1959).

Both issues – unilateral disarmament and Clause 4 – were raised stridently at the two-day Party Conference in 1959 – not least by Gaitskell, who suggested that the Constitution should be re-written. At the 1960 Party Conference at Scarborough, the Party voted unilaterally to renounce nuclear weapons. Various attempts at compromising the issue had been sabotaged not so much by the unilateralists as by Hugh Gaitskell.

Harold Wilson's reaction to this controversy was one of intense irritation. He was angry not so much with the Left, with whose views on both issues he completely disagreed, but with Hugh Gaitskell and his henchmen, with whose views on both issues he completely agreed. His political views were outweighed by his tactical outrage that the issues had been brought into the field of public squabble when they could have been compromised into the background.

Three years before the crisis, Wilson had had dinner with John Junor, editor of the *Sunday Express*. Harold Macmillan had just become Prime Minister, and Wilson was full of praise for the new Premier's tactics. 'You know, John,' (Junor remembers him saying), 'the man's a genius. He's holding up the banner of Suez for the Party to follow, and he's leading the Party away from Suez. That's what I'd like to do with the Labour Party over nationalization.'

Gaitskell's insistence on exposing the divisions in the Labour Party by re-writing the Constitution was, for Wilson, anathema. The Constitution, he claimed, was quite irrelevant to the policy which the Party should pursue. Not once since the war had the Party framed its policies according to the Constitution, and there was no reason why it should start to do so now. Labour could, he urged, continue with *Industry and Society* policies at home and Ernest Bevin policies abroad without changing the Constitution. The Party faithful could paste Clause 4 over their beds at night, but, provided no one re-wrote the Constitution, in the morning they would happily work for the opposite. Similarly with defence and nuclear weapons. Wilson boasted during the controversy that he 'could draft out at least seven defence policies on which the Party could unite'.

Any doubts Wilson may have had as to the relative importance of views and tactics must have been dispelled by a story which appeared exclusively in the *Sunday Times* on 15 November 1959, only a month after the General Election. According to the report, Hugh Gaitskell had held a meeting of some of his closest colleagues in Hampstead, and the meeting had decided to entice Wilson out of the Shadow Chancellorship with the offer of a job as 'Party overlord'. This plan was 'leaked' to Wilson, who immediately made it clear that he would have none of it. That year Wilson came top of the poll for the Shadow Cabinet, and second for the National Executive. He was too powerful to be shifted, but he realized, if he had not done so before, that Gaitskell and his friends were out to get him.

A month later, Walter Terry of the *Daily Mail* reported that Wilson had been holding meetings with left-wingers discussing opposition to Gaitskell on Clause 4. The report was angrily denied by Wilson, who stressed that 'nothing should be done at this critical time which would in any way imperil the unity of the Party'. Yet his language on public ownership became more militant than at any other time in the previous five years. 'We should say,' he told the Oxford University Labour Club in June 1960,

what we are going to nationalize and why. I myself am becoming far more impressed with the case for nationalizing the so-called defence industries of this country (*Daily Telegraph*, 4 June 1960).

His main theme was unity. He told a May Day rally:

The Labour Party is more united than it has been for some time past. Let us try honestly to reach the right decision with more regard for Party unity than the victory of one or other point of view (Coventry, 10 September 1960).

Let us have a clear decision that we can all respect so that all of us know where we are and that we can have Party unity (Farnworth, 18 September 1960).

And, at the Conference itself:

The sterile argument that started after the last election is over, and now we must make up lost time and face the future instead of the past (Labour Party Conference Report, 1960, p. 149).

Again and again, before the 1960 Conference, Wilson had begged Gaitskell to concentrate on those aspects of the defence issue which united the Party, not on those which divided it. He urged upon him the importance of the Party's policy to abandon the 'independent deterrent', of making a 'more viable conventional contribution' to NATO, of (that universal, utopian panacea) 'disengagement in Europe'. Gaitskell, quite rightly, regarded all this as political shadow-boxing. Verbal gymnastics, he argued, could not extract the Party from the theoretical impasse which it had reached. The only solution was to force the main arguments out into the open and decide them by the vote (or, if the vote went against the leadership, by whatever other means presented themselves). Arrogant as ever, he dismissed Wilson's pleas, and indeed attacked him on more than one occasion in public. Wilson in turn became more and more hostile and, at the Conference, conspicuously refused to join in the general hymn-singing to Gaitskell when the latter pledged himself to 'fight, fight, and fight again' against the majority decision of his Party.

Perhaps what irritated Wilson more than any other aspect of the controversy was that it forced him to take sides. At a party at Barbara Castle's Highgate flat two days before he finally decided to run against Gaitskell for the Party leadership, Wilson complained that he had no quarrel with Gaitskell over defence, and very little in common with the other guests except that they were the only people who treated him decently. Unfortunately, also, Anthony Greenwood, a Christian gentleman of the Left, had already allowed his name to go forward and the prospect of Greenwood reaping all the available left-wing sympathy was intolerable.

In the event, inspired, perhaps at the last moment, by a furious phone call from John Freeman, then editor of the *New Statesman*, Wilson decided to run against Gaitskell, in the annual election for Labour Party leader, and collected eighty-one votes from the Parliamentary Party – slightly less than half as many as Gaitskell.

During the course of his campaign for the leadership, Wilson enjoyed the declared support of Bevan's widow (Jennie Lee), Richard Crossman, Walter Padley, Anthony Wedgwood Benn, George Wigg, Barbara Castle, Michael Foot and Sidney Silverman. Yet immediately after his defeat, when the 'unilateralists' on the Labour Party Executive asked that a motion on hydrogen weapons should be argued, rather than simply stated, Wilson voted with the leadership and the majority.

His position in the Party, was, in the short term, greatly weakened by his stand against Gaitskell. In the elections for the Shadow Cabinet a week after the election, Wilson plummeted from top to ninth in the poll, and loyalists like Sam Watson rebuked him for double-dealing. Greatly disturbed by this treatment Wilson applied himself with renewed energy to heal the split in the party with two compromises.

The first compromise – on the Clause 4 issue – was successful. An executive meeting in 1960 unanimously approved a policy statement on Labour's aims. The key clause, suggested by Harold Wilson, stated: 'The Labour Party is convinced that these social and economic objectives can only be achieved through an expansion of public ownership substantial enough to give the community power over the commanding heights of the economy.' The Constitution was not re-written and Clause 4 was not removed from the Party cards (though it was soon relegated from the cover to the inside). In theory, the Party was still committed to the common ownership of the means of production, distribution and exchange and the best available system of democratic control thereof, but in practice its policy was to take into public hands 'the commanding heights of the economy'. As Harold Wilson made immediately clear, the two policies were very different. Taking over the commanding heights, he said, did not involve 'a sweeping programme of expropriation and nationalization of industry'. He explained:

The unresolved question is: what are the commanding heights? In the context of the plan, the commanding heights which would come into public ownership will clearly be those industries or undertakings which are required to be publicly owned if the plan is to be fulfilled. In recent elections the criteria adopted varied, and were not always easy to explain; this happens when you combine the minimum intention with the maximum of provocation.

To relate our proposals for extended public ownership to the fulfilment of a plan designed to restore Britain's place in the world will not only solve the problem of identifying the industries which are, in any real sense of the word, commanding heights; it will make the task of convincing the British electorate a great deal easier (*New Statesman*, 24 March 1961).

The 'commanding heights' *were never defined*. Neither the Executive statement which first used the phrase, nor the consequent statements of Harold Wilson and other Labour spokesmen indicated which industries would be taken over in the implementation of the 'commanding heights' policy. Both Left and

Right were appeased by Wilson's pledge that the proposals for public ownership would be linked to a plan 'to restore Britain's place in the world', and that the proposals would automatically 'solve the problem of identifying which industries are commanding heights'. Although the Executive statement was represented by the Left as a defeat of Gaitskell's intentions to abolish Clause 4, it was, from their point of view, a retreat even from *Industry and Society*. Whereas in previous election programmes the proposals for specific nationalization measures were included as the result of direct bargaining and argument from the Left, now the whole argument was abandoned for a meaningless military metaphor. *Signposts for the Sixties*, Labour's policy statement on which the 1964 election was fought, went no further than proposing the nationalization of road haulage and steel. And the document's language was even vaguer than before 1959:

> The forms of public ownership will vary widely. Already we can see it developing in various forms – nationalization of a whole industry or firm, State participation in industrial companies on a partnership basis, the establishment of State-owned undertakings competing with private concerns, municipal enterprise, and, finally, Co-operative ownership. All these kinds of social ownership have their part to play in meeting the dangers of monopoly, in achieving a fair distribution of the national dividend – and, most important of all, in helping to fulfil our national plan for economic growth.

With the single exception of the steel industry plans, the specific pledges had been replaced by general proposals. Yet, for the time being, they satisfied most people in the Party, who were grateful for Harold Wilson's part in papering over a nasty crack in the Party's solidarity.

The other compromise which Wilson supported was the 'Crossman-Padley' plan for defence and nuclear weapons. In a draft statement in 1961, printed in and supported by *Tribune*, Richard Crossman and Walter Padley demanded the abandonment of the independent nuclear deterrent, the removal of all nuclear bases in Britain, disengagement in Europe, but a continuation of Britain's partnership in a nuclear NATO. The draft statement was rejected by the Campaign for Nuclear Disarmament, and only just failed (according to some reports, by one vote) to get a majority on Labour's National Executive. On the nuclear weapons issue, Hugh Gaitskell had his way, and continued to mop up the crucial trade-union votes which gave him a handsome majority at the 1961 Blackpool Conference.

After these two partially successful attempts to solve the Party's two great debates by compromise, Harold Wilson retired from internal Party argument and submerged himself in his work as chairman of the Public Accounts Committee, chairman of the Party's home policy committee and as Shadow Chancellor.

By the time he was commending *Signposts for the Sixties* to the Labour Party Conference at Blackpool he had become once more a respectable and respected member of the leadership. 'The man who tried to depose Gaitskell less than twelve months ago,' mused a *Daily Telegraph* leader, 'was a reformed character' (2 October 1961). The Parliamentary Party thought so too. In November, Wilson jumped from ninth to first place in the elections for the Shadow Cabinet.

Yet Hugh Gaitskell could not forgive Wilson's opposition as quickly or as easily. In the autumn of 1961, he achieved what he had intended for some time: the removal of Wilson from the Shadow Chancellorship. Wilson had to be tempted with something apparently more prestigious and Gaitskell offered him the post of Foreign Affairs spokesman. The offer was a master-stroke, for Wilson had never been impressive on foreign affairs. This decision to accept the post, which gravely compromised him, was brought about more by his own conceit than by the machinations of the Gaitskellites.

In a discussion in the little House of Commons office of the Chairman of the Public Accounts Committee Wilson discussed the offer with a friendly journalist, Anthony Howard. Howard warned him at once that the offer was a trap to lure him out of influence with the Party, both in Parliament and outside. Wilson replied: 'I don't mind walking into a trap, provided I'm packing a Luger.' He accepted the offer.

The Luger, whatever its potential, never went off. Wilson's performances in the House of Commons on foreign affairs were at best predictable, at worst boring. His speaking style lost much of the rumbustious, populist wit which he had used in economic debates. Such frolicking, he considered, was not worthy of Her

Majesty's Opposition Spokesman for Foreign Affairs, and his language relapsed into Kiplingesque bombast. His name dropped from the headlines, while those of George Brown and Jim Callaghan (on economic policy) became more and more prominent. In the 1962 elections for Party office, Hugh Gaitskell was opposed for the leadership by Greenwood (who polled only two votes less than Wilson had the previous year) and Wilson fought Brown for the deputy leadership. Brown won this contest by the surprisingly large margin of thirty votes, and, despite a brilliant chairmanship of the 1962 Party Conference, Wilson's stock was at its lowest. He was still pontificating to no effect on foreign affairs; he had been beaten twice in vital elections in successive years; a substantial majority of the Labour Right saw him as a traitor to the leadership, and MPs of Right and Left dismissed him as an opportunist. Yet only four months later, after Hugh Gaitskell's death, Wilson was elected Leader of the Labour Party by a substantial majority. His success in that election was due partly to his clear personal superiority over the erratic and bullying Brown; partly to the split in Labour's right-wing caused by Brown's unsuitability; and partly to a brilliant campaign run by his old friends, Richard Crossman and George Wigg. Amid the general jubilation on the Left at Wilson's landslide victory (144 votes to 103), one voice was somewhat obscured. It was that of Peregrine Worsthorne, maverick right-wing commentator of the *Sunday Telegraph*, who could not contain his admiration and delight:

Harold Wilson is head and shoulders above all other possible choices . . . he somewhat resembles Lloyd George, violent and passionate in words, but sane and cautious in action . . . he looks like a possible national leader, who might rise to the challenge of the times, an estimate strikingly confirmed in today's Gallup Poll which shows him to be the Tories' favourite (*Sunday Telegraph*, 27 January 1963).

Harold Wilson lost no time in proving Worsthorne and the Tories right. Arriving back from America to fight for the leadership he told reporters:

I knew Hugh before we were in Parliament.[1] . . . Those of us who

1. Three months later, in a letter to Merlyn Rees, the Labour Candidate at Leeds South, Gaitskell's old seat, Wilson once again referred in glowing terms to Hugh Gaitskell, his oldest rival: 'The electors will give you a victory which will say to the Government: "Whatever you may do in Westminster

have to carry on are going to stand firm on the policy that has been agreed and remain fully united. The policy that was worked out under his leadership and which will remain the party's policy was designed to fit the age we are living in. Hugh Gaitskell will be chiefly remembered for keeping the Labour Party up to date (*Sunday Telegraph*, 20 January 1963).

On the day after his election Wilson was promising,
These policies will not be changed.

And Sidney Jacobson, editor of the *Daily Herald*, and a confirmed Gaitskellite, could assure his readers:

Harold Wilson will hold the Gaitskell line. There will be no policy swing to the left as a result of his election as leader.

Mr Jacobson's prediction was handsomely fulfilled. Party policy did not change before the next General Election, and in the few changes which were made unofficially, as over Commonwealth immigration or Aden, the policy swing was to the right. Yet in the twenty months of his Leadership of the Opposition, Wilson took complete control of the Party and forged it into an effective, united election-fighting unit.

This achievement was largely due to external political conditions: to the decadence and bankruptcy of the Tory Party; to the disillusionment, heightened by the Profumo affair, of the Tory militants; to the illness of Harold Macmillan and the appointment as Premier of Lord Home. Even more important was the tide of unity, which, as before all elections in the past, swept over the Labour Party, swamping discussion and debate. The mass of the Party *wanted* to follow Harold Wilson's lead and his peculiar genius for compromise and unifying rhetoric were never more gratefully received.

During this period, Harold Wilson relaxed his concentration on foreign affairs and returned to the issues with which he had been dealing in detail since 1955. The 1964 election was decided chiefly by old loyalties and old patterns, but Labour's economic policies as presented by Harold Wilson *did* attract a number of middle-

to obscure and deceive, we in South Leeds stand by the memory and values of Hugh Gaitskell and wish you to go quickly so that our national honour may be saved" ' (*Daily Telegraph*, 18 June 1963).

class floating voters. Wilson devoted most of those crucial twenty months to the economic policy which he and Hugh Gaitskell had instigated over the previous eight years. So crucial was this policy both to the election and to the future of Wilson's Labour Government that it deserves examination in some detail.

Labour's economic policy for the 1964 election, as outlined by Harold Wilson, was summed up in two words – 'planned expansion'. In all his speeches from 1957 onwards Wilson concentrated on the importance of drawing up a national plan for production and investment which would enable the economy to grow year by year without lurching into crisis as it had done since 1956.

Expansion was the *sine qua non* of Labour's economic policy. Again and again, Wilson made it clear that without expansion none of Labour's plans could be put into effect. 'We assert,' he told the 1957 Labour Party Conference, 'that there is *no solution* to our problems except on the basis of expanding output, expanding investment and rising productivity.'

The same theme straddled two election campaigns:

We believe there is no solution except by expanding production (ITV interview, 20 September 1957).
Everyone knows there is no solution to the problems of this country unless we do increase production (speech at Middlesbrough by-election, 4 March 1962).
We are going to provide funds for the expansion of industry. We are going to pay by expanding production. We are going to resume the steady rhythm of industrial advance that we had in the years after the war (speech at Prescot, 2 October 1959).

In a speech at Swansea in January 1964 in which he summed up Labour's economic policy, he declared:

The argument will be this: can the Conservatives or Labour best galvanize our sluggish and fitful economy into steady and purposive expansion?

He explained the necessity to 'stop the present boomlet grinding to a halt', and that, if necessary, the Labour Party would borrow funds and raise short-term interest rates to insure against excessive deflation. Yet in the long-term, he insisted, all Labour's economic policies: the Commonwealth Trade Councils, the speeding up of write-off for industry, increases in investment allowances, more help to import saving industries, legislation against tax avoidance, a capital gains tax, power to hold back office-building, power to stop monopoly and power to develop regions on the scale of the Tennessee Valley Authority in the 1930s – all these depended upon a 'steady rhythm of industrial advance'.

1. The Plan

The method and type of Labour's growth plan were described by Wilson in a long article in the *New Statesman* of 24 March 1961, entitled a 'Four-Year Plan for Britain'. The theory behind the article went like this:

The periodic reflation of the economy by the Tories (coinciding with election years) had been based upon unplanned consumer booms. These reflations were not planned, but were left to the mercy of the market. As a result, investment in Britain's 'industrial base' – so crucial to her 'competitive position' – was sacrificed to consumption and, at best, investment in consumer industries. Thus British industrial investment was, relatively, the lowest in Europe, and Britain's competitive position was consequently deteriorating. The first priority, therefore, was investment. A National Plan would concentrate first on raising that proportion of the national income which is invested. A National Investment Board should ensure that national investment took a further one per cent of the national income every year. The next priority was exports. 'Purposive' planning – for the first time perhaps the most famous of Wilsonian adjectives was thrown into the front line – could direct production, as it expanded, into the exporting industries.

The crucial difference, the article suggested, between Conservative and Labour economic policy concerned the degree of planning, the degree to which the state should intervene and establish economic priorities. 'In uncontrolled private enterprise, expansion programmes are uncoordinated in time and scale.' The fruits of expansion were 'dissipated on purposes which made no contribution to our economic development'. If the state intervened as it ought to, wrote Wilson, the priorities would be assured and expansion would be certain. Wilson proposed three main state weapons which should be used against private industry whenever they were required.

First, guaranteed Government orders for firms which had shown themselves progressive and willing to modernize; secondly, taxation 'directed towards penalizing the slothful and encouraging the enterprising and investment-minded' and, thirdly, the universal but undefined panacea – 'public ownership'.

Proposals for the wholesale nationalization of expanding, profitable and science-based industries were never part of his National Plan. Instead the Plan concerned itself with a multitude of methods by which the state could take the reins of policy and guide industry to increasing exports, investment and research. The Plan was based upon Harold Wilson's belief that the dynamic of modern capitalism, if properly guided and encouraged by the state, was sufficient to solve most problems fairly and well. The *New Statesman* article caused a considerable stir in political circles, not least in the Conservative Party, which had by now rid itself of its more conventional capitalist ideologues and was concerned with administering a complex, bureaucratic capitalism far removed from the free enterprise heaven of their forefathers. Before long the Conservative Government, to the irritation and derision of Harold Wilson, were experimenting in planning very much on the lines laid down by the Shadow Chancellor. They established the National Economic Development Council, with representatives from industry and trade unions, to discuss future developments in British industry and advise accordingly. They set up the National Incomes Commission, to investigate the merits of wage claims and awards, and advise accordingly. Accepting the recommendations of the Rochdale Committee, they effectively nationalized the country's ports. One after another, Conservative Chancellors announced, to the astonishment of the 'Enoch Powell school' (though Enoch Powell stayed in the Cabinet throughout this period), that they were 'not against planning, as such'.

Yet there *was* a difference between the 'plan' of Selwyn Lloyd and that of Harold Wilson. Lloyd, Maudling, and their party, took the view that the role of state bodies was merely to streamline the machinery of modern capitalism, to cut out the obstacles, to assist with industrial training, to place the valuable machinery of the civil service and state industry at the disposal of private industry so that it could most effectively plan its resources and improve its competitiveness. Harold Wilson, on the other hand, saw the state as the controller of the machinery. The basic decisions, he insisted, should be taken by the state. Moreover, the state by interfering and prodding should ensure the implementation of those decisions. In many cases, of course, the decisions of industrialists and the state would be the same. But in Wilson's plan, and not in Lloyd's or Maudling's, where the views of state and industry clashed, the state predominated.

Proposals to establish new, state-owned machine-tool plants to compete with private enterprise, and proposals to develop state-owned science-based industries in the development areas, for instance, were quite unacceptable to Tory aided capitalism, but fully consistent with Labour's state capitalism.

Harold Wilson summed up the difference between the two forms of 'planning' as succinctly as ever:

For the Conservatives the commanding heights of the economy are and should be in private hands, working for the consolidation of the existing order and with profit as the sole criterion. For them, too, the role of the state is confined to guiding, influencing and holding the ring – doing no more than prescribing the conditions in which that profit is made, always with the minimum disturbance to the existing order. For the Honourable Members on this side of the Committee, the commanding heights of the economy should be in the strategic sectors of industry, owned by and answerable to the community and working in its interests (House of Commons, 11 July 1960).

2. The Pound

Planned expansion and growth took priority over all other aspects of Harold Wilson's socialism, except one: the parity of the pound sterling. Throughout the period, Wilson defended the strength of sterling with all the enthusiasm of his Tory adversaries.

The Labour Party, no less than the Conservative Party, gives defence of the pound *the first priority*. We would be prepared to be very tough indeed in ensuring that the priority was implemented. . . . We shall need to *sacrifice all other considerations to make sterling strong* (Speech to Overseas Writers Club, Washington, *Times*, 11 February 1958).

'It is the duty of all of us,' he told the Commons soon after his appointment as Shadow Chancellor,

to put first the strength of sterling which is not a party asset or a Government asset but a national asset . . . we would pledge the support of this side of the House to any appropriate measures which the Chancellor chooses to bring forward (House of Commons, 4 December 1956).

And, following his leader who had made a spirited 'no devaluation' pledge in Washington some weeks earlier:

The strength of sterling must be our *first and primary consideration* . . . the strength of sterling and all that depends on it *must take priority over all other considerations*. I hope the Government will not doubt our sincerity and determination to make sterling our *first priority in all our calculations and actions* (House of Commons, 16 April 1958).

The defence of sterling, Wilson explained, did not entail deflation or economic stagnations. On the contrary, growth and a strong pound were highly compatible:

The pound should not be made a football of party politics in next year's election or in any events which might follow the election. The strength of the pound will always be *our primary consideration*, but we believed that this should not be the enemy of expanding production and full employment at home. Indeed we believe that these things are not incompatible with a strong pound but essential to it[1] (Speech to the American Chamber of Commerce, 10 December 1958).

And again,

We utterly reject this Tory notion that the pound can be strong only if the economy is weak. If the economy is depressed, if industry is working below capacity, then costs are increased. Furthermore, what is of great importance, productivity cannot increase unless the economy is expanded. Secondly, if the economy is depressed we fail to extend and to modernize the economy and, in the long run, we lose ground to all our competitors. We believe that we could have a strong pound and a strong economy only on the basis of expansion (House of Commons, 28 January 1959).

The theme persisted after the 1959 election. On an ITV interview Wilson, as leader of the Labour Party, optimistically forecast that 'as soon as the City and financiers overseas see that our

1. The italics in these quotations are mine.

policy is going to be one of expansion and a more vigorous attack on export markets, it will strengthen the pound, not weaken it', and after the 'pay pause' of 1961 Wilson summed up his arguments on devaluation:

All of us know, and the world knows, that a further devaluation would not be like the last one – a readjustment forced on us for years after the war by the consequences of the war and a hungry post-war world. A second devaluation would be regarded all over the world as an acknowledgement of defeat, a recognition that we were not on a springboard but on a slide (House of Commons, 26 July 1961).

Expansion would not, Wilson hoped, damage the strength of sterling, for he was committed to both. The double commitment, fortunately, made it unnecessary to choose between them. The pound was 'the primary consideration'; there was 'no solution' without expansion. But which, in the case of these conflicting, would take precedence?

3. The Incomes Policy

Another crucial aspect of the Wilson/Gaitskell economic policy forged in the last ten years of opposition was the incomes policy.

Labour's incomes policy grew in importance with the years of Opposition. In the earlier years of Wilson's Shadow Chancellorship it was easy enough to disguise policy difficulties on wages and salaries by attacking the class policies of a Tory Government. The engineering strike of 1957 was deliberately provoked by the Government, who quickly withdrew their support for the employers when the strike threatened to boil over. The Cohen Committee recommendations were so obviously biased in favour of the employers that it was possible to attack them without proposing a viable alternative. 'Last year,' Wilson told the House of Commons on 25 July 1957,

the Government lost the greatest asset that any Government could have in this matter of inflation – and which every Government has had since the beginning of the Second World War – and that is the support of the trades unions in wage restraint. I believe that the unions have shown great restraint since the war. In a sellers' market they could have made and exacted much bigger claims for their members than they have done. . . . Those who appeal for restraint in income must create a condition in which such an appeal can succeed.

When Government health officers were refused a negotiated award in November 1957, Wilson exploded:

We see now a direct blow against the system of collective bargaining in this country. The Government must realize that it cannot solve the problems of this country by armed conflict or a cold war with the trade unions (Hemel Hempstead speech, *Times*, 2 November 1957).

On the strike of London busmen in 1958, Wilson voiced similar solidarity:

Of course, all this is part of a showdown with the unions. It has been the London busmen who have borne the brunt of this struggle with a Government which was determined on a showdown and with a Minister of Labour spitefully refusing to carry out his duty to help reach a settlement (Northumberland Miners Picnic, 15 June 1958).

Similarly, after Selwyn Lloyd's deflationary measures in July 1961, Wilson and other Labour leaders shuffled off the problem of wage restraint under a Labour Government by attacking the 'unfairness' of the 'pay pause'. Much Wilsonian venom was reserved for the Conservative attempts to break the negotiating machinery for public employees:

Failing to get their way, like a wilful child they kick over the long-established machinery of the Burnham Committee. There may be a case for amendments in the negotiating machinery, but you don't shoot the referee just because you dislike the decision he gives (Huyton, 7 September 1961).

They say the country will be ruined if these people get a few extra bob on their £8 19s. 0d. a week, and in order to carry through this policy they do not hesitate to wreck arbitration and conciliation machinery which has taken fifty years to build (Darlaston, 21 October 1961).

We shall not be deterred by anyone from springing to the support of unions who find their wages and conditions prejudiced and their negotiation and arbitration machinery set aside by the diktat of a Government department (article in the *Daily Herald*, 2 February 1962).

Once again, the argument about wages in Labour's plan was obscured. 'The Government,' said Harold Wilson, 'is determined to hold down wages and salaries, saying they should be related to production. The Labour Party have been telling them this for years, but it is an argument, not for reducing wages but for increasing production.' Or, as he put it finally to the Transport and General Workers Union as leader of the Labour Party:

> We shall have to ask for restraint in the matter of incomes, but when we say incomes we mean *all* incomes. That means not only wages and salaries, but profits, especially monopoly profits, distributed dividends, yes, and rents as well. . . .
> The Tories' policy is to cut production down (except in election years) and then tailor the wage system to fit it. Our policy is to expand production and relate our national incomes policy to it (*Times*, 9 July 1963).

Such statements absolved Wilson and his colleagues from making any detailed statement about Labour's plans for wages. The Tory policy, they repeated, was unfairly concentrated on wages; Labour's policy of expansion would ensure more for all, and a wages policy would merely decide who gets more first. Thus, Labour's wages policy was sold by Wilson as 'a planned growth of wages', and accepted by the unions.

At the 1961 Labour Party Conference, Frank Cousins, general secretary of the Transport and General Workers Union, had stated in a militant speech:

> We are not willing to accept in any form, shape or disguise wage restraint.

The platform, led by Wilson and Gaitskell, cheered. A planned growth of wages, was, they assured themselves, an entirely different matter.

Two questions remained unanswered. First, how, in capitalist society, where profit is the criterion of success, can profits be controlled, curbed or penalized? Is this not 'encouraging inefficiency'? Secondly, if expansion did not take place or if it was postponed, what then was Labour's wages policy? An increase in production could lead to a planned growth of wages. But whither would a decrease in production lead? And what, in any event, was Labour's attitude to the 'time-honoured machinery of collective bargaining'? Harold Wilson fully understood the force of these questions long before he became Prime Minister. In November 1957, Transport House published a little pamphlet entitled *Remedies for*

Inflation – a reprint of three articles in the *Manchester Guardian* on the economic situation by Harold Wilson, with a glowing foreword by Hugh Gaitskell. Wilson concluded his articles:

> Success or failure in the battle against inflation would depend on its ability to secure an undertaking with the unions which would make wage restraint possible.

Over the next few years, Wilson indulged in a running dialogue with trade-union leaders, particularly with Frank Cousins, in an attempt to secure that undertaking. 'If the truth be known,' wrote the *Sunday Times* Student of Politics on 8 June 1958, 'the most assiduous student of Mr Cousins' struggles with his conscience against the pressures of wage restraint has been Mr Harold Wilson. . . . Unless Mr Wilson can get TUC cooperation on wage restraint, in return for his promise of a price freeze, stability cannot be assured.' Despite all the Wilsonian juggling with phrases – 'planned growth of wages', 'value for wages' and so on – Cousins consistently argued that the only conceivable condition for wage planning was expansion: and that without expansion of both production and productivity the unions would never agree to wage planning. As if to drive the point home, Cousins moved the resolution at the 1964 Trades Union Congress opposing all forms of wage restraint. Though he supported Wilson's formula of a 'planned growth of wages', Cousins and other trade unionists placed it firmly on record that they would in no circumstances agree to wage restraint. What Wilson in 1957 had accepted as a necessary condition for his new Britain – an undertaking from the unions 'which would make wage restraint possible' – had not been achieved.

4. The Decline of Welfare

An even more crucial question about Labour's planned expansion concerned its effects on the traditional egalitarianism of socialist thought and of the Labour Party. Moving the 1956 National Executive statement 'Towards Equality' at the Labour Party Conference, Harold Wilson had declared:

> Democratic socialism as we know it will be meaningless without a great drive towards equality. As we say on the first page of this pamphlet,

the pioneers of this party half a century and more ago 'proclaimed the need for a new and classless society based upon equal chances for the nation's youth, regardless of birth, sex or fortune; a fair division and a planned expansion of the nation's wealth; the right to work; the elimination of poverty, common ownership, control or dispersal of economic power; service, not greed, as the driving social purpose'. Those were among the ideals of the founders of this movement, and in this statement the NEC shows that we have not abandoned or weakened our resolve to achieve them.

A fair division *and* a planned expansion of the nation's wealth. How was Labour to achieve both? For, as Wilson himself pointed out in Parliament four years later,

In any period of economic expansion, there is a law of increasing returns to the rich; of an increased proportion of newly-produced wealth accruing to the owners of property whether in equity shares or land (House of Commons, 5 April 1960).

How was Labour to reverse that 'law', to maintain expansion and equality? For, as Harold Wilson was the first to agree, a necessary condition of *planned* expansion, as opposed to the *laissez faire* consumer boom expansion of the Tories, was the direction of more resources to investment, rather than consumption. This direction into investment, moreover, should be concentrated, again according to Harold Wilson, 'on the industries which strengthen our industrial base'. How was Labour to reconcile the direction of resources to investment, 'as a first priority', and the expenditure of large sums on the social services and other similar projects to establish a more universal prosperity?

In a Fabian pamphlet published in 1957, Harold Wilson analysed the post-war economic policies of Labour and Tory parties. 'The Labour Government,' he concluded, 'had subordinated housing and easier living standards to the paramount necessity of building up capital investment, especially in exporting and import-saving industries.' On the other hand, 'The Tory achievement of building well over 300,000 houses per annum was electorally popular and socially desirable, but it placed a great strain on our economic resources.' Had they built less houses, in short, and pandered less to electoral and social considerations they could have invested more money in strengthening Britain's industrial base, especially in the export industries (which un-happily do not include house-building).

This was the nub of the dilemma: the apparent contradiction between Labour's egalitarian welfare heritage and its dynamic, purposive policy of economic expansion. Shortly before the 1959 General Election, Peter Townsend wrote in the *New Statesman* one of the first criticisms of the new 'growth' hysteria which had gripped the Labour leadership. Townsend pointed out that social reform does not necessarily depend on growth. The sharing of the cake (to employ one of the more ghastly economists' metaphors) has no bearing on its size. In fact, as Wilson pointed out, basic in-equality and poverty in modern capitalist society tended to in-crease with economic growth. There were 'greater returns' from expansion for the rich. Townsend put the case for concentrating on social reform for its own sake, on egalitarian legislation as an end in itself, not as an incidental pay-off from economic ex-pansion. 'Can it,' (the next Labour Government), asked Towns-end, 'disengage itself from the cloying attention of those who think it better to invest in machinery than in people?' (*New Statesman*, 26 September 1959).

Harold Wilson replied the following week with 'an unequivocal Yes'. He was, he wrote, shocked that anyone should even ask such a question. He bore witness to

the burning desire among Labour Party members of all levels to end poverty and to advance far beyond the 1945–51 reforms to a much more real equality. The theme of all the campaign speeches I have heard has been not just 'expansion' or 'redistribution' but 'fairer shares in ex-panding prosperity'. . . .

Given a Labour victory, the test is this: will there be, twelve months from now, a narrowing of the gap between rich and poor, quite apart from any general upward movement there may be as the result of in-creased national production? The answer is, quite simply, that there will. This has been *the central theme* of both our election speeches and the party's television programmes (*New Statesman*, 3 October 1959).

To some extent, the assessment was a fair one, and Townsend's alarm was premature. Labour's economic policy for the 1959 election, though provisions for public ownership had been greatly watered down and nearly obliterated, was still shaped in the main by 'welfare' thinking. The new enthusiasm for 'growth' and 'purposive investment' had not superseded the old Fabian concept that equality and the obliteration of poverty and the provision of more adequate social and welfare services was 'the central theme' of any Labour economic policy. The central theme of the modern Labour intellectuals – Crosland in *The Future of Socialism*, Strachey in *Contemporary Capitalism*, and, later, Crosland again in *The Conservative Enemy* and Douglas Jay in *Socialism in the New Society* – was the erosion of inequality, poverty and social squalor.[1]

And in Crosland's controversial Fabian pamphlet *Can Labour Win?* (1960) only one of his eleven points for a 'radical party' mentioned economic growth – and that without great enthusiasm.

Perhaps the main change in Labour's home and economic policies between 1959 and 1964 was a shift in emphasis away from traditional welfare demands towards economic growth, efficiency and technocracy. Labour's policy statement for the 1959 election – *The Future Labour Offers You* – opened with sections on houses, jobs, schools, hospitals and old-age pensions, all illustrated with old-fashioned working-class families, all impressing on the reader Labour's commitment to bettering the lot of working people. *Signposts for the Sixties*, on the other hand, starts with an ode to etc. are all subsidiary to and in the context of the glittering, technological New Britain pictured in the foreword.

The Future Labour Offers You had stressed:

We can make such great social advances as bringing real security into our old age . . . we can cut down the size of school classes. We can turn our shabby old houses into modern homes.

1. 'The programme for economic growth of course remains important. Nevertheless from a socialist viewpoint it should increasingly be over-shadowed by the "social" policies outlined in Parts III and IV; and we should not now judge a Labour Government's performance primarily by its record in the economic field. . . . The pre-war reasons for a largely economic orientation are steadily losing their relevance; and we can increasingly divert our energies into more fruitful and idealistic channels, and to fulfilling earlier and more fundamental socialist aspirations. These have been defined in this book primarily in terms of social welfare and social equality' (C. A. R. Crosland, *The Future of Socialism*, Cape, 1956, pp. 517, 518).

While the theme of *Signposts for the Sixties* was well expressed by the complaint:

Our finance and industry need a major shake-up at the top. Too many directors owe their position to family, school or political connexions. If the dead wood were cut out of Britain's boardrooms and replaced by the keen young executives, production engineers and scientists who are at present denied their legitimate prospects of promotion, our production and export problems would be much more manageable.

The difference in the two campaigns was reflected in the manifestos and posters. The 1959 posters of old people in slums were replaced by gay young executives, forged in the white heat of the technological revolution. Labour's education policy was based, not on the need to end slum schools, but on the requirement of industry for more and more scientists. Labour's housing policy switched its attention from council-house tenants and slums to house-buyers and mortgage-holders.

Of course, the process was not complete. There were in *Signposts* the necessary references to the need 'to allocate more and more of the national resources to community services'. The old Wilsonian slogan, 'Fair Shares', was taken out, dusted and presented in the appropriate places. Labour candidates throughout the country felt themselves free to mouth the slogans of equality and social reform without, in their view, offending against Party policy.

From Harold Wilson himself, there were the carefully rehearsed expressions of dismay at poverty and squalor – including a well-timed visit to the Edinburgh slums during the campaign – and the usual references to individual cases of hardship and bureaucracy under the Tories (which, in Wilson's case, almost always concerned paraplegic ex-miners). Much of this was like singing the Internationale on May Day. In not one of his election speeches, nor in any of his 'blueprints for the New Britain', did Wilson refer, as he had done before the 1959 election, to equality and social reform as the 'central theme' of Labour policy.

Instead:

The *fundamental inspiration* of *Signposts for the Sixties* and the statement which followed, is the need to make Britain up-to-date, dynamic, vigorous, and capable of playing her full part in world affairs. The policy

breathes the ideals which have animated the Labour movement throughout its history but it is modern, relevant, and directed to problems which
call urgently for vigorous and radical solutions. It is an attack on the
complacency on the stagnation on the Edwardian nostalgia which seem
to underlie the attitudes and postures of the Macmillan Government.

We begin from the need to strengthen Britain's economy, to secure a
steady and purposive expansion in industrial production (*New York
Times*, September 1963).

The 'fundamental inspiration' to make Britain 'up-to-date,
dynamic, vigorous' had replaced the 'central theme' of the 1959
election – to close the gap between rich and poor. The accent had
switched from reform to efficiency.[1]

This change in emphasis was crucial to the development (and
decline) of socialist theory in the Labour movement, and therefore to Labour supporters' inability theoretically to cope with the
catastrophes which followed. Yet it was almost unnoticed at the
time, either by candidates or by the rank and file, many of whom
felt they were fighting a socialist battle with a more up-to-date,
dynamic leader. Harold Wilson was able to present Party policy
as a blueprint for revolution to the rank and file and a safe but
efficient panacea to the floating voter. The development from reform to efficiency was not all Wilson's work. It had been going on
gradually since 1945 and even before. What Wilson added to the
sickly brew of efficiency and economic dynamism was a new,
hitherto untasted sweetener: the technological revolution.

It is a common libel on Harold Wilson that he 'invented the
scientific revolution' for his speech at the Labour Party Conference in 1963. In fact, Wilson has always been deeply interested
in technological development. His father was an industrial chemist
whose work fascinated Wilson at an early age. At Oxford, in his
study of economics and politics, he concentrated on the pace of
technological advance. His winning entry for the Gladstone prize
in 1936 dealt in meticulous detail with the technological progress
of the railway companies in the early half of the last century. From

1. This basic change went unnoticed, even by political commentators of
the Right. In an article in the *Sunday Telegraph* three years later, Robert
Skidelsky wrote: 'In the pre-election period, the thinking, even of the
"Radical Right" was still orientated towards the problem of achieving social
justice within a mixed economy' ('Ramsay Macwilson', *Sunday Telegraph*,
19 November 1967).

the first, Wilson's politics were placed in the context of technological progress. His attacks on the Tories in the 1950s were
based on the latter's inability to understand and encourage
scientific advance. At his first meeting as Prospective Parliamentary candidate for Ormskirk, on 19 October 1944, when he
was twenty-eight years old, Harold Wilson declared:

During the war there has been a great industrial and technical revolution. Great changes have taken place in science, radio, electricity and
other directions. We are living in a totally different world. The Government is made up of tired old men. . . . (*Ormskirk Advertiser*, 19 October 1944).

And five years later he was telling his constituents:

You will not solve the problems of an atomic age in an atmosphere of
antimacassars, arsenic and old lace (Meeting at Maghull, *Ormskirk
Advertiser*, 15 September 1949).

During his time as President of the Board of Trade Wilson
frequently irritated his advisers with his concern for technological
detail. His liking for Mikoyan, and, later, for Kosygin was due at
least in part to the fascination which both Russians shared with
him for technological detail. Wilson's interest in technology was
encouraged during the 1950s by his two close friends and advisers,
Dr Tom (later Lord) Balogh, and Roy (later Lord) Fulton.

Wilson's Christmas message to his constituents in 1957 stressed
the advances of science:

It is the task of all of us to ensure that the great triumphs of the
scientist are controlled by mankind in such a way as to bring happiness
and not fear to all the peoples of the world (*Prescot and Huyton Reporter*,
20 December 1957).

'That is why,' he claimed, three years later

we say that socialism must be harnessed to science and science to
socialism. We have to appeal to the scientists. . . . We *base our case* in
the 1960s on a much more compelling demand. The world into which we
are moving is a world characterized by a scientific revolution beyond the
dreams of only a generation ago. The potential release of energy in the
widest sense of productive power, of facilities for material development
and leisure alike, defies the measuring rod of the market place or the
counting house or any system dedicated to private profit or speculative
gain (Labour Party Conference Report, 1960).

After the 1960 Conference, the National Executive of the Labour Party appointed a special sub-committee on science and industry, chaired by Harold Wilson. Wilson also chaired the sub-committee which drew up *Signposts for the Sixties*, and, no doubt, wrote the preamble to that ill-fated document. The preamble deals almost exclusively with 'the scientific revolution' and its relevance to modern socialism.

The Labour Party Conference of 1963 was crucial for the electoral success of the Party. Unity was assured. The arguments about the Bomb, public ownership and the Common Market had been 'settled' with compromises. The problem was how to build on this unity without appearing to be talking in the terms of the past. How to advance, electorally, without simply re-stating full employment, welfare reform and greater equality as Labour's 'central theme'.

The 'technological revolution' provided the modernization that was needed, and more. It provided an *ideal* – a Utopia where the machines did the work and men and women enjoyed their leisure. And it provided the conflict between the dynamic, up-to-date 'player' and the died-in-the-wool, old-school-tie 'Gentle-man'.

The first third of Wilson's famous 'science' speech at Scarborough is a description of the nature of technological advance, a beginner's digest of scientific progress, incorporating a host of dazzling facts about the speed of computers and the potential of unassisted production. All this, said Wilson,

put the whole argument of economics and socialism in a new per-spective . . . since technological progress left to the mechanism of private industry and private property can lead only to high profits for a few, a high rate of employment for a few and to mass redundancies for the many. If there had never been a case for socialism before, automa-tion would have created it. It is a choice between the blind imposition of technological advance, with all that means in terms of unemployment, and the conscious, planned purposive use of scientific progress to provide undreamed of living standards and the possibility of leisure ultimately on an unbelievable scale.

There was nothing new in any of this. If Harold Wilson had bothered to read on beyond page 2 of *Capital* he would have come across Marx's long chapter on 'Machinery and Modern Industry' in which Marx anticipated Wilson's observations in rather more readable prose:

> Machinery, considered alone, shortens the hours of labour, but, in the service of capital, lengthens them; in itself it lightens labour, but when employed by capital, heightens the intensity of labour; in itself it is a victory of man over the forces of nature, but, in the hands of capital, makes men the slave of those forces; in itself it increases the wealth of the producers, but, in the hands of capital, it makes them paupers (Charles H. Kerr edition, Vol. 1, p. 482).

And,

> Capitalist production develops technology only by sapping the original sources of all wealth – the soil and the labourer (Vol. 1, p. 556).

The socialist argument *has always been* that only under a planned publicly controlled and owned economy can technological resources be placed at the disposal of mankind; and that under the private-enterprise capitalist system the machines become the enemy of the people who operate them, since their produce is utilized only for the profit of their owners. The increasing pace of technological advance may make the argument more urgent. But it does not put it in a 'new perspective'. It is the oldest argument in the history of socialist theory.

Unfortunately, however, this traditional socialist view was not supported by Wilson's practical proposals. No attempt was made to explain how the 'mechanism of private industry and private property' was to be replaced. The speech made four proposals: to get more scientists; to keep them in Britain; to make more use of their work; and to apply the results of their research more 'purposively' to British industry.

Despite familiar genuflection to 'state activity' and 'state interference' there was not a single reference to take-over; no nationalizing of defence or chemical industries; no 'public ownership when an industry is failing the nation'. Instead, promises of 'prodding' and 'guiding' private industry into a more efficient and effective industrial policy. For this Wilson promised four new Ministries (of Science, Disarmament, Overseas Development and Higher Education), and a University of the Air. He promised new state-owned science-based factories for the development areas to compete with private enterprise. And he managed in the course of a speech allegedly about science to refer to such established Labour doctrines as the abolition of the 11-plus, the abolition of youth unemployment, the increase in overseas aid, and the provision of more universities.

Reading the speech four years later, it is almost impossible to credit the hysteria with which it was received. The long standing ovation was spontaneous and genuine. Almost every correspondent in the conference hall was instantly seduced by Wilson's pseudo-professional jargon. Every section of the Labour movement seemed delighted.[1] Why? What Labour needed to ensure electoral success was unity: unity on a fighting policy which was, above all else, uncontroversial. Nothing is as uncontroversial as fact. And the facts of technological advance, paraded with all the gritty dynamism of Harold Wilson's platform style, were a perfect substitute for the political proposals which had provoked so much dissent in former years. Their leader's assurance that 'you have computers at work now controlling a planned productive system of machine tools which have an impulse cycle of three millionths of a second. They do their calculations and take their decisions in a period of three millionths of a second', his promise of a New Britain 'forged in the white heat of a technological revolution', his proposal for 'a new breakthrough in marine propulsion, in aircraft guidance, in transport, in electronics, in agricultural or textile machinery' delighted the loyal Labour rank and file. It was all entirely new – no Labour leader had ever said it before. It was unquestionably modern. And, above all, it was uncontroversial. The 'sterile arguments' about the Bomb and Clause 4 had been drowned in a flood of technological data.

Yet the practical proposals arising out of Wilson's speech – the promotion of scientists, increasing their pay and conditions, levies for apprenticeship, taxes for more universities, state power over industrial decisions about priorities – chemical engineering was specifically mentioned – state control over the pace and extent

1. I was myself a delegate to the Woodside, Glasgow, constituency General Management Committee and I remember my own surprise at the conference report given to the committee by the newly elected MP, Neil Carmichael. Carmichael, the son of one of the 'Red Clydesiders', spoke with great emotion and sincerity. 'My whole conception of socialism changed as I listened to Harold Wilson's speech,' he told us. The sentiment was echoed in Labour Parties throughout the country.

of automation and re-training the redundant – all this required, at least, a new range of taxes and levies upon industry, considerable state representation on boards of directors and, in many cases, wholesale nationalization. Not once in his speech did Wilson indicate the extent to which his Government would interfere with industry. Vague reference to the 'profit system' told his audience nothing about how much Wilson's Labour Government would corrode that system, and with what he planned to replace it.

It would be wrong to write off Wilson's famous 'scientific revolution' speech as a public relations exercise, designed to win the 'floating' middle-class voter to the Labour cause, although in both capacities it was extremely successful. For Harold Wilson, modern industrial society is a vast machine, incorporating employers, workers and plant. The view that there is anything essentially contradictory about that machine is, for Wilson, dogmatic, theoretical, anti-pragmatic. There is, in his eyes, nothing wrong with the machine as such. What is wrong is the driver. And according to Wilson, only the Government has the power and the right to drive that machine. His aim was not to scrap the machine for another one, but to steer it round the obstacles in its path. It never occurred to Wilson that the machine might take control of the Government. Before the 1964 election, and for a considerable time after it, he passed on to his supporters his own passionate desire to steer the machine efficiently, humanely and accurately. He appeared before them, to his credit without pretending otherwise, not as a socialist confronting capitalists, but, to use his own favourite metaphor, as a player confronting Gentlemen.

Labour's triumph of the election in 1964 was won on the economic policies described above. The entire Labour movement, except a handful of 'splitters and sectarians', had swallowed the official economic policy without a moment's political indigestion. Yet, glossy and impressive though Labour's policy appeared, there were questions arising from it which should have been asked, if not answered, long before October 1964.

First, were the conventional Labour policies for welfare reforms dependent upon expansion, or to be enacted in their own right?

Second, was the pound more or less important than expansion?

Third, what was the difference between 'wage restraint' and 'wage planning'.

Fourth and fundamentally, would the Wilsonian policy of partnership and cooperation with private enterprise and private finance be any more successful than it was in 1945–51?

What, in summary, had happened since 1951 to indicate that those who hold the economic power would cooperate with a Labour Government, unless it offered them highly favourable terms?

As the election campaign reached its climax these questions were pushed further and further into the background. Harold Wilson eloquently reassured the few Labour doubters. The Tories, he proclaimed in increasingly confident speeches, were the creatures of the banks and big business. They responded to every situation in the manner which their masters in the Central Banks decreed. Labour, on the other hand, promised a New Britain, free from the shackles of Basle, Moscow or Washington. In a speech to a delirious rally in the Assembly Halls, Edinburgh, twelve days before polling day, Wilson issued a grimly accurate warning:

The people, when they vote, will have regard to the fact that there have been three sunshine elections – always followed by restrictionist policies. You cannot go cap in hand to the central bankers as they [the Tories] have now been forced to do, and maintain your freedom of action, whether on policies maintaining full employment here in Britain or even on social policies. The central bankers will before long be demanding that Britain puts her house in order and their ideal of an orderly house usually comes to mean vicious inroads into the Welfare State and a one-sided pay pause. The Government would then launch into savage cuts. The brunt will fall again on wages, on salaries, on the ordinary family struggling to make ends meet with cuts in the overtime that has financed their present standard of living.

Chapter 5
Eighteen Months at Dunkirk
October 1964–March 1966

I myself have always deprecated – perhaps rightly, perhaps wrongly – in crisis after crisis, appeals to the Dunkirk spirit as an answer to our problem because what is required in our economic situation is not a brief period of inspired improvisation, work and sacrifice, such as we had under the leadership of the Right Hon. Member for Woodford [Sir Winston Churchill], but a very long, hard prolonged period of reorganization and rededication. It is the long haul, not the inspired spirit, that we need (Harold Wilson, House of Commons, 26 July 1961).

I believe that our people will respond to this challenge because our history shows that they misjudge us who underrate our ability to move, and to move decisively, when the need arises. They misjudged our temper after Dunkirk, but we so mobilised our talent and untapped strength that apparent defeat was turned into a great victory. I believe that the spirit of Dunkirk will once again carry us through to success (Harold Wilson, Labour Party Conference, Brighton, 12 December 1964).

Fewer people voted Labour in the General Election of 1964 than in 1959, although the electorate was larger. The revolution which brought Labour to power after thirteen years in Opposition was accomplished because some two million Tory voters switched allegiance to the Liberals. Harold Wilson entered Downing Street, as he had originally entered Parliament, on a minority vote. The quirks of the British electoral system ensured him an overall majority of five in the House of Commons. No doubt, if the electorate had known the extent of the deficit on the balance of payments resulting from the Conservative Government's well-timed election boom, more would have voted decisively for an election alternative. The estimated deficit, on the balance of payments in 1964 presented to James Callaghan soon after he was appointed Chancellor of the Exchequer, was £800m. – by a long way the largest in British peace-time history.

The immediate necessity, as Wilson put it later, was 'to stop the bleeding'. At a meeting between Wilson, Brown and Callaghan in Downing Street on the evening of Saturday, 17 October, the most obvious remedy – devaluation – was ruled out. 'Wilson,' writes Henry Brandon,[1] 'came to the meeting with his mind made up. He was against devaluation. . . . The decision was finally taken, and it was Wilson who took it with impressive firmness. He said that from now on everybody must shut up talking about this subject, and it became known as "The Unmentionable" thereafter.' The views of Callaghan and Brown were not decisive. Neither, in fact, had completely made up his mind.

In a controversial article in *The Times* of 23 November 1967, Peter Jay, the paper's economics editor, revealed that on two occasions before the 1966 election Wilson refused to contemplate advice to devalue the pound from the economic advisers whom he had brought into the Government, and, on one occasion, had the relevant memorandum destroyed. Throughout the seventeen months of hair-line majorities, his loyalty to the parity of the pound never wavered. Over and over again, at home and abroad, he proclaimed his 'unalterable determination to maintain the value of the pound, and all the values that depend on it' (speech to the Economic Club, New York, 15 April 1965).

All this was quite consistent with Wilson's attitude to devaluation throughout his political life. He was, until the last moment, dubious about the 1949 devaluation and from 1955 to 1964 had consistently championed the 2 dollars 80 cents parity.

No less fervent, however, had been his pledges and plans for economic expansion. His apparently irrevocable decision not to devalue the pound did not, in his view, conflict with his original determination to expand the economy.

As for stopping the bleeding, the Government decided on a 15 per cent import surcharge and a re-examination of large Government contracts, notably for the Concord airliner, which were announced on 26 October. On the same day, Patrick Gordon Walker, the luckless Foreign Secretary who had lost his Parliamentary seat at Smethwick, stated in New York that the British Government had 'no intention of raising the Bank Rate'. Gordon Walker's indiscretion indicated clearly that his Government intended to pursue expansionary economic policies.

1. *In the Red* by Henry Brandon (Deutsch, 1966), p. 43.

'The first essential,' said Wilson in his first Prime Ministerial television broadcast about the economic situation, 'is a strong economy'.

This alone will enable us to maintain the value of the pound. The facilities for further borrowing which have been carefully and widely built up these past few years have given us a base from which we can advance without panic measures, without inflation, without stop-go policies and the rest.

He warned his audience, grimly and with some foresight, that 'you can't go on borrowing for ever', but went on to say that his Government was deeply concerned with social priorities:

If things are going to be tough, we as a national family must show that we care, that we care for the old, the sick and those in great need. That lies at the heart of all we want to do to make this country strong again.

On 1 November Wilson described the prospect before him as 'an exciting, challenging adventure', and the gold reserves fell £31m. to £876m. – the lowest since 1961. Undaunted, the new Prime Minister rose in the Commons on 3 November to make his speech on his Government's proposals for its first Parliamentary session. Despite the desperate economic situation, his speech promised more even than many of his essays into rhetoric during the election campaign:

The Chancellor of the Duchy of Lancaster [Douglas Houghton] in this Government will, among other duties assigned to him, have the task of coordinating the work of the social services to ensure that no longer do we have the scandal of poverty in the midst of great potential abundance or of an unbalanced social-service sector. . . .

From each according to his means, to each according to his needs, is the principle with which we approach this situation and the principle applies as much when things are tough as when they are easy. It is in our view a principle which is mandatory when the country is faced with economic crisis.

One choice was rejected. We decided firmly against going back to stop-go-stop policies. . . . Let me say what this would have meant. The effects on other countries' exports to us would have been just as great as the effects of what we have done, and more prolonged, because we have bitter experience that a decision to slam on the brakes leads to a prolonged stagnation and a prolonged restriction of imports. Secondly, we have learnt the hard way that deflation and contraction, so far from making us more efficient and competitive, have the opposite effect – costs rise; essential investment is discouraged; restrictive attitudes on both sides of industry are encouraged; a policy which relates incomes to expanding production is infinitely hard to achieve. Thirdly, we are not prepared to accept the unemployment and loss of production which defeatism of this kind entails.

All this was vindicated by James Callaghan's first Budget, announced eight days later on 11 November. It included a 6d rise in the standard rate of income tax the following spring; 6d on petrol; an increase in National Insurance contributions and advance warning of taxes on corporation profits and capital gains. To balance this, it also promised an increase in old-age pensions the following spring and the immediate removal of prescription charges on medicine.

The increases in pensions were covered to a large extent by the National Insurance contribution increases, and the loss to the Exchequer from the abolition of prescription charges was estimated at a maximum of £30m. This was not a reflationary Budget, yet it provoked an outraged hullaballoo from banking centres and businessmen all over the world. The following day the gold reserves slipped another £10m. and were saved from further pillage only by the week-end. The following Tuesday (17 November) Lord Cromer, the Governor of the Bank of England, deeply shocked at the proposed rise in pensions and the abolition of prescription charges, called on the Prime Minister and demanded an increase in bank rate. Wilson demurred. There was, he said, no need for such a drastic measure. Instead he sent a telegram to President Johnson requesting advice on the British economic situation, and stressed in his speech that evening at the Lord Mayor's banquet that the Government were determined at all costs to 'keep sterling strong'. Johnson's reply was delayed and indecisive, and when, on the Thursday, the bank rate remained at 5 per cent the international financial community erupted. The reserves sank by another £20m. – this time in an apparently endless slide. On the following day, Wilson and Callaghan agreed to raise the bank rate the next Monday by 2 per cent.

'The measures we have taken,' said Wilson, unabashed, to the Commons on the day of the increase, 'are relevant, and we believe that they have shown the determination of the Government and, I hope, of the entire House, to deal with the problem of defending sterling.'

Not, alas, so. The bankers and other holders of sterling were not in the least impressed. Having got their high interest rates, they started to howl for more. On Tuesday the reserves went down by £40m. and, on Wednesday, Lord Cromer was once more in 10 Downing Street, arguing stiffly with Wilson and Callaghan. There was, said Cromer, only one solution: to freeze wages and cut public expenditure. Wilson and Callaghan disagreed and advised Lord Cromer to investigate the possibility of a loan. The Central Banks, summarized Wilson, rightly, would pay up to save the pound, since, if the pound was devalued, they would all suffer. By 7 p.m. on 26 November, the Treasury and the Bank had notched up £1,000m. Sir Alec Douglas Home accompanied by Reginald Maudling visited Downing Street oozing bonhomie and promising Wilson all support in a coalition Government in the nation's hour of crisis. Wilson wiped the smiles off their faces with news of his massive loan. Home and Maudling left, still in Opposition.

Even the holders of sterling were reassured by the size of the loan, and, for a time, the pressure eased. Yet Wilson was severely shaken by the series of attacks made upon his Government by 'speculators' in his first month of office. Henry Brandon quotes him as saying, at the height of the argument with Cromer, 'we are fighting a war and we don't know who the enemy is'. He was delighted to have stalled 'the enemy' with his huge loan, but he had learned to treat it with greater respect. In a television interview on 3 December, he said:

I don't think foreigners are trying to dictate the economic policies of the British Government. But of course it's important to carry conviction abroad about the measures we're taking to make sterling strong and to build up our exports.

At the euphoric Labour Rally (in place of a Conference) at Brighton, Wilson appealed for the first time to the 'spirit of Dunkirk'. He assured his cheering supporters:

This is not a return to Selwyn Lloyd. We do not believe, as our predecessors did, that the way to deal with this kind of crisis is to bring the whole economy shuddering to a stop. . . .
What we have to tell the world is that this work has begun, and

begun with a will and a purpose, and that before long we shall have a dynamic, robust, thriving competitive economy (Labour Party Conference Report, 1964, p. 112).

Such promises did not impress the holders of sterling, who, in spite of the massive loan, started a small wave of selling shortly before Christmas – a move which inspired the Cabinet to launch a 'Spirit of Dunkirk Campaign' with plans for Ministers to speak all over the country. 'The campaign,' said one correspondent, 'it is hoped, will have an important influence at workshop level' (*Daily Telegraph*, 17 December 1964).

The Christmas crisis, however, was easily dealt with by prompt action from the Bank of England. At the start of 1965, despite the defeat of Gordon Walker at the Leyton by-election, Harold Wilson clearly thought that his troubles with sterling were almost over. In his New Year's message to the Labour Party, he declared:

Now that the decks have been cleared for action, I see every reason for confidence.

On 4 February he went further. In a speech at a Parliamentary Party meeting he was reported as saying:

The economic crisis, with the unpopular measures it has demanded, is now virtually over. The future is bright with promise (*Guardian*, 5 February 1965).

Lord Cromer, however, took a different view. Still smarting from his rebuke the previous November he made a public speech at an overseas bankers' dinner sharply criticizing Government policy towards public expenditure. While Wilson tried to explain the speech away to his back-benchers, Cromer repeated his attack a fortnight later, calling for more cuts in social expenditure if the country was to pay its way. For this he earned himself public rebukes from both Wilson and Callaghan. Wilson replied to the Cromer demands, which, needless to say, were taken up with enthusiasm by the Conservative Opposition, by insisting as strongly as ever on the importance of expansion and growth.

Let me tell the House what hon. members opposite would have done, faced with this situation and with an election behind them. They would have introduced panic measures as in 1957 and 1961. In 1957 and 1961, with a situation which was, both on trade and payments, incomparably less bad than that which we faced last year, they met the situation with a slamming on of the brakes, with three years' stagnation, each time resulting in unemployment and short-time working (House of Commons, 2 February 1965).

And again:

If the Rt Hon. gentleman is suggesting that the only way to get exports is to have deflation and under capacity working in this country, I believe that would be contrary to the interests of the nation (House of Commons, 25 February 1965).

Cromer's words, not Wilson's, were heeded by the holders of sterling, who once again started to sell sterling at an alarming rate. By mid-March sterling had reached its lowest point since the previous November's loan. The November borrowings expired, and the Central Banks agreed grudgingly to renew them after the British Government promised to borrow a further 1,400 million dollars from the International Monetary Fund. In May, as soon as it was drawn, the entire sum was immediately absorbed in the repayment of the Central Banks.

On 6 April, Callaghan introduced his second Budget, which was even more deflationary than the first. Taxes on cigarettes and whisky were increased, and hire-purchase regulations were strengthened. The corporation tax and capital gains tax were much milder than had been rumoured and, in the atmosphere of relief, sterling moved strongly upwards. In April Wilson assured financial leaders in France and America that sterling would definitely not be devalued.

As the Commons struggled slowly through the long and complicated finance Bill and a series of organized filibusters by the stockbrokers and industrialists on the Conservative benches, both Wilson and Callaghan began once again to believe that the sterling crisis was over. On 4 May Wilson told a rally in Hull:

We are going to honour our pledges on mortgages and our plans are ready to turn into legislation (*Daily Telegraph*, 5 May 1965).

Callaghan was even more confident. 'I think,' he opined on 7 June, 'we are now round the corner or turning the corner.'

The following week, however, the bankers studied the British trade figures for May and thought otherwise. They sold sterling.

Mr Callaghan, only a week after turning the corner, had to go back round it with further hire-purchase restrictions. At the same time he lowered the bank rate. In June, he travelled to America urgently to discuss a permanent solution to the sterling crisis. The American economic experts seemed strangely short of ideas, except, of course, that a strong incomes policy, if not a wage freeze, would help a great deal to restore confidence. Callaghan returned convinced that further deflation would not be necessary. On 15 July he told the Commons:

There is a temptation to assume that because the effects of these measures are not immediately obvious we should rush into further measures which have the effect of restraining the economy even more. This would be an unfortunate thing to do, and I am resisting the temptation to do it.

This resistance did not last long in the face of a new offensive from the holders of sterling. The day after Callaghan's statement, the pound fell to its lowest since 1 April. There was nothing for it. On 27 July, twelve days after his 'resisting temptation' speech, Callaghan announced drastic public expenditure cuts. Many Government schemes, notably for trunk roads, were delayed or cancelled. The local authorities' ability to borrow was curtailed, and hire-purchase restrictions were imposed.

'It was vital,' explained Wilson the following week, defending the Government's record in a strong attack on the Conservatives,

to reassure the world trading community and the holders of sterling balances of our utter determination to make Britain strong and sterling strong. For some months we have felt the effects of the American measures – the recall of profits and the reduction in working capital by subsidiaries in this country. We have also felt the side-effects of the American squeeze on Euro-dollars, which has led countries desperately short of dollars to convert marginal sterling holdings into dollars, just as our reserves were hit recently by the effect of Japan's grave dollar shortages on her purchases from Australia. Then, last week, came the impact of the Chinese gold-buying spree (House of Commons, 29 July 1965).

In the view of the holders of sterling, the Chancellor's July measures were not restrictive enough. By 2 August the pound was slipping again in the international markets, slipping crucially without Bank of England support. Devaluation rumours were rife. But Wilson and Callaghan decided to stick to their holiday arrangements. On 5 August, Cromer again went to Downing Street to emphasize the lack of confidence in the pound and to state his solution: a coalition Government. Once again, Cromer was shown the door.

Something drastic was clearly vital to protect the sanctity of the $2.80. Once again, Wilson based his hopes on American support. But by now the Americans were less keen to play the lifeguard, and conditions which before had been implied, now became specific. The American Government urgently demanded a 'tough' incomes policy, with some form of statutory control over wage increases. To this effect, George Brown met the TUC and the CBI on 26 August. Henry Brandon, in a dramatic account of this confrontation, tells us that Brown sought to bully the TUC into accepting a statutory incomes policy with threats of withdrawal of American support for the pound. Though George Woodcock, General Secretary of the TUC, remained sceptical, the tactic worked. Brown again met the TUC General Council in a marathon session shortly before their annual Congress in Brighton and persuaded the majority to accept statutory control of wages and prices.

Accordingly the National Board for Prices and Incomes was set up under the chairmanship of the former Conservative MP for Birmingham, Hall Green, Aubrey Jones. The Board had the power to examine all wage and price increases, but no power to hold them back or postpone them.

This was enough for the Americans. On 10 September, they initiated another massive and cleverly organized support operation for sterling. The holders of sterling were still hopefully selling when a further three-thousand-million dollar loan was announced. The operation cost practically nothing, and left the Labour leaders, not least the Prime Minister, fully confident that now, at last, they were free to get on with their plan for the economy, massively summarized the following week in the DEA's National Plan.

From the moment the support operation was assured, Wilson's speeches bristled with confidence. He told a Labour Rally in Bristol: 'I believe we are now at a turning point' (*Daily Telegraph*, 4 September 1965).

His faithful follower, Anthony Shrimsley, quoted him exclusively in the *Sunday Mirror*:

Now that the economic situation is improving, we are more than ready to move forward economically. We shall therefore get on with the job of economic and social advance (*Sunday Mirror*, 5 September 1965).

To the businessmen of Britain he spoke in the language of cops and robbers which they could understand:

Exports mean more than production schedules in the modern world. They mean a great deal of buccaneering and we need buccaneers at the top (Speech at the opening of a hall of residence for Leylands Motors, Preston, 17 September 1965).

The National Plan, he said at every meeting, was a 'national crusade for higher production', and in fashionable Dunkirk phraseology he condemned the 'idea that it's good for me and damn the nation'. At the Labour Party Conference at Blackpool, he made two massive speeches, one on home, one on foreign affairs, both of which received prolonged standing ovations. Optimism was the keynote:

After a year in which our first preoccupation was how to weather the storm, the whole world realizes that despite the sour pronouncements of our opponents, we are now getting within measurable distance of balancing our overseas payments. The economy is strong. Sterling is strong. Employment is strong. . . . [*Cheers*] (Labour Party Conference Report, 1965, p. 156).

At Walthamstow three weeks later he went even further:

Whereas over the greater part of the last year the work of reform was dominated by the need to get our economic situation right, now we are ready to swing into action. Our land proposals have already been published. . . . The Bill will soon follow. Dynamic new proposals to help the modernization of British industry will follow in the next few weeks (*Sunday Telegraph*, 21 November 1965).

In the House of Commons, the same theme of welfare reforms was consistently pursued. Wilson spoke of 'more public service pensions, teachers' superannuation, wage-related benefits in unemployment and sickness, legislation on industrial injuries, none of which will prejudice our proposals which will follow next year as a result of the searching review we are conducting of the social services'. In short, he concluded, 'we are carrying through one of the most massive programmes of social and economic reform in all our long Parliamentary history' (9 November 1965).

Speaking at Sheffield in mid-January, he said:

We shall have to go much higher than 500,000 houses in 1966 (*Times*, 15 January 1966).

And the following day at Huddersfield he aimed a powerful swipe at the 'speculators and sell-Britain-short brigade':

Let me warn them: this time we are in a position to deal with them from strength (*Times*, 16 January 1966).

By the end of January, Wilson had reached the peak of confidence and success. The resounding victory at the Hull North by-election was celebrated with a mass Labour rally in the Albert Hall on 29 January, where Wilson spoke in scenes of near-delirium. Once again he claimed:

After fifteen months of the Labour Government's purposive economic policies, we can claim that sterling is strong, that employment is strong and that they are both strong at the same time. . . .

The election campaign, made inevitable by the Hull North by-election result, was opened by Wilson on 1 March. The seventeen months of his Premiership had been dominated by the recurring sterling crises, the refusal of the overseas holders of sterling to be satisfied with regular and increasingly severe Labour measures to hold down the economy, and to concede vital policies in their programme such as the minimum income guarantee and the nationalization of steel. Throughout most of the period bank rate was held at 7 per cent. Yet in spite of these crises, the administration had been able to push through some of the promised reforms, mainly in the fields of housing and welfare. The most important of these was the Housing Subsidy Bill, announced in January 1966, which sought to level out interest rates on money borrowed for local authority housing at 4 per cent per year – some 3 per cent less than the market rate. The interest rate on money borrowed had, during the Conservative administrations, put increasing pressure on rates and rents, and the new Bill, though not yet enacted, measured a considerable advance. The Rent Act, which became law five months before the election, was probably the most popular of the reforms. It gave immediate security of tenure to tenants in almost all rented property and repealed the provisions for 'creeping decontrol' in the Conservative Rent Act of 1957. The Act had not run long enough for its bureaucratic weaknesses to be exposed. The nonsensical machinery of 'negotiation', rent officers, Rent Assessment Committees and Rent Assessment Panels was not yet in evidence. In addition there had been the promise to enfranchize leaseholders, of rating relief for the poor, the abolition of prescription charges, the abolition of capital punishment, the Race Relations Act (ineffectual though that measure was), the cancellation of TSR2, the imposition of corporation tax and capital gains tax, the maintenance of full employment, the steering of industry to the development areas, and an apparently determined stand on Rhodesia. Traditional Labour supporters could claim that considerable ground had been won, despite severe economic crisis and a tiny majority. Wilson himself was especially proud of the National Plan, which was based on 4 per cent growth for the next five years and a complete reconstruction of British industry. The Industrial Reorganization Corporation was another of Wilson's favourite innovations. The I R C had the power and the money to assist industrial take-overs. As Wilson assured the Birmingham Chamber of Commerce in January:

This is not nationalization by the back door. This is the rationalization of British industry.

Naturally enough, Wilson reiterated these achievements throughout the campaign. Yet he chose to devote the greater part of it to exposing the Conservatives. The Conservative Party had had a lean time during those seventeen months. The size of the 1964 payments deficit was attributed to their electoral tactics. Their unwillingness to vote against the repeal of their own Rent Act and against the increases in public expenditure of which they disapproved disappointed their militants; while their protracted assault on the corporation and capital gains taxes exposed their vested interests. They were split three ways on Rhodesia and their change of leader was not, according to the polls, for the better.

All this and their obvious distaste for the duties of opposition combined to make them easy targets for Wilson's invective.

The two main propaganda points employed by Wilson during the 1966 election referred to the Tory programme for the Welfare State and for the economy. 'The Tories,' he said in a speech at York on 13 March, 'will put up the cost of food and have a plan to destroy the Welfare State and replace it with a Means Test State'.

On the economy he was more specific:

At the election, there will be only one choice – expansion, economic strength and full employment on the basis of planning: or, with the Conservatives, a prolonged plunge into deflation and unemployment. For, underlying the whole Tory philosophy as it has emerged in these past few months, underlying their equivocation on prices and incomes, their refusal to plan – underlying all this is the deeper implication of deflation and depression, of the retreat from the expanding economy and the just society which we are in the process of creating (Speech at Middlesbrough, *Guardian*, 14 March 1966).

The Tories would make a wages policy effective, they tell us, by creating conditions of demand which would make it work. You know what that means. It means deflation (Speech at Preston, 25 March 1966).

Every word they utter, every piece of advice they are getting from their financial and economic advisers, the means they have blatantly stated they would use to enforce their incomes policy, their wages policy, all this points to a policy of deflation and unemployment. . . .

The Tories, faced with a crisis, have only one remedy. Ten men running after nine jobs. They have never succeeded for more than a few months at a time in creating more vacant jobs than unemployed men. For every time it happened, they ran into an immediate trade crisis. They have learned nothing. They have forgotten nothing. Their methods, if they were given the chance, would be to return to the old tactics of deflation and depression, unemployment and short-time working (Speech at Manchester, 26 March 1966).

These two bogeys, the Means Test State and the Inevitable Deflation, were used by Wilson consistently and at his own choice, throughout the campaign. At the same time the Labour programme which he held out to the electorate promised the same sort of welfare reforms which he had promised in 1964 – most notably a sharp increase in house-building. As he made those speeches Wilson can have had no inkling of the abyss into which he was about to stumble. When he told a television reporter on the eve of the election that 'a wage freeze, if by that you mean a law to hold back wage increases, that would be unthinkable' he was not bluffing. He meant it.

Yet the dominating feature of the first seventeen months as Prime Minister had been the extent to which he had, again and again, been blown off his original course by the need to defend sterling. From the raising of bank rate in November 1964 to the huge American loan of September 1965, almost all political decisions and directions were dictated by the sterling problem. Under each assault from the holders of sterling, Harold Wilson had given ground. On each occasion he had given ground less reluctantly than before. But after each surrender, he was able once more to proclaim, a little more cautiously, that now the decks were cleared and the action could start.

Harold Wilson ascribed the continuous attacks on sterling during those seventeen months to two basic causes. The size of the deficit when Labour took power, and the low Government majority in Parliament. These were external difficulties which could be remedied by lowering the deficit on balance of payments and by achieving a big majority. On both these fronts, Wilson was singularly successful. In 1965 the payments deficit was half what it was in 1964; and in March 1966 Wilson led his Party to their second biggest electoral triumph in history – with a majority over all other parties of ninety-seven. This success gave Wilson every confidence that he could proceed without difficulty and without further sterling trouble to rebuild the New Britain. Never at any stage did it occur to him that the attacks on sterling manifested a general distrust in financial circles for a Labour Government; or that the bigger majority he achieved and the more firmly he applied himself to the promised welfare reforms, the more savage would be the reaction of the international financial community.

The vast majority of MPs and rank and file Party members of Left and Right believed that his stewardship during the seventeen months had been almost impeccable. Hardly a Member of Parliament or a commentator had publicly argued for devaluation in that period. The snipers who had been suspicious of Wilson's alleged duplicity were silent. The few advocates of devaluation were locked in the silence of Whitehall. Only later were they to emerge to proclaim that devaluation should have come immediately after the election, or that the initial deflationary measures should have been much more savage.

In March 1966, no one except Christopher Mayhew and the First Sea Lord, who had resigned in quiet irrelevance in defence of an aircraft carrier, could find any serious criticism for Wilson. The Left, the Right and, most passionately, the Centre all agreed that Harold Wilson was the best leader the Labour Party had and the best it could have had. Scepticism and gloom about his leadership and Labour's wholesale support for it were confined, this time exclusively, to 'satirists and sectarians'.

Chapter 6
'Hard Pounding, Gentlemen!'
March 1966–March 1968

Of course the credit squeeze is unpopular. So are the hire purchase restrictions. So is the Capital Issues control. Nobody likes them. But they are necessary. As the Duke said at Waterloo: 'Hard pounding this, gentlemen; let's see who will pound longest.' Our fight against inflation is a hard pounding in a sense of which the Duke could scarcely have been thinking (Harold Macmillan, Chancellor of the Exchequer, at a Lord Mayor's banquet for bankers and merchants of the City of London, 9 October 1956).

We were not going to take the easy way out. The events of September and since show something of the resolution and determination of this country when up against it. More than once when the Chancellor and I were discussing the severity of the attack we were facing, I had occasion to quote the words of the Duke of Wellington at Waterloo: 'Hard pounding this gentlemen; let us see who will pound longest.' The world now knows who (Harold Wilson, Prime Minister, speech to the Overseas Bankers' Club, London, 7 February 1966).

October is the popular month for British elections. Elections in the spring disrupt Parliamentary routine, and, in the hour of his triumph, Wilson chose, as the Tories had done in 1955, to hold a mammoth eighteen-month session of Parliament from April 1966 to October 1967.

In his speech on the Government plans for this new session Wilson indulged himself in a long discussion of Parliamentary Specialist Committees, and outlined two basic aims: getting the balance of payments into surplus, and continuing policies of 'social advance'. Under the first heading he listed the work of the Industrial Reorganisation Corporation which would help to create monopolies; under the second, plans for a Land Commission; reform of local Government finance; leasehold enfranchizement and steel nationalization. Though he stressed the seriousness of the economic situation, there was not a Labour back-bencher who did not believe that the Government's first priority would be the long overdue and often promised measures for social reform.

Lord Cromer disagreed. The Governor of the Bank of England, who was not, we can assume, overjoyed at the election result, found himself knocking again on the door of 10 Downing Street demanding drastic measures to solve a new economic crisis. Cromer repeated to Wilson the 'basic facts' of the British economy which had been retailed by Heath with such little effect during the election. Wages, he complained bitterly, were rising faster than productivity. And unemployment was still shockingly low.

The remedies, Lord Cromer insisted, were obvious. Public expenditure should be savagely cut; a wage freeze should be instigated, and a pool of unemployed established. The bankers and holders of sterling at home and abroad, said Lord Cromer, who sold sterling 'to take precautions', were in their most precautionary of moods.

Once more, for the last time, Wilson resisted the Bank's advice. Once more he assured Cromer that there was no need for panic. The April trade figures were almost certain to be favourable. The Bank's remedies were, for any Labour Government, let alone a Labour Government with a majority of ninety-seven, 'unthinkable'. Harold Wilson had some other remedies in mind.

Lord Cromer left, never to return. On 24 April, he confirmed that he would retire when his term of office expired in July. The press discounted rumours of differences of opinion with the Government. Yet Cromer's relationship with the Labour leaders had been anything but friendly. Again and again, they had ignored his advice to deflate and freeze wages. Cromer has never forgiven Harold Wilson and his colleagues for the series of snubs he received at their hands, and, after taking a patriotic directorship in an American firm, he did not hesitate to return to the attack from the cross-benches of the House of Lords.

If Cromer's going came as some relief to Harold Wilson, he was not taking any risks. When Ladbroke's started taking bets on Lord Cromer's successor, Sir Eric Roll, the economic historian, radical Keynesian and Permanent Secretary at the DEA was a clear favourite after Cromer himself, whom most people thought would be asked to continue. Then, suddenly, on Saturday, 23 April, some £10,000 was placed on a dark horse – Leslie O'Brien,

Cromer's deputy, who jumped into the lead.[1] Someone had leaked. O'Brien got the job. The dangers of having anyone too unorthodox at the head of the Bank of England were too great, even with a majority of ninety-seven.

Harold Wilson believed he had a powerful alternative to Cromer's deflation. He called it an 'incomes crusade'. The crusade was launched in Aberdeen at the Scottish Trades Union Congress, where Wilson called for an 'end to bloody-mindedness on both sides of industry', and spoke in idealistic terms about the high-wage, growth-orientated Britain of the future. The following week he infuriated the National Policy Committee of the Amalgamated Engineering Union by saying that progress would start 'as soon as the rule book is relegated to the industrial museum'. 'I am here,' he went on proudly, 'to give the marching orders to industrial leaders in what must be for this country a crusade. It is a crusade on which the whole future of Britain depends' (*Daily Telegraph*, 30 April 1966).

By now a note of hysteria had crept into Wilson's and other Ministerial speeches. In a May Day speech, which had the full backing of the Prime Minister, Ray Gunter, the Minister of Labour, issued a solemn threat. 'The alternative to continuing our present slothful and selfish way, indeed our thriftless and dishonest way of living on foreign money, is in the end to have deflation forced upon us.' On 11 May, Wilson devoted almost all his speech to the Parliamentary Press Gallery to a frontal assault on 'restrictive practices' and called for a 'new spirit of anti-amateurism'.

Whatever the effect of this crusade among the mass of British trade unionists, it had little influence on the National Union of Seamen. For several months that union's negotiators had been seeking to improve on the agreement with the employers in 1965 which gave them just under £60 a month for a 56-hour week. The 56-hour week was regarded at the time of the agreement as a convenient formality, which would enable a ship's master to call on his seamen to work at any time in the week. The more unscrupulous shipowners, however, had instructed their masters to squeeze every minute's work from the 56-hours, with the result that dissatisfaction with the agreement was widespread. Ever since the

1. *Sunday Telegraph*, Mandhake, 1 May 1966.

outbreak of unofficial seamen's strikes in 1960, the situation within the union had been changing. By 1966 the old, anti-Communist leadership had to some extent been replaced by men who demanded a militant line with employers and drastic action to improve pay and conditions.

The seamen claimed a 40-hour week, instantly, and a rise of 12s. in the basic rate of pay. On 6 April, the employers offered no increase, and the 40-hour week in stages over three years. On 16 April, the seamen's union instructed its members not to sign articles of work after 16 May, and on that day the first national seamen's strike for fifty years duly started, to a howl of press abuse.

Wilson and Gunter had foreseen the strike and both saw their chance of accepting the advice of the *Economist* of 15 January:

The only way to achieve an incomes policy in 1966 is going to be by outfacing the trade unions in some big national wages struggle.

Accordingly, Gunter met the shipowners and persuaded them to lower their final offer to the seamen and accept a public inquiry into the seamen's case. The seamen's union, not surprisingly, would have none of this, but Gunter's approach made it clear that, from the outset, the Government intended to do all in its power to smash the strike.

Harold Wilson decided that the strike was important enough for a television broadcast. Though he claimed impartiality in the dispute, he stressed that it was the duty of the Government to resist the action because this was a strike 'against the state, against the community'. He went on:

What is at issue here is our national prices and incomes policy. To accept the demand would be to breach the dykes of our prices and incomes policy. . . . Our determination to insist on these principles when the cost is great will be taken by everyone at home and abroad as a proof of our determination to make that policy effective.

The broadcast shocked wide sections of the Labour movement – not least the 400,000-strong London Labour Party which unanimously carried a motion supporting the seamen. Its unashamedly nationalist and capitalist language compared interestingly with a similar broadcast in the summer of 1948 by the then Labour Prime Minister, Clement Attlee, when the London dockers were out on unofficial strike. Attlee attacked the dockers and called for an end to the strike. But he spoke in the terms of the Labour movement: 'The strike,' he said, 'is not a strike against capitalism or against the employer. It is a strike against your own mates.' Wilson found no such language necessary. He talked solely in terms of national policy.

From the outset, the weekly *Economist*, which had been campaigning for months against inflationary wage settlements, urged Wilson to 'expose' the ringleaders of the strike. In the early stages, Wilson was reluctant to take this advice. Instead he resorted to a well-tried remedy, favoured by his predecessor, Harold Macmillan: the Downing Street confrontation. After the 'independent' Pearson Report, which had made some concessions to the seamen's case, had been rejected by the NUS and accepted by the employers, Wilson summoned the entire NUS Executive to Downing Street and ordered beer and sandwiches. In urgent tones he pressed the seamen to accept the Report and go back to work. It was, he said, an hour of crisis. The pound was slipping once more in the markets. Could the seamen not do their bit for Britain by abandoning their strike and surrendering to the employers?

To his astonishment and rage the seamen replied that they could do nothing of the kind. They had, they explained, been bullied and exploited for years by reactionary employers and union officials. They had been on strike for four weeks and the militancy of the membership was increasing. On what possible grounds could they ask their membership to renounce this sacrifice? Certainly not for a few bromide phrases about their national duty. Joe Kenny, a Labour Party Member from Liverpool, made a particularly contemptuous reply to Wilson's plea. Wilson was outraged at being thus contradicted in his own Cabinet room. It was, no doubt, the snub he received at the meeting which determined him to play the final card and denounce the 'Red Plot'.

Four days later, he told the Commons:

A natural democratic revolt is now giving way, in the name of militancy, to pressures which are anything but democratic. The Executive last Friday knew the score and yet the combined advice and appeals of Government and friendly trade-union opinion was rejected as brusquely last Friday as the Pearson Report was rejected nine days earlier.

It has been apparent for some time – and I do not say this without having some reason for saying it – that since the Court of Inquiry's Report, a few individuals have brought pressure to bear on a select few on the Executive Council of the National Union of Seamen, who in turn have been able to dominate the majority of that otherwise sturdy union.

It is difficult for us to appreciate the pressures which are being put on men I know to be realistic and reasonable not only in their executive capacity but in the highly organized strike committees in the individual ports by this tightly knit group of politically motivated men who, as the last General Election showed, utterly failed to secure acceptance of their views by the British electorate, but who are now determined to exercise back-stage pressures, forcing great hardship on the members of the unions and their families, and endangering the security of the industry and the economic welfare of the nation.

And then, in a direct and wholly inaccurate reference to one of the speeches at the Downing Street confrontation:

Some of them are now saying very blatantly that they are more concerned with harming the nation than with getting the justice we all want to see.

These sentences caused a sensation in the press, most of which hurried into full-scale inquiries. Most newspapers came to the conclusion that the charges were ludicrous. Michael Randall, then editor of the *Daily Mail*, was given access to the 'evidence' for Wilson's charges, by courtesy of the Paymaster General, George Wigg. Randall refused to print anything based on what he regarded as, at best, exaggerated half-facts. Only the *Observer*, and to a lesser extent the *Guardian*, cooperated with the Prime Minister in his campaign against the militants.

On 29 June, in a debate on the Emergency Powers necessary to cope with the seamen's strike, Wilson 'named names' of the conspirators. The basic charge was that certain members of the Communist Party had been engaging in a desperate battle to extend the seamen's strike against the will of the NUS members. They had, in short, subverted democracy. But the lie was given to this allegation by the response of the rank-and-file seamen to the package deal finally accepted by their union.[1] In every major port, the vast majority of strikers voted against a return and many had

1. See, for full details, *The Incompatibles: Trade Union Militancy and the Consensus*, ed. R. Blackburn and A. Cockburn (Penguin Books, 1967), p. 169.

to be cajoled back to work by the men named by Wilson as subversives.

Wilson's experience of strikes and of rank-and-file trade unionism was almost negligible. The closest he came in his life to the rank and file of the trade unions was in his days at the Ministry of Fuel during the war, when he met the miners' leaders, sympathized with them and assisted them. For strikes, and particularly for unofficial strikes, he had nothing but contempt. Yet during the big official disputes of the 1950s – the engineering strike of 1957 and the London bus strike, Wilson managed to shuffle the blame on to the Tories. He became apparently genuinely angry in 1957 when a leading Conservative Minister, Lord Mills, warned industrialists to prepare for a showdown with their workers. And in 1958, without definitely taking the side of the busmen, he claimed that the Tories were deliberately interfering with industrial relations to bolster up their economic policy.

In summary, for all Wilson's hatred of strikes, he had never succumbed to the virulent anti-Communism of Labour Party leaders like Ernest Bevin and Hugh Gaitskell. When he visited America in the early fifties he came back genuinely depressed and concerned at the rise of McCarthyism. More particularly, he was quick to pounce on any of his Tory predecessors who sought to blame the failure of their own economic policies on the Communists.

In his denunciation of Selwyn Lloyd's pay pause in the summer of 1961 Harold Wilson, Shadow Chancellor, had declared his views on these matters in no uncertain terms:

Already, all over the country, employers are getting tougher, preparing for a bitter showdown. We warn the Government with all the emphasis at our command, while there is yet time, that if the Chancellor's policies and pressures lead to industrial strife, with all the damage which would entail to this country and its export orders, the responsibility will be his. Do not let him blame the trade unions. Do not let him look for Communist plots; he will not need them.

In May 1966, production was not expanding. All Wilson's earlier strictures of Lloyd applied to himself, and would apply with even greater force a month later. Yet, he chose to adopt Red-baiting tactics which were far less justified and far more savage

than anything engaged upon by his Tory predecessors since the
war.

The main reason was panic. His answer to the Bank of England's
insistence on deflation and a wage freeze had been an incomes
crusade. If the crusade worked, deflation, he believed, could be
avoided. The seamen's strike presented a practical opportunity to
demonstrate the Government's determination to hold incomes in
line. But the seamen were tough adversaries, and unwilling guinea
pigs. Every week a new batch of seamen came off the ships, reinforced with fresh pay packets and keen to inject a new dose of
militancy into their fellow-members on strike. Large sums of
money were donated by other unions to the seamen which prolonged their solvency. Moreover, most important, the seamen's
case was by any standard a good one, and, try as they could, even
the British press found it difficult to persuade their readers that
the seamen were wrong or subversive.

The extraordinary solidarity with which the seamen's leaders
rejected the Pearson recommendations suggested that the strike
might last into July and possibly longer. By then the ports would
be paralysed, and the effect on the balance of payments alarming.
If the 'incomes crusade' was to get a fair start, the immediate
defeat of the seamen was imperative. Thus Wilson lost no time in
resorting to smear tactics which had, in the past, disgusted him.
The tactics were highly successful. The seamen agreed to return
to work the following week. Despite the executive statement that
the 'revelations' had not affected their decision, the truth is that
the suspicions floated by Wilson succeeded finally in strengthening
the hands of the 'moderates' against the militants. For once the
moderates felt themselves justified in voting for a return to work,
though most of them must have known that they were voting
against the will of the rank and file. Ironically, Wilson himself
acted in precisely the same way as his 'politically motivated men'.
He had strengthened the hands of an unrepresentative group in the
union – the moderates – and enabled them to reach a decision,
which, as the subsequent meetings of strikers clearly showed,
was out of accord with the majority of seamen.

Nevertheless the price was heavy. For the first time, the left
wing of the Labour Party began to view Wilson with a real
suspicion and concern. Speeches in the House of Commons by

Eric Heffer and Michael Foot sharply criticized the 'revelations' and exposed their groundlessness. Writing in *Tribune* several months later, Anthony Arblaster described the Prime Minister's reaction to the seamen's strike as 'surely the most sordid episode since Labour came to power' (17 March 1967). In reality, it was yet another example of 'the economic situation dominating every decision we took' – a further instance of the pressure on sterling forcing Wilson into speeches and postures against his better judgement and past commitment.

Despite the seamen's return to work, there were still grumblings (notably in the *Economist*) that the settlement was 'too inflationary'. The bankers and holders of overseas sterling were unimpressed, and the publication of the June reserve figures did little to help.

On 7 and 8 July, Monsieur Pompidou, Prime Minister of France, arrived in London for a two-day visit and talks with Wilson and George Brown. The communiqué issued on 8 July which referred to the talks was non-committal. Its one definite proposal was to proceed with the Channel Tunnel. One cryptic sentence at the end of the communiqué indicated, however, that the talks had been a great deal more important than the communiqué suggested.

The Prime Minister described the rigorous measures which Britain had taken to strengthen her economy and redress the balance of payments. The French Prime Minister expressed his Government's interest in the success of these measures.

What dominated the discussion was the European Common Market and the prospects of British entry. Pompidou – never ecstatic about Britain's chances of entry – urged upon Wilson the need to strengthen the economy, and referred to the French success with their drastic devaluation in 1958. Devaluation, suggested Pompidou, might well be a precondition for entry. Only through devaluation could the British economy hope to solve its recurring balance of payments crises.

Wilson appreciated the argument, but disagreed. Devaluation, he insisted, was no more than a short-term gimmick. It was also a 'feather bed' for exporting industry. He would continue with his 'rigorous measures' to restore a balance of payments surplus, attempting meanwhile to refit British industry to make it genuinely competitive. The French Prime Minister duly 'expressed his Government's interest' in these measures and returned to Paris. Almost immediately the selling of sterling started with renewed intensity – much of it in Paris. By Monday, 11 July, senior economic advisers were already talking about and advising devaluation. The selling continued relentlessly on Tuesday. Wilson was dumbfounded. There was absolutely no chance of a further 'support operation' without strings. The choice was coldly clear: devaluation or deflation. The American Government, and particularly the President, were adamant for deflation. The French Government, and all his own economic advisers, recommended devaluation. The Cabinet, which met on the 12th and 14th to discuss the economic situation, was split. Several of the more coherent Cabinet Ministers, notably Anthony Crosland and Roy Jenkins, argued along the same lines as Pompidou: for devaluation and the Market. Bewildered and angry, Wilson stormed down to the Guildhall arriving late for a dinner engagement in honour of the recently retired Prime Minister of Australia, Sir Robert Menzies. In his prepared speech of welcome he inserted a long section which surprised Sir Robert and the journalists there by its irrelevance to the speech's theme. It began:

Britain, not the real Britain, the defeatist fringe, our detractors at home and abroad, have recently been going through one of the periodic phases of knocking her . . . with defeatist cries, moaning minnies and wet editorials. I believe there is a determination in this country to strengthen our economy. But the sell-Britain-short brigade seem to be incapable of looking beyond their noses. We met the shipping strike with determination, but when the cost to our reserves of one month of the seven-week strike was published we heard the wailings and moanings of short-run calculators. They did not see that this was a price to pay for maintaining the vigour of the incomes policy and the fight for economic solvency. I give an assurance that the value of sterling will be maintained. We shall not shrink from any further measures, however severe or unpopular, that may be necessary. Anyone who doubts our ability or resolve entirely misjudges the temper of the British people and the British Government.

This panic attempt to 'stop the bleeding' impressed neither the bankers nor the holders of sterling, nor the minority in the Cabinet urging devaluation. At the Cabinet meeting the following day a deep split emerged between the devaluers and the deflaters (or loyalists, for Wilson's own mind was made up). The deflaters won. In the Commons that afternoon, Wilson announced an increase of bank rate from 6 to 7 per cent, and promised the following week, on his return from Moscow, to make a statement on a new package of squeeze measures which would demonstrate, once for all, the Government's 'determination to solve the balance of payments crisis and maintain sterling'. The following day, he left for Moscow assuring a television reporter that his new package would not be the result of 'the old scratching together of panic measures'.

During his visit to Moscow the members of the Government who favoured devaluation and who disapproved of Wilson's leadership met to discuss the situation. This meeting was later 'disclosed' in the press as a plot to get rid of Wilson. It did not go as far as that, although clearly there was, for the first time since Labour achieved power, a genuine possibility that Wilson could be a casualty of the new unity between Left and Right against deflation. As it was, James Callaghan went to see Wilson on the Monday morning after Wilson's return from Moscow, determined to argue the matter out to the point, if necessary, of suggesting Wilson's resignation. Callaghan left the meeting convinced that Wilson should be supported. Thus, in the Cabinet meeting on the following day, Tuesday, the 19th, only six Ministers held out against the deflation package – Brown, Crosland and Jenkins from the old Right; Crossman, Castle and Greenwood from the old Left. Of these, only Brown threatened to resign and he was finally persuaded not to by a 'whip-round' letter from back-benchers. Harold Wilson had survived the reversal of every policy he had uttered over the past ten years with his Cabinet intact.

The package had to be announced quickly. In the renewed selling on Tuesday, 19 July, the pound hit a new low. The announcement was made by Wilson himself on Wednesday, the 20th. It amounted to the most severe deflation of the British economy since the war. More than £500m. were taken out of the economy. Hire purchase, building, defence, travel allowances, Government and local authority spending were all severely cut or pruned. Finally, to the delight of the *Daily Mirror*, Wilson announced a legally binding freeze on all wage increases in the next six months, to be followed by a period of severe wage restraint.

Wilson's economic lecture which preceded the Commons announcement dealt mainly with the reasons for the sterling crisis: the seamen's strike, the American withdrawal of Euro-dollars, high interest rates in America and so on. There was none of the harsh talk about speculators which had so surprised Sir Robert Menzies the previous week. More seriously, there was nothing of any intellectual quality to explain the contradiction between everything Wilson had said previously and what he was now saying. Wilson had always argued that deflation discouraged productivity and encouraged restrictive practices. He had said that the only way to social justice was through economic expansion. He had said that the Labour programme depended on the National Plan because only through the Plan's growth could the programme be paid for. He had said that the Government could ask for wage restraint only in an atmosphere of expansion. He had spoken again and again in the most scathing terms against Government interference with arbitration agreements between trade unions and employers. He had attacked high interest rates because they attracted hot money which was no use to any economy. Expansion was the be-all and end-all of Wilsonian economic policy. It was his central theme from the moment he became Shadow Chancellor in 1956. Now he was abandoning growth for stagnation, social justice for a strong pound and freely negotiated agreements for a wage freeze. Every aspect of his policy was now reversed – with hardly a word of intelligible analysis or justification.

Indeed, the one attempt at justification in terms of anything more than the balance of payments crisis measured the extent of the reversal:

There are abundant market opportunities abroad for British products which are competitive enough in terms of quality, performance or price, but are being lost owing to the shortage of labour. Hours of work have been reduced and incomes have been rising faster than productivity. What is needed is a shake-out which will release the nation's manpower, skilled and unskilled, and lead to a more purposive use of labour for the sake of increasing exports and giving effect to other national priorities. This redeployment can be achieved only by cuts in the present inflated level of demand, both in the private and public sectors. Not until we can get this redeployment through an attack on the problem of demand can we confidently expect growth in industrial production which is needed to realize our economic and social problems.

In his pamphlet *Remedies for Inflation*, written in 1957, with a foreword by Hugh Gaitskell, in which he had laid down Labour's economic policy for economic expansion over the next decade, Harold Wilson had written:

The supporters of this type of policy [deflation] urge that to hold down production leads to healthy redeployment of labour in more essential industries. But there is no evidence to support this. In 1955–6, the first two years of the Butler-Macmillan squeeze, the biggest increases were not in essential industry but in 'distribution' (78,000), and in 'professional, financial and miscellaneous' (64,000). There was a heavy loss of women workers in industry and the major cut in manufacturing was in automobiles, the one industry which has expended most in the Butler boom. As we have frequently urged, to squeeze workers out of wrong industries does not always mean that they will go with the right ones; and a financial squeeze, in any event, provides no guarantee even that it will be the wrong ones from which they are squeezed.[1]

1. Neither of these wholly contradictory analyses was confirmed by the facts after the July 1966 deflation. There were fewer people employed in Britain in June 1967 than there were in June 1966, yet the category 'professional and scientific', as in the first year of the Butler-Macmillan squeeze ten years earlier, had increased sharply – in this case by 107,900. Distributive trades, on the other hand, and 'miscellaneous' industries had lost labour heavily, as had construction. To some extent this was due to the Selective Employment Tax, imposed in the 1966 Budget, which discriminated in favour of manufacturing industry and against the distributive and service industries. To some extent, too, the widely publicized work of the Industrial Reorganization Corporation, assisted by similar acts of 'rationalization' set up by the Conservatives, such as the Industrial Training Boards and the National Economic Development Council, ensured a trend towards manufacturing industry. Even so, however, the big manufacturing industries listed under Vehicles, Engineering and Electrical Goods and Metal Goods all lost labour (though less drastically than distribution and construction). The truth almost certainly was that Wilson's initial contention – that throwing people out of work does not of itself ensure a boost in productivity or exports – was as accurate in 1966 as it was when he first formulated it in 1957. What changed the situation was the 'rationalization' effort, of which the SET and the IRC were the most important. In themselves, the 'shake-out' and the 'redeployment' myths were as great as they had been under Macmillan, Butler and Selwyn Lloyd. In 1966, as in 1956, 1957 and 1961, the Government had deliberately created unemployment for no other purpose than that of solving the immediate balance of payments crisis.

The following week, on 27 July, in another long, fumbling speech, Wilson groped for some qualitative difference between his deflation package and that of his Tory predecessors. The only one he could find, apart from the sophisticated argument that housing, school and hospital building would be 'contained within their existing programmes', lay in the way in which Labour would *come out of* the deflation. Referring to the thirteen wasted years of Tory rule, Wilson explained:

As it [deflation] became increasingly intolerable, action was taken. But the action taken was simply to reverse the restrictions in demand. Hire purchase had been cut; hire purchase was restored. Government expenditure had been cut. Government expenditure was increased. We had this in 1958 and 1963. . . .

Now, however, Wilson promised 'a planned expansion of these elements in the economy which can make the biggest contribution to exports'. In other words, the Tories had deflated the economy and the social services and created unemployment. When they took off the brakes, they increased funds for social services, lowered taxes and relaxed hire-purchase restrictions. Labour, too, had deflated the economy, held back the social services and created unemployment. But when Labour took off the brakes, they would do it first in the export industries. This crucial distinction between the two parties' economic policies was rather different to 'the vast chasm between us and the Tories' proclaimed by Wilson at the 1966 General Election.

Perhaps the saddest personal aspect of the 27 July speech was its complete abandonment of the cheeky language with which Wilson had, on occasions, mocked the received doctrines of the Bank of England, and sterling speculators. Only a week previously, at Menzies' dinner, he had savagely attacked speculators and the rest of the 'sell-Britain-short brigade'. Now they were all, for Wilson, honourable men. In language which must have delighted even Lord Cromer, Wilson told the House that the run on sterling was not a 'machination of some bearded troglodytes deep below ground speculating in foreign currencies for private gain. . . .' The selling of sterling was on the contrary 'precautionary'. People, after all, had to protect their money, and it was now up to Wilson's Government to prove to them once for all that their sterling was safe at the existing parity. Hence the deflation and the effective abandonment of Labour Party economic policy since the war.

Devaluation, for all Wilson's pledges, would not have so devastated Labour's promises and hopes as did the July measures. As Sir Stafford Cripps admitted during his 1949 devaluation broadcast, pledges on devaluation have to be made whether or not they are honoured. Wilson would certainly have had to face the wrath of the Confederation of British Industries, the Bank of England (and the *Daily Mirror*, whose proprietor was a Bank of England director) and the Conservative Party. Yet the core of his economic policy – expansion – would not have been affected. He could be sure of support for devaluation from the most coherent and intelligent members of his Cabinet. And the Party at large could have been coaxed to interpret the decision as a bid to outplay the bankers at their own game and to slaughter the sacred cows of the City of London. Finally, devaluation would have disposed of the principal French argument against British entry into the Common Market for which Harold Wilson's enthusiasm was mounting weekly.

Why, then, did he not devalue? Certainly not because he was afraid to face Conservative anger. The one charge which cannot be made against Wilson is that he is afraid of the Parliamentary Conservative Party.

First, he was personally opposed, on intellectual and strategic grounds, to devaluation. Secondly, more important, his decision not to devalue ensured him the continued support of the White House. Wilson opposed devaluation not because it meant, at any rate in the short run, an attack on home demand and on the standard of living of working people; not even because it would damage Labour's electoral chances or because it would imperil the dollar, but most of all because he has always regarded it as, in his own phrase, 'a feather bed'. Exporters, he believes, should fight for markets with other exporters. Devaluation, basically an export subsidy, is, in Wilson's view, an unnecessary subsidy for people, who, once subsidized, will not make the necessary structural alterations to assure sustained success in export markets.

Secondly, the American Treasury were still terrified of the consequences of sterling devaluation. Most of their experts, however, understood the appalling consequences for Britain of the deflationary alternative. Thus President Johnson, who had grown fonder of Wilson, personally intervened to assure him of support in the most glowing terms:

'England,' said Johnson at a White House dinner in Wilson's honour nine days after the measures had been announced,

is blessed with a gallant and hardy leadership. In you, Sir, England has a man of mettle, a new Churchill in her hour of crisis.

She is blessed with a leader whose own enterprise and courage will show the way. Your firmness and leadership has inspired us deeply in the traditions of the great men of Britain (*Daily Telegraph*, 30 July).

Even these words can have been of little comfort to Harold Wilson, who, for all his prevarication, was well aware that the July measures were the opposite of Labour's economic policies. He was, for some time, depressed by the hopelessness of the prospect before him, and his natural political resilience failed him. By way of compensation for the gloom at home, he turned his political attention away from home affairs, and lost himself in exotic fantasies about British 'merchant venturers' crashing through waves of competitors and conquering new export markets in Europe; in dreams of technological power-houses of Europe, led and dominated by British know-how and British scientists; in productivity conferences, suitably televised; in dramatic eyeball to eyeball confrontations on the high seas. From his speech to the Commons on the economy on 27 July 1966 to his speech on the Middle East on 31 May 1967, all Wilson's contributions in the House of Commons concerned Rhodesia and the Common Market. Even outside the Commons he returned to the economic situation, grudgingly and without enthusiasm or accuracy. His speech to the Labour Party Conference at Brighton was a shoddy affair, laying emphasis, as he had done in the Commons, not on the stop but on the go. The July measures were, he said,

not a backward reversion to Tory stop-go policies, but a necessary condition for national advance . . . . The July measures must now provide us with a once-for-all opportunity to break the whole miserable cycle we inherited. So far from being a rejection of expansion they create an opportunity to continued expansion.

Such sophistries read very differently to the triumphant declarations made only six months earlier at the general election.

Gone was the talk of the Means Test State and the Inevitable Deflation. Instead:

The Conservative Party was defeated in 1966 by the new realization of a common interest between those who wished to use their skills – managerial, professional, technical, industrial – to help solve Britain's problems, by those who realized that thirteen years of Conservative policy. . . .

and so on and so on, all of it adding up to a magic political formula: the consensus:

The Parliamentary programme of which this Report represents one year's progress, is part of a continuing, consistent and conscious policy. Within that continuing policy we each have our own special personal priorities. These subjective priorities find general acceptance in a consensus acceptable to the entire Movement.

At the few big constituency rallies at which he spoke, Wilson sought new scapegoats for the hardship which his policies were causing:

The discipline following our policies has meant hardship, particularly in the motor industry. And to the problems the industry is facing are added the self-inflicted wounds caused by unofficial strikes, which have needlessly thrown tens of thousands out of work [*Cheers*] (Meeting at Poplar, *Daily Telegraph*, 12 November 1966).

Most of that gloomy winter, with unemployment figures rising to more than half-a-million, was spent in a 'whistle-stop' tour around Europe, ending in the formal request for permission to enter the Common Market. Gradually, as the economic situation appeared to brighten, the Prime Minister regained much of his former confidence. The Chancellor assured him that the reaction of the economy to the July measures had been quicker than planned, and the prospects for the balance of payments by the end of 1967 were far better than they could have hoped. A display of economic knowledge and political sleight of hand in a big television performance on the Common Market and the continued failure of the Conservatives to make any impression upon British public life combined to push him back into favour, at least with the public opinion polls. Spring had calmed the foul winds of the previous July. 'We are back on course,' Callaghan trumpeted.

'The ship is picking up speed. The economy is moving' (speech on the Budget, 11 April 1967). By May Day, 1967, Wilson had discovered a new rationale for his Government's policies, a new hope to hold out to his followers. Speaking in Leeds, he outlined a programme of three stages which, he alleged, Labour had carefully followed since taking office: the battle to save the pound (Part 1); the 'refit' of the economy (Part 2); and the 'great leap forward' (Part 3). The Government, he said, had completed Part 1 successfully, and were at present passing through Part 2. The decks would soon be cleared for the 'great leap forward'.

> The vision your Labour Government holds out to you is this. That a Britain strengthened by the firm measures of these past two years will be able, as year succeeds year, to move forward at a still more rapid pace into the third major phase of building the New Britain (*Daily Telegraph*, 8 May 1967).

Wilson's renewed confidence and his obsession with technology and Europe were given a severe jolt by the publication of the August unemployment figures which, at 550,000, were the highest for August since the 1930s. It was clear that, without drastic action, unemployment the following winter would rise above 1963 levels – which Wilson had described as 'deliberate Tory inhumanity'. Wilson responded to the challenge in the Cabinet re-shuffle at the end of August by making himself 'overlord' of the Department of Economic Affairs and bringing in one of his most trusted lieutenants – Peter Shore – as Secretary of State.

Three days after the re-shuffle, Wilson appeared in his new guise as expansionary overlord. He announced that the relaxation of hire-purchase restrictions announced for motor cars the previous June would apply across the board, thus relaxing the pressure on home demand.

Thirteen months previously, Wilson had scoffed at the previous Tory reflations:

> As it [deflation] became increasingly intolerable, action was taken. But the action taken was simply to reverse the restrictions in demand. Hire purchase had been cut; hire purchase was restored. Government expenditure had been cut. Government expenditure was increased. We had this in 1958 and 1963 ... (House of Commons, 27 July 1966; see p. 183).

Now Wilson was doing it in 1967. Deflation was becoming increasingly intolerable, so he was taking action simply to reverse the restrictions in demand. Hire purchase had been cut in the 1966 deflation. Now hire purchase was being restored. The previous year, Wilson had argued that the Government's moves *out* of the deflation would distinguish it once for all from its Tory predecessors. Now, to the last detail, he was aping past Tory practice.

The reflationary moves infuriated Wilson's hard-headed Keynesian economic advisers, who had placed all their faith on an export-led reflation, and a continued depression of domestic demand. More importantly, it horrified the holders of overseas sterling for whom the prospect of lower unemployment and in-creased domestic consumption was intolerable. With his first act as economic overlord, Harold Wilson put an end even to his own meagre aspirations.

Yet still he hoped that the balance of payments deficit would, by some miracle, in spite of the Middle East crisis and the closure of the Suez Canal, be righted. In a speech at Newport he declared that his Government, at long last (and once again), had reached the 'turning point'.

For three years the Government, industry and the people have shown their determination to pay our way. We have pursued this objective ruthlessly, regardless of political popularity. We have had to ask for efforts and for sacrifices – for hardships, even, and we have not yet seen the end of the hardship which may be necessary, although the measures which made it necessary are bringing us through. . . . Overseas pay-ments have reached a position of basic balance and growing strength. The fact that Britain has been able to take the Middle East crisis in her stride is a measure of her basic strength. If these events had fallen upon us in any other summer in recent years, I doubt whether it would have been weathered so robustly.

We now face a turning point in that we can advance in production and in the productive use of our capacity. Since July 1966, there has been in countless British firms and productive centres an unprecedented drive for efficiency, an unparalleled drive against waste, whether of physical or human resources. Production can now increase without plunging us into the overheating, wasteful use and indeed famine of labour which, in the past, have plunged us into crises (*Daily Telegraph* and *Times*, 9 September 1967).

The 'turning point' had been reached, conveniently, in time for the Labour Party Conference. As the delegates assembled at Scarborough for the most gloomy and dispiriting conference since the 1930s, even the most illusionist of loyalists could conjure up little socialist achievement from the first 1,000 days of Labour Government.

The economic policy of the Party in Opposition had been abandoned. Sterling was still weak, and, as the period for repayments approached, was bound to get weaker. The Department of Economic Affairs, which had been created to manage the promised growth in the economy, had been decimated, and its planners festered in a political backwater. The National Plan which the DEA had produced with such a flourish two years previously had been written off in its entirety. The Ministry of Overseas Development had been humiliated. The Minister of Disarmament existed only in name. The Ministry of Land and Natural Resources had been abolished. The Ombudsman was a bureaucratic farce. The University of the Air had been twice postponed. Rent control was paralysed by the Rent Act's regulations for application and appeal. In many towns and cities, rent officers had dealt with less than twenty applications in the Act's first eighteen months' operation. Steel nationalization had provided effective stability for the steel-owners. Not only were they paid enormous compensation – totalling more than £450m. – but they had retained control of the industry by their appointments to the key positions of power. Lord Melchett, the Conservative merchant banker, had been appointed chairman of the British Steel Corporation. Niall Macdiarmid, chairman and managing director of Stewarts and Lloyds, and William Cartwright, former managing director of the Steel Company of Wales, both ardent opponents of nationalization and renowned for their 'toughness' with the trade unions, were brought into key executive and managerial positions in the new Corporation, while the only job held open at the top for a trade unionist was the post of labour officer. Aubrey Jones, a former Tory Minister, was chairman of the Prices and Incomes Board. Ronnie Grierson, a Tory merchant banker, was managing director of the Industrial Reorganization Corporation. Sir Henry Wells, a prominent chartered surveyor and estate agent, who had been appointed chairman of the new Land Commission, declared on taking office that his Commission would operate 'according to the laws of the market' and was little more than an agency to facilitate the buying and selling of land. While Wilson had promised that a Land Commission would usher in the 'nationalization of urban land', Sir Henry declared his total opposition to all forms of nationalization, especially in land. The review of the social services, painstakingly prepared by Douglas Houghton for two years, had been scrapped, and Patrick Gordon Walker had been brought back into the Cabinet to turn the Welfare State into a Means Test State. Lord Hill of Luton, formerly secretary of the British Medical Association (in which post he had conducted a bitter wrecking campaign against Aneurin Bevan's National Health Service proposals after the war) and formerly Conservative Chancellor of the Duchy of Lancaster, had been appointed chairman of the BBC Board of Governors, and Lord Harlech, deputy Conservative leader in the House of Lords, was chairman of the consortium of assorted actors, opera singers and Wilsonite socialists which had won the independent television contract for the West and Wales. Abroad, the Smith regime, inspired by Wilson's dithering, had taken firm control of Rhodesia. A Fascist revolution in Greece had been condoned by the British Government and the American Government, with the unswerving support of British Labour, had doubled the number of its forces and the ferocity of their methods in Vietnam.

The Scarborough delegates responded to all this with a standing ovation. Their leader told them

> We are now able to look forward to the rising production and rising employment which increased productivity has made possible. Production has already begun to increase. For the first time for nearly eighteen months the number of jobs available has started to increase (Conference Report, 4 October 1967).

And, even as late as 17 October, Wilson was telling motor industrialists that

> Industry is now more streamlined, and productivity has risen in an unprecedented way. The motor industry in particular can now expand without any loss of competitiveness in world markets.

By mid-October, however, the situation suddenly changed. The publication of the bad September trade figures, the outbreak of powerful dock strikes in London and Liverpool in protest against the introduction of the sacred 'Devlin Proposals', and the private forecast to the Chancellor that the balance of payments deficit for the year, so far from being cleared, would probably exceed £400m. indicated that the turning point was still some way off. Wilson reacted ferociously to the dock strikes, which coincided with the end of a year-long dispute on the Myton's building site on London's Barbican. Myton's bovine efforts to open up their site had provoked the pickets to violent disturbances outside the gate. Ray Gunter, the most consistently reactionary member of the Cabinet, blurted out the familiar charges. 'The Communists,' he said, 'are planning a winter of disruption.' Wilson immediately agreed. 'Everyone here,' he said with some confidence, since he was speaking at a tercentenary celebration for London wine merchants, 'will endorse his [Gunter's] words' (*Times*, 19 October 1967). There was, he told the Commons a week later, 'abundant evidence' of a winter of disruption.

No evidence, however, was produced, for the reason that there was none. The strike leaders in the Liverpool docks were militant Protestants. In the London docks, Jack Dash, chairman of the London port-workers committee, was a well-known Communist but had never found it easy to force his political views on the London dockers against their will. Dash's personal following among the dockers, regardless of his politics, was proved conclusively, when, after a nine-week strike in which he had been ruthlessly vilified and abused in the press and on television, he was elected by the dockers to the post of dock shop steward. Once again, the *Sunday Times*, after careful analysis, discounted the Wilson/Gunter 'Red Plot' and the *Observer* tried unsuccessfully to substantiate it.

In the seamen's strike, eighteen months previously, Wilson had invented a Red Plot only after all other tactics had failed. On this occasion, there was no delay. A strike was holding up exports in a critical period for sterling. It was therefore a Red Plot from the beginning.

This time, however, the allegations failed. The strike went on, and so did the sterling crisis. Harold Wilson had fired his last round at a mythical scapegoat, and missed. In his speech to the Lord Mayor's Banquet on 13 November, Wilson broke off from euphoric meanderings about the European Technological Institute to assure his audience that the October trade figures, to be published later in the week, were caused almost entirely by the Middle East crisis and the dock strike. But already he had come round to the view that the devaluation which he had fought so tenaciously for so long was inevitable.

The decision to devalue the pound was taken by the Cabinet on Thursday, 16 November, and it was announced the following Saturday evening. The machinery of the civil service, however, had been set in motion long before that. For some six weeks a handful of highly vetted experts in the Treasury had been working out the practical problems of devaluation. Yet Wilson kept the option open until the last possible moment. By all accounts, he was the last of senior Cabinet Ministers to accept devaluation. For weeks he clung to the hope that the figures, by some miracle, would right themselves and the pound would rise again in the world markets. The devaluation was, ironically, a much greater personal blow to Wilson than it was to James Callaghan or any other of the Senior Ministers who had staked their political reputation on the \$2.80. Wilson told his interviewers on Rediffusion's 'This Week', on 23 November, that 'the last two weeks has been hell. . . . They've been the worst two weeks I've known.'

His commitment to the existing parity was not, as was Callaghan's, purely sentimental or even electorally opportunist. As he explained on 'This Week', the objection was also intellectual and economic:

> It [devaluation] does give us a chance to break out, but by God it does mean that we've got to take the opportunity of breaking out, we can't regard it as a feather bed. One of my feelings in 1964 against devaluing was the danger that it would be regarded as a feather bed by British industry on both sides who might feel that they could just sort of sink back and not bother. If anyone takes that view now, we face a very, very serious situation. It is an opportunity, but I don't in any way deny it was a setback.

Setback or not, the purpose of devaluation was to provide a substantial enough boost to British exporters to wipe out the balance of payments deficit. The extent of devaluation – slightly under 15 per cent – had been kept down deliberately to prevent a dollar devaluation in its train. It was therefore all the more necessary, if devaluation was to work, further to 'hold down home demand' so that industry concentrated on export markets. For a brief moment, Wilson appeared to believe that the 8 per cent bank rate, announced simultaneously with devaluation, and further minor moves to squeeze credit would be enough. But before long, as Mr Callaghan left the Treasury for the Home Office to be replaced by the younger, and even more ruthlessly orthodox Roy Jenkins, Wilson was forced to announce that his Cabinet were preparing another big 'package' of deflationary measures, to be announced after the Commons had re-assembled after the Christmas recess.

The package, when it finally came, wiped out all the remaining advances in social reform which the Wilson Labour Government had accomplished since 1964. A charge of 2s 6d (with suitable exemptions for the old and unemployed) was imposed on all health prescriptions – a higher charge than that imposed by successive Conservative Governments for thirteen years. A meagre £5m. was saved in the abolition of free secondary school milk, a welfare service which Wilson himself had defended in the most moving terms in 1957 and in 1961. Even more absurdly, the raising of the school leaving age was postponed from 1971 to 1973. This last measure invoked the widest anger in the Labour movement. Apart from the resignation of Lord Longford, Lord Privy Seal and Leader of the House of Lords, whose removal from the Cabinet had been predicted by the press for several months, among Labour educationists, most of whom were sworn loyalists and devoted right-wingers, the protest was more powerful and more meaningful. Tyrrell Burgess, who stood in 1964 as Labour candidate for Croydon North East, and had sat on committees for the formulation and development of Labour's education policy, outlined in uncharacteristically reckless prose his total disillusionment with the Labour Government:

Post-war educational building has been one of the triumphs of public administration. It is now in jeopardy. Nor is it an exaggeration to say that in spite of the promises, the chief victims of withdrawing the leaving-age money will be slum primary schools. I do not believe that Ministers have been telling lies in the House of Commons. It is clear from what they have said that they really believed that postponing the raising of the school leaving age would leave other educational programmes intact. They took that decision out of unsullied ignorance. I am trying to keep at bay the suspicion that all the other decisions announced on black Tuesday were of a similar quality (*Guardian*, 2 January 1968).

Such disillusionment was even more serious for Labour than John Morgan's cry of 'Black Wednesday!' at the time of the deflation in July 1966, for Burgess represented the loyalist reformers in the Labour Party – the influential intellectuals who had sunk their differences in the conviction that a Labour Government would carry out substantial reform in the areas of social policy which mattered most – in Burgess's case in education. The only genuine support left in the Labour Party came from careerists, sycophants and paid Party officials.

The Government's determination to prove to the world, and particularly to the International Monetary Fund, that it had no further time for social reforms was extended to housing. All his political life, the Prime Minister had regarded the housing programme as a 'special area' of social reform, to be treated gently in time of deflation or national economic crisis. In 1965 and 1966 the number of houses built in Britain, although it did not rise in the spectacular manner promised and envisaged by the Prime Minister prior to 1964 and in spite of some rather dubious juggling with the established minimum standards for size and height of council houses, had increased steadily towards the Labour target of 500,000 houses a year by 1970. In an election meeting in Bradford in March 1966, the Prime Minister promised:

> This is not a lightly given pledge. It is a promise. We shall achieve the 500,000 target, and we shall not allow any developments, any circumstances, however adverse, to deflect us from our aim.

In 1967, as though to establish the point, for the first time the total of house-completions rose over 400,000. On 18 January 1968, however, Anthony Greenwood, Minister of Housing, in an astonishing display of public masochism, called a Press Conference to announce that the target of 500,000 houses by 1970 had been abandoned. 'There are,' said his statement, 'too many uncertainties for it to be possible for anyone to say exactly how many will be built in 1970' (*Daily Telegraph*, 19 January 1968).

By now, the Prime Minister had forged an invigorating partnership with his new Chancellor, Roy Jenkins. Three years previously, the gap between the two men was a wide one. Jenkins had little contact with the rank and file of the Labour movement. Though his father was a miner, and a union official, Jenkins had studiously avoided the trade-union section of the Labour Party. He was an 'intellectual', sought after in London's fashionable drawing rooms and dinner parties, and an excellent House of Commons man. His politics were shamelessly liberal. He had never any time for socialist theory, and his early essays into egalitarianism were quickly abandoned. His biography of Asquith referred only sketchily and in passing to the tumultuous developments in the Labour Movement, to the strikes and poverty and industrial upheavals which so dominated the political scene in Asquith's lifetime. In his book *The Labour Case*,[1] written before the 1959 General Election, he had said that the Labour Government of 1945–51 'tilted the balance too much towards the austerity of fair shares'.

Harold Wilson had believed in and defended 'the austerity of fair shares'. Even in his period as Prime Minister he had stressed, at each crisis, that the nation should respond as a family and share the burden equally. Until the 1967 devaluation Wilson had striven to combine his interest and concern for tough technology with a sentimental concern for the poor, the sick, the old and the badly housed. This concern had gradually drained from him through the recurring financial crises of his Premiership. By January 1968 he was sufficiently cleansed of reformist sentiment to agree with Jenkins – unequivocally – that what was good for the balance of payments was good for British Labour.

In the period following the package of cuts in state expenditure, there was a great deal of speculation in the press about the Prime Minister's chances of survival. Commentator after commentator alleged that Wilson's credibility had vanished and that he was on the way out. Alan Watkins, the *New Statesman*'s political commentator, noted that Wilson had 'lost control of the Centre' of his party.

If such speculation was accurate, it was unfair. The decision to devalue the pound had been inevitable, and had been accepted unanimously by the Cabinet. Only one Cabinet Minister had resigned over the January cuts. The only real complaint about the

1. Penguin Books, 1959, p. 74.

package from most senior Ministers was that the decision to abandon our role of East of Suez was a breach of commitments made to 'our friends overseas'. Pressure on Wilson, in short, was stronger from the Right than from the Left, but the collective responsibility of all the Labour Ministers for the package and its effects was beyond question. Wilson was no longer in a position to take big decisions by himself as he had done in July 1966. In spite of widespread press speculation, the only Labour MPs who openly attacked the Prime Minister were Desmond Donnelly, who resigned the Labour Whip and was subsequently expelled from the Labour Party, Reginald Paget, who had resigned the whip over Rhodesia and asked for it back again some months later, and John Cronin. Within a few weeks, the speculators about Wilson's resignation had changed their tune. Wilson had 'recovered his nerve'. As I write, and inopportunely break off this story, sterling is rising firmly in the world money markets, Britain's gold reserves are increasing, the prospect of a 'tough' Budget is eagerly anticipated in the Central Banks, and the stage is set for Harold Wilson to announce, in several months time, that his Government have reached 'the turning point', and that 'the decks are cleared ready for action'.

In an interview with three journalists on the Rediffusion programme 'This Week' eight days after devaluation, Harold Wilson was asked what he thought was his Government's biggest mistake since taking office.

I think perhaps the biggest mistake that I would feel is that I underrated, we underrated if you like, the power of speculators at home or abroad, even when our balance of payments was improving as it was last year, to put the pound in jeopardy and force us into short-term measures which were injurious to this country. Yes, I think that was our biggest mistake. But we have now learnt that lesson, and we have decided . . . to get rid of the root cause of the problem, their feeling that they could speculate the pound out of existence.

The expression 'speculator' was, as so often, misleading. It conjured up images of greedy gnomes, shiftily shuffling sterling in the underground. In fact, the people who sell sterling are, by the values of the society which Wilson himself upholds, highly respectable. They are both generals and subalterns of the world's financial citadels. The process of selling sterling takes place, not in the underground, but in the banks and bourses of the free world.

The men who deal in these financial 'bargains' are traditionally fickle. They respond speedily and without much rational argument to crises and rumours of crises and, consequently, their political sensitivity is sharper than that of industrialists or entrepreneurs. While an industrialist, in otherwise favourable circumstances for industry, might agree to overlook, for example, the abolition of prescription charges or a subsidy Bill to help local authorities to build houses, a financier will be outraged.

For the first three years of Harold Wilson's Labour Government, the manufacturers of Britain treated the British Labour Government with remarkable respect. In the early months, particularly, when Labour's parliamentary majority was negligible, investment in private industry rose sharply and there was seldom a suggestion among the captains of industry of a conspiracy to bring the Tories back. On the contrary. In many industries the advent of the Labour Government, promising and providing generous investment allowances and a much tighter hold on the trade unions was greeted with some relief. The financiers and money-marketeers, on the other hand, responded with traditional hysteria whenever Labour moved even slightly in the direction of social reform.

In many respects, the situation was much the same as in the 1945–51 Labour Government. For the first three years, private industry had cooperated with the Government (and with Harold Wilson, President of the Board of Trade).

Only then, provoked by the announcement of further measures, notably widespread nationalization, did the industrialists unanimously campaign against the Government. In 1968, there were no such measures to provoke such a reaction. Nevertheless, an ominous development for Harold Wilson and his Government was the growing testiness of the Confederation of British Industries. At a meeting of the CBI Economics Committee on 5 December 1967, a paper was read by Eric Caswell, a member of the CBI council and chairman of the Metal Window Association. Caswell's paper launched a violent attack on the Labour Government and drew unfavourable parallels with the previous Conservative administration. The paper asked pointedly how long industrialists could continue to cooperate with the Labour Government, and, in the discussion which followed, there was much support for an open campaign by British industrialists to rid the country of its infamous Government. Only references to the treasonable nature of such a proposal from the more urbane (and more powerful) industrialists present prevented such a campaign. Similarly, a few weeks later, the Road Haulage Association, in the course of its campaign against the Labour Government's Transport Bill – a bromide measure by comparison with Labour's nationalization of road haulage in 1947 – was forced to dissuade its militant members from sponsoring a national stike of road hauliers in opposition to the Bill (*Daily Telegraph*, 5 February 1968).

If Wilson and his Government can convince British industry that their interests are, and always will be, the same, the Labour Government and Party could survive, even if they forfeit the socialist aspirations of their rank and file. On the other hand, if the political militancy of the Confederation of British Industry and its members grows, and if British industrialists join their financial brethren in an assault on Labour of 1949–51 proportions, Harold Wilson's next turning point will be his, and Labour's, last.

Chapter 7
America, Commonwealth or Common Market

1. America

When Harold Wilson was at the Board of Trade, he agreed with his hero, Sir Stafford Cripps, that the recovery of Britain was to a large extent due to what Wilson called 'the far-sighted generosity of the American people'. In the famous debate on Marshall Aid in July 1948, where a band of Tory extremists joined Communists and fellow-travellers in opposing the project, Wilson explained that the Americans obviously expected some return for their money.

> The United States Government are concerned, not unnaturally, at the running down of their stocks and lest there should be depletion of their natural resources which are at present being exploited – a number of metals and minerals essential for the fulfilment of the Aid programme. There are some in respect of which they foresee a continuing shortage unless new sources of supply are developed. They want our cooperation in building up essential resources in the Empire, both to avert shortage and as a contribution to our own economic recovery. They are anxious and rightly anxious, that in cases where American firms want to engage in new projects contributing to those ends, they shall be free to do so (House of Commons, 6 July 1949).

The penetration of the British market and the sterling area by the Marshall Aid programme, however, did not, in Wilson's view, 'in any way affect the steps necessary for further development in the Commonwealth' or the doctrine of imperial preference. Nor did it affect further cooperation with Western Europe. As an example of the coincidence of interest between Western Europe and the Commonwealth Wilson referred to the 'port difficulties' in the independent colony of Southern Rhodesia. 'The need for cooperation with other European countries is well exemplified by the work that is now going on between this country and Portugal to get the necessary work done in Beira.'[1]

In short, Wilson, at the outset of his political career, welcomed

1. Seventeen years later, as Beira became the main port of supply for the rebel Rhodesian regime, Wilson must have regretted this cooperation.

all three developments – closer ties with the Americans, closer cooperation with Western Europe and further economic concentration on the Commonwealth. As the months in office wore on, however, he became increasingly obsessed by 'the crucial problem for this country and Western Europe' – the dollar balance of payments. 'We shall need the maximum effort in exports to the dollar areas if we are to succeed.' American investment to Britain was more than welcome. 'We are prepared,' he said on 28 January 1949, 'to consider and to welcome any scheme for US investment on its merits, dependent on the contribution it makes to viability by 1952.'

In April he gave an account of the dividing of the American market into four segments, and the collecting together of a small group of 'merchant-venturing' firms and bankers who would attack the market simultaneously. In July he was referring to 'the grave increase in the dollar deficit' and was quoting Paul Hoffman, master-mind of the Marshall Plan: 'All Europe needs to do is to find ways of attracting an additional one per cent of the American national income for the purchase of her wares and the problem is solved.' An increase in dollar exports, said Wilson, was, at the same time, a short-term and a long-term solution to the problem.

All through this period Wilson's attitude towards America was wholly friendly. He accepted the majority view in the Cabinet that the road to economic advance lay in genuine and planned cooperation with the Americans. What shook him from this view was the devaluation in the autumn of 1949, of which, as we have seen, he did not approve as whole-heartedly as did some of his Fabian colleagues. Wilson was genuinely shocked at the ease with which the American business world forced devaluation on an unwilling Government. Like Cripps, he saw devaluation as a national disgrace, and again and again in his future assessments of the 1949 devaluation he referred in scornful tones to the speech of the Secretary to the United States Treasury which, in effect, provoked the last decisive wave of pre-devaluation selling. From that moment, Wilson's language and attitude towards the Americans, while staying very firmly within the boundaries of diplomatic courtesy, lost the ring of gratitude with which he had welcomed the Marshall Plan. For the devaluation debate Wilson was saying: 'We have to reduce by alternative sources of supply our abnormal dependence on dollar sources of supply' (28 September 1949). In the remaining eighteen months of Labour Government, Wilson was struck more and more forcefully by the sensitivity of the British economy to economic twists and turns in the United States. On the few occasions in the Cabinet when he spoke up in opposition to the Party leadership, he complained that no real steps had been taken to break the American stranglehold on the British economy.

Much of this disillusionment came out into the open after Wilson's resignation in April 1951. In a speech on economic affairs in July of that year Wilson assured the House that he was 'not making an anti-American speech'. He went on:

There might be some honourable members who thought that it was anti-Americanism on our part to resist this onslaught on Imperial Preference, but I believe that the interests of the free world cannot stand this gratuitous and unnecessary attack on the economic links of the Commonwealth. Our American friends must realize that, just as our trade with the Commonwealth provided the key to an economic recovery in 1945–50, as it did, yet further development, yet closer links with the Commonwealth will be necessary in the darkening economic situation which we face today.

Nowhere in his speech did Wilson analyse the cause of this 'onslaught on Imperial Preference', nor remind the House that he himself had warned that American economic penetration of the sterling area was an inevitable consequence of Marshall Aid. Instead his speeches argued for breaking away from American economic domination. Later in July he told the Commons:

Our dependence on the American economy is so great that even a small percentage move either way could have a disastrous effect on the situation in this country . . . without independence of external aid there can be no real independence in foreign affairs and Britain will be prevented from exercising that great moral influence which she can exert in the councils of the world (29 July 1952).

In September 1952, *Tribune* published a pamphlet by Harold Wilson entitled *In Place of Dollars*. 'The first aim of Britain's economic policy,' stated the foreword, 'must be to achieve independence of aid from abroad at the earliest possible moment.' The free-trade conditions of the American loan, explained the pamphlet, despite its author's advocacy of them at the time, were 'intolerable'. What was necessary was to concentrate almost exclusively on Commonwealth trade and Commonwealth production in order to build an alternative economic bloc to the United States.

Writing in *Reynolds News* the following December about the Commonwealth Prime Ministers' Conference, Wilson gave some indication of the sacrifice necessary to put his views into effect:

> It will take perhaps ten or fifteen years of Commonwealth development to reduce the sterling area's dependence on dollar supplies to manageable proportions. But this conference should agree on a plan to set us on the road (7 December 1952).

His attacks on the United States and the Government's dependence on them became more and more persistent:

> We must go on strengthening the Empire and Commonwealth and should not have to follow the policy of the United States of America (*Prescot and Huyton Reporter*, 21 September 1951).
>
> Would Mr Churchill have flown to America last December to restrain some of the hot-heads of American militarism who wanted to carry the war from Korea to China? (ibid., 5 October 1951).
>
> Last year Mr Churchill's policy was simple: 'We must follow America at all costs'. But that is not the way to bring peace (House of Commons, 25 July 1952).
>
> The Government is not exercising that restraining influence on the United States which will be necessary if we are to win through to peace. It is not clear even if they are trying . . . (Speech at Canterbury, *Manchester Guardian*, 12 February 1953).
>
> The biggest danger to world peace is that the Conservatives would follow America and be dragged at America's heel instead of starting independently to build up a system of world peace (House of Commons, 14 May 1954).

With these generalizations went more specific criticisms of specific policies. The barriers set up against trade with Russia and China particularly irritated Wilson, and when the Americans refused to sell a disease-fighting helicopter to the Russians, he exploded:

> The US administration has reached an all-time low in ineffective vindictiveness (*Daily Telegraph*, 6 July 1953).

Throughout those Bevanite years Wilson consistently attacked American foreign policy, and reserved his more powerful rhetoric for American policy in South East Asia, more particularly in Indo-China. Almost as soon as the Labour Government lost the 1951 election, Wilson was championing the cause of the Vietminh and other South East Asian nationalists:

The speeches of Mr Dulles and Senator Taft show the clearest danger of the Korean war escalating into the rest of Asia, and of an intention to impose Chiang Kai Shek on China. It must be the duty of the British Parliament, and the British Labour Movement in particular, to make it clear that if any section of American opinion sought to extend the area of fighting in Asia, they could not expect us to support them (speech at Coventry, *Daily Telegraph*, 18 February 1952).

The controversy warmed up at the beginning of 1954, as Dulles insisted on the formation of the South East Asian Treaty Organization, and the encirclement of China with 'friendly' puppet states. At the May Day celebrations of that year, Harold Wilson surpassed himself in tub-thumping rhetoric. In Liverpool, at a big meeting outside St Geoge's hall, he proclaimed:

Not a man, not a gun must be sent to defend the French in Indo-China. We must not join with nor in any way encourage the anti-Communist crusade in Asia, whether it is under the leadership of the Americans or anyone else. We must remember that the road to peace in Asia is the way of Nehru, not the way of Dulles. There will be no peace if we talk of arming the Asians to fight one another. It is tractors and measures to raise the abysmally low standard of life in Asia, not tanks, guns or military alliances that are our best defence against Communism. The world is now ready to chart out the road to peace. That will not be made possible by following what is said by Washington or Moscow. I believe it is this country which must give the lead to peace-loving nations and see that the world can go forward in peace (*Liverpool Daily Post*, 3 May 1954).

And again in Manchester:

The Government should not further subordinate British policy to America. A settlement in Asia is imperilled by the lunatic fringe in the American Senate who want a holy crusade against Communism. Not a man, not a gun must be sent from Britain to aid French imperialism in Indo-China. Nor must Britain join or encourage an anti-Communist alliance in Asia. Asia is in revolution and Britain must learn to march on the side of the peoples in that revolution and not on the side of their oppressors (*Daily Telegraph*, 3 May 1954).

In July of 1954, as a member of the Shadow Cabinet, Wilson visited China and was granted an interview with that country's Premier, Chou En Lai. In an article in the *Manchester Guardian*, Wilson gave an account of his interview:

I asked him: if the outcome of Geneva were to be a truce in Indo-China with no political settlement in Korea could there be peace in Asia on the basis of peaceful coexistence? He was emphatic that there could, provided there was no intensification of American intervention (3 June 1954).

In the few further comments which Harold Wilson had to make about American foreign policy during that period he indicated that he agreed with Chou: that peace, especially in Vietnam, was perfectly possible, in spite of the division between North and South, provided there was no further intervention by the Americans.

He enthusiastically supported the Geneva Agreements of 1954, which promised future elections, and as the hope of elections failed to materialize, he attacked the Americans for deliberately sabotaging the agreements. In March 1955, he put down a question in the House asking the Foreign Secretary 'what representations he had made to the Government of the United States of America about their discussions for an agreement between the United States of America and the Government of Laos for military assistance, drawing their attention to the breach involved of the Geneva Agreement over Indo-China to which the United Kingdom was a party'.

Even more explicitly, in September 1955, he wrote a long letter to the *Manchester Guardian*, arguing for elections in Vietnam, as laid down in the Geneva agreements:

It is true, as you indicated, that Mr Diem[1] never considered himself bound by the Geneva Agreement and his intransigence has been shown recently by his claim (denied in London) that the Western powers have some sympathy with his position.

We are put in an impossible position if steps are not taken to ensure

1. Then Prime Minister of South Vietnam.

that the agreement is honoured and if it is possible for Northern Vietnam to point to a failure to carry out the terms of the agreement. One understands that this matter was discussed informally between Mr Molotov and Mr Macmillan. Surely the Government ought now to make a statement defining their position and the steps they are taking to avoid any further breach in this matter (8 September 1955).

But by now Harold Wilson had 'got over' his Bevanism and was looking to higher things. From the summer recess in 1955, he moved closer to the Labour leadership, and concentrated less and less on foreign affairs. His business life with Montague Meyer became less hectic, and his trips to the East, and to China, which had inspired so much of his indignation over US foreign policy, less frequent.

Somewhat naturally, perhaps, his conviction over American policy in Asia began to fade as he became absorbed in the more mundane duties of Shadow Chancellor, and as the opportunities for outspoken opinion became less frequent. From 1956 to 1961 there is hardly a reference in any of Wilson's public speeches or writings to American foreign policy in South East Asia, and only in occasional speeches did he wander far from his economic brief. In April 1958, for instance, he declared that the 'Government is an utterly unpredictable satellite of American foreign policy' (*Daily Telegraph*, 28 April 1958).

Much of his former antagonism to American foreign policy was transferred to American penetration of the British economy. He was irritated by the increasing influence of American finance and industry in British industry. Again and again, he attacked the Government for agreeing to the sale of British firms, or substantial shareholdings in British firms to American interests. When the then Chancellor, Harold Macmillan, agreed to the sale of the Trinidad Oil Company to the Americans for £176m., no one in the House was angrier than Harold Wilson:

The Government are transferring a vital British interest into other hands . . . this is a regrettable transaction, which has caused dismay and despondency throughout the country and I believe in more than one quarter of the House. . . . Was there any alternative? We believe that there was. We believe that the Government should have provided the capital for the Trinidad Oil Company by taking shares in the company. Is there anything revolutionary or shocking in suggesting that the

Government should have stepped in on this important development?...
the Rt Hon. Member for Woodford [Winston Churchill] did it before
the war when he took shares in BP (or Anglo-Persian as it was then
called). Disraeli has been almost deified by the Party opposite for his
brilliant opportunism in buying Suez Canal shares, but these tired and
unimaginative followers of his, these drooping primroses, have tamely
let the initiative fall from their palsied hands (House of Commons,
20 June 1956).

When the Conservative Government, shortly before the 1959
election, sold all the shares of a highly successful state-owned
instrument-making firm, S. G. Brown, to private enterprise,
Wilson exclaimed:

How does he [the Civil Lord of the Admiralty – T. G. D. Galbraith]
know that having disposed of the firm to a perhaps reputable British
firm that it will not in twelve months, two years or some other time be
sold to a consortium, possibly dominated by American concerns? There
have been some amazing success stories on the part of American share-
buying in the past few months.

Indulging for a brief moment in satire, Wilson mocked the
Government's policy:

The Americans can have our oil, they can have our vital defence firms,
but our ' gins and bitters ' – never! (House of Commons, 28 June 1959).

Seventeen months later, when the Ford Motor Company of
Detroit moved to take 100 per cent holding of their already
majority-owned Ford of Britain for £129m., Wilson responded
typically:

We have already had Trinidad, British Timken, British Aluminium,
S. G. Brown where there was a very substantial American minority
shareholding. We are bound to ask: where will this end? What assurance
is there that Dagenham will not be sacrificed to Cologne? What guarantee is there that Dagenham products for third countries will not be
sacrificed to the interests of Dearborn, Michigan?... I want to make it
clear that we on this side of the House are not against American investment in this country. There has been a great deal of it. But we are against
a major industry being owned by the Americans (ibid., 21 November
1960).

The abandonment of Bevanism had made little difference to
Wilson's own distaste for the American way of life under Eisen-

hower. Eisenhower represented that old-school-tie incompetence among Western leaders which Wilson so despised and in a number of speeches he attacked Eisenhower personally. His attitude towards the Americans and American society earned him the sharp disapproval of the other Labour leaders, and the fact that he allowed his anti-Americanism to shine through indicates how strong his feelings were. Even at Labour Party conferences Wilson rarely failed to introduce a snide reference to the American way of life, and, of course, in the short period when he challenged the leadership, his views were permitted full expression:

We are building up an Americanized society and the Tories are revelling in it. Some of our own colleagues welcome it. Our sense of values is wrong. We must stress the ethical basis of our socialism more than ever. . . . (Speech at Hendon, 25 February 1960).

Late in 1960, such complaints suddenly stopped. The reason was simple. The American electorate had thrown out Eisenhower's nominee, Vice-President Richard Nixon, and replaced him with a 'dynamic' young millionaire who had blown them up with rhetoric about 'a hundred days of dynamic action' and 'storming the new frontier'. Wilson observed the new President, John Kennedy, with an admiration which developed rapidly into hero-worship. For the British Shadow Chancellor, the young President incorporated all the political virtues. Here was the 'new broom sweeping out the cobwebs of hereditary Government', the brash electioneer who could gather to himself, without bothering with Congress and the Senate, a gang of like-minded intellectuals to assist him in Governmental decisions. Kennedy could absorb vast volumes of detail with incredible speed. He was energetic, vital, technocratic – vain and sentimental. The image which he created, fostered so lovingly by the prince of sycophants, Theodore White, fascinated Wilson as no politician had fascinated him since Sir Stafford Cripps.

Suddenly all Wilson's inherent anti-Americanism, dating back to the 1949 devaluation crisis, passed from him. In his speeches both as Shadow Chancellor and as shadow Foreign Secretary, the former citadel of capitalism and militarism became the bright land of purposive dynamism.

In a crucial debate on economic affairs he told the Commons:

Now in America, under a new and youthful President, they are flexing their muscles once again. They are looking to new frontiers, while this tired, discredited, caste-ridden Government, boasting of nothing but a certain amount of Edwardian elegance, allows Britain to lag behind (7 February 1961).

Wilson's year as Shadow Foreign Secretary was dominated by speeches in praise of American foreign policy. He carefully avoided detailed analysis of American policy in the Congo and in Cuba and excused American policy on China ('the total reversal of American China policy is not a practical possibility at the moment'). But the basis of his speeches was praise. On 24 May 1962 he delivered himself of a panegyric on American foreign policy everywhere.

On Laos:

The American position today has considerably changed. . . . I am completely convinced of American sincerity in this matter of attempting to secure this coalition Government . . . I think there may be some plot, but I personally do not believe that the US Government are in any way involved.

On Thailand:

The United States was quite right and so are we.

On Berlin:

The hopeful feature is that America's firm reply to Dr Adenauer has made it clear to the Russians for the first time that American policy in Europe is not dictated by Dr Adenauer. That is a welcome development from the days of Foster Dulles.

Even the Cuban crisis that autumn did not detract from Wilson's support for the new American Government. 'We should welcome,' he lectured the Commons, 'President Kennedy's rejection of the characterization of the Cuban confrontation as Good versus Bad' (31 October 1962).

His job as Shadow Foreign Secretary gave Wilson much more chance to visit America and to speak to American leaders. He was in America when the news of Gaitskell's death reached him, and he lost no opportunity, after becoming Leader of the Party, to visit America again. His visit in the spring of 1963 was put across by Wilson's public relations staff as the visit of a Kennedy man, with Kennedy ideas, discussing the future of the world, and the US–British relationship, in modern, purposive terms. In a long interview with the *New York Times* on 1 April, Wilson stressed:

The centre of our foreign policy is NATO. Labour's *main point of difference* with the Conservative Government is a feeling that Britain is not making a sufficient contribution to NATO in conventional terms.

His speech to the Washington Press Club and his genial behaviour, particularly to journalists, drew the warmest praise. A leader-writer in the *New York Times* wrote:

Mr Wilson is trying out some eloquent vows of affection for the United States and President Kennedy's policies. Mr Wilson has confirmed reports from London suggesting a gradual shift in his views from the extreme Left towards the centre of Labour sentiment (2 April 1963).

Wilson and Kennedy found, as expected, that they did get on together; that their attitudes to politics and industry were remarkably similar and that they shared many personal qualities, such as an excellent memory and the ability to absorb themselves in detail. Ever since Eisenhower's first victory in 1952, it had been taken for granted that the American Government preferred the Tories in power. Now, for the first time since Attlee and Truman, it was clear that the White House showed a distinct preference for Labour.

Kennedy's death in November 1963 was therefore, in more than one sense, a tragedy for Wilson. Not only did he feel a genuine personal loss. Kennedy's successor, Johnson, had little in common with Wilson, and his generally reactionary background, education and early business life prejudiced him the other way. Wilson never again recaptured the rapport which he had had with Kennedy. Yet he continued to foster the notion that Democratic America wanted a Labour Britain. He stressed on every possible occasion that Labour's policy to abandon the independent deterrent – the only foreign policy of the Labour Party which differed in any meaningful way from that of the Tories – was wholly approved by Washington and the White House. They too, Wilson urged, wanted more conventional forces from Britain and less 'vain nuclear posturings'.

Though Wilson's enthusiasm for the 'new America' became less apparent than in the days of that country's 'youthful leader', he scrupulously avoided the anti-American rhetoric at which he had been so expert for so long. Only occasionally, with the odd reference, were the old passions aroused.

At the Labour Party Conference of 1963, for instance, at the height of his technocratic triumph, there was still a glimpse of the old Harold:

> Advanced capitalist countries are maintaining full employment today only by virtue of vast arms orders and panic would be the order of the day in Wall Street and other stock markets the day peace breaks out.

Only once in his short period as Opposition leader did Harold Wilson allow his former antagonism to United States policy to suppress his better judgement.

In June 1964, the American Chrysler Corporation bought a 49 per cent shareholding in the British car firm, Rootes Motors. Under the agreement, Chrysler nominated three of the seven directors. An assurance was given by Chrysler that they were not seeking overall control of Rootes and a spokesman for Rootes told *The Times*: 'We can be quite confident there will be no change in control.'

Wilson was furious. In an angry speech at St Helens, he scoffed:

> We shall not know more about control than we know now, not forgetting that when the American firm concerned took a minority interest in a leading French firm [SIMCA] it was not long before that minority interest became a majority controlling interest. Mr Heath [then Minister for Trade and Industry] should not forget that a great deal of taxpayers' money went into the Rootes plant at Linwood. What is going to happen to that? Everyone recognizes the central role of the motor car industry in production and employment and we must view with concern the fact that more and more of it is falling into foreign hands. We are entitled to know – and I challenge Sir Alec Douglas Home to tell us – which firms they will guarantee – if by any mischance they remain in office – will not be allowed to fall into the hands of either financial manipulators in this country or American, German or other foreign interests (*Times*, 8 June 1964).

Many of Wilson's colleagues were horrified. For the first time since becoming leader, they felt, he had made a serious mistake.

Shadow Chancellor James Callaghan begged Wilson not to raise the matter centrally in Parliament. Other colleagues urged him to recognize that Rootes would certainly perish without capital investment from Chrysler and to attack the Chrysler stake was tantamount to endangering the jobs of thousands of men, some of them in marginal seats.

Yet Wilson insisted that the matter be raised in Parliament, and that Callaghan himself criticize the Chrysler investment. The Tory Chancellor made the most of a fine opportunity to attack the Labour front-bench for putting sectarian nationalism before full employment. Even then, Wilson returned to the attack, though less frontally, at a meeting at Derby:

> The Tories in their present mood have shown that if United States Steel or Krupps were to make a take-over bid for one of our big steel companies, they would fall over themselves to accept it (*Times*, 15 June 1964).

Despite this lapse, however, Harold Wilson and his colleagues remained consistently loyal to the American Government and the 'Americanized society' which had so revolted him in the fifties. On the issue of the war in Vietnam, which increased in ferocity soon after the assassination of Premier Diem in 1963, the Labour leadership remained strangely silent. Only by the odd question or emphasis did Wilson suggest that Labour took a different view of the Vietnam war from that of the Tories. On 30 June 1964, for instance, Wilson asked whether Sir Alec Douglas Home if the Prime Minister would 'make it clear – as we asked him to make it clear in March – that he would not support any extension of the war into North Vietnam'.

Yet throughout this period all Wilson's old rhetoric about the 'revolution in Asia' and about 'being on the side of the peoples in their revolution, not on the side of their oppressors', his enthusiasm for the Geneva Agreements, his pride at Britain's role as co-chairman, his horror at the American breach of the Agreements, his demands for Vietnamese elections – all these had vanished.

Any remote doubts which might have worried Wilson about American attitudes and American policies must have been dispelled almost as soon as he gained power by the discovery that the

Americans were opposed to the devaluation of sterling. So opposed, in fact, that they were prepared, apparently indefinitely, to bale Britain out of balance of payments and sterling crises with massive loans. This was no doubt, for Harold Wilson, yet another manifestation of what he himself had described, in relation to Marshall Aid, as 'the far-sighted generosity of the American people'. Just as Marshall Aid had brought with it the right of the United States economically to penetrate the sterling area and the lucrative markets of the Commonwealth, so the American loans and promises of loans strengthened what used to be called 'the special relationship' between the two countries.

On 6 December, six weeks after he had assumed office, Wilson set off for Washington with one of the biggest retinues ever to accompany a Prime Minister on a trip abroad. He clearly regarded the confrontation with the American President as crucial to the whole of Labour's foreign policy – a foundation for the rebuilding of a 'special relationship' in a constructive and radical form. To his surprise, however, Johnson was abrupt, almost rude. He harped again and again on the sterling crisis and the dangers to the international monetary system in a British devaluation. He reminded Wilson that while in crisis Britain depended almost entirely on American support to keep sterling strong, and urged the British Prime Minister to construct a foreign policy in keeping with Britain's economic situation. Wilson gave assurances that Britain's 'commitments' in the Far East, the 'defence' of Singapore and other expensive idiosyncrasies of Empire, would scrupulously be maintained. Above all, he promised support for the American cause in Vietnam. In return, the President agreed to reconsider the Kennedy plan for a multi-lateral nuclear NATO force, with multi-national teams manning nuclear submarines in the Atlantic. Instead, Wilson proposed an Atlantic Nuclear Force, which excluded the Germans and the French. The British contribution to the ANF, promised Wilson, would be the V-bomber fleet and the full complement of Polaris submarines, whose building would go ahead as planned. Thus the promised 'renegotiation' of the Nassau agreement turned out to be a proposal to remove 'the German finger from the nuclear trigger', and the explicit promise that Britain should stop making her own nuclear weapons was clearly broken by the decision to continue with the building of the British

Polaris. Moreover, Johnson gave no express pledge that the ANF would be accepted. For a possible, and, as it turned out, illusory advantage, the 'so-called independent so-called nuclear so-called deterrent' continued in manufacture. In spite of Wilson's assurances to a Press Conference that the talks had been 'completely successful', he was more than a little depressed at Johnson's suspicion. According to a typical (and therefore unsubstantiatable) *Sunday Times* Insight report much later, he told an aide, on his return:

> Johnson's gone mad. We'll have to find a new ally (7 May 1967).

Whether or not 'the aide' who leaked this reaction to the *Sunday Times* remembered his lines correctly, the December confrontation did not shake Wilson from his main scheme: that an economic military and diplomatic special relationship with the United States should form the basis of British foreign policy.

That had been the basis of Ernest Bevin's foreign policy from 1945 to 1950 and it had, as Wilson remembered it, worked very well indeed. It had also carried distinct advantages for Britain in the world's council chambers. Wilson recalled with meticulous accuracy the details of Attlee's frantic dash to Washington in order successfully to persuade President Truman not to use atomic weapons in Korea. This story, which has only a slender basis in fact, rapidly became part of the mythology of the Labour leadership and gave rise to a myth more general and more dangerous: that of the 'eyeball-to-eyeball' confrontation. Building up a new partnership with America would, dreamed Wilson, as many supporters of Britain's nuclear deterrent had dreamed before him, enable the British Prime Minister, in times of international crisis, crucially to intervene with the American President and change the course of history.

Henry Brandon (*In the Red*, Deutsch, 1966) reveals, almost in an aside, the first catastrophic attempt by Harold Wilson to follow Attlee into an 'eyeball-to-eyeball' confrontation. The occasion was a similar one – the bombing of North Vietnam in February 1965 after the North Vietnamese attack on an American ship in the gulf of Tongking. On the evening of the bombing Wilson picked up the newly installed 'hot line' to Johnson and begged the President to arrange an 'eyeball-to-eyeball' confrontation in

Washington so that he, Wilson, could intervene to stop the bombing. The President was furious, and rudely cut off the conversation with the harsh comment that adventurism of that kind was out of the question. The decision to bomb North Vietnam had been taken by the President of the United States and had nothing whatever to do with Harold Wilson. The relative failure of this eardrum-to-eardrum confrontation encouraged Wilson to pledge his unconditional support for the American bombing of North Vietnam, and for their entire Vietnam policy.

So far as Her Majesty's Government are concerned, I repeat, as I have said many times before, that we have made absolutely plain our support for the American stand against Communist infiltration into South Vietnam. . . . The people of South Vietnam, like the people of North Vietnam and every other area, are entitled to be able to lead their own lives free of terror, free from the danger of sudden death or from the threat of a Communist take-over, and the Government of South Vietnam are entitled to call in aid allies who could help in that purpose (House of Commons, 1 April 1965).

Almost always, during statements such as these, ghosts rise up in Harold Wilson's mind of arguments which he has put with equal vehemence for the opposite view. On this occasion he must have recalled how he and his friends, ten wasted years previously, had ridiculed talk about 'rights' and 'freedoms' of the Indo-Chinese peoples when they were not permitted to test their rights and freedoms with elections. Now he told the House:

The hope of an early election covering the whole area – particularly if one felt it could or would be conducted in a democratic way – was far too optimistic a hope in the conditions of that area. Democracy was not ingrained in the southern part of the country. Nor could we claim that the then South Vietnam Government fulfilled the requirements of democracy in the sense that we understand it. Having regard to the characteristics of the country in the North, conditions were not there for an election as we in this House would understand a democratic election (1 April 1965).

So clear a refutation of the arguments for elections which he had put ten years previously warmed the hearts of President Johnson's administration, which had decided to pursue the war as relentlessly as the military situation demanded. Harold Wilson, moreover, continued to insist on keeping troops 'East of Suez' and maintain Britain's allegedly peace-keeping role all over the world. Some 70,000 'peace-keeping' troops were duly despatched to Borneo and Sarawak to defend the borders drawn up by Duncan Sandys when he was inventing the most bizarre of all his Federations – Malaysia.

Somewhat naturally, perhaps, President Johnson's suspicions of Harold Wilson and his Labour administration decreased. Wilson's visit to Washington in December of 1965 marked a new peak in the relationship between the two men and the two Governments. Johnson was delighted with Wilson's assessment of the world situation, and Wilson told the Commons on his return:

We have reached a clearer understanding than probably at any other time since the Second World War (21 December 1965).

There was also:

Complete agreement in Washington with the British Government's decision to continue to maintain a world-wide defence role, particularly to fulfil those commitments which, for reasons of history, geography, Commonwealth association and the like, we, and virtually we alone, are best fitted to undertake.

Two months later, his admiration for President Johnson knew no bounds:

I made clear then the desire of the American Government to bring this fighting to an end and I am absolutely convinced about the sincerity of the President in this matter. I could not be more convinced about anything (House of Commons, 8 February 1966).

The above speech on Vietnam represented the foreign policy of the Labour Party as it fought the 1966 election – almost total allegiance to America. The 'special relationship' was still the core of Wilson's foreign policy. When the 1966 election result was announced in America, Johnson took special trouble to add a note of personal congratulation to the formal one drawn up by the White House bureaucracy.

Almost immediately, however, the special relationship was threatened by another sterling crisis and the renewed propaganda of the Common Marketeers. In July, the Americans bombed oil installations in and around Hanoi and Haiphong, slaughtering

North Vietnamese civilians on a large scale for the first time. Cleverly timing the debate to coincide with the visit of M. Pompidou, the French Prime Minister, Wilson disassociated the British Government from the bombings. Even so, his speech was cautious. He attacked what he called the 'cynical attitude' of his former friend, Chou En Lai, and repeated his conviction that the American presence in Vietnam was entirely justified.

In July 1966, however, as he was forced to jettison all his economic policies in order to maintain the special relationship, Wilson must have looked back with some misgivings, if not frustration, at the development of his foreign policy and the economic *cul de sac* into which it had led him. Nearly two years of unequivocal support for the Americans, of praise and panegyric from both sets of leaders and of blind agreement with policies in South East Asia, San Domingo, the Congo and almost everywhere else had not enabled Harold Wilson to shape history in the council chambers of the world. Despite Johnson's flattery, the 'eyeball-to-eyeball' dream had not come true. Worse than ever, the economic dependence on America had led him into the most severe deflation since the war.

In the search for a substitute policy, there were many documents at Wilson's disposal, notably the pamphlet *In Place of Dollars*, by Harold Wilson, published in 1952, and a host of other articles and speeches by the same author reiterating the theme that American domination over the British economy could lead one way only – to disaster. The progress of one firm in particular must have jogged his memory about all those warnings. Rootes Motors, still under British management, had failed to take advantage of its new structure, and the investment funds necessary to keep the firm in the international motor-car rat-race were not available to the family firm which controlled it. The Chrysler Corporation were prepared to make the investment funds available, but, not unreasonably, only on condition that they took over full control of the firm. In the Cabinet and other discussions on Chrysler's bid, Anthony Wedgwood Benn, the Minister of Technology, backed initially by Wilson, fought for a single, massive British motor-car company which would absorb Rootes. Leylands and the British Motor Corporation were approached with the idea, without success. Finally, the inevitable was accepted and permission to sell out to Chrysler, with a face-saving £15m. investment and representation on the Board for the Government-owned Industrial Reorganization Corporation, was granted.[1]

Did Harold Wilson remember his vitriolic attacks on his Tory predecessors for selling out Rootes to the Americans? Certainly the Chrysler purchase of Rootes was the signal for a spate of anti-American rhetoric such as Wilson had not uttered since Kennedy was elected six years previously.

On the day that the Rootes take-over was announced, Wilson told a lunch of businessmen and politicians in Rome:

While Her Majesty's Government are loyal to NATO, we do not believe there is anything in NATO which requires us to accept the domination of European industrial and economic life by American industrial agencies (*Daily Mail*, 18 January 1967).

And, six days later, in Strasbourg:

Loyalty to the Atlantic alliance must never mean an industrial helotry, under which we in Europe produce only the conventional apparatus of a modern economy, while becoming increasingly dependent on American business for the sophisticated apparatus which will call the industrial tune in the seventies and eighties (*Daily Telegraph*, 24 January 1967).

This sort of language marked all Wilson's foreign policy statements during the remaining winter and spring of 1967. When the Russian Premier, a personal friend of Wilson's from his Board of Trade days, Alexei Kosygin, visited Britain in February 1967, Wilson made a last, almost desperate bid to invoke the 'eyeball-to-eyeball' principle. Cornering Kosygin in Claridges hotel after a dinner, he urged upon him an anodyne draft stating 'general principles' for a cease fire in Vietnam. Johnson was contacted on the 'hot line' and agreed, in some bad temper, to consider the proposals. But by the time Johnson came back with an answer Kosygin had gone to bed. The Vietnam truce to celebrate the (Chinese) New Year was duly called off. Hostilities re-opened and chances of a peace initiative vanished. Johnson, rather than Kosygin, had ruined Wilson's initiative, and the 'eardrum-to-eardrum' confrontation had failed again.

1. Benn's dream eventually came true. BMC and Leylands merged in January, 1968.

Wilson duly hardened his determination to discover an alternative to Britain's 'industrial helotry', and relations between the two leaders deteriorated. By the next sterling crisis, the Americans had grown accustomed to the idea of devaluation, and Wilson's last card – the threat to devalue – was no longer a trump. Reluctantly, the Americans agreed to a devaluation too small properly to solve the British payments problem, but small enough to enable the US Treasury to beat off speculation against the dollar. Johnson, however, could hardly contain his fury when George Brown arrived in Washington with the news that, as part of the devaluation package, Britain was abandoning her 'East of Suez' role, and withdrawing troops from the Far East and the Persian Gulf, and, for good measure, was cancelling the contract to buy fifty American F111 jet fighters. The President and his advisers had other economic problems, notably concerning their balance of payments deficit, and in January 1968 they announced a squeeze on overseas investment by American firms. Britain, Japan and other countries whose Governments supported the Americans in Vietnam were among the 'specially favoured' countries, but Wilson reacted angrily by threatening to reimpose the export rebate on British exports. Clearly his faith in the special relationship had been dimmed, if not extinguished.

2. The Common Market

The famous speech by Sir Winston Churchill, then leader of the Opposition, at Fulton in 1946 in which he argued for a 'new Europe' to arise, united, out of the ashes of the war had little influence with the post-war Labour Government. In the process of rebuilding British industry and shifting priorities from war to peace production, the vast market of the Commonwealth, almost unaffected by the war, provided a useful and sufficient outlet. The question of a customs union for Europe was seldom, if ever, discussed, and even Sir Winston and the Opposition front bench did not regard it as a central economic issue. While President of the Board of Trade, Wilson was instrumental in the signing of the treaty of economic cooperation with Western Europe, which took place with some ceremony in April 1948. In his speech on the Budget on 16 April 1951, only four days before he resigned from the Government, Wilson boasted of the Government's achievements in establishing greater European unity:

When the economic history of these past years comes to be written, a great place will be given to what Marshall aid and the assistance from Canada had achieved in helping Western Europe to save itself by its own exertions, and not less in providing a degree of economic cooperation through the OEEC never before seen in the Western European Community.

Ernest Kay (p. 49) tells us that his hero

steered Britain into signing, along with France, Belgium, Holland and Luxembourg, the first Brussels treaty for economic cooperation; and denied categorically that he was opposed to a customs union for Europe.

But Wilson's own attitude to a free market in Europe at that time was probably best summed up by a speech he made to his constituents in Ormskirk in January 1948, shortly after becoming President of the Board of Trade. A member of the audience asked him whether or not the British Government had missed an opportunity to establish a customs union for Europe. Wilson replied:

No, we did not miss an opportunity. There are enormous difficulties and problems. There must be a will for a political union before it is possible to get an economic union. I hope the time will come when there will be a customs union for all Europe, linking up East and West. I would much prefer that to a customs union for Western Europe (*Ormskirk Advertiser*, 15 January 1948).

Conventional ideas about Imperial Preference and the sterling area persisted throughout the early years of the 1951–5 Conservative administration. Between the years 1951 and 1956, European Free Trade was never a central political issue. Both major parties and even the Liberals watched with patronizing indifference while the other industrial countries of Europe prepared an Economic Federation.

This complacency was shattered by the meeting in 1956 at Messina of representatives of the six major industrial countries of Western Europe, where final proposals for the signing of a Common Market Treaty were drawn up. The meeting panicked the Conservative Government into proposals for a loosely knit

European Free Trade Area, incorporating the Six, Britain and some of the smaller countries. In a debate on the 26 November 1956, these proposals were submitted to the House of Commons, and Wilson spoke on them for the Labour Party.

His speech, perhaps necessarily, failed to make it clear whether or not the Labour Party favoured the idea. 'What we are debating this afternoon,' he said, obviously in some relief, 'is not a common market or a free trade area. It is an area of tariff-free trade and that is as far as it goes. The Chancellor said at the beginning of his speech, and I think we agree with him, that we are not contemplating adherence to the Messina scheme, or to the Messina "six-power club".' On the other hand: 'We must go into the talks not in any mood of obstruction or delay, but positively, in the hope of working out a European arrangement. Can we afford to stay out? I am sure the answer is that we cannot afford to stay out.'

Wilson then laid down stringent conditions for the negotiations. Britain, he said, should retain and expand all the existing free-trade arrangements in the Commonwealth; agriculture and horticulture should be excluded from the talks; all rights to plan the economy and to maintain balance of payments surpluses should be protected; there should be no cheap labour and no cartels.

In the same vein, a few months later, Wilson wrote an article for the right-wing *Sunday Dispatch:*

There is no suggestion that Britain should join the Common Market. For one thing we have vast trading connexions not only with the Commonwealth, which accounts for half our trade, but with almost every other country in every part of the globe. It would be impossible for us to keep our intricate system of Imperial Preference if we were part of a European trading scheme which involved a single uniform tariff on each item we imported from the outside world (27 January 1957).

Labour Party policy on Europe did not take any definite shape before the 1959 election. In a big Commons debate on European Free Trade in February 1959, Wilson spoke more favourably about free trade in Europe. He pointed out that exports of new consumer goods in the Common Market would increase very much faster than would British exports of similar goods if Britain remained outside the community. He warned the Government not to conceive of the Free Trade Area as a purely negative, liberal, tariff-free European economy ... it ought to be positive, expanding and based not merely on the doctrine or theory of full employment but with provision written into the treaty binding each country individually and the group as a whole to take all steps necessary to maintain full employment on the basis of an expanding economy.

The original dreamers and idealists who threw up the Common Market and the EEC have put in these highly realistic ideas for investment banks, social funds, greater credit and the rest.

On the Common Market itself, Wilson expressed 'doubts whether we would be welcomed. If we made an application – and I am not recommending that to the Government – there is some doubt whether it would be accepted.' Nonetheless:

There is a strong desire for a really effective and intimate basis of association between Great Britain, and Scandinavian countries on the one hand, and the community of Common Market countries on the other.

When the re-elected Tory Government announced plans for a smaller European Free Trade Area, incorporating Scandinavia, the neutral countries of central Europe and Portugal, Wilson, without opposing it, called it 'a second-best, a perhaps useful but scarcely adequate substitute for a more generalized European Free Trade Area'.

In another debate in July 1960, Wilson outlined the two arguments on Europe which were pulling him (and the Labour leadership) in different directions. On the one hand:

There is a real danger that Western Europe will attract more 'know-how' and new techniques, and in a world of rapid scientific advance, there is always a real danger that if Britain is not in the main stream we shall become, relatively speaking, a backwater. Some of the investments on sheer technical grounds have got to be on a vast scale. They are capital intensive, so if they are sited in the Six the rest of Europe might be neglected. ... The Six have created a virile, expanding, dynamic community ... and some of the arguments used two or three years ago against joining the Community are less strong now than they seemed then.

The agricultural objection, thought Wilson, and those relating to social services were 'no longer true'. And the Commonwealth had 'something to gain as well as to lose'.

These, said Wilson, were 'formidable arguments', but the balance of the argument was 'perhaps the other way'. First there was the problem of Commonwealth preference; secondly, conflicting commitments with EFTA; and thirdly, the possibility that planning control might move from Westminster.

Wilson's speech in 1960 shows him in a genuine dilemma, prejudiced neither one way nor the other, seeing advantages and disadvantages in both courses of action. He was greatly attracted by the expanding, 'virile' new market of the Six, but resented the encroachment on British institutions like the Commonwealth and Parliament.

Over the next three years, Wilson's position on the Common Market hardened into virulent opposition. Although he invariably included the *caveat* that 'if we can get the terms, then we go in', he emphasized the terms with such force that no one reading on listening to his speeches could doubt that he was opposed to the 'European idea'. In his early speeches on the subject he still agreed that 'in terms of our own industry and our trade in Europe we may gain from being in Europe'. But soon even these concessions to the argument were left out. By the end of the period, he was attacking the Market without quarter.

The Conservative application for Common Market entry was made on 31 July 1961. The Labour Party was recovering from internal dissension, and badly needed an issue with which to fight the Opposition with Left and Right united. Hugh Gaitskell, who himself had been doubtful on the issue for some years, made up his mind to stress the conditions for entry rather than support the Conservative initiative, and, in his speech to the 1962 Party Conference, declared himself in all but words opposed to the Common Market venture. The mass of the Party rallied to his philanthropy and his chauvinism. In one much-quoted passage, Gaitskell brought the conference to its feet with a historical call to arms:

We at least do not intend to forget Vimy Ridge and Gallipoli!

None cheered more loudly than Harold Wilson, the Party Chairman. When Gaitskell went on to suggest that joining the Common Market could involve the sacrifice of 'a thousand years of history' (taking Britain back to the days of Alfred the Great), the conference and its chairman were moved to scenes of near-delirium.

The new-found unity of the Labour Party on the Common Market issues, coupled with the obvious difficulties encountered by the Conservative negotiators in Brussels, helped to convince Harold Wilson. As Shadow Chancellor and as Shadow Foreign Secretary, he marshalled a vast array of arguments against entry, which increased in vehemence as the negotiations floundered.

First, there were the conventional arguments.

On agriculture:

The agricultural Common Market is restrictive, autarchic, and Schachtian and is an offence to the trading interests of the free world. It will divide, not unite. We should have no part in it (House of Commons, 13 December 1962).

Or on the Commonwealth:

The Commonwealth, as we know it today, cannot survive if Britain continues her breakneck rush into Europe on these unacceptable terms (*Sunday Express*, 16 September 1962).

Or on the economy and wages:

Although some employers look forward to a bigger market, many look forward to it as a means of depressing wage standards by the back door method when they have failed at the front (Annual Conference of Boilermakers Society, 2 June 1962).

There are some employers who are looking forward to the Common Market primarily as a means of strengthening their hands in a showdown with labour ... as the means of enforcing the general wage freeze which the Government has been trying to get ever since the Prime Minister was Chancellor of the Exchequer (House of Commons, 7 June 1962).

Or even on defence:

The breathless rush to get into Europe on any terms has caused the Government to support the French deterrent (Letter in *The Times*, 20 October 1962).

Then there were the sentimental arguments, the appeal to the chauvinism which Gaitskell had so successfully evoked at Brighton. In one remarkable and much quoted sentence, Wilson managed to combine anti-German prejudice with anti-consumer-goods prejudice with old-fashioned military chauvinism.

We are not entitled to sell our friends and kinsmen down the river for a problematical and marginal advantage in selling washing machines in Düsseldorf (3 August 1961).

Nor did Harold Wilson forget the starving millions:

The Party is a moral crusade or it is nothing . . . and we are not going to join any rich man's club if it means turning our back on the rest of the world (Chairman's address, Labour Party Conference, 1962).

There were also constant references to the danger of 'national humiliation', warnings which were based on the knowledge of a man who knows his history:

I do not remember the Lord High Admiral of those days, Lord Howard of Effingham, negotiating with another power for the weapons with which to defeat the Armada; or saying that we must have them if we were to have an independent defence policy (House of Commons, 13 December 1962).

But probably what convinced Harold Wilson most of the case against the Common Market, apart from his admiration for Kennedy and his confidence in the 'American alternative', was the feeling that the Common Market threatened the powers of Parliament, and that a Labour Government's powers to act would be trimmed by European Assemblies. Quoting Dr Erhard, then the German Finance Minister, that 'a nationally planned economy is incompatible with the Common Market', Wilson inveighed against the concept of supra-national European control:

The plain fact is that the whole conception of the Treaty of Rome is anti-planning, or at any rate anti-national planning. . . . What planning is contemplated is supra-national, not national, but it is planning for the one purpose of enhancing free competition. . . . One cannot then use the public sector for planning purposes, for the establishment or enforcement of priorities, for anything which involves discrimination against private industry (7 June 1962).

The dominating principle in Wilson's (and Labour's) economic thinking up to that time and up to the 1966 General Election was the belief that Labour could, should and would intervene crucially in the industrial machinery of the nation state in order to make it more efficient and effective. This state capitalism was fundamental to Wilson's political faith. And he rightly saw in the

Treaty of Rome a rejection of state capitalism for free enterprise capitalism. 'Planning' under the Treaty of Rome meant organizing a more efficient atmosphere in which capitalism could prosper. 'Planning' for Harold Wilson meant intervention by the state 'in the national interest', if necessary to change the course of private enterprise. Wilson spoke about the potential corrosion of Parliamentary powers with genuine distaste and even passion. 'Mr Macmillan,' he wrote, suitably in the *Sunday Express* (16 September 1962), 'is seeking to involve us all in a decision which will for all time fetter and cripple the working of our British Parliament, without seeking the authority of those who elect that Parliament.'

Any doubts about these policy statements were very soon dispelled by the French veto on the British application in January 1963. Harold Wilson, by now leader of the Party, pounced on the enfeebled Tories with all his arguments reinforced. In a rash moment he even used the most dangerous word in the politician's dictionary: 'never'.

Never again must a British minister be put in a position of sitting outside in a cold anti-chamber while six European nations decide the fate of his country. We must make it clear that we are not going to have another eighteen months of negotiation as happened last time. One of the tragedies of the negotiations was the impression given by the Government that we were turning our backs on the Commonwealth both economically and politically. A great deal of harm has been done. The future of Britain is in the re-creation of our links with the Commonwealth. We believe that the Government cannot do that now because of the harm that has been done (*Guardian*, 23 February 1963).

And, on May Day, at Coventry:

Last year, the Prime Minister was falling over himself to get into Europe on terms which would have allowed German or other European combines to take over British industries.

From the outset, Harold Wilson threw the Common Market into the forefront of his long election campaign:

Will he [Sir Alec Douglas Home] give a pledge that no Government of which he is the head will consider entering the Common Market on terms which would reduce Britain's freedom to trade with the Commonwealth? I have three times challenged the Prime Minister to state publicly where he stands on this question. His answers have been evasive, equivocal and contradictory. In his by-election he finally settled on a formula which said it would be for Parliament to decide. But he knows perfectly well that Parliament does not decide these things on a free vote (*Daily Telegraph*, 20 January 1964).

The alternative, Wilson made clear, was obvious – a mixture of better terms with America and wider trade with the Commonwealth. On his visit to the United States in March 1964, Wilson gave a Press Conference in Washington. *The Times* correspondent in that city summed up the conference as follows:

His basic assumption – and here he went further than Sir Alec Douglas Home – was that the movement for a United Europe was dead and that future efforts should be devoted to strengthening the Anglo-American relationship in cooperation with the Commonwealth. This was a constant theme. At his Press Conference, Mr Wilson opposed supra-national control and said that Britain did not want to be corralled into Europe.

The Times correspondent noted, however, as Wilson apparently did not, that 'his suspicion of Europe disturbed officials' in the Administration (4 March 1964).

The arguments which Harold Wilson had used against the Common Market while leader of the Opposition continued to be used long after he became Prime Minister. Sir Alec Douglas Home, the Conservative leader, had described the issue as 'a dead duck', and for a long time after becoming Prime Minister Wilson agreed. Indeed throughout the whole of the seventeen months of his first administration, Wilson referred to Europe only in answer to questions. To a questioner at a public meeting in Church House, Westminster, in February 1965, Wilson replied:

Entry into the European Economic Community is at the present time not a real issue. If it were to become one, we should be prepared to consider negotiations for entry if, and only if, we can secure the conditions vital to British interests, vital to Commonwealth interests and vital to the pursuit of an independent foreign policy which we have laid down and which we have all agreed (*Daily Telegraph*, 21 February 1965).

In the House of Commons, the questioners were all Conservative back-benchers who put entry into the Market top of the country's economic priorities. One such was Neil Marten, who was told on 25 February 1965:

There is no question whatever of our being invited or of having any opportunity for discussing at present the question of adherence to the Treaty of Rome or in other ways to join the European Economic Community.

Another was Sir Richard Nugent, who asked in April about a statement by the Foreign Secretary, Michael Stewart, in the United States, which appeared to favour entry into Europe. Wilson repeated firmly:

There is no question whatever of Britain either seeking or being asked to seek entry into the Common Market in the immediately foreseeable future ... the terms on which the last Government tried to crawl in were completely unacceptable to the Commonwealth ... they would involve the complete disruption of Commonwealth trade.

In a debate on the Commonwealth in June 1965, Wilson jeered at Sir Alec Douglas Home for raising the Common Market issue, so recently a 'dead duck':

What I said in the election was what Hugh Gaitskell said at Brighton, what I said in Rome and what I said at EFTA last week. We have said the conditions on which we are prepared to go into the Common Market. There is a difference between that and going in on terms which would totally disrupt foreign trade. The Rt Hon. Gentleman is prepared to sacrifice the Commonwealth for going in. We are not ... (1 June 1965).

In August, again in answer to questions, Wilson dismissed any question of entry. As late as December 1965, only three months before the General Election, Wilson returned to the issue of Common Market entry, again not on his initiative but in answer to questions from a pack of young Conservative MPs who were howling for the Market at any price. Nicholas Ridley asked about a speech made by Michael Stewart, Foreign Secretary, which made distinctly favourable noises about the Common Market. The speech, said Ridley, was 'inconsistent with the Labour Party's five principles'. Wilson insisted that there was absolutely no question of entry into Europe while her agricultural tariff policy threatened primary producers in the Commonwealth.

In February 1966, when Patrick Jenkin, Conservative MP for Woodford, again asked him about European entry, Wilson, very slightly, but crucially, shifted the emphasis:

I hope that honourable members would agree that we should join if we can get the right conditions to safeguard British interests . . . the position is that we shall go in if we can get the right terms (House of Commons, 10 February 1966).

Already, then, before the 1966 election Wilson's attitude and reaction to the Common Market was less hostile than in the past. According to the *Sunday Times* Insight investigation on his conversion, Wilson told George Brown in late January 1966: 'George, I've got news for you. You'll be startled by what I'm going to say. We're going in' (7 May 1967).

There were, at root, two main reasons for this change of mind. The first was the conversion of Michael Stewart at the Foreign Office. The prodigious efforts of Sir Con O'Neill, Permanent Secretary at the Foreign Office and for a long time a European diplomat in Brussels, to persuade Stewart of the case for the Market had had miraculous results. The promotions of Roy Jenkins and Anthony Crosland to the Cabinet, respectively in December and January, 1965, shifted the anti-European bias of Wilson's original cabinet. As George Brown's obsession with home economic policy eased, he redoubled his former efforts to push Britain into the Common Market. Former anti-Marketeers, or neutrals, notably Richard Crossman and Denis Healey, made it clear that much of their former antagonism was on the wane. The shift of emphasis in Wilson's answer to a question in February 1966 probably reflected the feeling in the Cabinet more than any fundamental change in Wilson's personal views. The theory, proposed by the *Sunday Times* survey, that his mind was, at that time, already made up is not borne out by the facts. Almost all Wilson's big speech on foreign affairs on 21 December 1965 was devoted to Rhodesia and the American alliance. His meeting with Johnson that month had been the most successful yet, and he had told the House 'there is a clearer understanding than probably at any time since the Second World War'. As he prepared for the 1966 election, Wilson's mind was still not made up on the Market issue. He saw the force of some of his colleagues' argument, but still believed that a partnership with America and the Commonwealth provided the best possible basis for British economic policy.

In the early weeks of the election, the Common Market was hardly mentioned. That was how Harold Wilson wanted it. As long as it could be kept out of the controversy, he could concentrate solely on the thirteen wasted years and the seventeen magnificent months; on the Tories' plans to create unemployment and dismantle the Welfare State. The Labour Manifesto referred to Europe in only the briefest terms, making entry conditional on the preservation of existing arrangements for Commonwealth agricultural products.

Then, unexpectedly, at a Ministerial Conference of the Western European Union, the French delegates made speeches which indicated a softening in the French approach to British entry. Immediately, Edward Heath demanded an enthusiastic Government response to the speeches, or an admission that Labour were opposed to the European idea. Wilson replied with a speech at Bristol which indicated clearly that, although he was keeping his options open, he was still opposed to British entry on the Conservative terms:

> The Government's position, as we have stated again and again, is that we are ready to join if suitable safeguards for British interests, and our Commonwealth interests, can be negotiated. But, unlike the Conservative leader, we shall not proceed on the basis of an unconditional acceptance of whatever terms are offered us. . . . Given a fair wind, we will negotiate our way into the Common Market, head held high, not crawl in. And we shall go in if the conditions are right.

The Tory proposals, warned Wilson, meant huge increases in the cost of living, wages and export costs; an unacceptable increase in our export bill 'which would ruin any chance of paying our way', and 'a total disruption' of the Commonwealth.

The condition which Wilson stressed more anxiously than ever before however was that entry should only be sought from a position of economic strength. Despite the 'strong industrial arguments' for entry,

unless we continue, as we have done in the past eighteen months, to strengthen sterling and our balance of payments, then the Common Market choice is simply between being a backwater inside Europe and backwater outside Europe (*Guardian*, 19 March 1966).

Most of the press noted that Wilson's attitude towards Europe was more friendly than in the past. But the unanimous view of the British speech was that it held over an application for entry to the Common Market for an indefinite period. Certainly, Mr Heath and his colleagues took the speech as an opportunity to 'run' the issue of Europe centrally in the Conservative campaign, thus earning the plaudits of the *Sunday Times* Insight team, who somehow discovered that the decision to 'run' Europe had 'set the campaign alight'. Certainly, too, the left-wing anti-Common Market section of the Labour Party jubilantly concluded that Wilson had slammed the door on the Common Market.

Wilson preferred the issue closed, and even issued instructions to major Ministers and campaign organizers that the Market issue should be kept well in the background. No doubt Wilson noted that despite the singular failure of the Market issue to catch the electorate's imagination or their votes, this was the one issue upon which Conservative policy was different, and, in the suffocating terms which Wilson himself uses, 'more dynamic'.

In the Cabinet constructed for the long Parliamentary session after the election, Wilson paid lip service to the growing pro-Europe feeling by appointing George Thomson Chancellor of the Duchy of Lancaster, with special responsibilities for Europe. Mr Thomson was instructed to move around the European capitals 'sensing European opinion' and 'forging new links' between Europe and Britain. In an article in the *Sunday Times* on 1 May, James Margach reported:

> With hand on heart the most dedicated Europeans in the Cabinet will tell you that 'Harold is now the most distinguished convert to the great ideal and vision of the United Europe'. But who says so? Certainly not the Prime Minister himself.

Wilson's approach remained equivocal. Certainly the arguments for entry seemed to grow with the weeks. His Cabinet was now almost entirely pro-Europe. Only Douglas Jay, Fred Peart and Herbert Bowden remained firm against entry. Patrick Gordon Walker, not the most inflexible of politicians, had openly declared that Britain would be in Europe before the next Parliament. The new Labour intake included many bright Fabian graduates who had no time for the old Gaitskellite sentimentality towards the Commonwealth and national sovereignty. Even the Labour Left, until then solid against the Common Market, showed signs of a split. Eric Heffer, formerly a militant Liverpool shop steward, and Paul Rose, a young left-wing MP from Manchester, both argued that the anti-Europe stand by the Left was chauvinist and narrow-minded. Heffer and Rose were joined by a select few from the Party's centre-Left.

Further, perhaps even more importantly, the attitudes of General de Gaulle, his nationalism, his suspicion of the supra-national idealism of the Treaty of Rome, and his opposition to supra-national political organizations must have had some attraction for Harold Wilson.

All these arguments pushed Wilson in the direction of Europe. In his speech on the Queen's speech he reported:

In the reorganization after the election, we have now made full provision for ensuring that any opportunities that do present themselves in Europe can be quickly seized upon so that they can be evaluated. We shall neglect no opportunity of finding out what those opportunities are (21 April 1966).

But on the other hand:

It looks at present as if it will be some time before any serious opportunity will emerge of our being able to engage in any effective negotiations for British entry.

Four days later, he was again called to answer for a speech of his Foreign Secretary about Europe, this time from the left-wing Mrs Renee Short. There was, said Mrs Short, 'growing concern in and out of the House at the speeches that are being made by Ministers implying that Britain's choice is made and that our entry is decided upon'. Mr Wilson: 'The five conditions are still operative, but there have been certain changes in Europe itself, not least in relation to EFTA, which make some of them no longer such impediments as they seemed to be $3\frac{1}{2}$ years ago' (House of Commons, 5 May 1966).

On 10 and 19 May, he answered further sets of questions from all parts of the House and managed with some difficulty to steer a middle course between the views of the veteran reactionary, Emmanuel Shinwell, who opposed European entry, and the young reactionary, Stanley Henig, who supported it. Throughout this period he shrunk from a final decision. As so often before, he kept both options open, until the pressure of events forced him to declare himself. In this case, the decisive factor was almost certainly the visit of the French Prime Minister, M. Pompidou, on 7 and 8 July and the economic crisis which followed.

The various reports of the Pompidou talks differ in detail but on the main point they are unanimous: that the bulk of the talks were taken up with bitter controversy about the prospects for British entry into the Common Market. Both sides were surprised – the French by the determination with which the British argued the case for British entry: the British by the toughness of the French conditions. The French, driven by their obsession to damage the dollar through the pound, insisted that entry into the Market would not be possible without a savage sterling devaluation followed by drastic deflationary measures. No doubt M. Pompidou, himself a banker, pointed out the different experiences of the two French devaluations of 1957 and 1958. The first had not been accompanied by deflation, and had failed. The second had included the most drastic attack on home living standards in France since the war, and had succeeded. Action like that, urged Pompidou, might make Britain a suitable candidate for the European family of nations.

Whatever the reaction of George Brown, it is a fair guess that Wilson was horrified by these demands, which involved a combination of the two economic policies he had dreaded and derided most. Yet, still, he urged the French not to close the door, to wait awhile and see if some compromise proposals could be agreed upon.

Almost as soon as Pompidou returned to Paris, the irresistible wave of sterling-selling started – much of it from Paris. French diplomatic gossip in Europe insisted that Britain had deceived the French about European entry, the pound dropped further still, and Wilson was forced into the deflationary measures he had so consistently opposed. The reaction, almost certainly, was to revive in his brain the grim prophecies which he himself had made fifteen years previously about dependence on the American economy.

The analysis which he outlined to the House of Commons of the nature of the economic crisis rang all the old bells about dependence on the dollar. On 20 July he referred to the 'American withdrawal of Euro-dollars' and the high interest rates in America made necessary, in part at least, by the Vietnam war. A week later, he expanded a little:

The big international companies with American roots have been under the strongest pressure from their own Governments, as a result of the United States balance of payments position, to transfer profits more rapidly to the United States and certainly to keep their sterling holdings to a minimum. In a very real sense, sterling has been in the front line, taking part of the attack which is basically, if not equally, directed against the dollar (House of Commons, 27 July 1966).

The argument was that economic dependence on America – the backbone of British foreign policy in Wilson's first two years of office – had resulted in the collapse of all his economic policies. Politically, a new initiative abroad was crucial if only to disguise the failures of domestic economic policy. There can be little doubt that the 1966 sterling crisis, and the decisions resulting from it, was the decisive factor in switching Wilson's attention to the grand technological vistas of the European Economic Community.

Even those who had predicted that Harold Wilson would change his mind on the issue of the Common Market had no inkling of the degree to which he would commit himself to entry. The statement announcing that exploratory talks would begin on Britain's application was made on 10 November 1966. Throughout all the following winter and spring Wilson devoted himself almost exclusively to preaching the European cause. Much of his time was spent in visiting Common Market capitals with his Foreign Secretary. At home, and particularly in Parliament, almost all his statements and his answers to questions – he did not speak in a Parliamentary debate from November 1966 to May 1967 – were devoted to the European application.

In the course of this conversion, and by way of explaining it, Wilson stressed three main themes. The first, as already mentioned, was the fear of industrial domination by the Americans. In his speeches about the economic measures of July 1966, he explained that the high interest rates in America were a disincentive to investment in Europe: the 'squeeze on Euro-dollars' indicated all too clearly the 'industrial helotry' to America into which Europe was slipping. 'I had very much in mind,' he told a meeting in Rome, 'the specific factors of the Chrysler–Rootes situation in which there had been a total breakdown of management and where there was no question of selling out a technological industry. The Government have shown that they mean business about this by the way in which we have saved our own computer industry unlike others from the predatory actions of certain American firms.' The unsuccessful attempt by IBM to take over ICT and the entire British computer industry had been one of the decisive factors in switching Wilson's attention away from the Anglo-US partnership of which he originally had dreamed.

This theme persisted through 1967. In April, he complained to the Commons:

> We have not always got the dividends on what we have taught them, and in many cases we are still paying royalties to the Americans for inventions which began in this country (20 April 1967).

And, as late as November, he spoke to the Parliamentary Press Gallery:

> Time is on our side in a narrow sense, but it is not on the side of those who want to take European action to stop the technological and industrial gap between Europe and America widening year by year, indeed month by month. It is not on the side of those whose concern about US domination of our national industries has been shown not by words but by deeds (*Daily Telegraph*, 30 November 1967).

Secondly, the Labour application to enter the Common Market robbed the Conservative Party of their most distinctive policy. Heath's public relations success during the election when he raised the Common Market issue was observed with some irritation by Wilson, and 'dynamic' commitment to the Common Market presented the Tories with an identifiable distinctive policy. It made the Conservatives modernizers, and associated Labour with sentiment. For Labour to hold high the banner of entry into the Common Market was an act of thunder-stealing, and one which greatly appealed to Wilson's political instinct.

Thus Harold Wilson was able magnanimously to patronize Edward Heath's former efforts to negotiate entry for Britain.

> I am not going to make any contrast between this operation and what happened four or five years ago. There were difficulties then which do not exist now; there are difficulties now which did not exist then. The Rt

Hon. Member for Bexley [Mr Heath] faced great difficulties and no one said that sooner than I did when negotiations broke down (*Hon. Members: 'Oh'*). My words are on the record indicating the sympathy that I expressed to the Rt Hon. gentleman at the time. The previous Conservative Government made their effort in their way. We intend to make our approach in our way, and we only hope that, as a result of it, we shall get the answers that most of us want (House of Commons, 10 November 1966).

The achievement of maximum Conservative discomfort by stressing the need for a consensus has always been one of Harold Wilson's favourite tactics while Prime Minister, and, in his treatment of the European issue, he excelled himself.

Yet, as the trips round Europe drew to a close and a decision to apply for membership was taken; and as the cry of N O N! from Paris became louder and louder, one theme in Wilson's speeches and attitudes came to dwarf all the others. It was a theme, which, as he rightly pointed out, he had stressed when Europe was first discussed as a major political issue, though he came to drop it in his years of opposition to the European idea. It was a theme which incorporated two striking aspects of Harold Wilson's politics: his interest in technology and his romantic notions about a new Great Britain.

Wilson first articulated this theme in a speech to the Lord Mayor's banquet at the Guildhall only four days after his decision to seek entry:

We are embarking on an adventure of the kind that enabled merchant venturers of the City of London and other cities in time past to win treasure and influence and power for Britain. We go forward in the same spirit of enterprise today. I believe the tide is right, the time is right, the winds are right to make the effort.

I would like to see a drive to create a new technological inventiveness in Britain and other European countries, to enable Europe on a competitive basis to become more self-reliant and neither dependent on imports nor dominated from outside but basing itself on a competitive indigenous European industries (*Times*, 15 November 1966).

Again and again, throughout the following year, Wilson sang different harmonies to this extravagant theme:

The importance of greater technological strength in Europe, such as could result from our proposals, on hopes of getting a wider Europe both economically and politically played a central part in our discussions in Paris and again in Brussels. This has been more and more one of the chief motifs of these discussions. . . . Technology and Market must go together (speech on visit to Brussels, House of Commons, 2 February 1967).

We discussed the question of a technological community at considerable length and we were agreed about the very great importance of this concept (speech on visit to The Hague, House of Commons, 28 February 1967).

Really effective technological cooperation, the pooling and the creation of new technological products on a joint basis, is possible only if we are in One Market (16 March 1967).

When announcing his decision to negotiate for entry Wilson slipped neatly over the difficulties presented by agriculture and deflected a question as to his conversion. It all, he said, came down to one thing in the end:

The enormous possibilities which an integrated strategy for technology can create. I am glad to say that my right honourable friend and I found that this concept has made a great impact throughout Europe (21 May 1967).

The 'great impact' did not, apparently, have any lasting effect in Paris, where General De Gaulle and his Foreign Minister, M. Couve de Mourville, kept up a barrage of negative replies whenever the issue was raised in public. Wilson replied that he was not taking '*Non*' for an answer, that the British application 'lay on the table', and would stay there until the processes for negotiations as laid down by the Treaty of Rome had been properly exhausted.

'In one sense it can be said that time is on our side,' he told the motor manufacturers on the eve of the Earls Court Motor Show. 'But it is not on the side of all of us in this country and the rest of Europe who believe that the industrial and technological strengthening of Europe is really urgent if Europe is to exert its rightful influence in the counsels of the world' (*Sun*, 18 October 1967).

The only intelligible sense in which time could be said to be on Wilson's side was that the French Government would in time give way to the French Left Federation, which supported Britain's application. Apart from a few odd rumours – one of them originating in the BBC – that General de Gaulle's death was imminent, there was, unhappily for Wilson, no sign of the French Government's collapse. His only answer, therefore, was to muse in still more fanciful terms about the importance of technological co-operation with Europe. In his speech at the Lord Mayor's banquet, in the shadow of the biggest economic crisis since the war, Wilson confidently offered Europe a Technological Institute and tediously listed the twelve points on which this 'exciting project' could advance. Undeterred by devaluation and the total lack of response to his proposals for an Institute, Wilson returned to this theme again and again, notably in a fantastic speech to the leaders of the British export drive only a day after devaluation.

Throughout this technological dream, Wilson's ordinarily unimaginitive language rose to exotic, even poetic heights. In his speech to the European Assembly at Strasbourg in January 1966 he stressed the altruism of the European idea, condemning the notion that economic motives were the only genuine ones behind the movement. In one passage he went so far as to quote Wordsworth:

> [High heaven rejects the lore
> Of nicely-calculated less or more.

And he indicated that the motives for European entry stretched back in historical and traditional ties of brotherhood which outweighed any narrow economic consideration. Unhappily, however, high heaven apart, the French Government were very much impressed by 'nicely calculated less or more', and Britain's chances of entering the Market, as far as they were concerned, were less rather than more. Their almost inevitable veto of the British Market application will, of course, enable Harold Wilson to refer back to his past speeches and once more warn the country against 'the marginal advantage of selling washing machines in Düsseldorf'.

3. The Commonwealth

'If Mr Harold Wilson,' promised (or threatened) Crossbencher of the *Sunday Express* on 2 May 1948, 'succeeds in convincing the socialist Government to go forward on the Empire Free Trade policy, he must not be surprised if he gets support from a source that might be unexpected – the *Sunday Express*.' Succeed Wilson did in that respect, and the *Sunday Express* was as good as its word. Throughout his career Harold Wilson has consistently argued for expansion in Commonwealth trade. 'I profoundly believe,' he told the Commons in 1950, 'that the fullest development of trade with the Commonwealth must be the cornerstone of economic recovery.' And Wilson personally supervised many of the fifty-one long-term contracts and even more of the bulk-buying agreements entered into by the Labour Government.

As these agreements were rapidly sabotaged by the ensuing Conservative Government, Wilson responded predictably by castigating the Tories as 'anti-Commonwealth'. His theme on this subject was quite consistent throughout the fifties and early sixties. Labour, he promised when Shadow Chancellor, stood for an increase in Commonwealth trade and a building-up of the links between the 'great family of nations'. Labour, he promised, would revert to special contracts and bulk purchase; would set up new publicly owned factories in the development areas to manufacture the products that the underdeveloped countries of the Commonwealth needed; Labour, he promised, would unleash a 'dramatic expansion of capacity to produce machine tools, fuel and power plant, steel and chemical plant-making equipment, agricultural and earth-moving equipment and other items which are and will be in urgent demand in world markets, not just in those of the affluent West' (*New Statesman*, 24 March 1961).

This distinction between the ugly contemporary affluent society and the clean healthy world of the Labour future was constantly drawn by Wilson in his articles and speeches about the Commonwealth. The 'candy-floss economies' of the West, he said, were founded on 'orange squash and washing machines', while the New Britain would be founded on earth-moving equipment and machine tools. 'A Labour Government,' he told a Cardiff audience, 'would not hesitate to build state-owned factories and industries to prepare equipment needed by Commonwealth countries.'

In the year before the 1964 general election, Wilson adopted the rejuvenation of the Commonwealth as one of Labour's central themes. In speech after speech he emphasized the crucial importance of reversing the decline in Commonwealth trade since 1951 and of building up the Commonwealth as a force for multi-racialism and peace.

In February 1964, he personally instigated a full-scale Commons debate on the subject of Commonwealth trade, and denounced the Conservatives for allowing the Commonwealth to slide into the economic background. At the end of his speech he outlined ten proposals for dealing with the problem of Commonwealth trade. They were:

(a) Special meetings to try to arrange 'special contracts' for Britain.

(b) Guaranteed markets for Commonwealth primary produce in this country.

(c) The expansion of those sections of the British economy 'where existing capacity is inadequate to meet Commonwealth needs'.

(d) Joint work for stabilization of commodity prices.

(e) Taking the initiative with the US to expand world liquidity.

(f) An intensified programme of higher education in the Commonwealth.

(g) More scientific information between Commonwealth countries.

(h) A system of 'adoption' by British towns of Commonwealth towns and villages 'to help them with the provision of industrial and agricultural equipment'.

(i) A pensionable career service in the Commonwealth public service.

(j) 'To enlist the enthusiasm of young people in a service dedicated to aiding Commonwealth economic and social development.'

Harold Wilson's Commonwealth emerged very clearly from that speech. It was, essentially, the old Commonwealth, based upon old ideas and old traditions. The economic proposals – special contracts, bulk purchase, guaranteed markets – were all borrowed from the days when the links between Britain and the Commonwealth were the links between stern mother and growing child. A rigid preference system, with high external tariffs erected against the outside world, harked back to the days when Britain was the workshop of the world and her dependents were the suppliers of that workshop's materials.

In September 1964, Harold Wilson enlarged on his views on the Commonwealth for the Fabian Society journal, *Venture*. In an article entitled 'Machinery for the Modern Commonwealth' Wilson guardedly welcomed the proposal for a Commonwealth Secretariat, but declared:

The truth about the Commonwealth is that attitudes come first, and institutions follow only as a reflection of those attitudes.

Wilson understood that the proposal for a Secretariat could well conflict with his own ideas about the Commonwealth. The Secretariat grew out of the increasing irritation of the new Commonwealth members with the patronage of the British Commonwealth Relations Office. The CRO's refusal to place Rhodesia on the agenda for the 1964 Commonwealth Prime Ministers Conference had convinced the Canadian Government of the need for a Commonwealth Secretariat, which would arrange its own agenda and discussions and in which Britain, instead of laying down the law, would have only one voice in a democratic process of decision-making. Harold Wilson preferred the old system. His thinking about the Commonwealth was based on the mother/ family concept and the demotion of the mother to child status did not appeal to him. Labour's 1964 Manifesto, *The New Britain*, written largely by Wilson, called for a 'coherent policy at the centre' of the Commonwealth.

In his *Venture* article Wilson made still further proposals for an inward-looking Commonwealth based on Empire Free Trade. He called for a Commonwealth Exports Council, a Commonwealth Development Council, a Commonwealth Career Service, even a Commonwealth Consultative Assembly:

For many years there has been a Consultative Assembly of European MPs meeting at Strasbourg as part of the Council of Europe. Why couldn't we try to create the same kind of Parliamentary institutions to draw Commonwealth politicians more closely together? . . . With the Prime Minister's Conference acting as a Council of Ministers on the Strasbourg model, there could be gradually built up a full-scale Council of the Commonwealth.

Though Wilson has since denied that he saw the Commonwealth and the Common Market as alternatives, it is clear from his *Venture* articles that he seriously considered the Commonwealth as a new force in world affairs, not merely in diplomatic circles, but as a huge power block, tightly built on economic and political lines, perhaps even challenging the might of America and Russia for the leadership of the world.

A more concerted policy, which will not be possible until we have a Government at Westminster which is prepared to come to terms with the world we are living in, will enable Britain in and through the Commonwealth to exert an influence in world affairs far greater than Her Majesty's Ministers are capable of realizing. As Lord Attlee pointedly reminded the Lords it is through our attitude to the Commonwealth, and the influence this can bestow, not through nuclear posturings, that Britain will once again be great (*Venture*, September 1964, p. 10).

This statement represented, in his hour of triumph, the quint-essence of Harold Wilson's ideas on foreign policy and on Britain's role in the modern world. Nothing, not even the NATO alliance and certainly not the European Common Market, was as important to Britain as her Commonwealth, through which, with the right Government, her leaders could shape world events as once they had when Britain ruled the waves. In every pragmatist there is a romantic trying to get out. The romance of Harold Wilson, always considerable, was allowed to run riot whenever he thought of the Commonwealth.

In the short term, his article in *Venture* earned him some criticism from that paper's Fabian editors. According to an editorial the following February, entitled 'Harold Wilson's Commonwealth':

There is a tendency to let the Commonwealth become a figleaf for chauvinism. . . . The Labour Government, particularly in view of its current emphasis on being strong East of Suez, could give the impression that it was more interested in patching up British prestige than forging an instrument for peace and economic development.

The more intelligent Fabians, in other words, had written off the Commonwealth as an economic, or even a political movement. They saw it more, as the *Venture* article put it, as 'an effective communications system helping to close the gap between rich and poor, white and coloured' (though *how* it would help to close the gap was not specified). Invocations of Gallipoli and Vimy Ridge stuck in their sophisticated throats. With their eyes fixed on

Europe, the 'radical' Fabians argued for association with Europe for African states along the lines of the 1963 Yaoundé Convention for the French colonies associated to the EEC. When Nigeria applied for associate membership in 1965, the European Fabians rejoiced. Even the old 'Gaitskellite' Fabians who were opposed to the Common Market, argued that the best hope for the under-developed countries lay not in tight preference systems as in Harold Wilson's Commonwealth but in world-wide agreements to stabilize prices and tariffs.

Despite these criticisms Harold Wilson's faith in his Commonwealth was not shaken for many months after taking power. In February 1965, answering questions about long-term economic contracts for the Commonwealth, he admitted:

It is not so easy now to revert to a system once it has been scrapped and speculative markets have been set up. . . .

But on the other hand:

The agricultural policy recently agreed in Brussels would mean that, if we were to adhere to that kind of policy on the lines which some right hon. gentlemen advocated, and still advocate, the result would be total disruption of our trade with the Commonwealth (House of Commons, 9 February 1965).

On 1 April, he repeated:

We shall certainly do what we can to halt the decline and reverse the trend. . . . I cannot accept the view that if a Commonwealth country is developing its own industry we can no longer sell in that market but can sell only in the most highly developed countries, which are those of Western Europe.

And on the 13 April he satisfied a Labour left-winger with the assurance:

We are hard at work to see what can be done to stop the rot and decline in trade between Britain and the Commonwealth.

In June, the Government permitted a full-scale debate on Commonwealth trade, in which Harold Wilson proudly restated the position which he had held consistently for twenty years. He savaged the Tories for their 'dismal record' in Commonwealth trade, pointing out that the proportion of Britain's exports and imports going to and coming from the Commonwealth had fallen drastically in the thirteen years of Tory rule. 'It may,' he opined, 'have been due to a feeling by our Commonwealth partners, especially after the unfortunate Commonwealth Prime Ministers' Conference in September 1962, that as a nation we are turning our backs on them.' For all this, Wilson could promise only one positive move to 'reverse the downward trend' of Commonwealth trade – the establishment of a Commonwealth Exports Council.

In that summer of 1965, Harold Wilson engaged on his most daring effort to prove to the world that the British Common-wealth of Nations was no cipher. At the Commonwealth Prime Ministers' Conference he proposed a 'Commonwealth Peace Mission' to Vietnam, which would visit both sides, the capitals of China, Russia and the United States, and would attempt to negotiate a settlement. The chairman of the Mission would be Harold Wilson, and it would include Prime Ministers as politically incompatible as Sir Robert Menzies and Kwame Nkrumah. From his statements about the Mission, Wilson appears genuinely to have believed that neither side could afford to turn away from an initiative from so powerful a body as the Commonwealth. His announcement of the Mission in the House of Commons on 17 June rang with confidence:

We shall have asserted the role of the Commonwealth in the world.

The Americans quickly agreed to cooperate with the Peace Mission, but the Chinese and North Vietnamese turned it down flat. In a brief statement, the North Vietnamese Government indicated that any initiative from Britain could not possibly be impartial, since the British Government unequivocally supported American policy in Vietnam. The inclusion of alleged neutrals, such as Kwame Nkrumah, then President of Ghana, made no difference to the fact that Britain supported the Americans. Until that support was withdrawn or qualified there would be no question of access to Hanoi. After a vain attempt to ignore this snub, Wilson agreed to abandon the project. The role of the Commonwealth had been asserted in the world. In the reality of power politics, particularly in wars, sentimental attachments and past glories carry little influence.

The Queen's speech of November 1965 included a vague pledge to increase Commonwealth trade, but as far as it is possible to judge from the record that was the last time 'the family of nations' was taken seriously by Harold Wilson or by his Government. From that month, the romance of Harold Wilson's Commonwealth vanishes from the public record. In the years 1966 and 1967 there were no Parliamentary debates on Commonwealth trade, still less any restatement of his Commonwealth faith by the Prime Minister. All the pledges disappeared into limbo. There were no meetings to discuss special contracts, and no special contracts signed. There were no special agreements with Commonwealth countries for bulk purchase of goods. There was no Commonwealth Development Council; no careers service for the Commonwealth; no adoption of villages in the Commonwealth by British ones, save those sponsored by War on Want in a scheme started in Tory 1962; no guaranteed markets for Commonwealth produce; no intensified programme of higher education in the Commonwealth; no recognizable move to obtain more exchange of scientific information between Commonwealth countries; no increase in the enthusiasm of young people in a service dedicated to aiding Commonwealth social and economic experiment; no mention of a Commonwealth Consultative Assembly, still less of a Commonwealth Grand Council.

The Commonwealth Exports Council, the establishment of which Wilson had so proudly announced in June 1965, and which had been his main practical suggestion for improving Commonwealth trade, had died an unnatural death. The Commonwealth Exports Council held its first meeting in the offices of the British National Export Council on 4 March 1965. All the people at the meeting were members of the BNEC, to which the new Council was affiliated. The chairman, Lord McFadzean, who was also chairman of the BNEC, announced that the new Council had been set up on the personal request of the Prime Minister. After some desultory discussion, the meeting broke up. A second meeting was held on 20 July 1965 and attended by the same people. The discussion centred on the Commonwealth Prime Ministers' Conference the following autumn. The minutes of the meeting record a unanimous request that, at the next meeting, there should be more time for discussion.

There never was another meeting. According to a spokesman for the BNEC:

It was allowed to lie, as it were. You see, most of the work which the Council would do, is already done by the area Committees of the British National Export Council. I suppose the new council felt itself redundant.

As for 'reversing the trend' away from Commonwealth trade, the figures read as follows:

1961	1962	1963	1964	1965	1966

Exports to Commonwealth as percentage of UK exports

30	30	29	28	28	25

Imports from Commonwealth as percentage of UK imports

31	31	31	30	29	27

Percentage of Commonwealth countries exports sent to UK

22	22	21	20	18	16

Percentage of Commonwealth imports supplied by UK

21	19	18	16	16	14

In almost every area of trade with the Commonwealth the figures show the same decline, ending with a catastrophic fall in 1966, which, on the provisional figures, continued still further in 1967. The extent of British trade and the 1966 deflation are irrelevant to this trend, since it is presented in percentage terms. In boom or recession, the figures all point the same way. As the Commonwealth Economic Committee, now absorbed by the Commonwealth Secretariat, put it in their report, *Commonwealth Trade*, for 1965:

The movement is a continuation of a long-term downward drift in the Commonwealth share of UK imports which had been temporarily checked between 1961 and 1963.

To some extent, the steep drop in the percentage share of British trade enjoyed by the Commonwealth can be attributed to the Rhodesian crisis, and the economic sanctions declared by Britain on Rhodesia. Peter Younghusband, the *Daily Mail*'s Africa correspondent, reported from Lusaka in January 1967, for instance, under the heading 'Britain is Losing African Trade', that an oil pipeline contract and another for building a dam on the river Kafue had been taken away from British firms, and given to

Italians; a French mining concern had been invited to develop a new coalfield at Siankadoba and even Chile had been handed contracts previously reserved for Britain (*Daily Mail*, 9 January 1967).

Yet against the loss of these prestige projects and the loss of some £10m. a year in exports to Rhodesia must be balanced the increased trade with Zambia and the surrounding countries. In 1966, when British trade with the Commonwealth decreased, both imports and exports between the United Kingdom and Zambia, Tanzania and Malawi all increased, sometimes considerably. The figures for Zambia are as follows:

	1964	1965	1966
		£ m.	
Exports to UK	54	72	78
Imports from UK	13	21	27

The Rhodesian crisis explains only a very small part of the overall decrease in Commonwealth trade. More crucial are the historical and geographical developments in world trade which Harold Wilson mocked in Opposition. The patterns of world trade are changing with political and imperialist patterns. The pull of Britain for the trade and merchandize of the Commonwealth in the last century is losing effectiveness. The countries of the Commonwealth are turning to different markets. Australia, New Zealand and Malaya are turning to Japan. Even New Zealand, the old Commonwealth country most dependent on British trade, doubled her exports to Japan between 1960 and 1964. In 1966, for the first time, Japan overtook Britain as Australia's main trading partner. Canada has become more and more dependent on America, which takes 61 per cent of her exports and supplies more than 70 per cent of her imports. Similarly, the United States is taking more and more Indian and Pakistani exports, has already overtaken Britain as the main receiver of Indian exports and provides more than a third of both countries' imports. Ironically only South Africa, removed in 1961 from the Commonwealth for political reasons, maintains the old imperial relationship and expands trade in the old tradition. Elsewhere the trend away from the imperial relationship is as inevitable as the increases in percentage of British trade with Europe. It is the re-alignment of modern capitalism with geographical and technological reality. In these circumstances the grand myth with which Harold Wilson lulled his supporters before the 1964 Election – the idea of a reinvigorated Commonwealth forged in the white heat of imperial preference and making history in the council chambers of the world – was certain to vanish with the advent of pragmatic Government. The astonishing aspect of the end of Harold Wilson's Commonwealth dream is that no one, neither Tory, Labour or independent commentator, was wise or bold enough to wake the Labour Party up while they were dreaming it.

The current fashion for industrial and financial mergers on a grand scale has evoked differing responses from the trade unionists in the merging firms. Many have sought to identify with their firm, and to assess the effect of the merger on the firm's performances in the future. Others have contented themselves with sentimental reminiscences about the good old days before the merger. In all these cases, the chief casualties have been the workers. Redundancy and loss of earnings have followed without effective protest.

The intelligent, responsible trade unionist has sought neither to defend nor oppose the merger. He has accepted it as inevitable, and has applied himself immediately to forging new links with the trade unionists in the new firm in order to protect *both sets of workers* from redundancy and loss of earnings, and to build a powerful new front with which to confront the merged employers. In this way, and in this way alone, the workers' interests, which should be the main concern of trade unionists, are assured of protection.

International mergers of capital like the European Common Market, the European Free Trade Area or the proposed North Atlantic Free Trade Area present very much the same problem to the socialist. Many socialists react to such a merger by assessing its effect on national capitalism by identifying, not with the workers and poorer sections of the community whom they represent, but with the 'nation', which invariably means the nation's industrial and financial leaders. The assessments, therefore, are discussed in purely capitalist terms and have purely capitalist objectives. Inevitably, they ignore the welfare reforms and social benefits which should be the main short-term objectives of a socialist.

Other socialists react to the proposal for a merger with a mixture of chauvinism and sentimentality, and call for 'an independent Britain, free from the shackles of other capitalist countries'. These demands are not only impracticable, and therefore useless as an alternative. They serve also to divide socialists by nationality and may, as a result, if Britain enters, postpone a common fight by united socialists in the new community to extend the area of social reform and international planning. As with the trade unionist, the only practicable socialist reaction to such a merger is neither to oppose it nor to defend it but to concentrate upon forging new links with socialists in the new association to defend and protect the mass of working people from the ravages of the free market, and, eventually, to abolish the free market on an international scale.

Nothing proves the force of this 'old-fashioned' argument better than the history of Harold Wilson's reactions to the various economic alliances entered into and suggested for Britain in the last two decades. He has followed both the above disastrous courses with predictably disastrous results. In power, he has identified throughout with British capital. The indecisiveness of British capital – whether to form a tariff-free association with America, or to join the Common Market – has been reflected in the indecisiveness of Harold Wilson. When British industry decided that an American association would allow American capitalism too much power over their British colleagues, so Harold Wilson came to the same conclusion.

In Opposition, he reverted to sentimental visions of an independent Britain planning her own socialist economy in a world of capitalist chaos. He dreamt of a new Commonwealth rising out of old imperial associations. And he reacted to American foreign policy with all the fury of the traditional Left. Once he was in power the visions vanished with as little explanation as they had appeared. Shorn of its sentiment, Harold Wilson's pragmatic foreign policy was left with nothing but the conflicting, vacillating aspirations of British capitalism. The casualties are the working people who put Wilson in power.

Chapter 8
The Hottest Place in Hell: Race, Rhodesia and Southern Africa

This is not to say that Mr Wilson was trimming his own beliefs. He genuinely hates racism. That is one of the dominant features of his political life. Anybody who thinks otherwise doesn't know him (Terence Lancaster, *The People*, 17 December 1967).

Mr Wilson is case-hardened to being called devious, tortuous and gimmicky as a professional operator, but he is not prepared to tolerate the innuendo that on apartheid, colour and race he is ready to compromise his moral judgement (James Margach, *Sunday Times*, 24 December 1967).

This Conference makes us know that Mr Wilson is coming to be a racialist (Simon Kapwepwe, Zambian Foreign Minister, after the Commonwealth Prime Ministers' Conference, 1966, *Times*, 14 September 1966).

One of the more consistent themes in Harold Wilson's politics is his Christianity. In the numerous interviews about himself and his politics he seldom fails to mention the Christian origin of his political principles. As early as 1948, preaching in the Milnsbridge Parish Church which he attended while a boy, he told the congregation:

> My own party is based more on Christian teaching than the teaching of Karl Marx. All the pioneers were local preachers. No one should be in a political party unless he believes that party represents his own highest religious and moral ideas (*Daily Mail*, 21 June 1948).

Over and over again in his political career Harold Wilson has fallen back on his Christian principles to guide him through crisis, or assist him in decision. A typical instance was that of the Polaris missile. In a speech to the 1960 Christmas Fair at St Paul's Church, Prescot, he remonstrated:

> This is not the occasion to talk about the Polaris base – but I am sure we all feel something abhorrent about it being in an area called the Holy Loch (*Prescot and Huyton Reporter*, 25 November 1960).

On the rare occasions when he has introduced the issue of race into public debate, he has almost always done so in terms of his Christian faith. In his regular speeches, for instance, to the Prescot Brotherhood in his constituency, Wilson returned again and again to the race issue:

Politics cannot be divorced from spiritual and ethical standards . . . Love thy neighbour does not mean the white race, but people of all colours (*Prescot and Huyton Reporter*, 24 January 1954).

And, four years later, speaking to the text 'He has made of One Blood all the Nations upon Earth':

No one can stand aside. Many of the [race] problems arise from intolerance and lack of Christianity in the hearts of men. In 1906 religion and politics were closely linked. . . . A blot on our national life is intolerance and a growing colour prejudice (*Prescot and Huyton Reporter*, 16 May 1958).

Christian teaching on the race issue through the centuries has, unfortunately, been somewhat inconsistent. One of its most striking characteristics is its relevance to the area and racial situation in which the doctrine is preached. To the Christian missionaries in the West Indies in the eighteenth century, for instance, as they hurriedly baptized the newly arrived slaves before the branding and whipping ceremonies, the doctrine of racial equality was heresy. Similarly today in the white Anglo-Saxon Protestant Southern States of America, or in the white Christian civilization of Southern Africa, the Almighty, while recognizing that all men are of one blood, inclines to the view that the colour of their skin is more important. Racial equality – the irrelevance of skin colour and racial origin to social status – is, however, preached unequivocally by Christians in those places where the problem does not arise.

In Britain, for instance, received Christian doctrine has for decades been implacably opposed to racial segregation and racial inequality. The practice and principle of equality between white and coloured people were, until recently, facilitated by the absence of all but a handful (and a fairly civilized handful at that – students, cricketers and so on) of coloured people.

From 1948, however, the issue has presented many British Christians with a quandary. 1948 was the first year of large-scale immigration from the Commonwealth of coloured people seeking jobs in the expanding industries of Britain. The industries expanded faster than acceptable living standards were provided for their workers, and, as a result, prejudice built up against the immigrants. Ill-informed, opportunist politicians pressed the claim that widespread shortages in housing, hospital beds, school places and transport facilities were caused by the immigrants.

From the outset, the Labour Party opposed this propaganda, and argued that no restrictions should be placed on immigration from the Commonwealth. Arthur Bottomley, Labour spokesman on Commonwealth affairs, told the Commons on 5 December 1958:

> We on this side are clear in our attitude towards restricted immigration. We are categorically against it. The central principle on which our status in the Commonwealth is largely dependent is the 'open door' to all Commonwealth citizens. If we believe in the importance of our great Commonwealth, we should do nothing in the slightest degree to undermine that principle.

In the autumn of 1961 the Conservative Government announced its intention of introducing a Bill to control immigration from the Commonwealth. Immediately, the Labour Party opposed the measure. The Leader of the Party, Hugh Gaitskell, wound up for the Opposition in the Second Reading Debate on the Commonwealth Immigration Bill with one of the finest speeches in his life, indicating that the measure was racialist in inspiration, irrelevant to social problems and economic nonsense. The fight against the Bill continued through a Committee of the whole House, in several full days of debate (which eventually forced the Government to introduce the 'guillotine') and more than a hundred speeches from Labour MPs. The campaign was taken into the country. Everywhere local Labour parties and Young Socialist branches took up the arguments against the Bill.

Two months after his election as leader of the Party, Harold Wilson agreed to speak at a mass rally sponsored by Anti-Apartheid, in Trafalgar Square. 'One of the greatest of the many inspiring acts of Hugh Gaitskell's leadership,' he said 'was his fight against the Commonwealth Immigration Act.' Chapter and verse for this inspiration, however, as it affected Wilson himself, are difficult to find. Not one of Wilson's published speeches in the Commons or outside was devoted to supporting Gaitskell's 'free-entry' line.

The Gaitskell policy had been clear from the outset. Cyril Osborne, a leading Conservative campaigner for immigration control, had written to Gaitskell on 23 May 1958 asking for a statement on Labour's policy towards Commonwealth immigration. He received a reply on 2 June from the secretary of the Parliamentary Labour Party:

> Mr Gaitskell has asked me to thank you for your letter of 23 May. The Labour Party is opposed to the restriction of immigration as every Commonwealth citizen has the right as a British subject to enter this country at will. This has been the right of subjects of the Crown for many centuries and the Labour Party has always maintained it should be unconditional.

That was Labour's policy in 1961 and 1962 upon which the Commonwealth Immigration Bill was fought, and which Harold Wilson consistently supported in the lobbies (though not in speeches).

As a result of a successful Labour amendment to the Act, it came up in November 1963 for renewal under the Expiring Laws Continuance Bill. After a rearguard action by a small right-wing group, the Parliamentary Labour Party decided to oppose the continuance of the Act. Yet the terms in which it was opposed by the then leader of the Party, Harold Wilson, differed sharply from those expressed by Hugh Gaitskell. While Gaitskell had rejected the need for any control of Commonwealth immigration Wilson told the House:

> We do not contest the need for control of Commonwealth immigration into this country (Hansard, 27 November 1963).

According to Wilson, the main objection to the Commonwealth Immigration Act was that there had been no consultation with Commonwealth Governments before the controls were imposed. He offered not to oppose the continuance of the Act if the Government would agree to consult the Commonwealth on the nature of the controls. This offer was brusquely rejected by the then Home Secretary, Henry Brooke, who showed with little difficulty that the chances of any effective controls through consultation were minimal. India and Pakistan, he said, had already tried con-

trolling immigration at source, and had failed. Wilson's new immigration policy – to keep the Act while attempting to get
immigration control by Commonwealth Governments – was both
futile and hypocritical.

Indeed in several crucial respects Wilson argued for tightening
the provisions in the Immigration Act:

> I must point out that there are loopholes in the Act and we would
> favour a strengthening of legal powers. . . . We believe that health checks
> should become more effective. We would be prepared to support a
> change in the law relating to deportation. At present the Act provides
> this limit of five years' residence in this country. If an individual found
> guilty of certain crimes has been in this country for more than five
> years, he is excluded from the operation of parts of the Act (Hansard,
> 27 November 1963).

Statements like these showed how wide was the gulf between
Wilson's and Gaitskell's thinking on the immigration issue.
Wilson was talking about tightening health checks, extending
deportation powers, accepting general control, while his predecessor had dismissed health checks resulting in deportation as
inhumane, and had attempted in every possible way to whittle
down the deportation provisions.

Wilson's speech was made only a few weeks after the 1963
Conference at Scarborough when the Labour Left were performing
the rites of Wilson-worship. Complaint and criticism about the
erosion of the Party's principled stand on immigration was confined to 'sectarians'. From that moment, all arguments and discussion about immigration policy in the Labour Party was effectively stifled. The orders went out to and from Transport House
that on no account was immigration policy to be raised on the
platforms of prospective candidates. In the eleven months
between Wilson's speech and the General Election, there was no
Labour Party pronouncement of any kind on immigration. The
only rebuke for this silence came from the Fabian Society's
journal, *Venture*, which demanded an end to equivocation and a
restatement of the Gaitskell line (September 1964).

Immigration policy presented a nasty problem for the writers of
the Labour Party 1964 Manifesto – Peter Shore, Head of the
Research department at Transport House, and Harold Wilson.
The relevant paragraph read:

Labour accepts that the number of immigrants entering the United Kingdom must be limited. Until a satisfactory agreement covering this can be negotiated with the Commonwealth, a Labour Government will retain immigration control.

Anthony Howard and Richard West tell us that the final draft of the manifesto had only been seen by Wilson, Shore, George Brown, Richard Crossman and Len Williams (Labour's General Secretary) before it was submitted to the NEC for their approval on 8 September. The NEC had only half an hour to read the draft before submitting criticisms, and the manifesto went to the printers that night. If any Member of the Executive had any qualms about the unexplained reversal on immigration policy, there was hardly time to raise the matter.

Almost as soon as the Labour Government took office its Ministers started to 'improve on' the sections of the Commonwealth Immigration Act which they had three years ago so violently opposed. By March 1965, Wilson himself was wailing to the Commons about 'fatal erosion' of the Act. 'Since the Act is not working as intended,' he told the House on 9 March, 'a fresh examination of the whole problem of control is necessary.' This amounted to a high-level mission, led by Lord Mountbatten, who was briefed to travel around Commonwealth capitals 'to discuss whether new methods are needed to regulate the flow of immigrants into the United Kingdom'.

The Mountbatten Mission, like the Commonwealth Peace Mission and so many other of Wilson's prestigious delegations, was a total flop. It returned with the predictable news that the Commonwealth Governments concerned refused to contemplate any further immigration control, and regarded the Mission as beneath contempt. Wilson responded with the respect for the Commonwealth of which he had consistently boasted. He agreed to the proposals of his Home Secretary, Sir Frank Soskice, for further drastic measures to control Commonwealth immigration. The proposals – announced in a White paper on 5 August – cut the number of working Commonwealth immigrants down to 7,500 a year (plus a thousand from Mountbatten's old base at Malta). It further proposed tightening the deportation and health provisions. Part 3, which dealt with ways and means of avoiding discrimination in Britain, scrupulously omitted the possibility of legislating against discrimination in the two most crucial social areas – housing and employment. Remarkably for a Government document which was clearly the responsibility of the Home Office, the Immigration White Paper was issued specially from the Prime Minister's Office.

The White Paper was greeted with a howl of rage by the immigrant organizations and a large number of Labour Parties and trade unions. An emergency resolution at the 1965 Labour Party Conference urging the Conference to withdraw the White Paper mustered a million and a half votes. Replying to the general criticism, Harold Wilson started naturally by expressing his disgust at racial discrimination and his Government's determination to halt it. 'We repudiate,' he went on, 'and let me say for my part I resent the accusation of illiberality or of any desire whether on the part of the Home Secretary or of the Government as a whole to act in an arbitrary manner. Our concern was with evasion. . . .'

Slightly more than a month later, Wilson appointed a new Home Secretary – Roy Jenkins – who brought to the Home Office a whiff of liberalism which it had not smelt for fifty years. Under Jenkins' insistence, the original, mealy-mouthed and utterly ineffective Race Relations Act – which has been used in the main against demonstrators and coloured people – was strengthened to include housing and employment. Jenkins also persuaded the Government to accept a report by the Wilson (not Harold) Committee, which recommended a right of appeal for potential deportees, particularly of immigrants arriving at London Airport, whose numbers have increased substantially since the Labour Government's White Paper. It seems unlikely that the 1965 White Paper would have been so crude in content and brutal in effect had Jenkins been Home Secretary at the time. Yet Harold Wilson was prepared to accept Soskice's proposals just as he later accepted Jenkins'.

In January 1968, Jenkins was promoted to the Treasury, and was replaced at the Home Office by James Callaghan, who, almost at once, introduced an Immigration Bill to control the entry of British passport-holders in the Commonwealth and colonies who, for one reason or another, were not covered by the Immigration Act of 1962. Most of these were Kenyans of Asian origin who, in justified scepticism about their own future under Jomo Kenyatta's 'Africanization' policies, had opted to retain their British passports and citizenship when Kenya became independent in 1963.

Racialism was specifically written into the new Bill, whose provisions did not apply to passport-holders who could prove 'a substantial connexion' with the United Kingdom. The new category of British citizens, which, by dint of herculean powers of imagination, the Government estimated at some two million, was restricted to 1,500 work vouchers a year. The Bill also tightened still further the provisions of the 1962 Act, barring all dependants between the ages of sixty and sixty-five, and children joining single parents. As a result some 150,000 Kenyan Asians, who had chosen British citizenship on the understanding that they would be permitted free entry to Britain, were rendered effectively stateless.

Political pressure for the Bill had been restricted to the wildest elements in the Conservative Party, led by Duncan Sandys, whose scare talk about the 'flood' of Kenyan Asians free to enter without restriction had not, before Callaghan came to the Home Office, had much effect, even in the local authorities. The chairman of the Conservative-controlled Birmingham Education Committee, who approved the Bill, admitted that 'the suggestion of an avalanche of newcomers as a result of the Kenya problems had not materialized'. No one close to the problem doubted that a firm statement categorically committing the Government to honouring their commitments to the Kenyan Asians would have had an immediate stabilizing effect on the panic 'Beat Control' rush of Kenyan Asians to Britain.

The Bill was rushed through in less than a week in scenes of unusual Parliamentary decadence. The Liberal Party, 35 Labour MPs, 15 Conservative MPs and more than 80 peers opposed it in the lobbies against the advice and votes of both front benches. Outside, the opposition was more vocal and more permanent. The Archbishop of Canterbury, chairman of the National Committee of Commonwealth Immigrants, and Mark Bonham Carter, chairman of the Race Relations Board, voiced the unanimous view of race relations workers that the new Bill would do irreparable damage to race relations in Britain.

The Bill caused consternation in the most loyal wing of the Labour Party, the 'principled' Right. Resignations were reported all over the country from intellectuals and Fabians. *Socialist Commentary*, the monthly theoretical journal of the Labour Right, published an article by Nicholas Deakin which established in bitter language its author's contention that 'their [the Government's] performance on this Bill displays evidence of bungling, cynicism, opportunism and malice'. Deakin himself resigned from the Labour Party, which he was about to represent in the 1968 local authority elections in a safe Labour seat in the Borough of Camden. This was one of many such resignations from Labour intellectuals who, in the old days of controversy about the Bomb and public ownership, had sided unequivocally with the Labour leadership.

In the Cabinet, however, the measure was opposed only by the Lord Chancellor, Lord Gardiner, and George Brown. Throughout the debates, in public and elsewhere the Prime Minister maintained a cosy silence.

The cheering crowd in Trafalgar Square in March 1963 who heard the Labour leader pay such generous tribute to his predecessor's 'fight against the Commonwealth Immigration Act' could hardly have been aware that the same man would administer that Act with more severity and more unconcern for the human beings involved than its Tory initiators would ever have dared, and would then initiate a second Commonwealth Immigrants Act even more racialist in motive and effect than its predecessor.

Immigration from the Commonwealth, for the first time, brought the colour problem into domestic British politics. Yet the issue has arisen again and again in post-war British politics, largely through the disintegration of the British Empire, most notably in Africa. In most of Africa, the process took place without violent racial upheaval or antagonism. Even in Kenya the white settlers eventually came to terms with their former tormentor – Jomo Kenyatta – and in most of the countries of North Africa white people formed too small a minority to create a powerful pressure group against independence and black majority power.

Southern Africa presented a different picture. In South Africa itself, three million whites had devised a system of oppression and segregation called 'apartheid' which ensured their domination over eleven million black Africans. Further north, the white minorities sought similar security. In the Portuguese colonies of Angola and Mozambique, the Portuguese Government had deliberately encouraged large-scale white immigration and the breeding of half-castes to ensure the continued suppression of black nationalism. In the three British colonies of South and North Rhodesia and Nyasaland, the tiny white minority had sought a more subtle method of ensuring their continued rule – a method, moreover, which by its very structure recommended itself to the British Colonial Office and Commonwealth Relations Office – the Federation.

The concept of a Central African Federation seemed to make economic sense. The difficulties were political and racial. In Southern Rhodesia, 250,000 whites were powerful enough to retain racial control and power over four million Africans. In the other two countries a handful of whites formed no more than an administrative skeleton.

The proposal for a Federation, therefore, which came originally from Salisbury, laid down roughly the same voting system for the three countries as then obtained in Southern Rhodesia – thus ensuring for an indefinite future control over all three countries' economic and social affairs by the Southern Rhodesian white minority, led at that time by Sir Roy Welensky.

The proposals, first put in 1950, commended themselves to the British Labour Government, notably to Patrick Gordon Walker, then Secretary of State for Commonwealth Relations. With the loss of office, however, the mood of the Labour Party changed, and in 1953 the Opposition spokesman on Colonial Affairs, Jim Griffiths, on behalf of the Parliamentary Labour Party, opposed the Tory plans to establish the Federation. His case was based entirely on the undesirability of white minority power. A number of Labour members abstained in the vote – including Patrick Gordon Walker and George Brown. Harold Wilson, however, then a Bevanite, voted with the majority, and, though he seldom raised the issue in public, clearly opposed the formation of the Federation.

Throughout the 1950s the Labour Opposition firmly supported the African Nationalists in Central Africa who, in all three Federation countries, opposed the Federation. In 1959, six months before the British General Election, the Government ordered the arrest in Nyasaland of leading African Nationalists, notably Hastings Banda. The Labour Party led the outcry against the arrests. Once again, Harold Wilson, Shadow Chancellor, supported the Party line without raising the matter more than casually in or out of Parliament or his constituency. The inevitable collapse of the Federation forced the Southern Rhodesian whites into further isolation and supremacism. A succession of elections led to the eviction of 'moderates' like Welensky, and their replacement by increasingly racialist Governments, culminating in that formed in 1964 by the Rhodesian Front, led by Ian Smith. The Conservative Government warned Smith against any rash declaration of 'independence' from British Colonial rule. Such independence, warned the Commonwealth Relations Office, could only come if and when the Africans were properly represented.

If the Tories had any plans to let Smith and Southern Rhodesia off the colonial hook, they can have been in no doubt about the mood of the Opposition. The Labour Party had consistently opposed the 1961 Constitution for Southern Rhodesia, which even the Tories explicitly ruled out as a basis for independence. In March 1963, the new Labour leader, Harold Wilson, declared:

We have said that no constitution is defensible which fails to allow the people of those territories to control their own destinies. We have bitterly attacked the Southern Rhodesian constitution for that, and a Labour Government would therefore alter it – let me make that very very plain.

On 11 April, he demanded in the House of Commons:

Will Her Majesty's Government give the House a clear assurance that there will be no question of granting independence to Southern Rhodesia until the country has a constitution which enables the mass of the people to govern themselves? Is he aware that there should be no question of granting independence under a constitution where 250,000 have the right to rule three million people?

Only a fortnight before the General Election of 1964, Wilson wrote a letter to Dr E. Mutasa, a member of the Rhodesian Committee against European Independence, who had asked for Labour's policy on Rhodesian independence:

The Labour Party is totally opposed to granting independence to Southern Rhodesia so long as the Government of the country remains under a white minority.

Somewhat embarrassingly, perhaps, for the new Prime Minister, Dr Mutasa issued the letter publicly to the press as soon as the Labour Government took office.

All those who had feared continued white supremacy in Rhodesia were cheered by the Labour victory. The left-wing *Tribune*, in the third issue after the election ('the only paper to publish the full text of Harold Wilson's attack on Tory mismanagement') printed a jubilant report from a correspondent in Rhodesia:

Ian Smith was in chastened mood. The bouncing self-confidence, the defiance had all but disappeared. The narrow, tapering shoulders, the sullen, unsmiling face was a figure of pity. In Harold Wilson, Ian Smith had met his match (6 November 1964).

The 'figure of pity' soon shook off his melancholy. In the first year of Labour Government Ian Smith's Rhodesian Front grew in confidence and strength, and, after various visits to London by Smith and his leading colleagues, independence for Rhodesia was unilaterally and illegally declared by Smith on 11 November 1965. Every possible effort had been made by Wilson in his meetings with Smith shortly before UDI and in a long telephone conversation on the morning of the declaration to introduce a compromise whereby independence would be granted following a Royal Commission Report on what the Rhodesians wanted. Wilson had even chosen a prospective chairman of the Royal Commission, Sir Hugh Beadle, the Rhodesian Chief Justice.

The reaction of the British Prime Minister to the declaration was suitably shocked and patriotic. He told the Commons:

It would be unworthy of this Government, of any British Government, as it would be unworthy of this House, to allow this challenge, offensive as it is to all our cherished traditions, and to the wider aspirations of the whole of mankind, to go unchallenged ... we shall face this challenge with courage and determination. Whatever measures the Government, with the support of this House, judge are needed to restore Rhodesia to the rule of law, to allegiance to the Crown, these measures will be taken ... we shall have the clear and decisive verdict of history (House of Commons, 11 November 1965).

On a national television broadcast that evening, widely regarded as his best up to that time, and in his many other public statements on Rhodesia Wilson appeared to take a tough line with the rebel regime. He showed nothing but contempt for those elements in the Conservative Party, anxious about their investments in Central Africa, who claimed that sanctions would not work and advocated their removal. The sanctions which he announced on 11 November were very quickly tightened, and the general view of the financial Press was that the Rhodesian economy could not stand up to them. On 21 December, nearly six weeks after UDI, Wilson rounded on the Tory right wing, who had suggested that sanctions could not work, and had called for negotiations with Smith:

The hottest place in hell [he said, quoting Dante] is reserved for those who are neutral in a moral crisis. . . .

Quite apart from the repugnance, which I hope we all share, about negotiating with the illegal regime, the very idea that it would be successful, that we could ask the rest of the world to reserve the policies they carried out at our request, that we could ask other countries to hold their hand while we parley with Mr Smith and his colleagues, is the product of the most woolly-minded thinking I have come across.

There may be some honourable members who would be prepared to negotiate with a burglar on the basis that they would allow him to retain his illegal gains, provided that they did not stay illegal, by changing a theft into a gift. That is what negotiation on Mr Smith's terms would mean (21 December 1965).

Yet, in spite of this language, there were from the outset signs that Wilson's resolution in face of the Rhodesian rebellion was not as tough as had appeared. His determination to preserve an all-Party 'consensus' on the Rhodesian issue, coupled with his own admiration for the majesty of the monarch, pressed him time and again into sentimental genuflection before the Queen, the Governor of Rhodesia, Sir Humphrey Gibbs and the Chief Justice, Sir Hugh Beadle.[1]

Advice from harder colleagues that the Gibbs–Beadle partnership would inevitably fall victim to the Smith regime, that their 'loyalty' was, as far as any final solution was concerned, futile, were brushed aside. Sir Humphrey and Sir Hugh were officially honoured and, in the Prime Minister's speeches, lavishly praised.

1. The fortnightly satirical paper *Private Eye* pictured him on its cover shaking hands with the Queen, saying, 'We can't go on meeting like this.'

At the outset, Wilson clearly relished the atmosphere of national crisis. He referred to Rhodesia as 'my Cuba' and he delivered himself of some choice Churchilliana. His Commons speech on Rhodesia in December ended with the following hilarious passage from Abraham Lincoln:

I will do the very best I can, the very best I know how. And I mean to keep doing so until the end. If the end brings me out all right, what is said against me now won't amount to anything. If the end brings me out wrong, ten angels swearing I was right would make little difference.

More important, perhaps, for the final outcome of the Rhodesian situation, was Wilson's personal decision to rule out the use of British troops to enforce constitutional Government. He had committed himself against the use of force before the declaration of independence, and he remained faithful to his pledge.

The UDI announcement – on 11 November – was met by the Labour Government with a declaration that the regime was illegal, and a series of mild economic sanctions, which were strengthened a month later. From the outset, Harold Wilson declared his Government opposed to the 'use of force' in Rhodesia. In 1964 he had called for more helicopters to assist British troops fighting Adeni and Yemeni nationalists; had argued in the same year that it was time for Britain to 'get tough' in Cyprus and send in tanks; had consistently in his year of office given full support to the American Government's massive array of force in Vietnam. In Rhodesia, however, for Harold Wilson, force became an intolerable remedy – a resort to un-Christian violence.

It was also, apparently, an irrelevant issue. Economic sanctions would, Wilson assured Commonwealth leaders in Lagos the following January, bring the rebel regime to its knees 'in weeks rather than months'.[1]

Unfortunately, however, as the weeks and months rolled on, the rebel regime gained in confidence. No one sustained that con-

1. Wilson's Lagos conference was hailed by the Labour Left as proof of his political courage and virtuosity. The *Johannesburg Star*, the paper with the largest circulation in South Africa, was also delighted. 'He succeeded,' it said, 'in his main objectives – the buying of time, damping down of the near-hysterical demands of the African states for military action, and preservation of the Commonwealth's existing membership. On the face of it, it was a considerable achievement.'

fidence more than the British Government, who hastened, at every conceivable opportunity, to make it clear to the 'rebel regime' and, more importantly, to the business community of Salisbury, that they were anxious to scuttle for a settlement.

In April 1966, for instance, immediately after an election in which Labour had gained its second biggest victory in history, Ian Smith, somewhat worried by the election results and anxious lest sanctions should be extended internationally, approached the Governor, Sir Humphrey Gibbs, and suggested that talks might be instigated between the 'rebel regime' and the British Government. Immediately, only four months after his no-negotiations pledge in the Commons, Wilson agreed to the proposal. Wilson's private secretary, Oliver Wright, and a group of senior CRO officials were dispatched to Salisbury for a long round of 'talks about talks'.

At the 'talks about talks', the Rhodesian representatives maintained a rigid line. Not a single concession on a return to constitutional rule or advancement in African education or electoral power was granted. The civil servants pursued their ludicrous task for two months, and it was only after some pressure from the Commonwealth Relations Office that Wilson agreed to recall them at the end of July. The 'talks about talks' had served their purpose for the Rhodesian Government. They had shown that the British Government was far from determined to smash the regime, and would, at the slightest provocation, come to the conference table and make concessions. Business confidence in Salisbury soared. The entrepreneurs who, some months before, had worried about permanent closure of the British market and international sanctions, shook off their doubts and applied themselves with renewed vigour to prising open the numerous cracks in the sanctions wall.

In spite of all this, the following month Wilson decided to send back three of the civil servants for more 'talks about talks' with the 'rebels', and was only thwarted from continuing the absurd discussions by the passing of the frankly racialist Constitutional Amendment Bill, which forced the civil servants to return without a day wasted in negotiation.

Wilson however, was determined to get Rhodesia off his back by the end of 1966. In the Cabinet re-shuffle following the July measures of 1966 he sacked the faithful Arthur Bottomley, who had publicly branded Smith as a liar and had argued passionately against negotiations with his regime. In his place, Wilson appointed Herbert Bowden – who was for fifteen years a Labour Whip, and had learned the dangers of expressing independent judgements against the views of the majority. Bowden travelled to Rhodesia in late September with a new package deal drawn up by Wilson. It was the 1961 constitution, dressed up with 'entrenched clauses' ensuring black majority rule some time in the future.

Even Herbert Bowden, the ex-Whip, found Smith difficult in negotiations, and, after an unhappy few days in Salisbury, he returned to advise Wilson that the Rhodesian regime refused all concessions, and that any further negotiations would serve further to improve the confidence of businessmen in Rhodesia. Wilson responded to this advice by insisting on a 'dramatic' man-to-man meeting with Smith on board the cruiser *Tiger* in the Mediterranean. The meetings took place between 2 and 5 December 1966.

The purported pretext for the *Tiger* confrontation was the need to reconcile with Smith the British Government's stated six principles for constitutional independence in Rhodesia. These were:

1. Unimpeded progress to majority rule.
2. Guarantees against retrogressive amendment of the Constitution.
3. Immediate improvement in the political status of the Africans.
4. Progress towards ending racial discrimination.
5. A basis for independence acceptable to the people of Rhodesia as a whole.
6. Regardless of race, no oppression by majority of minority or *vice versa*.

Since Harold Wilson claimed in the House of Commons that his proposed settlement on the *Tiger* amply met all six principles it is worth dealing with the *Tiger* discussions in some detail.

Pages 84 to 90 of the official document on the *Tiger* discussions[1] contains the draft Independence Constitution which the British Government proposed to Smith as a basis for a settlement. The constitution was based on the one framed by Duncan Sandys, then Commonwealth Secretary of State, and Edgar Whitehead, then Prime Minister of Rhodesia, in February 1961.

1. *Rhodesia. Documents Relating to a Proposal for a Settlement*, Cmnd 3171.

The 1961 constitution established a legislature of 65 seats, 50 elected from the 'A' Roll, and 15 from the 'B' Roll. The electorate of the 'A' roll were all qualified to vote by educational and property-owning achievements. They were, with a tiny handful of exceptions, all white. The 'B' Roll electorate, on the other hand, were almost all black. The first principle, unimpeded progress to majority rule, was said by the document to be 'enshrined' in the 1961 constitution, because, as Africans got better educated, more and more of them would qualify for voting on the 'A' Roll, until they outnumbered whites. Sir Edgar Whitehead had put the likely date of majority rule under the Constitution as 1977 – which was, for the Africans, optimistic. To get a bare majority on the 'A' Roll the Africans needed to win 18 seats out of 50 on the 'A' Roll, 36 per cent of the 'A' roll seats.

Wilson's *Tiger* Constitution, however, made majority rule much more difficult. It increased the total legislature to 67, constituting 50 'A' Roll seats, 17 of which could be filled only by Europeans. Thus there were only 33 'open' 'A' Roll seats. The African representation was increased to two by increasing 'B' Roll seats to 17. To get a bare majority, therefore, the Africans had to win 17 out of the 33 open 'A' Roll seats – 51.5 per cent compared with 36 per cent under Sandys! Moreover the 'delimitation' proposals in Wilson's constitution cleverly ensured that the Africans qualified to vote in the 'A' Roll seats should be 'spread evenly' throughout the constituencies, and therefore, as their prospects became better, would be less and less likely to win the vital seats.

The basic clauses in the 1961 Constitution could be altered only if approved by a one-man, one-vote referendum of all four races voting separately. In so far as it is possible with Constitutional safeguards, which can always be annulled once power has been transferred, this gave an absolute guarantee that the Constitution would not be changed to favour either whites or blacks.

These provisions were scrapped on the *Tiger*, and were replaced by a complicated set of proposals for a Senate consisting of 12 elected whites, 8 elected blacks and 4 chiefs. Constitutional change of the so-called 'specially entrenched provisions' was only possible if voted in by three-quarters of both houses, Senate and Legislature, voting together. This 'ensured' that the elected black Africans, who held more than a quarter of all the seats, could not be outvoted on the 'entrenched clauses'.

The South Africa Act of 1909, granting independence to that country, laid down two 'entrenched clauses' which could *in no circumstances* be changed by the Legislature. These clauses 'ensured' the multi-racial nature of legislation. The clauses have since been coolly ignored, to the impotent fury of constitutional lawyers. Wilson's confidence that his own feeble 'guarantees' against constitutional change satisfied his Government's 'second principle' was no more than verbal shilly-shally.

The third principle – immediate political improvement for Africans – was, as we have seen, effectively negated by the new proposals for the legislature which made it more difficult for Africans to get a majority. Even more startling was the total lack of insistence in the Wilson constitution on any special efforts to advance African education, or worse still, to lower the educational qualifications for the franchize, under which only about 5,000 out of a million and more African adults qualified for voting on the 'A' Roll.

The principle that only properly educated, propertied people had a right to vote was proudly stated in the *Tiger* document: 'The British Government repeatedly said that majority rule could not come about immediately but should be reached through merit and achievement' (p. 6).

The principle represented a complete departure from British colonial practice. Every grant of independence until the *Tiger* talks (most of them under Conservative Governments) had been accompanied by universal suffrage in the newly independent country. As one of the most experienced of British colonial servants has written:

I am convinced by experience in the West Indies and in Africa that restrictions on the franchize, whether by property or income or literacy tests, except as a temporary measure, are fundamentally wrong. In Jamaica, the people who would have been excluded from the vote by the restricted franchize were some of the best people on the island – the sturdy, independent, self-respecting people of the hills. Had restrictions in the franchize been maintained, political power would have been withheld from the countryside and handed to the towns. But why should clerks be enfranchized and cultivators excluded? The illiterate hill cultivator in Jamaica is just as capable as anyone else in the world of exercising the basic function of democracy, the function of choosing whom he wishes to speak for him. The fact that a man or woman is poor and illiterate makes it more and not less necessary that he should have the right to choose. The vote is to him not a luxury but a necessity (Hugh Foot, *A Start in Freedom*, Hodder, 1964, p. 126).

These were the principles which had dominated British thinking in framing constitutions in Africa, the West Indies, Asia and even Cyprus. Harold Wilson, however, had put an end to such idealistic ravings. In Rhodesia, as far as his Government was concerned, the franchize, and majority rule, were available only by 'merit and achievement'.

The next two principles – an end to racial discrimination and the assurance that a settlement was acceptable to the Rhodesians as a whole – were surmounted by a familiar Wilsonian remedy: the Royal Commission. One Royal Commission would travel round the country making sure that the Rhodesian people accepted the constitutional proposals; another would sit 'for several years' (Wilson's own words during the *Tiger* discussion) to find ways and means of ending racial discrimination. The Smith regime had the right to veto nominations for the Commissions. The reasons why it is easier to find out peoples' views through a Royal Commission than through a referendum of the whole population were not discussed on the *Tiger*.

The only principle which was maintained on the *Tiger* was the sixth and last, included solely to comfort the white minority. The dangers of 'oppression of minority by majority' had been scrupulously avoided by the suggestion, never before included in an African independence constitution by a British Government, that special seats in the legislature should be reserved for Europeans only. With this exception, every one of the six principles was broken by the *Tiger* talks, and in every particular the Wilson *Tiger* Constitution was more reactionary and more acceptable to the racist Rhodesian's white minority than the Tory Constitution of 1961.

The talks themselves went all Smith's way. Before he left London, Wilson had promised Mrs Judith Hart, his Minister of State at the Commonwealth Relations Office (who would certainly have resigned if the *Tiger* proposals had been accepted), that he would insist on a military presence in Rhodesia while the Royal Commission was finding out what the people wanted. Somehow, during the *Tiger* talks, a combination of Wilson's realism and Smith's racialism pushed this promise off the agenda.

Sir Edgar Whitehead, whose pragmatic preference for white supremacy has long since been outpaced by the more ideological racialism of Mr Smith and his colleagues, condemned the Wilson Constitution on the *Tiger* as 'greatly postponing the possible date of African majority rule almost certainly beyond the end of this century'. Once again, Edgar Whitehead erred on the side of optimism for the Africans. Leo Baron, a white Rhodesian lawyer, who spent most of the first year after UDI in Smith's jails for the crime, for which he was not charged, of defending Africans in the courts, described the position taken by the British Government on the *Tiger* as 'the blackest page in the whole of British colonial history' (*Guardian*, 28 July 1967). It is difficult to imagine a graver charge – nor one more accurate.

The proposals put to Smith on board HMS *Tiger* had been composed on the initiative of Harold Wilson. Throughout, he personally claimed full credit for them. He freely admitted that he had changed his mind about negotiating with Smith and never once, before or since the *Tiger*, has he indicated anything but intense disappointment that the proposed settlement was rejected.

When Wilson returned from the *Tiger* on 5 December, he was jubilantly confident that his proposals would be accepted. From their first meeting, Wilson had formed a high regard for Smith and liked his 'tough, no-nonsense approach'. On the day after the Commonwealth Prime Ministers' Conference that autumn a BBC interviewer had asked Wilson what he thought of Smith. He replied:

> I've got great respect for him. I believe that with the right influences around him, as a member of a much more broadly based Government than this extremist, racialist Government, I believe there could be a future for Rhodesia provided that they are prepared to recognize the kind of world and the kind of century we are living in (*Daily Mail*, 16 September 1966).

These views, and the obvious delight of Smith at the *Tiger* terms, made Wilson sure that the acceptance by the Rhodesian

Cabinet was a mere formality. Yet within twenty-four hours the answer came back that the *Tiger* terms were 'unacceptable' to the Smith regime. The concept of a 'broadly based' government and that of a Royal Commission were 'intolerable'.

The rejection of the *Tiger* terms can be explained by the extremism of the ideological racialists in the Smith Cabinet, of whom the most persuasive was Gerald Lardner-Burke. Lardner-Burke argued that acceptance of the terms could provoke the Africans into excessive demands, and the danger of an African uprising would become greater. More realistically, perhaps, Lardner-Burke and his friends saw in the proposals their own demise. For no 'broadly based' Government, however widely the phrase is interpreted, could include Lardner-Burke. No doubt Smith's original enthusiasm for the settlement was heightened by the possibility under its terms of ridding himself of men like Lardner-Burke.

Lardner-Burke and his followers, notably the farmers and financial supporters of the Rhodesian Front, soon swamped the pleas of Smith and the 'moderates'. The Rhodesian whites, some of them a little sadly, rallied to the extremism of their leaders. Those businessmen who mourned the continuance of sanctions could take some comfort from the fact that, however long the sanctions lasted, the British Prime Minister was always ready to negotiate.

Harold Wilson, once he had recovered from the shock, reacted with typical resilience and vigour. His speech to the Commons on the *Tiger* negotiations and their unsuccessful outcome was, once again, a restatement of his Christian faith in multi-racialism in Southern Africa. Gone was all hope of compromise, he thundered. The slogan now was NIBMAR – No Independence Before Majority Rule. Astonishingly, a number of Labour backbenchers cheered.

As a reprisal for the *Tiger* breakdown, Wilson asked his representatives at the United Nations to call for international mandatory sanctions against Rhodesia. No one knew better than he that such measures were little short of useless. There were, he must now have realized, only two methods of bringing down the rebel regime. The first involved the use of British troops. The second was a showdown with South Africa. From the outset it had been plain to even the most amateur student of the sanctions game that the main reason for the sanctions' impotence was that South Africa ignored them. Both in the supply of oil in huge quantities through the Smith regime's front organization, Genta, and in the syphoning out of crucial Rhodesian exports, to be exported elsewhere as South African, the South African bourgeoisie – shouting racial solidarity and pocketing vast profits – saved the Smith regime from economic collapse.

By the *Tiger* meeting, some 22 per cent of Rhodesian exports were finding their way to unsuspecting customers through South African middlemen. If the South African breaches in sanctions could be closed, the Rhodesian regime would surely perish.

South Africa

Harold Wilson summed up his attitude towards South Africa and the racialist Government as early as 1948, when he was President of the Board of Trade. In a speech only three months after joining the Cabinet, he said:

Within the sterling area itself, there is one market of particular importance in view of its position as an important gold producer – South Africa. Exports to this market may indeed not only save dollars, but earn us gold, and in view of its importance as a long-term market it can be placed pretty well on a par, though for different reasons, with the three permanently important markets (*Daily Telegraph*, 20 January 1948).

Never was a more accurate assessment made of the economic relations between Britain and South Africa. From the earliest days, the economic destinies of the two countries have been indissolubly linked. No partnership thrived more on the relaxation of tariffs imposed by Empire Free Trade, and when South Africa left the Commonwealth for political reasons in 1961, 'Commonwealth preference' was left intact. Today South Africa is Britain's second biggest customer. It is no exaggeration that the entire British export programme and potential depends on the South African market. However, 'on the figures,' wrote a leading expert in these matters, 'South Africa is far more dependent on her trade with Britain than Britain is on her trade with South Africa. South Africa sells one third of her total exports, including gold, to Britain and buys 28 per cent of her total imports from Britain.'

More than £1,000m. of good British money is invested in South African industry, which is able permanently to undercut world prices through the liberal use of racial segregation, and consequently of cheap labour.

No one understands the importance of the economic links between the two countries more than Harold Wilson, and he has always been careful to draw the distinction between expanding trade between the two countries and political criticism of apartheid. His Christian conscience is revolted by South African racialism, but his common sense about economics reminds him that a great deal of British money is invested there. Condemnation of the South African regime is required by Nonconformist teaching, but that condemnation should on no account endanger the balance of payments. Thus Wilson, when he was Shadow Chancellor, steered clear of the South African issue. From 1954 to 1961 there is hardly a mention in his speeches of increasing racialism in Southern Africa. In his year as Shadow Foreign Secretary (1961– 62) he concentrated in the main on the Common Market, Berlin, and the Far East. In October 1962, he called for an immediate embargo on all arms to South Africa, and attacked the West German Government for sending arms. West Germany, he said, is 'the universal provider of arms to trouble spots'. References to South Africa, however, even when he was Shadow Foreign Secretary, were extremely rare, and all were kept well within the limits of Party policy. No observer could have guessed that the new Labour Party leader, elected in February 1963, was guided by a single-minded passion to put an end to apartheid in South Africa.

Shortly after being elected as leader of the Labour Party, however, Wilson agreed with his old friend and supporter, Barbara Castle, then President of the Anti-Apartheid Movement, to speak in Trafalgar Square, at a mass rally attended by some 20,000 people.[1]

Since the speech represents the high peak of idealism in the post-war Labour movement, and is also one of the few unequivocal attacks on the South African Government by Harold Wilson, it is worth quoting at some length:

1. The Anti-Apartheid Movement have done a considerable service by reprinting the full text of Wilson's speech as an Appendix to their excellent pamphlet by Anne Darnborough: *Labour's Record in Southern Africa*.

Things have gone from bad to worse in South Africa. Dr Verwoerd's regime now has all the odious trappings of a police state. . . . Even in the past year we have seen more and more brave believers in liberty put behind bars, or in one case condemned to death. The great leaders of South Africa – Luthuli, Sobukwe, Mandela – are all denied their liberty. . . .

There are more men under arms in South Africa than ever before. In two years their defence Budget has doubled. French Mirage jet fighters, Fouga jet aircraft, Lockheed Hercules transport planes, British Buccaneer military aircraft and many other means of destruction have either been delivered or are on their way to South Africa. We know of the role played by British-made Saracen armoured cars in the brutality we condemn today. . . .

Let me repeat where the Labour Party, for whom I am speaking today, stands on this issue. Under Hugh Gaitskell's leadership we condemned the supply of arms to South Africa as long as apartheid continues. That is the policy of the Labour Party today. It will be the policy of the Labour Party when we are called upon to form the Government of this country. And lest there be any doubt, we shall apply exactly the same policy in respect of arms supplied to the Portuguese Government for use in territories they control in Africa.

Towards the end of the speech came the inevitable holy text:

One of the formative influences of my life was a sermon I heard preached at a scout service by a colleague, now a leading Nonconformist Minister. He took as his text 'He hath made of one blood all nations of men to dwell on all the face of the earth'. That is the faith in which we stand. And we shall be judged as hypocrites if that faith is for export only.

The Trafalgar Square rally greatly strengthened the Anti-Apartheid Movement, and aroused much enthusiasm and idealism in the Labour movement. A special committee of the United Nations came down deliberately, and with great force, in favour of economic sanctions to squeeze the South African regime into changing its racial policies. 'Boycott South African Goods' movements gained strength throughout Britain. Some local authorities, notably Liverpool and Aberdeen, decided not to stock or to order South African goods.

In June 1964, Wilson reaffirmed his position on the arms embargo in categorical terms, in a television interview with one of his greatest admirers, Anthony Wedgwood Benn. It was in this interview that he talked of following President Kennedy's 'hundred days of dynamic action'. Benn asked him about Labour's opposition to the sale of arms to South Africa and to the sale of frigates to Spain. Wilson replied:

> I would never support the principle of the selling of arms to Fascist or Communist countries. This is a principle. Not everyone will agree with our view of what is an issue of principle, but when you are faced with a basic principle, if you try to tamper with it or compromise with it the only thing you can do is to get out of public life (*Daily Telegraph*, 16 July 1964).

Such principles, however, were not extended unreasonably. At the eighth meeting of the Socialist International in September 1963, the British Labour Party opposed a Scandinavian resolution calling for economic sanctions against South Africa. On 13 April 1964, Wilson told a meeting of Western European socialist leaders that a trade embargo, if effective, 'would harm the people we are most concerned about, the Africans and those whites fighting to maintain some standards of decency'. And, the following day, he sent a message to the International Conference on Economic Sanctions, which had opened in London.[1] 'Sanctions which hit at the people of South Africa,' he wrote, without reference to the fact that African leaders had called unanimously for economic sanctions, 'without influencing its Government would be futile and tragic.' Labour's attitude to South African trade was of great importance to that growing group of British businessmen who traded with South Africa. Many sought out Harold Wilson to probe his views on the crucial issue of trade with South Africa. At the select businessmen's lunches presided over by Wilson in London's most exclusive hotels, the matter of trade with South Africa was raised with concern, even threats.

Wilson's reaction was instantaneous. He passionately assured all who asked that on no account would trade or trading relations with South Africa be tampered with by a Labour Government. On the contrary, he made it clear, it was Labour's policy to expand trade with every area, not least with an area of such economic importance as South Africa.

The businessmen were convinced. In October 1963 Cyril

1. The proceedings were later published in book form: *Sanctions against South Africa*, ed. Ronald Segal (Penguin Books, 1964).

Lord, a textile manufacturer, declared publicly, 'Harold Wilson would do nothing to undermine trade relations with South Africa.' Never has a prophecy been so rigorously vindicated, and never has Harold Wilson so firmly kept a political pledge.

Three years after the Labour Government's coming to power, its Minister of State at the Board of Trade, Lord Walston, could proudly tell a businessmen's dinner that trade with South Africa had grown at a remarkable speed. In two years South Africa had jumped from fourth to second in the table of Britain's largest customers. British exporters, said Lord Walston, had made every use of the new machinery supplied by the Labour Government for facilitating South African trade, in particular the South African Section of the British National Exports Council. The BNEC was set up in the spring of 1964 by Edward Heath, who was then Minister for Trade and Industry. Some of Mr Heath's closest friends and admirers became leading officials in the BNEC, which at once established special Committees to deal with trade with the United States and most European countries. The Conservatives, however, did not sponsor a South African section of the BNEC, perhaps for fear of criticism from the then Opposition that they were thus actively assisting apartheid. The South African Section was set up in February 1966 under a Labour Government, under the chairmanship of W. E. Luke, Chairman of Lindustries, a constant and popular visitor to South Africa.

All these organizations were, of course, greatly assisted by 'Imperial Preference' between the two countries, which, although South Africa had left the Commonwealth in 1961, by mutual consent was never removed. When, three months later, a left-wing Labour MP asked the Prime Minister why he would not 'withdraw the benefits of Imperial Preference from the Republic of South Africa', Wilson replied: 'This would involve the denunciation of our trade agreements and I see no case for it.'

One of the more bizarre examples of the extraordinary increase in business communication between Britain and South Africa in the first three years of Labour Government was the delegation to South Africa from the Birmingham Chamber of Commerce in November 1966. The mission was headed by Oscar Hahn, a prominent and distinguished liberal businessman. Mr Hahn had a busy week. Three days before he took off for Johannesburg he had been appointed chairman of the Birmingham Conciliation Committee of the Race Relations Board. The conciliation committees were set up under the Government's Race Relations Act, in order to investigate cases of racial prejudice or discrimination in places of public resort. Nothing more clearly indicated the Labour Government's (and Harold Wilson's) flexible approach to race relations than the activities of Oscar Hahn – busily promoting trade with a country whose social system is based on racial discrimination and returning home to help the Government smooth out the wrinkles of racial discrimination at home.

Yet in spite of all the hard work and effort undergone by the Government to improve trade with South Africa, the businessmen were still not entirely happy. What worried them was the arms embargo which, as he had promised, Harold Wilson announced to the Commons soon after taking power. The embargo, however, was not total. Announcing it, Wilson surprised his more faithful supporters by saying that 'existing contracts will be honoured', and, more particularly, that the sixteen low-flying Buccaneer strike bombers on order by the South African Government would be delivered. 'Her Majesty's Government, will, of course, allow the shipment of spares for the sixteen Buccaneers as and when required,' Wilson went on.

Only a year previously, Mrs Barbara Castle had summed up Labour Party policy on this matter for the National Executive to a cheering Labour Conference:

> We know that the Buccaneer aircraft are still being made in British factories for South Africa. The order has not been cancelled. We say that a Labour Government would cancel that order and substitute a better one, because there are many better purposes to which those aircraft could be put – for example defending the frontiers of India against aggression (Labour Party Conference Report, 1963, p. 223).

In June 1965, permission was given to Vauxhall Motors to sell £400,000-worth of four-wheel drive chassis for armoured cars or motor lorries for the South African army. No mention was made of what Harold Wilson eighteen months earlier had described as 'the role of British armoured cars in the brutality we condemn today'.

By these direct examples, and a host of other more subtle ruses, such as the building of British equipment by licence in other countries, the assistance given by British firms to the building-up of South Africa's expanding home-based armaments industry, and the widespread use of legal fictions to include sales under the heading 'existing contracts to be honoured', British businessmen have contrived to avoid the harsher excesses of the arms embargo.

None of this, however, succeeded in stopping the whining of the industrialists. Mr Luke, for instance, chairman of the South African Section of the BNEC, mourned the great damage done to trade and profits in both countries by the embargo. In a speech in Glasgow in late September 1967, he said:

> It is not for me to tell the Government what to do. They are adhering to undertakings they have given. . . . The results, unfortunately, are likely to mean a permanent trade loss for this country. The Government is well aware of our views on this matter. Some people in South Africa bitterly resent the implementation of the arms embargo and, when other countries step in, trade links are created which spread like measles to non-embargoed goods.

Mr Luke might easily have had his way. For a long time before his Glasgow speech, and probably unknown to him, the British Government had been plotting to swap a relaxation of the arms embargo for assistance in a solution to the Rhodesian impasse.

One of the most startling aspects about Harold Wilson's speeches on Rhodesia after the declaration of independence was their reluctance to mention South Africa, or in any way to censure that country for deliberately and openly defying the express wish of the United Nations. In his speech to the House of Commons in December 1965 he referred to the possibility that Rhodesian exports could seep through South Africa or Mozambique:

> Honourable Members opposite entirely misconceive the whole feeling in Africa and in the United Nations if they think that in the event of such a seepage nothing would be done about it.

Precisely what would be 'done about it' asked a Tory back-bencher, interrupting, if South Africa tolerated or encouraged such a seepage? Wilson answered:

> I do not speak for South Africa. I cannot forecast what its attitude will be. I would feel that South Africa would behave with great prudence and caution in this matter concerning Rhodesia. South Africa has not recognized the illegal regime (House of Commons, 21 December 1965).

From the start of the Rhodesian crisis, Wilson's attitude towards South Africa was extremely cautious. He relied throughout on seducing the South Africans to keep out of the Rhodesian crisis, and to maintain the status quo. The only other reference to South Africa in all Wilson's thousands of public words on the Rhodesian crisis is even more illuminating. Once again, it arose after an interruption from the Tory benches – in the debate on the Queen's Speech immediately after Labour's election victory in 1966:

> We are in discussion with the South African Government at this time. We have had two series of exchanges, and there will be more exchanges. We must await the result of those exchanges. I will not be pushed by the Rt Hon. Gentleman into stirring up unnecessary trouble with another country (House of Commons, 21 April 1966).

George Woodcock, then General Secretary of the Trades Union Congress, once remarked in a famous summary of modern politics that his movement had moved out of Trafalgar Square into the committee rooms. The spectacle of Harold Wilson, former scourge of the South African Government in Trafalgar Square, indulging in committee-room 'exchanges' and begging the Tories meanwhile not 'to stir up unnecessary trouble' is surely the best available example of the Woodcock rule.

What was at stake in those committee-room exchanges was the settlement of the Rhodesia problem – a settlement which, in spite of the continued and open support given to Smith by South African merchants and middlemen, was of crucial interest to the South African Government.

For some years before UDI, the South African Premier, Dr Hendrik Verwoerd, had pursued a policy of 'friendly relations' with the African Governments of the British Protectorates immediately to the north of his country. On 25 April 1964, he had asked the South African Parliament 'if it was not realistic to accept that the people of the Protectorates wanted self-Government and that the best thing possible was to lay the foundations for good neighbourly relations with them. . . . He expressed confidence in the integrity of the African leaders not to become Communists' (*Johannesburg Sunday Times*, 25 September 1966). Accordingly, shortly before his assassination, Verwoerd met

Chief Leabua Jonathon, Prime Minister of Lesotho, in the Union Buildings, Pretoria, on 2 September 1966. As a result of the meeting, in spite of Jonathon's expulsion from the white section of a Bloemfontein bank by a manager who regarded him as a precocious kaffir, Lesotho became independent.

This policy was followed by Verwoerd's successor, the more pragmatic and brutal racialist, John Vorster. In March 1967, Vorster welcomed a trade delegation from Malawi, comprising three Cabinet Ministers, including the Minister of Trade and Industry, Jeremy Kumbweza. The delegation was feted by the South African Government and was persuaded with little difficulty to sign a trade and friendship agreement with the South African Government. The visit brought it home forcefully to the Vorster Government that it was safer, easier and more profitable for them to bribe black majority Governments than to prop up white minority Governments. The economic helplessness of the black nations in the North made their dependence on South Africa inevitable. Their colour and majority support not only secured the economic situation, but also distracted international moral outrage. Apartheid, in short, though clearly crucial in South Africa, was quite unnecessary and even a nuisance elsewhere.[1]

The *Tiger* proposals on Rhodesia would have been welcomed by the South African Government. They would have stabilized the economic situation, without any immediate revolutionary upheaval, and removed the threat of international economic sanctions from the area. The only difficulty was the ideological and racial solidarity shown by so many white South African citizens towards Ian Smith, reinforced by the large profits made out of sanctions by South African merchants. By early 1967, more than a quarter of Rhodesian exports passed through South African middlemen. What was required was some back-door method by which some of the economic loopholes in economic sanctions could be

1. When Joe Kachingwe came to Cape Town to take up his post as First Secretary at the new Malawi mission in South Africa a secluded house in a white suburb was found for him by the Ministry of Community Development. White neighbours in the area agreed that Mr Kachingwe – the first African diplomat even to take up residence in South Africa – would be welcome. Willie Maree, the Minister for Community Development, said that a lot of money had been spent isolating the house, and the whole matter was being treated 'with discretion' (*Observer*, January 1965).

tightened, thus squeezing the Smith regime into a possible settlement.

The 'exchanges' which Wilson had announced in April 1966 continued throughout the summer. In October, the Foreign Secretary, George Brown, discussed Rhodesia with his South African counterpart, Dr Hilgard Muller, a former Oxford rugger blue and an Anglophile. No doubt on all these occasions the South Africans contributed much of their constitutional expertise, particularly about 'entrenched clauses', towards framing the *Tiger* proposals. The rejection of the *Tiger* plan was mourned by both British and South African Governments. Nevertheless, both still held out hope. In May 1967, Robert Farquharson, First Secretary at the Foreign Office, until that time head of the sanctions department of the FO, was transferred to the post of 'assistant consul general' in Johannesburg.

The Foreign Office insisted that the appointment bore no relation to Mr Farquharson's former work. Yet many aspects of the appointment surprised diplomatic correspondents. Farquharson's former job had invoked the highest political decisions and was of supreme international and political importance. There was, in fact, no more crucial job in the service. His new job, on paper, was no more than that of glorified salesman. It was, on the face of it, a demotion.

More realistically, some correspondents suggested that Farquharson's new job was not entirely unconnected with his expertise in the field of sanctions against Rhodesia. And that every effort would be made by the new 'assistant consul general' in Johannesburg to close some of the vital loopholes through which Rhodesian exports were escaping.

If Mr Farquharson was examining these loopholes, his reports home during the spring and summer of 1967 must have become increasingly depressing for the British Government and Prime Minister. Rhodesian exports increased, South African loopholes widened, and business confidence in Salisbury and Bulawayo reached an all-time high. In the late summer, further meetings were arranged between the British Government and the South African Governments, from which it became entirely clear, first that the chances of the South African Government effectively 'squeezing' the Smith regime were growing smaller every week;

and secondly, that if anything was done, the South Africans would expect a *quid pro quo*. The only *quid pro quo* which the British Government could provide was a relaxation in the arms embargo.

In late August, Harold Wilson changed Commonwealth Secretaries once more and made a further bid to negotiate a Rhodesian settlement. The faithful Bowden, who had proved so stubborn over Rhodesia, was rewarded with a peerage and the chairmanship of the Independent Television Authority. In his place, George Thomson announced soon after his appointment that he would be making a tour of Africa in November, visiting, among other countries, Rhodesia.

Before Thomson's visit, communications between the British and South African Governments on Rhodesia rose to a crescendo. On 10 October, Dr Hilgard Muller visited Wilson in Downing Street for 'friendly talks'. 'Mr Wilson,' reported the *Daily Express*, 'told Dr Muller that if South Africa stopped trading with Rhodesia then it would not be long before the illegal regime collapsed.' A meeting was also arranged in Pretoria between Mr Vorster, Mr Muller and Ian Smith. Reports of the exchanges were not helpful, but most commentators indicated that Vorster and Muller urged Smith to settle with the British Government on something rather more favourable to the Rhodesian whites than the *Tiger* proposals.

Yet, once more, Rhodesian racialism had outpaced the will to compromise. Even if Smith himself agreed with Vorster, he could not afford to concede an inch from his position after the *Tiger* meeting.

Mr Thomson, who arrived in Salisbury on 28 October, was greeted cordially, but firmly. Though Smith no doubt took note of the fact that the British Government were prepared not only to shelve the 'NIBMAR' pledge, but also to go further than on the *Tiger* to meet the regime's demands, the answer was No. Thomson reported to the Commons later that the regime had refused to move at all from its position before the *Tiger* confrontation.

The failure of the Thomson mission and the inevitable, if rather less strident, reassertion of NIBMAR, indicated that for the time being the chances of squeezing Rhodesia through South Africa were slim. Nevertheless, the South Africans, having sensed the possibility of a relaxation of the arms embargo, kept up the pressure. They argued that the extension of the naval base at Simonstown, which had taken on added importance since the closure of the Suez Canal the previous June, and the wider role which they envisaged for the Cape as a route to the East, justified the sale by Britain to South Africa of a wide range of naval equipment which had been cut off by the arms embargo. Many of the 'contracts' made before the embargo had now been honoured, and it was time to make some more: notably for a few more Buccaneer jets.

Accordingly, the South African Admiral Heinrik Biermans arranged to visit Britain in mid-December to discuss the matter with British Chiefs of Staff, and a deadline for a final British decision was set for 31 December 1967.

The matter came up at the Cabinet Overseas Policy and Defence Sub-Committee on Friday, 8 December. The Committee was presided over by the Prime Minister and attended by the new Chancellor, Roy Jenkins; Anthony Crosland; the Lord Chancellor, Lord Gardiner; Michael Stewart; Richard Marsh; Lord Longford; Dennis Healey; George Brown; and George Thomson. There were also present a number of junior Ministers, including John Stonehouse, deputizing for the Minister of Technology. When the South African arms issue was discussed, a majority of Ministers took the view that in her present crisis Britain could not afford to continue the embargo rigidly, and an exception might well be made in the case of naval equipment and the Buccaneers. Wilson's position, according to the authoritative account by Alan Watkins in the *New Statesman*, was equivocal. He said little or nothing about the actual embargo, and accepted the majority view that the South Africans should be asked to postpone their 'deadline' by a month.

In the next few days the press was full of Government doubts about the arms embargo. Mr Callaghan, who was not at the original meeting, told a dinner of young Labour MPs that the embargo could not be sacrosanct. Mr Gunter and Mr Gordon Walker joined the ranks of those who wanted to lift the ban. On the other hand, the Parliamentary Labour Party indicated clearly that the vast majority of Labour MPs firmly backed the embargo. A motion reaffirming support for the embargo received 130 signatures and only 6 of those approached refused to sign. At a full Cabinet meeting on Friday, 14 December, the group of Ministers who wanted to relax the embargo were in a minority, but the decision of the Overseas Policy Committee to seek a delay of a month was upheld after a vote.

This decision was again agreed to by the Prime Minister.

That weekend, almost all the newspapers carried stories which had clearly been placed by the Ministers opposed to the embargo. Wilson, declared the press, had suffered a grave defeat. Some papers, notably *The Times*, the *Evening News* and, in headlines, the *Sunday Telegraph*, suggested that Wilson had lost his authority in the Cabinet, and that he might even be replaced.

Stung by these Press reports and encouraged by the advice of Lord Wigg of Dudley, Wilson summoned a further meeting of the Cabinet on the morning of Monday, 18 December. He insisted that his position was now intolerable. Rather sheepishly, with the single exception of George Brown, the Ministers agreed, and accordingly Wilson announced in a few short sentences to the cheers of the Parliamentary Labour Party that the arms embargo to South Africa remained firm and unequivocal. That evening, at a party given for lobby correspondents at 10 Downing Street, Wilson turned from one correspondent to the next complaining bitterly about the press coverage of the Friday Cabinet meeting. He left the newspapermen in no doubt that the Cabinet meeting that morning had been called solely because of allegations in the press about his personal position.

It would be wrong, however, to conclude that Harold Wilson would never have consented to lifting the arms embargo. On the contrary, if the Rhodesian crisis could have been settled as a result, Harold Wilson would almost certainly have relaxed the embargo without undue qualms and without undue publicity.

As if to prove the point that no generalization about the arms embargo was possible, two Sunday newspapers on Christmas Eve, 1967, reported that the Government had approved the sale of eighteen Beagle light aircraft to the South African Government, but that the American Government, under whose licence the Beagle engines were manufactured, had vetoed the sale. The vote, it was reported, followed an American investigation proving that the Beagle aircraft would be used for military or internal security purposes.

Six days later the *Daily Mail* reported that the British Government were furious with the American veto, particularly as the Americans had been selling a number of their Cessna light aircraft to the South Africans. The Cessnas, apparently, although sold only to private enterprise in South Africa, had been purchased by the South African Army and used as 'spotters' and carriers in internal security. The British Government, reported the *Mail*, were convinced that the American veto was inspired by the aim further to open up the market for Cessnas. The evidence of British officials proved beyond all reasonable doubt that the Beagles too, if they had been bought by the South Africans, would almost certainly have been used for military or internal security purposes. Indeed the Beagle 206 had been specially reconstructed for military use and twenty of them had already been bought by the RAF.

The Beagle sale had arisen first when Michael Stewart was Foreign Secretary and had been considered for a long time by the Government. The initial inclination was to ban the sale under the South African arms embargo, but in 1966, under the inspiration of the Ministry of Technology, the Government bought the Beagle company and became entirely responsible for its financial affairs.

The South African sale then became crucial to the survival of a new Government firm, and eventually, after solemn guarantees that the planes would be used only for 'air-sea rescue work and fishery patrols', the Government agreed to sanction the sale. The Government, in short, did not take a 'dogmatic view' about South African arms. Each case was considered 'on its merits'.

The meaning of the word 'racialism' varies widely with the user of it. If it means an ideological commitment to the theory that black men are inferior to white, and that therefore they should be treated in a less privileged fashion, Simon Kapwepwe's definition of Harold Wilson at the head of this chapter is wrong. Wilson is not ideologically committed to any theory of racial inferiority. On the contrary, he 'believes' that all men are of one blood, and, other things being equal, his political responses correspond with that belief. While most other British politicians describe themselves as multi-racialists, Wilson goes out of his way to proclaim his fundamental belief in racial equality. Shortly after his election as Prime Minister in Autumn 1964 he astonished the diners at the

Guildhall Lord Mayor's banquet with a speech devoted almost exclusively to attacking racialism, including racialism in the Smethwick Labour Club. And when Peter Griffiths came to the House of Commons after his flamboyant exploitation of the race issue in October 1964, Wilson attacked him bitterly, and called on the Tories to treat him as 'a Parliamentary leper'. Both these speeches won Wilson the respect of Liberals in the Labour Movement, but neither cost him anything in money or in votes.

Yet, if Simon Kapwepwe is wrong, the other commentators quoted at the head of the chapter are wrong too. For the gap between statements about multi-racialism and political activity to promote it is a wide one. It is true that 'other things being equal', Harold Wilson will act for racial equality. But 'other things' are usually not equal. More often than not other factors intrude upon a straight choice between racialism and multi-racialism. The electorate, for example, may not agree with a rational case for unlimited immigration. A policy of unlimited immigration, though unanswerable in logic or in principle, may lose votes. The offer of a council house to a black man may cause ill-feeling which did not exist before. Subjection of the Rhodesian regime with troops could strain the loyalty of Her Majesty's regiments. Sanctions against South Africa could ruin the balance of payments . . . and so on. In all such instances, a logical and principled line on race matters involves acting in a way which may be harmful in some other directions. And it is in such instances that Harold Wilson has preferred the easy way out. The August 1965 Immigration White Paper, which he sponsored, abandoned former policy and principle for electoral gain. The *Tiger* meeting with Smith was in itself a breach of a pledge never to negotiate with a rebel, and the terms on which Wilson was prepared to settle made nonsense of everything promised by Labour to the Rhodesian Africans.

The soft-soap treatment of the South African Government during the Rhodesian crisis, and the gradual corrosion of the arms embargo, were part of an attempt to subdue one racialist regime by appeasing a worse one. In only one issue – that of the South African arms embargo – has Harold Wilson placed multi-racialist principle before electoral or balance of payments considerations. And even his stand on the arms embargo was hedged about with conditions and vacillation.

Perhaps the clearest example of the collapse under pressure of Wilson's Boy-Scout Christian values on race was the Commonwealth Immigrants Act 1968. Large numbers of Labour Party members, and most Labour MPs, would have been delighted if the Government had turned down the demands for control of the Kenyan Asians. Labour Ministers were presented with a moral crisis from which, had they chosen to oppose control, they could have emerged with their principles unscathed and their electoral position almost undamaged. In the event, they chose the weak and easy course. And in that choice, their leader was silent, effectively condoning the measure. In this moral crisis, as in so many others, Harold Wilson had remained neutral. If his own quotation from Dante was accurate, he had booked himself a reservation in the hottest place in hell.

Chapter 9
War and Peace with World Poverty

Harold Wilson's interest in the plight of what are now termed 'the underdeveloped countries' was first aroused in February 1947 when, as a junior Minister, he led Britain's delegation to the United Nations World Food and Agricultural Preparatory Commission Conference. The Conference was one of the many idealistic ventures engaged upon by the United Nations and its subsidiary organizations in the flush of internationalism following the UN's foundation. It was called by Lord Boyd Orr, the first Director General of the Food and Agricultural Organization, and its aim was to discuss a detailed and radical plan drawn up almost entirely by Boyd Orr himself, 'to make sure,' as Wilson later explained to the Commons, 'that the shortage of food for ordinary people of the world will come to an end as food production increases and not continue for twenty-five years.'

Boyd Orr's plan started with the necessity of ensuring adequate distribution throughout the underdeveloped world of food surpluses in agriculturally rich countries – a problem which did not immediately affect Britain. But it moved on to recommend sweeping action in the field of international prices, which, in effect, amounted to a massive subsidy of poor by rich to enable the poorer countries to develop their economies in a secure international economic setting. Prices of the basic equipment, mainly machinery and manufactured goods, suggested the Report, should be held at artificially low levels, their losses sustained by a World Food Board which would be financed from contributions from the rich countries. Similarly, international prices for raw materials and primary products from underdeveloped countries should be fixed to avoid the poorer countries being penalized by sudden gluts and falls in prices of their basic goods.

Both these proposals were rejected by the Conference, whose decisions depended on the agreement of the large industrial nations. On the price proposals, Wilson explained to the Commons after his return, 'It is a plain fact that our own foreign exchange position would not enable us to be a party to an arrangement of that kind' (6 February 1947). Similarly, Boyd Orr's World Food Board was whittled down by the Conference to a much less powerful Food Council, with no powers on prices and very few powers of international levy. The proposal for instance for buffer stocks to be held by an international body, financed by the industrial countries, was rejected in favour of national buffer stocks, whose size and distribution would be controlled by the Food Council. Nevertheless, Britain did accept certain aspects of the food plan – notably the need to initiate big schemes for food development in the poor countries, and the desirability of long-term contracts. Wilson initiated both politics and proudly announced to the Commons that 'the big scheme for the development of ground-nut production in East Africa is one of the most important things ever done in this field'. He concluded:

The Report [of the Conference] provides a new deal in the world food and agricultural situation. We have taken Boyd Orr's great conception and have produced from it a practical scheme which we believe will work. . . . There are hundreds of millions of people in the world who under the plans of this Government and under the international arrangements in the Report have a far brighter prospect of adequate food supplies for their families (House of Commons, 6 February 1947).

Wilson's undoubted interest in and concern for the problems of the underdeveloped countries was soon submerged in administrative work at the Board of Trade – first as Secretary for Overseas Trade and then as President. He watched however with some dismay as the Government's policy, which he had proudly proclaimed in 1947, gradually collapsed. Direct assistance for food production in the Commonwealth was compromised by the bureaucratic disaster of the ground-nuts scheme, and the policy of building buffer stocks never started to succeed. The Food Council declined from the powerful body Boyd Orr had envisaged into an administrative bureaucracy at the mercy of the agricultural policies of the big industrial nations. Only in their reliance on long-term contracts with Commonwealth countries did the British Government act in the spirit of the 1947 Conference.

When Wilson resigned from the Government in 1951, his interest in the underdeveloped nations revived. In May 1951, he was approached by the publisher Victor Gollancz, who had formed an organization called the Association for World Peace, and asked if he would prepare a report on the problems of world development on behalf of the Association. The following month he took the chair at a committee of businessmen and trade unionists from different parts of the Western world whose purpose was to discover how the money at that time being devoted to world rearmament could be spent on development in the underdeveloped countries. This last step got a mixed response. The American trade union leader Walter Reuther, who served on it, described its purpose as 'to combat Communism', while the Communist Party regarded its main intention as 'to involve United States Big Business' (*Daily Worker*, 8 June 1951). The Committee recommended that at least a quarter of the money at that time spent on arms could and should be spent instead on world development.

World poverty soon become Wilson's central theme. He told his constituents:

Stalinite Communism is an idea, but you don't kill an idea with guns, tanks and bombing planes. You have to destroy it with a better idea, a stronger faith. In the backward areas of the world, social justice, a higher standard of life, is the best answer to Communism (Prescot meeting, 9 September 1951).

The work of the first committee was published in the middle of 1952, and by now Harold Wilson had become deeply involved in his subject. Speaking at a socialist youth congress in Vienna he proclaimed:

Build up our national defences, yes, but once the minimum necessary for repairing gaps in our national defences has been achieved, then I believe another pound, another dollar, another franc spent on the machinery and materials of world development are a better guarantee of peace than the same money spent on guns and tanks and bombing planes (*Manchester Guardian*, 8 July 1952).

The title of the pamphlet produced by Wilson's committee was *War on Want* – the name eventually given to a charity which grew out of the Association for World Peace. Yet Wilson's views on the underdeveloped countries at that time, though often expressed in religious and charity terms, were essentially political, dealing with political and economic solutions in the long term. The pamphlet

War on Want was, on Gollancz's suggestion, enlarged by Wilson into a full-scale book, *The War on World Poverty*, which Gollancz duly published in 1953. *The War on World Poverty*, which was written several years before the 'Third World' became a fashionable subject for academics, is an excellent statement of the appalling division between the world's rich and poor and the importance of international action to deal with the problem. It is distinguished from many other works of Harold Wilson in that the careful detail and argument is supported, unquestionably, by a horror of the poverty, squalor, disease and illiteracy which it unveils.

There is one reason above all others why the world should be mobilized against human poverty. It is not a question of self-interest or power politics. It is a moral imperative. We are rich and they are poor, and it is our duty to help them (p. 25).

Nor does help in this context mean buying off individual consciences with three-guinea cheques to Oxfam. On the contrary, as Wilson goes on to explain, it means international trade agreements to stabilize prices of primary products. It means world mobilization for investment in education in the underdeveloped areas 'on a scale never previously contemplated'. It means a transfer of capital from rich to poor countries of at a minimum two per cent of the national product of the rich countries, a re-dedication to bilateral colonial development programmes such as the Colombo Plan, and, above all, the creation of a World Development Authority.

For, Wilson argued, 'bilateral' aid policies were 'involved in national strategic considerations'. The war on world poverty, on the other hand, was justified in itself, and could only properly be fought by an international agency, equipped and financed by money from the rich countries.

This would involve a contribution by the advanced countries of, on the average, about three per cent of their national income, though, of course, on the principle of equal sacrifice the richest nations could afford not merely a higher absolute contribution, but a higher proportion of their national income (p. 175).

Britain's contribution to the World Development Authority, suggested Wilson, should be 'of the order of £350m. to £400m. a year'. Moreover, if the United States and others refused to join such an Authority, Britain should 'go it alone'. For 'it is in such a policy that Britain's duty lies'.

The book ends with an orgasm of idealism. Quoting from Louis Blanc, 'From each according to his ability, to each according to his means', Wilson wrote:

> Men of goodwill in Britain, and particularly the Labour Movement, have prided themselves on the fifty year's march out of nineteenth-century industrialism and inequality towards social justice and the welfare state. More than half a century ago, the pioneers of this movement, seeing all around them the ugliness, the squalor, the misery, the want and poverty which Victorian capitalism had brought in its train, dedicated themselves and those who came after them to the creation of a New Britain in which hunger and poverty would be no more. Their dream has been very largely realized. Now those who honour their memory must look to wider horizons: their mission in the second half of this war-torn century must be to carry the war on poverty and want to the uttermost ends of the earth. . . . The war on world poverty, which must be Britain's historic mission in what remains of the twentieth century, is the only way in which we in the more favoured countries can fulfil our obligations to 1,500 million people all over the world; and, lifting our eyes above the tensions and struggles of world politics, we shall find that in fighting this war we are treading the way – the one way only – to peace and a more abundant life for all mankind (p. 203).

The War on World Poverty foreshadowed the approach of the Labour Party in Opposition towards the end of empire. As the years went on, Labour committed itself more and more firmly to a policy of aid for development in the underdeveloped countries. In 1957, the Labour Party National Executive approved the document *Economic Aid and Labour's Colonial Policy*, which was approved unanimously by the Labour Party Conference of that year. The document committed the Labour Government to an expenditure on public economic aid of at least one per cent of the national income over a period of years. Explaining the policy to the Conference, on behalf of the Executive, Barbara Castle said:

> One or two delegates from the rostrum said: 'What does it mean? Is it going to be a fiddle?' I will tell you exactly what it means, and why we put in the words 'over a period of years'. It *does* mean that the Labour Chancellor will earmark the equivalent of one per cent of the national income, which at present levels of income would mean something in the

neighbourhood of £160m. a year, as our yearly contribution; but he is not, and cannot be, committed to make that allocation necessarily in the first Budget; he wants freedom of planning – which is fair enough – to see that this annual contribution is spent in such a way that best fits in with the domestic problems we shall meet when we come into power, whether they be inflation or deflation. He must have manoeuvrability. But over five years a sum totalling £160m. per year will be spent on developing our colonies. That is a very specific commitment and a very important one. We know the priorities are piling up on Harold Wilson as next Chancellor of the Exchequer for our own social services, but we do here today specifically say, however clamorous the demands from our own people for increases in social services, that the colonies should have an equal priority in the demands on the next Labour Chancellor (Labour Party Conference Report, 1957, p.198).

Harold Wilson must have cheered loudly at that commitment, though the £160m. demanded by his colleague on the NEC was less than half the £350 to £400m. he himself had demanded four years previously in *The War on World Poverty*. But at least here was an official Labour endorsement of the importance of aid and the fight against poverty which he had so passionately proclaimed.

Throughout the 1950s and early 1960s Harold Wilson stuck closely to this theme. Most of his economic speeches, in and outside Parliament, referred to the puny efforts being made to bolster the underdeveloped world, and his complicated plans for reforms of world liquidity were inspired primarily by the need to finance more investment in the poor world.

In 1963, shortly after becoming leader, he wrote a long essay for the *Encyclopaedia Britannica* on the meaning of British socialism, which was subsequently published in this country as a book called *The Relevance of British Socialism*. The book contains a short chapter entitled 'The War on World Poverty', which makes sad reading after the explosive passion of its longer and more idealistic namesake. Indeed the best that can be said for the chapter is that it restated the British Labour Movement's concern for the problem of world poverty, and indicated its intention to deal with it more ambitiously than hitherto.

Gone are the demands for massive mobilization of capital from the rich countries to the poor. No specific sum or percentage for aid from rich to poor is specified. Gone are the threats to 'go it alone' in establishing international machinery for aid and development. The World Development Authority is mentioned, in passing, without any commitment to the amount of money it would need, or to how it should be set up. Instead the section welcomes the increase in public aid to the underdeveloped world; explains that private investment is not enough; attacks the commercialization of aid through the charging of high interest rates; predicts (wrongly) that 'bilateral' aid will inevitably be superseded by multilateral aid; and argues in great technical detail for 'regional planning' continent by continent with preferential tariffs within and without the regions so as to assist in investment, in industrial substructure and agriculture. Finally the essay makes a plea for cooperation between East and West to turn the arms race into a 'friendly development race, where East and West can vie with each other, on the basis of their contrasting forms of society, to see which can do the more to drive poverty and hunger from the world' (pp. 96, 97).

The War on World Poverty, written in 1953, was a combination of careful analysis and militant demands. Its successor, ten years later, applied a familiar Wilsonian recipe: safe, technical demands overlaid with idealistic rhetoric. Only the rhetoric had persisted, again convincing all but the 'sectarians'. Wilson told the euphoric 1963 Conference at Scarborough:

Labour means business about world development. We are going to establish a full-scale Ministry of Overseas Development, with a Minister of Cabinet rank, to join with the Ministry of Science in mobilizing Britain's scientific wealth for the task of creating, not the means of human destruction, but the munitions of peace.

Again and again the pledge was repeated throughout the long election campaign of 1964. In January he wrote an exclusive article for the *Daily Herald* entitled 'Operation Adventure' reiterating the bogus idealism which heralded Kennedy's Peace Corps and calling on British youth to dedicate themselves to Labour's plan for reinvigorating the underdeveloped world. Unhappily, however, the meaty proposals Wilson himself had made in 1953 had degenerated into electioneering slogans. The Labour Manifesto was quite unspecific on what exactly the Government plans and commitments were for 'Operation Adventure'.

In the first Labour Cabinet appointments announced in October 1964, Mrs Barbara Castle, Wilson's most consistent admirer throughout the years, was given the post of Minister of Overseas Development in the Cabinet. The new Ministry took on work previously administered by the Foreign Office, the Commonwealth Relations Office, the Ministry of Agriculture, the Ministry of Education, the Colonial Office and, chiefly, the Department of Technical Cooperation. A host of experts, mainly economists, were taken on, particularly in the Economic Planning Department headed by Dudley Seers.

Mrs Castle set about her task with characteristic energy and enthusiasm. In the first six months of office she visited India, Pakistan, Jordan and most of the countries in East Africa. She persuaded Zanzibar to accept £300,000 of aid from Britain, previously classified as imperialist. She also persuaded the chiefs in the Arusha district of Tanzania to stop evicting white farmers. Despite protests, mainly from the Ministry of Education, recruitment to teaching and technical training jobs in underdevelopment countries was stepped up. A corps of specialists for work overseas was set up, as was the home-based Institute of Development Studies at Sussex University. The staffing of British embassies with people who knew about aid problems was started in those months, and the Caribbean Development Division – a perfect example of 'regional aid planning' – was established.

By far the most concrete achievement was the announcement on 19 June 1965 – only nine months after the Government took office – that most loans to underdeveloped countries would, from that date, be interest-free. This was a dramatic and meaningful reform, which brought the average interest rate payable on British loans down from 5 per cent in 1963 to 1 per cent in 1967. Given the state of the economy at the time and the sensitivity of the balance of payments, the 'interest-free loans' announcement was a remarkable tribute to Mrs Castle's negotiating powers.

Indeed most of Mrs Castle's time at the Ministry of Overseas Development was spent in argument with her fellow Ministers in an attempt to maintain and increase the existing aid commitment. The most important argument – and the most tedious – concerned the extent to which aid was a drain on the balance of payments. With a hail of carefully argued memoranda and much bullying in the corridors of power, the Ministry of Overseas Development established its case with the Treasury: that aid does not consititute a serious balance of payments drain; and that in the long run it can only be for the benefit of everyone. Signs that the Treasury were at last convinced by this argument gave rise to considerable confidence in the new Ministry, which prepared its first White Paper in an atmosphere of excitement and idealism.

For the first time, aid became the subject of a coherent and intelligible economic plan. After a preamble, which reads today like a clarion call, the White Paper stated:

> We shall need to plan our aid with great care. In the immediate future, the shape of our programme will be largely determined by existing commitments, but, as time goes by, our ability to modify it will increase progressively as new decisions have to be taken. We shall aim to develop a long-term strategy for aid, so that we don't simply react to past decisions and pressures of the moment. Our main guiding principle will be to channel our aid in directions in which it will make the most effective contribution to development.

This new idea that aid should not represent an automatic response to political activity or capitalist enterprise in the colonial world – an 'independence' grant here, a harbour to assist mining interests there, a steelworks somewhere else – but a planned attempt properly to tackle development was by far the most encouraging feature of the White Paper.

Yet in spite of the Treasury's apparent conversion to such enthusiasm, and in spite of Mrs Castle's success in staving off demands for cuts in aid commitments in the economic 'mini-squeeze' of July 1965, an ominous threat to the work of the new Ministry presented itself suddenly from a totally different quarter – the Department of Economic Affairs. There, George Brown and a team of economists rather different in their political conviction to those hired by Mrs Castle had been immersed in the preparation of Britain's First (and possibly last) National Plan.

The aims of the National Plan were quite simple – to switch resources in Britain from consumption to investment and to build up the sub-structure of British industry. It was, in fact, as its name implied, first and foremost a *national* plan. It was therefore not at all concerned with international obligations, still less with the plight of the poor and the hungry abroad. Indeed even the British poor and hungry were almost completely overlooked by the Plan, which concentrated solely and exclusively on growth.

Whatever the force of the argument, which had convinced the Treasury, that aid was not a drain on the balance of payments, the bright, dynamic economists in the DEA would have none of it. As she presented her White paper to the Cabinet, Mrs Castle discovered that her main enemy was George Brown, the First Secretary in charge of Economic Affairs. Brown insisted that the commitment to more aid should be taken out of the White Paper. He then proceeded to argue against the general tone of the document and the call for 'new initiatives'. Such initiatives, he argued, were totally incompatible with his National Plan. Economic growth, for Mr Brown, was a serious business. Skilled economists and scarce investment resources should not be sliced off the national cake merely to feed hungry foreigners. As it turned out, Brown's forecast that the aid White Paper would contradict the National Plan were vindicated. The White Paper was published after much Cabinet argument, on 3 August 1965. The National Plan was published a month later. The latter contained two brief, contemptuous references to aid. First, 'aid to developing countries will be restrained, and the effectiveness of each pound of aid increased' (p. 17), and secondly, 'the size of the aid programme will be reviewed periodically in the light of progress made in overcoming our economic problems; meanwhile the Plan makes provision for only a small rise over the levels of the current year' (p. 75, para. 39).

The crude contradiction between the attitude of the DEA and that of the new Ministry provides a clear insight into similar contradictions in the attitudes of the Prime Minister. The National Plan, though constructed by George Brown, was Wilson's favourite conception. It represented all he had argued for since his famous *New Statesman* article in 1961. All his plans, all his speeches, all his propaganda had been based on a new national plan to build up investment and technology and to thrust the New Britain into the jet age. In these terms the DEA had supplied him with exactly what he wanted. On the other hand, for much of his life he had made repeated pledges to relieve the starving millions.

In the Cabinet argument on Friday, 29 July 1965, Wilson supported his old ally Mrs Castle. Yet he saw the force of Brown's arguments, and was loath to do anything to damage the National Plan. He proposed a compromise, whereby the publication of the White Paper should go ahead as planned and the National Plan would follow, its attitudes to aid unaltered. Like so many Wilsonian compromises the result was a ludicrous and indefensible contradiction in Government policy, which, fortunately for the Prime Minister, escaped the notice of the Press.

Even Mrs Castle was set back not a little by the coarse language of the National Plan. She had not long to brood. Shortly before Christmas she was removed from Overseas Development to Transport, and replaced by another 'left-winger', Anthony Greenwood. Greenwood by nature is more polite and less argumentative than Mrs Castle. He was, and is, less eager to interfere in Cabinet discussions, still less to oppose its unanimous decisions. His time at the Ministry was short and undistinguished by any new policy departure. In the re-shuffle following the 1966 squeeze measures he was promoted to the Housing Ministry. His replacement was Arthur Bottomley, formerly Commonwealth Relations Secretary. Bottomley, who had been singularly intransigent with the Smith regime in Rhodesia, was slung out of the Cabinet. The 'voice in the Cabinet' which Wilson had stressed at the 1965 Party Conference had been silenced. A quiet word from Wilson to his old friend Arthur Bottomley assuring him that the Overseas Development Ministry would never lose the Prime Minister's special favour was not enough to conceal the importance of the demotion. A Minister speaking in the Cabinet on behalf of aid can alter marginal decisions on cuts in the aid programme. Once the Minister is out of the Cabinet, the other Ministers, each anxious to preserve his own Budget, can more easily ignore their consciences about the underdeveloped world. Under Bottomley the considerable enthusiasm engendered by the Overseas Development Ministry quickly evaporated. Dudley Seers gave up his administrative post in the Ministry and passed on to the academic pastures of the Institute of Development Studies of Sussex University. Several other founder members of the Economic Planning Staff left in disillusionment. In 1967 the Ministry published its second White Paper which was summarized by the independent Overseas Development Institute in its Annual Report as follows:

It could not announce any single important new initiative. What was most disappointing of all was that the promised rethinking did not emerge from the document. It appeared that hardly any progress had been made for more than a year in coming to grips with the requirements of tackling world poverty in a concerted manner. . . . The geographical reallocation of the aid programme in line with development needs was certainly complicated by the shortage of new funds, but the lack of more clearly thought-out criteria for allocation resulted in new aid tending to go where there were specific short-term pressures.

This means that the pattern for the future, rather than being rationalized, was being laid down by the pressure of forces, many of which were ephemeral in character.

The promised 'policy of aid' in short, had become what it had always been under the Tories. The volume, distribution and allocation of aid and specialists merely reflected political and climactic developments. When Britain left Aden, Aden got an aid grant. When she moved into Bahrein, so did Bahrein. When BP invested in Eastern Nigeria, the Nigerian Federation received aid. An earthquake in India produced a slight increase in aid – and so on.

In the autumn of 1967, in another re-shuffle, Bottomley was removed to the back-benches and a new Minister, Reginald Prentice, was appointed. Prentice stayed out of the Cabinet. The Ministry had had four Ministers in less than three years – only one of whom, Barbara Castle, had stayed long enough to achieve anything. The Ministry, like the Department of Education and Science, had become a rung on the ladder on which Ministers 'on the up' could make their names and Ministers 'on the down' could nurse their grievances.

This state of affairs was clearly reflected in the Prime Minister's attitude. After announcing the 1966 deflation, Wilson seemed to lose all interest in overseas development. In October 1966, he brushed aside a question from a Labour back-bencher with the bland assurance that 'we are already attaining our target of one per cent of our national income in overseas aid . . . when we have had to count every penny of overseas expenditure, it was inevitable that some restriction on the increase – not a cut – had to be laid down for aid'.

The one per cent referred to by Wilson does not refer to public aid, given by the Government. It refers to all aid, which, by a curious twisting of the meaning of the word, includes investment by British private enterprise in underdeveloped countries. Since this is obviously not aid at all, but merely investment for profit, the percentage of national income normally used in this context refers to public, official aid. For instance, the 'one per cent' pledge by the Labour Party in 1957 referred explicity to public aid – and Harold Wilson's Government is as far, indeed slightly further, from achieving that 'target' as its Tory predecessor.

The figures for official aid for the last three years of the Conservative Government and the first three years of the New Britain indicate very clearly the extent of the revolution in aid which Wilson had promised:

	Total official aid (*gross*) £m.	*as percentage of National Income*
1962	164	0.64
1963	163	0.60
1964	194	0.66
1965	196	0.61
1966	209	0.60
1967	209 (est.)	0.59

The squeeze measures of July 1966 had resulted in a cut in the 1966–7 aid target of approximately 10 per cent, bringing the figure down to what it is above. In September 1967, the Voluntary Committee on Overseas Aid and Development, a central committee for all organizations interested in alleviating world poverty, formed in 1966 on the initiative of Mrs Castle, wrote a long memorandum to Wilson, pointing out the urgency of the situation and urging him to restore the £20m. cut of July 1966. Wilson replied early in October, eagerly approving the Committee's activities but refusing them their demands. 'This Government,' he wrote, inevitably 'have the unenviable task of making unpleasant choices between the many competing claims for the limited resources available, and I can only ask you to accept that the decision to make the reduction in the aid target was taken not because the Government ignored the considerations you mention. . . .'

The 'devaluation package' of cuts in public expenditure an-

nounced by Wilson in January 1968 did not include the aid programme – a tribute, no doubt, to the tenacity of Reginald
Prentice, the new Minister, who had argued in full Cabinet
meetings, to which he was specially invited, that any substantial
cuts would be disastrous. Recalling, no doubt, the evidence of the
opinion polls that the public would welcome cuts in the aid programme, the Government issued special instructions to the
Ministry for Overseas Development banning publicity about the
absence of aid cuts.

The fact that the aid programme had not suffered from the
measures was greeted with some delight in Labour left-wing circles
(notably by the *New Statesman* in an editorial of 2 January 1968).
Hardly had this chorus died down, however, than the Overseas
Development Institute issued a report indicating that devaluation
itself had slashed the aid programme by up to 10 per cent. The
ODI report declared that this decline in real value meant that
British aid 'had been required to carry its full share of the Government economies' (*Financial Times*, 25 January). After three years
of the New Britain, in fact, the combined efforts of Harold Wilson
and his new Ministry had succeeded in slashing the aid programme
by two separate cuts of 10 per cent each.

The Food and Agricultural Organization of the United Nations
celebrated the twentieth anniversary of Harold Wilson's first
visit to the organization by stating that the world population would
increase from 3,400 million to 5,000 million by the end of the century. 1,000 million of the extra 1,600 million will be in the underdeveloped countries, mainly in the poorer areas of Asia. To feed all
these at their present starvation level, world food production
must increase by 4 per cent per year. Since 1958 it has increased
on average by 2.6 per cent and even that rate may not be maintained.

'If the rate of food production,' said B.R. Sen, Director General
of FAO, in October 1966, 'cannot be significantly increased, we
must be prepared for the Four Horsemen of the Apocalypse.'

Per capita income in the underdeveloped countries will, it is
estimated, rise from £43 per year to £61 per year in 2,000, while
per capita income in the US will rise in the same period from
£1,270 to £2,685. Meanwhile, the advanced countries will decrease
their dependence on primary products from the underdeveloped

world. Already they have achieved 88 per cent self-sufficiency in oils, 83 per cent in fats, 73 per cent in cotton, 90 per cent in sugar and are rapidly replacing raw materials like cotton and rubber with synthetic substitutes. World trade has increased between 5 and 7 per cent per year since 1960, but raw material exports have increased by only 1 per cent. The proportion of world exports in trade between industrialized countries increased from 37.1 per cent in 1953 to 45.5 per cent in 1964, and the backward countries' share fell from 27 per cent to 20.2 per cent (14 per cent without oil).

All the trends are in one direction: the isolation and, consequently, the economic suppression of the underdeveloped world by the advanced countries. The process leads inevitably to mass starvation on a scale which will make the rigours of nineteenth-century capitalism appear gentle by comparison.

The Governments of the advanced countries cheered on by 'moderate' and 'progressive' economists are meeting this crisis by spending 120,000 million dollars a year on the means of destroying one another, and some 10,000 million dollars a year, most of which returns to them, in aid to the underdeveloped countries.

Harold Wilson's approach to these matters is now clear. When the British economy is growing, all its resources must be geared to creating a more efficient and technological industrial structure. Any unnecessary expenditure of capital or exports elsewhere is therefore to be discouraged. When the British economy is stagnating, resources spent elsewhere serve only to worsen the balance of payments position. Every effort should be made meanwhile to develop indigenous British technology so as to make the country no longer dependent on imports from outside. A synthetic rubber complex in Grangemouth may throw rubber workers in Malaya out of work but it helps the balance of payments. A 'vast smelter' in Invergordon may damage the chances of industrialization in Bolivia or Indonesia but it assists the British balance of payments. The starvation of half the world's population may cause some distress in the universities, but it makes no difference to the solvency of the New Britain. In short, Harold Wilson has grown up. The utopian ravings of an adolescent have developed into a rich, pragmatic maturity.

Chapter 10
Harold Wilson and the Labour Left

I've never known anyone able to mask an argument by taking refuge in words (Harold Wilson in an interview with Richard Clements, editor of *Tribune*, on that paper's thirtieth anniversary, 28 April 1967).

When the buggers are giving you trouble, give them a mass meeting (Attributed to J. H. Thomas, 1931).

Bevanite fury at the rightward drift of official Party policy after the 1955 election did not last long. The Suez crisis of late 1956 and the economic recession which followed exposed the fallibility of Tory economic policy and forged the Labour Party into a new unity. Even Aneurin Bevan agreed to cooperate with a leadership with which he fundamentally disagreed. Bevan's public disavowal of the 'unilateralists' at the Brighton Conference of 1957 and his acceptance of the post of Shadow Foreign Secretary encouraged his followers to fall grudgingly into line with Party policy for the 1959 election. At the Scarborough Conference of 1958, controversy was sacrificed to unity. Only the public schools provoked a genuine revolt against the leadership. 'Unilateralist' motions on defence were defeated by votes of six to one and the Executive statement on economic policy, *Plan for Progress*, moved by Wilson, summed up by Gaitskell and supported by Frank Cousins was carried unanimously. It was only after the election had been lost that the left-wing re-grouped and fought again.

By now, Aneurin Bevan was dying, and it was by no means certain who should take his place as the Left's candidate for the Party leadership. Harold Wilson was still an enigma. His association with Bevan in the early 1950s had not been forgotten and most of the left wing still regarded him as their man in the Shadow Cabinet. Others remembered his sponsorship of *Industry and Society* and his tacit support for the Executive on nuclear weapons. In 1958, Wilson came fourth in the elections for the constituency section of the Executive – the lowest place he had occupied since 1955.

His decision to stand against Gaitskell for the leadership in 1960, and against Brown for the deputy leadership in 1962 rallied the Left to him. He received the declared support of all Parliamentary left-wingers and of *Tribune*, around which the Parliamentary Left rallied. Other journals of the Labour Left, however, were not so enthusiastic. The *New Left Review*, for instance, whose circulation had risen sharply with the rise of the Campaign for Nuclear Disarmament, attacked him sharply: 'If the Labour Party ends this week facing two directions,' it declared before the 1960 Party Conference, 'it is certain that the figure of Mr Wilson will be there – at the end of both of them.'

On Gaitskell's death in 1963, the Left rallied without hesitation to Wilson's candidature for the leadership. After his election as leader they abandoned their accustomed role as critics of the leadership, and became instead its most enthusiastic supporters. Michael Foot, who, with four other MPs, had had the Labour Whip withdrawn for opposing the Tory defence estimates in 1961, wrote a long article on *Tribune*'s front page, listing Wilson's qualifications for the job:

> [He has] not only qualities of political acumen, political skill and survival power which no one denies him. Other considerable qualities too for a Labour leader – a coherence of ideas, a readiness to follow unorthodox courses, a respect for democracy. . . above all a deep and genuine love of the Labour movement.
>
> We are told he is tricky, untrustworthy, an addict of political infighting. Of course he is canny, ambitious, often cautious, always cool, usually calculating. And why not? They say that he does not make up his mind, that he sits on the fence. It was not true when he resigned in 1951. It was not true when he opposed German re-armament (22 February 1963).

Walter Padley, the 'centre-Left' General Secretary of the Shopworkers Union (USDAW), and MP for Glamorganshire, Ogmore, told his union conference: 'In Harold Wilson we have a leader fully worthy of the tradition of Clem Attlee and Keir Hardie.' This sentiment commended itself to Frank Allaun, a hardy warrior of the Left, who wrote an article for the Labour Press Service which was circulated to all trade-union journals. 'Harold Wilson,' the article started in what was intended to be a compliment, 'is the best Labour leader since Keir Hardie.' Shortly before the Scarborough Conference of 1963, Frank Cousins called a Press Conference to assure the nation that any suggestion of a quarrel between himself and Wilson was totally unfounded. 'There is,' he said, 'no difference, nor can anyone manufacture a difference between us.' The *New Statesman*, which had assaulted Gaitskell in the most decisive language during the 1960 controversies, stated in their leader of 10 March 1964:

Mr Wilson has set his party a fine example. Like Gladstone he believes in appealing to the highest instincts of the public, and his speeches have a cogency and authority unrivalled in recent years.

Even James Cameron, the idealist journalist, who had bitterly opposed the Gaitskell leadership, exclaimed in the *Daily Herald* after Wilson's speech at the 1963 Scarborough Conference:

Harold Wilson will not be just a good Prime Minister. He may well be a great one. . . . Harold Wilson's startling essay into political science-fiction may well be held by experts to be the most vital speech he has ever made. Here at last was the twentieth century (2 October 1963).

In the following months *Tribune* confined itself to praising Wilson and publishing his speeches. Anxiously it assured its readers that, despite outward appearances, Wilson's intentions were all for the good:

Mr Harold Wilson's remarks to the T & G W U conference have been widely misinterpreted. He did not, as the *Daily Worker* headline suggested, advocate a wage freeze. 'When we say incomes,' he said, 'we mean all incomes – not only wages and salaries but profits, especially monopoly profits, distributed dividends and, yes, rents (12 June 1963).

And Clive Jenkins, militant general secretary of ASSET, wrote after the 1963 Trades Union Congress:

Mr Harold Wilson is opposed to wage restraint.

After the 1963 Labour Conference, Jenkins complained:

A circumstantial story that a Wilson Cabinet will hold back wages for the first eighteen months of his Government is, incredibly, being peddled. It is a lie. The Scarborough decision is a real gain over the re-drafted paragraph on wages finally approved by the T U C (*Tribune*, 11 October 1963).

Jenkins' support increased during 1964. On Wilson's speech to the TUC in Blackpool the following year, he wrote:

Harold Wilson's well-keyed and emphatic speech on Monday was brilliantly expressive of the taut, yet flexible pregnant relationship between the unions and the Labour Party to power (11 September 1964).

And, after Labour's election to power,

Everything in the Queen's speech is first-rate and demands, firstly, our support and our appreciation of the firm leadership being shown. The task of transforming our country has been very well begun indeed (6 November 1964).

Plaudits for Harold Wilson in *Tribune* throughout those months can be found even from such devoted militants as Ian Mikardo and Fenner Brockway. In the nineteen months of Wilson's Leadership of the Opposition, *Tribune* devoted only a few random sentences to criticism of Harold Wilson or his policies. When, for instance, Wilson called for more helicopters to assist the British troops fighting against nationalists in South Arabia and Aden, *Tribune* complained: 'Hasty statements like Mr Wilson's this week will not help.'

The compliments heaped on Harold Wilson by the Labour Left were not always returned. During the election campaign for the Labour leadership after Gaitskell's death, the editor of *Tribune*, Richard Clements, decided to publish Commons speeches on defence policy by the two principal contenders, Harold Wilson and George Brown, to demonstrate the differences between them. Accordingly, Clements sent them both proofs of the edited versions of their speeches, and telephoned them to check that the editing met with their approval. Brown agreed instantly, as did Harold Wilson, who was full of praise for the standard of the editing. As Clements was about to hang up, Wilson asked urgently: 'You're not supporting me, are you, by any chance?' Not at all, replied Clements. The speeches would be published without editorial comment. In some relief, and with further effusive praise and thanks, the conversation ended.

By the time Wilson became Prime Minister in October 1964 he had contrived to unite the Labour Party and its affiliates as it had never been united since 1945. Even before the 1945 and 1929 elections a substantial minority of critics continued to attack central aspects of official Labour Party policy, and the Labour leaders. Before the 1964 election the silence of the consensus was broken only by the thin wails of 'satirists and sectarians'.

In normal circumstances such unanimous approval and praise from the Left would almost certainly provoke an opposite reaction from the Right. Yet during the same period the Labour Right was equally uncritical. This was not merely because an election approached and most of the right-wing leaders were guaranteed a place in a Labour Cabinet. It was also because in the twenty months of Tory Government following Gaitskell's death Labour Party policy did not change in detail or in emphasis.

The few policy changes which did take place, notably over immigration, Cyprus and Aden, were clear moves to the Right. The right-wing leaders may have disliked Wilson and distrusted him. But they could hardly forbear to support him when he contrived to unite the Party behind a policy which was slightly to the Right of that approved by Hugh Gaitskell. The Left, in the meantime, concocted a myth which was to sustain them for several years:

> By the early 1960s the Labour Party had decided that revisionism was not on the agenda and the slow struggle back to power began. Under a new leadership and with a programme which made a clear challenge to the 'You've never had it so good' society which had been created by the Tories, the party won the election of 1964 (*Tribune* editorial after the 1966 election, 8 April 1966).

In fact, of course, revisionism had in no sense, and not for a single moment, left the agenda. Gaitskell's policy on the Bomb had triumphed and the party's policy on economic affairs was still based on the ultra-revisionist *Industry and Society*. In more ways than one, as shown in Chapter 4, the policy of the Party, as opposed to the electoral rhetoric of its leaders, had swung if anything rightwards since 1959. The magical transformation in Party policy which accompanied the election of Harold Wilson to the leadership did not take place, except in the minds of the Labour Left.

The enthusiasm for this mythical revolution swept the Labour ranks even further Left than *Tribune*. Tom Nairn, a prominent writer in the *New Left Review*, wrote in the symposium *Towards Socialism*, written before the Labour victory of 1964, but coming out after it:

> There is no doubt that, relatively, with regard to the past annals of the Labour leadership, Wilson represents a kind of progress. Wilson constantly professes the habitual Labour contempt for theory – 'theology' as he calls it – but has far more theoretical grasp than any previous leader. Unlike so many former left-wing figures who have moved towards power, he has never actually renounced or broken with his past; he is likely to be much more open to left-wing ideas and pressures than his predecessors. In contrast to Gaitskell and Attlee, Wilson seems singularly free from the bigoted anti-Communism which has been a surrogate for thought and action in many social-democratic movements.

The almost unanimous inclination of the Labour Left to turn their attention from the written policy to abstract rhetoric about 'commanding heights' and 'nationalization of urban land' enabled Harold Wilson during his twenty months as Leader of the Opposition to fulfil his promise of remaining loyal to the policy of Hugh Gaitskell while at the same time convincing Gaitskell's enemies that Gaitskellite revisionism 'was not on the agenda'. His ambition, as expressed to John Junor, to hold high the banner of nationalization while leading the Labour Party away from it had been fulfilled.

This achievement was sustained in the immediate afterglow of the 1964 election victory. Only a few Labour MPs complained about the delay of six months in paying the proposed pensions increase, and even fewer objected to the decision to send Buccaneer aircraft to South Africa. Throughout November, *Tribune* republished Harold Wilson's main speeches, explaining that the differences between the paper and the leader were 'of emphasis rather than of principle' (20 November 1964). The paper's clerical correspondent, Dr Donald Soper, who was shortly to receive a peerage from the Prime Minister, declared his New Year's resolution on 1 January 1965: 'to support the Government more fervently'. And when George Brown had enticed the leaders of the trade unions and of industry to sign a declaration of intent to formulate an incomes policy, he received uncritical support from *Tribune*'s two economic correspondents from Sheffield, Michael Barratt Brown and Royden Harrison, who were not ashamed to cloak Mr Brown and his advisers in the mantle of Marxist orthodoxy: 'The scene,' they wrote, 'is once again set for a decisive victory for the political economy of Labour' (*Tribune* 8 January 1965).

Summarizing Labour's first hundred days, *Tribune*'s editor concluded: 'It would be grossly unfair to turn upon the Government now and rend it.' Any minor errors, he was sure, would soon be put right. After all,

Given the spirit which Harold Wilson has most notably displayed on many previous occasions, there is no reason why the Government could not and cannot recover all the ground lost in the past weeks, and capture much more territory in the months ahead (*Tribune*, 29 January 1965).

And so it seemed, for a few months at any rate. The publication of 'Dick Crossman's brilliant housing Bill', the 'welcome Race Relations Bill', the plans for steel nationalization, the Budget, and the long Commons battle with Tory stockbrokers, all put heart into the Labour Left. *Tribune* proudly published interviews with leading Ministers, notably one with Anthony Greenwood, the new Colonial Secretary, who astonished the paper's readers in British Guiana by his enthusiasm for the Duncan Sandys Guyanese Constitution (described by Harold Wilson at the time of its publication as 'fiddled') and his description of the Guyanese Prime Minister, Forbes Burnham, as 'a socialist'.

More important matters, however, soon arose to ruffle the solidarity of the Labour Left. First was the Government's immediate and unequivocal support for the Americans in their war in Vietnam, particularly their support for the American bombing of North Vietnam, which started in February. Second was the immigration White Paper in August. Third was the series of nibbling deflations, culminating in the big £100m. bite at the end of July. Fourth was the Government's decision, in the light of the abstention of Desmond Donnelly and Woodrow Wyatt in the House of Commons, to shelve the nationalization of steel. And fifth, perhaps worst of all, was the National Plan, published in September. All these, in one form or another, were attacked by the Labour Left, though none of these attacks took the form of Parliamentary votes or abstentions. The National Plan particularly irritated those who had hoped for a genuine economic programme based on social justice, welfare and equality. The Plan, complained *Tribune*, 'is a non-plan with its priorities badly wrong. George Brown should go away and think again.' As for deflation, the Left's alternatives did not (yet) include devaluation. John Mendelson, left-wing MP for Penistone, argued both in Parliament and outside for import controls and overseas investment checks. On the issue of the incomes policy, the Left was split. Clive Jenkins, who had argued so furiously a year earlier that Harold Wilson was opposed to wage restraint, found that George Brown's plan for an Incomes Bill was 'fundamentally authoritarian and anti-trade union. It should be spurned as a hobble for free men – a device which perpetuates inequality in British society' (*Tribune*, 17 September 1965). The academics of the Left, however, still believed that the Government would produce a 'socialist incomes policy'.

The extent of the Left's reaction to these measures differed sharply. Some were so shocked and horrified that they cried halt to all support for Labour. Malcolm Caldwell, a dedicated Labour campaigner, voiced the most extreme disillusionment in a letter to *Tribune* on 20 August:

Socialist principles have been tossed aside with almost indecent cynicism and casualness. Racial discrimination in Britain has been condoned and strengthened. American butchery in Vietnam has been actively supported and encouraged. Social welfare and economic development in Britain have been sacrificed to carry out a reactionary economic programme at the behest of international finance capital. What of the Left leaders in Parliament? Tell them off on your fingers, comrades, and think of their words and deeds in recent months while the Labour movement has been sold down the river. It is a sad picture and I can personally neither see nor offer any excuses. Are we finished, we of the Labour Left?

And, the following month, Alan Dawe, *Tribune*'s education correspondent, announced his resignation from the Labour Party:

We are not right to view the Labour Party and its latter-day works as having anything to do with socialism. They don't, they won't and it is time we faced up to it (*Tribune*, 24 September 1965).

Such voices were, at the time, isolated heralds of the massive disillusionment that was to follow. The editor of *Tribune* received a great many more letters complaining about his attacks on the Labour Government and was forced to write an editorial explaining the need for dissent. And, even in that unhappy summer, the left-wing Labour MPs could take solace in the wizardry of their leader:

> He [Wilson] commands more widespread support within the Parliamentary Labour Party and in the country than any other leader the Labour Party has had. He fights the Tories and enjoys it. . . . The atmosphere [at the P L P meeting at the end of the summer Parliamentary session] was euphoric. Miraculously the gloom was banished. . . . Everything in the garden seemed to be looking, well, if not exactly lovely, at least a good deal greener than when Callaghan was wielding his axe six days before (Michael Foot in *Tribune*, 6 August 1965).

As the economic crisis was temporarily dispelled, and, as Parliament met again in the autumn, the atmosphere of euphoria drugged the Labour Left. The total disarray of the Tories, under a new and indecisive leader; Harold Wilson's two vast speeches at Party Conference and his apparently tough line on Rhodesia; the promotion of Barbara Castle and Anthony Greenwood; and a number of important welfare reforms, notably rating relief and local-authority interest-rate subsidy, combined to convince the Left that the Government was on the right road. When Richard Gott decided to stand as Radical Alliance candidate in the by-election in North Hull, he was severely rebuked by the Labour Left. 'Do not destroy the Government!' bellowed *Tribune*:

> Every socialist has the right to criticize the design and performance of the Labour automobile – so long as he also helps to put some petrol in the tank (7 January 1966).

Two months later, with the decision to hold another General Election, all criticism was thrown to the winds in a stampede to get as much petrol into the tank as possible. Even Clive Jenkins' carping about the incomes policy was stayed. For the new Labour Manifesto, *Time for Decision*, *Tribune* had nothing but praise:

> The Labour manifesto is not only an interesting and stimulating document. It is also, in essence, a socialist one. The answers are inescapably egalitarian. There is some self-congratulation, but is it not justified? (11 March 1966).

As election day approached the enthusiasm became feverish: Michael Foot wrote:

> March 31st will mark one of the essential dates in the forward march. It is an opportunity which only incorrigible sectarians and nihilists, the best allies of the forces of reaction, will not wish to seize (*Tribune*, 25 March 1966).

It is hard even for an incorrigible sectarian to read *Tribune* before and after the March 1966 General Election without a lump rising in his throat. On the day of the election, *Tribune* brought out a special front and back page which shouted in savage exultation at the impending destruction of the Left's enemies:

> . . . Who doesn't want a landslide? We see you, Desmond Donnelly, with your *Spectator* pals – well, here it comes and you'll be buried in steel. . . .
>
> Pensions up, Rent Act Security, Unemployment down, Prescription Charges off, who cares! We do . . . and so do millions . . . now, for bigger advances, VOTE LABOUR!

It was the triumphant, almost incredulous shout of thousands of men and women in the Labour movement who had worked all their lives without compensation for the return of a Labour Government in prosperous peacetime. The quarrels, the arguments, the strikes and lock-outs, the bitter theoretical wrangles of the last thirteen years, had been smoothed over and by-passed with the injunction: 'Get the Tories Out'. In the past seventeen months of miniscule majorities, the injunction had been reiterated even more earnestly. For the 50,000 or so readers of *Tribune*, the hard core of Labour's rank and file, a Parliamentary majority for Labour *was* the first solution and *did* promise a more libertarian, more egalitarian society.

No wonder in the hour of victory, that *Tribune* bellowed: SOCIALISM IS RIGHT BACK ON THE AGENDA . . . and that their columnist Francis Flavius could argue that the election results marked 'a significant watershed in British politics' (8 April 1966).

The Labour Left and *Tribune* took the 1966 election result more seriously than anyone else in the land. The press, who had whipped up a violent campaign against Labour in 1964, and the industrialists (even the steel masters who knew that a big majority would bring steel nationalization) were silent. The flow of big money into Tory Party funds, even from the steel masters, all but dried up. Political commentators reported 'a boring election' and predicted 'no change'.

And, in the event, nothing changed. The course of British politics was not altered in the slightest degree by Labour's landslide victory of 1966. After a brief moment of euphoria, Harold Wilson and his henchmen continued their propaganda about restrictive practices on both sides of industry, their paranoiac defence of the pound sterling and their attacks on the trade unions.

Once the axe started to fall, it fell quickly. In May, the seamen went on strike to be met with fierce resistance, smears and abuse from the Labour Government. In early July, Frank Cousins, hero of the Labour Left, resigned from the Government over the publication of the Prices and Incomes Bill. In mid-July another sterling crisis pushed the Labour Government into a wage freeze and the most ruthless deflationary measures since the war.

The Left reacted to all this in shocked astonishment. 'There has been,' complained *Tribune* in June, 'no glimmer of a changed strategy, no enlarged vision since the General Election of March 1966.' John Morgan, a devoted socialist with a strong left-wing bias, greeted the July measures with a melancholy cry which must have touched the hearts of the Labour Left throughout the land:

It isn't just emotion that moves the socialist to rage and sadness now – not that there would be anything wrong with emotion. Dismay springs from the knowledge that a good, coherent programme for modernization existed, even exists, which has been abandoned without even being tried. When Harold Wilson began speaking on the stage of the Brangwen Hall, Swansea, on the afternoon of 25 January 1964, he was not only establishing himself as a national leader, he was winning the people to sensible ideas. It was an important moment in British politics. . . . The speech became the basis of the National Plan. It demonstrated how the recurring difficulties of the balance of payments could be defeated, how increased production could be the basis of a new society (*Sunday Times*, 24 July 1966).

John Morgan represented the Labour Party members who had been won over to what he called 'that series of great speeches in the early months of 1964'. The dreary semi-Keynesian technocracy of

Harold Wilson had inspired men like John Morgan, just as John Kennedy's preposterous New Frontier had inspired the soft American Left four years previously. Now with the Government's collapse into Conservative remedies and Conservative reactions the Labour Left was utterly disillusioned without anything to offer as a half-credible alternative.

In his *Sunday Times* article, in fact, John Morgan argued that the pound should have been devalued in 1964. Along with many others on the Left and Right who argued along the same lines, Morgan had advanced no such argument in 1964. *Tribune* opposed devaluation in 1964, 1965 and in July 1966; only in 1967 did the majority of the paper's economic correspondents support a floating rate for the pound. And even then the Labour Left argued, quite dishonestly, that devaluation need not involve deflation. (See the *Tribune* pamphlet *Never Again*, published in July 1967.)

The July measures of 1966 forced the hard-core Labour Left into almost permanent opposition to their Government. The Prices and Incomes Act (on which some thirty Labour MPs abstained in August and October), the Vietnam war, the Common Market (for entry to which the Government applied in November), rising unemployment and a continuing squeeze on the social services all provoked more and more protest. Fortunately for the left-wing MPs, the policy of the Whips, laid down by Richard Crossman and John Silkin, was to run the Parliamentary party on a light rein, and abstentions were permitted against angry protests from the more 'loyalist' back-benchers and from the chairman of the Parliamentary Labour Party, Emmanuel Shinwell, who eventually resigned. All the Left assumed that Harold Wilson strongly approved this 'liberal' policy. In May 1966, for instance, Hugh Jenkins, the MP for Putney, had argued: 'Years of hostility and repression have bred in the old Parliamentarians (who are still the most courageous and resolute of the lot of us) conspiratorial habits which are no longer necessary under the tolerant regime of Harold Wilson' (*Tribune*, 29 May 1966).

Yet in March 1967, after sixty MPs had abstained after a defence debate in protest against the refusal to make further defence cuts, Wilson rounded on the Left at a Parliamentary Party meeting, warning them that 'a dog is only allowed one bite' and threatening them with a General Election unless they came to heel. Though the discipline issue faded for several months after this outburst, it arose even more seriously in early 1968 as the hard core of the Parliamentary Left voted against every one of the Government proposals for cuts in social services, announced in January, and against the Immigration Act 1968. Once again, the Parliamentary Party, with Wilson's approval, turned the discipline screw.

Yet throughout the entire period of disillusionment and near-despair, there was one threat which never failed to ensure the loyalty of the Labour Left: a threat to the personal leadership of Harold Wilson. In the aftermath of the 1966 July deflation, a rumour gained ground in Labour circles, which was substantially true, that a meeting of back-benchers and some Ministers had been held to discuss the possibility and the means of replacing Harold Wilson with James Callaghan. As soon as *Tribune* caught hold of this rumour, it exploded with rage.

Similarly, after the 1967 devaluation, during the controversy on arms for South Africa, when a bid was made to replace Wilson with Callaghan, the Left rallied to Wilson. Three months later, when further moves were made to promote Roy Jenkins or Anthony Crosland to the Treasury, a group of ninety-one MPs wrote a letter to *The Times*. The letter was headed 'Comfort for Mr Wilson' and it took issue with the *Times* political correspondent, David Wood, who had reported the previous day that 'his [Wilson's] own rank and file have no confidence in him'. 'We do not know,' ran the letter, 'how Mr Wood came to this conclusion, but it certainly was not in speaking to any of the undersigned, *proof enough that his sweeping generalization has no basis in fact*' (12 March).

The signatures had, reported the letter, been 'gathered in a very short time', and they included familiar loyalists and former 'young eagles'. Yet they also included such bastions of the Parliamentary Labour Left as Russell Kerr, John Mendelson, James Dickens, Eric Heffer, Peter Jackson, Norman Atkinson, Michael Foot, Andrew Faulds and Ben Whittaker.

The official argument for the letter was that the Left's quarrel with the Government was about policies, not personalities, and that any attempt to introduce personalities into the argument should be immediately scotched.

The Left however had not scrupled in the past to attack personalities responsible for reactionary policies, and to call for their removal even if only as a gesture of disapproval of those policies. In 1959 and 1960, *Tribune* and its followers had consistently attacked Gaitskell and had called again and again for his removal from the leadership. Again, on 6 January 1967 *Tribune* had demanded, in a front page headline: 'CALLAGHAN MUST GO'! and had claimed that although the removal of the Chancellor would not of itself right the wrongs of his policies, it was necessary as an indication that policy changes were intended.

The obsession of political correspondents with personalities is infuriating for all politicians who seek to discuss policy issues. Yet the MPs' letter to *The Times* of 12 March 1968 did not diminish the personality aspect; it increased it. If the left-wing MPs who signed the letter had genuinely not cared about personalities, they would have written to *The Times* not to declare their confidence in their leader but to disavow all interest in the leadership issue. The truth was, as it had been for several years, that the Labour Left felt deep down that Harold Wilson was 'one of them'. This myth had outlived the apparently endless list of anti-socialist measures enacted by Harold Wilson's administration.

Old ghosts still jibbered in the theoretical graveyard. 'Gaitskellism,' wrote Michael Foot in March 1967, 'like Stalinism, cannot easily be restored.' Yet what, in the reality of March 1967, did Gaitskellism mean? What further horrors could it wreak? Would Gaitskell perhaps have introduced a wage freeze for a year or permanently brought wage negotiations under the control of the law courts? Would he have imposed prescription charges, postponed the school leaving age, cancelled free school milk in secondary schools? Would he have based his industrial policy on mergers and monopolies supported by Government finance and Government orders? Would he have supported the Americans in Vietnam? No doubt, Gaitskell would have pursued all these courses, as would Callaghan, Jenkins or Crosland. But Wilson had done all these things – and more. Where was the evidence – save only in the quarrel on South African arms – that 'the Gaitskellites' would have proved better Tories than Harold Wilson? Essentially, their policies would have been the same. The direction of the Labour Government, under Gaitskell, Wilson, Callaghan, Jenkins or

Crosland or any of the other alternatives would have been equally disastrous. The leadership issue, in short, compared with the political issues in which the Government was involved, was almost if not completely irrelevant.

The tenacious hold which Harold Wilson exercised on his former friends and supporters in the Left had a deeper, more political root than the fear of a mythical Gaitskellism. The reactions of *Tribune* and the Parliamentary Left to Wilson's Government was based throughout on the political theory of another era. Where the Government took action which offended against the old traditions and the old theory of the Labour Left, the Left responded immediately and courageously with clear and untrammeled opposition. *Tribune*'s reaction to the seaman's strike of 1966 was unconditional: 'SUPPORT THE SEAMEN!' When unemployment was created, the Government was sharply censured. When the health charges were reimposed, *Tribune* shouted 'THE SHAME OF IT ALL!'

Certainly no one could blame the Labour Left for a lack of resolution, courage and determination in their efforts to swing the Government away from these old evils. Yet at the same time, the Wilson Government was pursuing policies of a more subtle and sinister nature which seem to have escaped the attention and the criticism of the Labour Left.

These policies can be listed under the heading of corporatism. The encouragement of vast mergers and monopolies under the aegis of the Government-financed Industrial Reorganization Corporation; the complex planning machinery of the little Neddies and of the geographic planning councils; the incorporation of the trade-union leadership into the network of planning on the bogus pretext of 'incomes policy'; the interference of the state with almost every major wage dispute through the Prices and Incomes Board – these new, drastically dangerous corporatist developments were not identified by the Labour Left, and therefore not opposed. When Alan Dawe had resigned from the Labour Party in 1965 he had complained in *Tribune* about that paper's obsession with state ownership and state control:

There is nothing socialist about the commanding heights now. For this Government is trying to create a power elite, more cohesive and omnipotent than any we have seen in recent British history . . . this is the ultimate significance of the attempt to forge a consensus of opinion and action between the leaders of Government, industry and the unions. . . .

Yet the Left around *Tribune* overlooked this problem. They rejoiced when, in the autumn of 1967, the Queen's Speech included references to an Industrial Expansion Bill,, whereby the state would take minority shareholdings in crucial industries and appoint minority directors to the Boards. The measure was marginally less drastic than the proposals in *Industry and Society* which the Left had so violently opposed ten years previously. Nevertheless, at the suggestion that the Industrial Expansion Bill should be dropped or postponed, *Tribune* frothed with fury. Harold Wilson's knowledge of 'public ownership' rhetoric, gleaned with such care during his period as a Bevanite, served him in good stead as Prime Minister, and continued to bamboozle many of his former left-wing colleagues into the belief that the vast, undemocratic corporatist machinery which he was setting up was in some sense a move towards socialism. In fact, of course, the 'planning' of Selwyn Lloyd and Maudling was taken over and speeded up by Harold Wilson – even to the extent of nationalizing the steel industry and appointing the steel bosses to run a new, dynamic, streamlined single unit called the National Steel Corporation. The Government's decision to include provisions in the steel legislation for the election of trade unionists and rank-and-file workers to the local steel boards was hailed by the Labour Left as a victory.[1] In fact, it was nothing of the kind. As became clear at once, the 'concession' served merely to incorporate some of the more politically conscious workers into the labyrinthine apparatus of the Corporation machine. The Steel Corporation rapidly became the most transparently corporatist, or state capitalist industrial unit in the country.

The grand illusions which, both before and after 1964, rallied the Labour Left to the Wilsonian recipes of state ownership and automation were not entirely due to the skill of the illusionist. Rhetorical sleight-of-hand, however brilliant, could never of its own have brought about so great a conversion. The truth was that Harold Wilson's pragmatism burst on the Labour movement at a moment of theoretical impasse. The violent changes in capitalism, in the relationship between the state and private industry, had

1. See Ian Mikardo, 'The Left in 1967', *Tribune*, 23 December 1966.

thrown the Labour Movement into theoretical disarray. The Labour Right had responded by abandoning 'the means' of public ownership and fixing their sights on a more humane capitalism, prodded and pushed by a Labour Government. The Left, in fury, responded by re-stating 'the end' – socialism – while becoming increasingly vague as to what it meant, and increasingly unable, therefore, to propose any comprehensible means. The argument, symbolized by two 1960 Fabian pamphlets, *Socialism in the Affluent Society*, by Richard Crossman, and *Can Labour Win ?*, by Anthony Crosland, dragged on for several years, with both sides hopelessly missing the mark. In the event, both sides were exhausted by irrelevance, and Harold Wilson's 'dynamic', essentially capitalist terminology filled the vacuum.[1]

The new corporatism which Wilson had consistently proclaimed for so many years led to a development which was even more significant for the Labour Left: a decline in the power and importance of Parliament. Classical capitalism of the Adam Smith variety, with its warring factions and devotion to competition between individual firms, allowed considerable scope for debate, discussion and even power in Parliament. Similarly, in the early days of universal suffrage, and particularly in the post-1945 era when private, pre-war capitalism was in jeopardy, the power of Parliament was, relatively, considerable. With the closing of the capitalist ranks in national, corporate monopoly, and, more importantly, with the increasing power and confidence of the monopolies, the power of Parliament declined. The big decisions left to Government became increasingly secret, increasingly the preserve of the Executive, which did not always mean the Cabinet.

1. Needless to say, the few socialists who recognized the real situation were 'incorrigible sectarians'. Alasdair McIntyre, for instance, had written in the aftermath of Wilson's Scarborough speech, in an article which was vindicated by subsequent events in every particular: 'From Togliatti to Wilson the cry goes up across Western Europe that socialism is now state-sponsored planning plus automation. It is sad that neither Wilson nor Togliatti is a keen student of Hegel's dialectic, for it would be a great comfort to those who believe that opposites become one in a higher synthesis to realize that oddly enough capitalism too is now state-sponsored planning plus automation. To accept Wilsonism is to have moved over to the Right at least for the moment, no matter what other professions of socialism are made. . . . ' ('Labour Policy and Capitalist Planning', *International Socialism*, Winter, 1963, pp. 5–9).

The big decisions were taken by Cabinet committees, sometimes even by individuals, and even then many of these decisions depended on expert advice from the men who wielded economic power. As shown above (Chapter 2), the decision to devalue the pound in 1949 was taken by four or five men, and the Cabinet were not told until six weeks after the decision had been taken. The choice open to Cabinet members at that stage was to accept a *fait accompli* or to resign. Similarly, in 1967, the devaluation decision was taken several weeks before the Cabinet knew anything about it. In 1965, the National Plan, which was intended to shape the nation's economic future for five years, was released in the Parliamentary recess, without recourse to Parliament or even to the Parliamentary Labour Party (still less to the Labour Conference). These were all decisions which were still formally the province of Parliament. In the meantime, the big decisions in the nation's economic and industrial life moved away even from the Executive. The almost laughable antics of the Monopolies Commission indicated, if proof were needed, the full extent of the impotence of Parliament over the nation's industrial affairs. The more the mergers, the bigger the monopolies, the greater the power of industrial and economic bureaucracies. The absorption of trade-union leaders and the official trade-union machinery into these bureaucracies shifted the centres of resistance into small pockets of revolt: into isolated unofficial strikes, tenants committees, students' demonstrations. Even inside the Party, however, the real shift to the Left was to be seen not in Parliament but in the trade unions. The election of Hugh Scanlon as President of the AEU in 1967, the growth in membership and militancy of the small white-collar worker unions, notably the Draughtsmen and Allied Technicians Union and the Association of Scientific and Managerial Staffs, indicated a sharp shift away from the Labour establishment in the area in which hitherto it had been most firmly entrenched; the trade-union leadership.

In the meantime the Parliamentary Left and *Tribune* seemed to focus even more closely and intently on traditional, Parliamentary forms of political activity. There was no attempt to reform the *Victory for Socialism* Group or the *Appeal for Unity* which had been formed in the late 1950s and early 1960s in an effort (which was not very successful) to organize the rank and file for a campaign against the Labour Right. In 1967, an effort was made to re-start the *Tribune* Brains Trusts of the early 1950s. By April, 1968 about twenty of these Brains Trusts had been held, their success depending on the strength and militancy of the sponsoring constituency parties. The left-wing MPs were forced, by the logic of their position, to concentrate on Parliamentary tactics. In August 1966, John Horner, left-wing MP for Oldbury and Halesowen, wrote an article in *Tribune* attacking the new wage freeze and incomes policy and calling for rejection of the policy at the forthcoming Trades Union Congress. When Francis Flavius, *Tribune*'s columnist, referred the following week to Horner's 'campaign', John Horner replied in some urgency: 'I should hate Francis Flavius to give anyone the idea that I am now calling for mass action from the trade union movement against it [the incomes policy]' (*Tribune*, 2 September 1966).

Moreover, as Ralph Miliband has shown in his comprehensive analysis *Parliamentary Socialism*, the Parliamentary road to socialism is fraught with dangers – not least the danger of personal absorption into the machinery of Government. From the very beginning of the Labour Government in 1964 the Left was split between, on the one hand, the resolute older Parliamentarians and the new trade union MPs who were prepared to fight decisions with which they disagreed through the established Parliamentary machinery, and, on the other, a group of younger men who hoped, in some unspecific way, to find 'new ways' of proclaiming their opposition. One idea was to establish a 'Parliamentary Forum' – a permanent debating chamber at which the Left could thrash out a new strategy and a new theory.[1] Allegations were made by these younger men of 'pussyfooting' – a disparaging reference to Michael Foot and the older Parliamentarians.

Harold Wilson, who had so much experience of such splits and divisions, watched with considerable interest, and, as soon as an able young Left MP fell out with his colleagues, he was swept into the Government. As early as 19 February 1965 a group of young back-benchers joined with two Labour veterans, Philip Noel-Baker and Arthur Henderson, in writing a letter to *The Times* urging the Government 'to take an immediate initiative to achieve a

1. One Labour wag named the proposed organization the Parliamentary Institute for Socialist Studies (PISS).

cease-fire [in Vietnam] and a conference in which the principal participants can search for a political solution'. They were Peter Shore, David Ennals, Shirley Williams and Jeremy Bray. The following August, the latter three of the four signed a letter from back-bench MPs calling on the Government to 'scrap the immigration White Paper'. Jeremy Bray spoke at the 1965 Labour Party Conference on behalf of his union, the Transport and General Workers, whose million votes he pledged against the White Paper. The most anxious and dedicated opponent of the immigration White Paper was Reginald Freeson, MP for Willesden East, whose constituency housed one of the largest immigrant populations in the country (and who subsequently tripled his majority in the 1966 election). Another signature on the letter was that of the young barrister MP for Lincoln, Dick Taverne. The immigration policy was also attacked in a brilliant and bitter speech late at night in the House of Commons by the MP for Renfrew West, Norman Buchan, perhaps the ablest of all the left-wing intake in 1964.

Two years later, Shore (Minister of Economic Affairs), Bray (Technology), Mrs Williams (Education), Freeson (Power), Taverne (Home Office), Ennals (Home Office) and Buchan (Scottish Office) had been absorbed into the Government. Neil Carmichael and Ioan Evans, who had associated themselves with the Left, notably on Vietnam and defence, had also accepted jobs in the Ministries of Transport and the Whips Office respectively. The 'pussyfooters' had been left to carry on the fight against their accusers.

The offer of such a job places a left-wing MP in an intolerable dilemma. In the first place, the logic of his place in Parliament tells him that he must accept a place in the Government. How, he argues, can he press for more left-wing policies from a Government, and then refuse to join the Government when offered a place in it? Moreover, particularly in offices like the Scottish Office and the Ministry of Transport, the political complexion of an Under-Secretary can make a difference to a host of administrative decisions. As against that, the Minister is silenced on the broad issues. He has no voice in the Government, which never meets. And, whenever necessary, he can be hauled out to vote for the Cabinet's policy.

The spectacle, for instance, of Norman Buchan and Reginald Freeson failing to oppose the frankly racialist Immigration Act of 1968 was as nauseating for their supporters as it must have been galling for themselves. Yet only once, in the case of Eric Heffer, who was offered a Government post in 1967, was the offer of such a job turned down by a left-wing MP.

Yet, in the final analysis, the central criticism of the Labour Left under Harold Wilson's leadership does not concern their Parliamentary tactics nor the difficult decisions whether or not to vote against the Government, or to accept a post within it. In the 1930s Sir Stafford Cripps had posed to his followers in the Socialist League, many of whom were prominent in the Labour Left in the 1950s and 1960s, central questions about power in modern capitalist society, based on his view that the 'idea that the wielders of economic power will cooperate with a Labour Government is quite fantastic'.

'Can socialism come by constitutional means?' he had asked, and had replied in the affirmative only on the condition that the most drastic measures to control private economic interests were undertaken immediately by a Labour Government. The power of Parliament, argued Cripps, had to be exerted to the full against private economic and industrial interests *if that power was to survive*. The slightest wavering in the face of those economic interests would mean the inevitable bondage of Parliament.

Had Cripps's case been eroded in the thirty years between 1933 and 1963? Had capitalism become less powerful, more subservient to the whims of Parliament than in the 1930s? Were the great corporations of the 1960s more democratic and more easily controlled than the demoralized industries of the 1930s? Had the conflict between economic interests and socialist aims diminished, so that the powers necessary to fulfil the latter and control the former were in some sense less crucial? These questions had been raised to some extent, though in less specific and more diluted language, in the big arguments of the late 1950s. At the 1958 Labour Party Conference, for instance, Trevor Park, the delegate from Darwen, later MP for South East Darbyshire, had declared:

I am not interested merely in a better organized society; I am not interested merely in working capitalism more efficiently than the capitalists themselves. I am interested in a society which is based upon cooperation and not upon competition. . . .

There is a fundamental conflict here.

The aims of those who evolve the plans – Government and the public authorities – are very different from the aims of the private capitalists who control industry. No matter how many social controls and regulations we create, there will still be attempts to evade them and discover ways and means by which the instruments of social interest can be evaded. . . .

Sooner or later we shall be brought back to this fundamental issue: are we interested only in making capitalism more efficient; are we trying to out-do the Tory Party in what is their own territory; or are we preparing for the next stage in the march forward to socialism? (Labour Party Conference Report, 1958, pp. 163–4).

Under the leadership of Harold Wilson, these questions, despite their increasing relevance, were not asked. Instead the Left concentrated on the mechanics of Parliamentary victory rather than the policies by which the 'fundamental conflict' between Labour's aims and private economic interests could be resolved. The hysteria about the importance of electoral victories reached a climax at the General Election in 1966, which quickly emerged as the unhappiest paper victory in Labour history. Under the hypnosis of Wilsonian rhetoric about public ownership, peace and technology, in the vacuum created by the irrelevance of old slogans and old analyses, and in the Gadarenian stampede to party unity at election time, the Labour Left forgot about or ignored the 'fundamental conflict' and were therefore theoretically and practically unprepared for defeat in it.

Harold Wilson's uncanny knowledge of the Labour Party and its left wing, most of it gained from his association with the Bevanites in the early 1950s, was consistently applied to obtaining the support of left-wing MPs, though his policies only very rarely leant leftwards. Ruthlessly he played on the Left's most fatal weakness: its sentimentality. Wilson knows that the Labour Left responds more enthusiastically than the Right to calls for party unity at times of crisis (especially at elections), to vague phrases about public ownership and moral crusades and helping the starving millions. In the generalized sloganizing of the Labour Left Harold Wilson has always been an expert, and he never scrupled to wrap it in the shroud of Aneurin Bevan. Both before and after his accession Wilson deployed a familiar, but highly successful rhetorical technique, attaching the name of Aneurin Bevan to the most banal clichés.

Why, Aneurin Bevan asked, look into the crystal ball when you can read the book? (Swansea, 25 January 1964).

We know, as Nye Bevan said, that politics are about power (London, speech to the Society of Labour Lawyers, 20 April 1964).

Nye had a word for it, as always: why look in the crystal ball when you can read the book? (Blackpool Labour Party Conference, 29 September 1965).

If I may quote Nye again, we are not gigolos (ibid., 29 September 1965).

As Nye Bevan reminded us in the last speech to the House of Commons, one of the defects of our post-war democracy has been that it has not yet proved that it can voluntarily save itself from drift, decline and disaster by imposing the necessary disciplines in time (TUC, 5 September 1966).

Howard and West tell us (p. 30) that after the first ballot for the Labour leadership election in January 1963, in which Wilson had fallen only eight votes short of an overall majority over his two rivals, Callaghan and Brown, he repaired with his two campaign managers, Richard Crossman and George Wigg, to Crossman's house in Vincent Square. There Wigg assured them that at least twelve of Callaghan's votes were committed to Wilson, who had, in effect, won the election. At this, Wilson 'raised his glass and proposed a toast to Nye Bevan's memory'.

Wilson, supported by Crossman, had taken Bevan's place on the Shadow Cabinet in 1954, when the latter had resigned on a principle held by both of them. Wilson had actively supported Gaitskell for the Party leadership against Bevan in 1955 and 1956. Wigg had resigned from the Keep Left Group in 1951 out of loyalty to Emmanuel Shinwell and the latter's defence budget, which Bevan opposed. Yet, in a sense, the toast was justified. For without the mantle of Nye, and the deep attachment to Bevan's memory (and to those who had supported him in the past) among the Labour Left, Harold Wilson would never have been able to appeal to the Left as one of their own.

The appeal to the sentimentality of the Left was to serve Harold Wilson even more handsomely in the future. At the 1966 Labour

Party Conference, for instance, at which he tried to explain away
the collapse of all his policies, Wilson turned, at the end of a long,
pedantic speech to quote from a living hero, from Lord Soper,
formerly the Rev. Donald Soper, personally ennobled by the
Prime Minister himself as a mark of Wilson's respect for the
'Nonconformist conscience' of the Labour Left:

At a 'service of dedication' in the crypt chapel of St Stephens
Church, Mary Undercroft, in the Palace of Westminster, Wilson
recalled Soper pronouncing a prayer:

Oh, God, grant us a vision of our land, fair as it might be;
A land of righteousness where none shall wrong his neighbour;
A land of plenty where evil and poverty shall be done away;
A land of brotherhood where all success shall be founded on service, and
  honour shall be given to excellence alone;
A land of peace where order shall not rest on force, but on the love of
  all for the common life and weal;
Bless our efforts to make the vision a living reality;
Inspire and strengthen each one of us that we may give time, thought
  and sacrifice to speed the day of its coming.

When the time comes [Wilson went on] I would want this Government, this Movement, to be judged by not only the British Nation, but
by history, by our success or failure in turning this prayer into a reality.

No one was sick.

The Conference, whose left-wing element had been distinctly
restive throughout Wilson's speech (one incorrigible sectarian had
even been moved to heckle), was silenced. And, to a man, the
delegates rose for the solemn ritual of the standing ovation.

Chapter 11
The Futility of Pragmatism

Harold Wilson's success in the Labour Party before 1966 is due to the same contradiction in his political personality as his failure since then. In a reply to Norman Hunt, in a BBC interview six months before he was elected Premier, Wilson declared:

> My conception of the Prime Minister is that if he is not the managing director, he is, at any rate, and should be, very much a full-time executive chairman.

The business of Government, in other words, was for Wilson similar to that of a private firm, with the Cabinet as members of the Board and the Prime Minister as executive chairman. This was the primary role in which Wilson saw himself. His mission in this role was to increase exports and improve technology; to 'cut out the dead wood' in industry and the civil service and to ensure continuing and permanent economic growth.

Economic growth was the first principle in Wilson's politics both before and after 1964. And from this first principle there flowed a number of demands and priorities which Wilson accepted, tacitly before 1964, openly after 1966. A programme committed to economic growth depended, first, on balancing payments, which in return meant a cut in home demand and a 'shake-out' of labour. It depended on an incomes policy with the accent on wage restraint. It meant increases in profits, and, after devaluation, of prices. It meant putting investment before consumption. It meant an increase in arms sales abroad and the appointment of an arms salesman. It meant a resurgence of nationalist rhetoric, and playing down the importance of international organizations. It meant moving towards freer trade with the rich industrial Western nations either in Europe or the United States. It meant streamlining industry with mergers and monopolies. Logically, too, it meant that welfare programmes and the social services would have to be treated with care. 'An income guarantee,' said the Growthman's Charter, the 1965 National Plan, 'would not contribute towards economic growth' (National Plan, Cmnd 2764, p. 204).

Then there was another Harold Wilson, who told the 1964 Scottish Labour Party at Rothesay and repeated *ad nauseam* until the 1964 General Election:

The Labour Party is a moral crusade or it is nothing. We shall not suffer this Party, on which the hopes of millions depend, to become either a soulless bureaucracy or a vote-dealing Tammany Hall.

Or similarly, as Prime Minister:

In the part of the world I come from, men are very ruggedly equal. The Yorkshire Socialist reacts from poverty not so much because it is a product of inefficiency and a badly run social system, but because it is a crime against God and man (Speech at Newport, 8 September 1967).

Harold Wilson, Yorkshire socialist and Moral Crusader, believed in the 'leavening of humanity'; in multi-racial societies everywhere, in uncompromising attacks on South Africa and Rhodesia, on arms salesmen and private arms manufacture; in opposing American military and financial imperialism in the Far and Middle East and in Latin America; in the United Nations as 'the cornerstone of our foreign policy'; in increasing aid to the underdeveloped countries; in building more houses, hospitals, schools; in improving welfare programmes; in collective bargaining and profits control; in a minimum income guarantee; in the Commonwealth before Europe or America; in tightening monopoly legislation and abolishing cartels.

The contradictions in these two sets of attitudes and demands could, Wilson believed, be resolved either in verbal gymnastics or by drastic state intervention and planning under a Labour Government. Such planning would coordinate with private enterprise, and, where necessary, override it in the interests of efficient *and* humane government.

The two years of Labour Government from March 1966 to March 1968 have seen the death of Harold Wilson, Yorkshire socialist and Moral Crusader. Every one of his priorities have been reversed or abandoned. Racialist minorities in Southern Africa have been appeased. The American Government, with his support, have trebled their fire-power in Vietnam. Programmes for overseas aid, housing, hospital building, school building, a minimum incomes guarantee have been abandoned or slashed. Even the existing welfare services – free health prescriptions, free school milk in secondary schools, sick pay in the first week off work – have been trimmed, or threatened with trimming. Collective bargaining has been replaced by wage restraint. Europe and America have taken precedence to the Commonwealth. Almost every week a new industrial merger has been provoked by the Government and financed by its merchant bank, the Industrial Reorganization Corporation. The Monopolies Commission has sunk into limbo.

Harold Wilson, Growthman and Technocrat, on the other hand, is still there, bruised and almost punch-drunk by balance of payments crises, but mouthing the technological slogans of Scarborough, 1963. Economic growth, the *sine qua non* of his economic policy, has, as yet, not been achieved. Nevertheless, in terms of industrial reorganization and increases in productivity, Wilson has some successes to his name, and will, no doubt, short of further sterling crises, notch up a few more before his time is out. The moral crusade has been abandoned before it could be started, but the technological crusade continues.

In this process, there have been many casualties, of which one of the worst, for Harold Wilson, is his reputation as 'scourge of the Tories'. 'Whatever you say about Harold Wilson, he hates the Tories,' was a common theme among the Labour Left at least until July 1966. Some enthusiasts went further, and described Wilson's attitude towards the Tories as inspired by a genuine class antagonism, based on a theory of class politics.

Wilson's bitterness towards the Tories in the 1950s and early 1960s was no more than a meritocrat's irritation with an incompetent and amateur aristocracy: the cry of the scholarship boy angrily knocking at the bolted door of the bourgeoisie. Wilson was genuinely infuriated by the cocksure arrogance of aristocratic, public-school politicians. Harold Macmillan's predilection for packing his Cabinet with old school friends and in-laws presented an irresistible target to Harold Wilson, who scored on it with almost every major speech, inside and outside Parliament:

We meet the challenge of the modern world with an effete Venetian oligarchy,[1] a Government who themselves reflect the nation's besetting weakness of family connexions and aristocratic recruitment (House of Commons, 18 April 1961).

Such attacks rose to a crescendo with the appointment, in the autumn of 1963, of Lord Home as Prime Minister. This was the last fling of the old aristocratic Tory Party, and everything about the appointment provoked Harold Wilson's contempt and ridicule. A month before Home's appointment, Wilson had attacked his attitude to the United Nations:

Lord Home and the effete establishment, which represents the entire horizon of his life and thought, cannot begin to come to terms with a world and a world organization where the vast majority of nations are not even European. . . .

On Home's appointment, Wilson jibed:

The selection had been through the machinery of an autocratic cabal. I am worried to know how a scion of an effete establishment can understand the scientific revolution. After half a century of democratic advance the whole process has ground to halt with a 14th earl (Speech at Belle Vue, 19 October 1963).

This theme ran through all Wilson's attacks on the Tory Party and upon the industrial establishment which supported the Tories. The crucial distinction, for him, was between gentlemen and players. The joint stock banks, for instance, Wilson once declared, are gentlemen; the merchant banks are players. The brewers were an 'old-established hereditary squirearchy, run very largely by Old Etonians' while the timber industry was run by professional grammar-school boys. The accent was always on 'cutting the dead wood' out of the boardrooms and Ministries and replacing it with men chosen for their ability. Effete, aristocratic

1. Those puzzled by the expression 'Venetian oligarchy' should read their Disraeli: particularly *Sybil*, where the hero exclaims: 'England has been burdened by Dutch finance, a Venetian oligarchy, French wars and a German King!' Indeed, admirers of Harold Wilson's political style would profit from a wide reading of Disraeli. Disraeli's constant references to a 'national idea', and his belief that the working people will believe anything if assaulted by 'One Nation' propaganda and a streamlined public relations machine show that Harold Wilson learned a great deal from those leather-bound volumes of Disraeli, purchased at Oxford with the winnings of the Gladstone Prize.

cabals would then be replaced by dynamic, meritocratic cabals.

There was, in all this, not a hint of class antagonism or class politics. There was never any question of Harold Wilson supporting workers against employers in class confrontation. What worried him was that the distribution of power within the ruling circles was weighted heavily against grammar-school boys; that Macmillan and Home would not have been Prime Minister had they not gone to Eton. The difference was between *caste* bitterness and *class* antagonism. Yet, once again, Wilson's invective against Tory nepotism was sufficiently savage to satisfy the Labour rank and file.

All this came to an end with the election, in August 1965, of Edward Heath as Conservative Party leader. The caste differences between the two Party leaderships immediately vanished. Heath, like Wilson, had been educated at state schools, and had made his way to fame at Oxford from the bottom. Heath entertained the Tory plutocracy in his father's semi-detached in Ramsgate. He was a man of modest, almost puritanical habits, and had nothing in common with an 'effete establishment' or a 'hereditary squirearchy'.

At the outset of his leadership, the sameness in background and approach of the two men did more damage to Edward Heath. The tide was running against his Party and his own breathtaking *gaucherie* helped it along. Yet Wilson's early triumphs against Heath could not disguise for ever the fact that Wilson's main argument against the Tories had been knocked from under him. In the 1966 election campaign Wilson relied on his Party's commitment to full employment and the Welfare State to distinguish him from Edward Heath, but as this commitment was abandoned in Government and as Wilson applied for British membership of the Common Market the real differences vanished.

In his speech to the 1966 Labour Party Conference Wilson referred to the 'main enemy – Conservatism'. The real threat from Conservatism, he explained, was in industry, where employers and workers were not responding quickly enough to the need for technological innovation. Industrial and technological change, he declared, was Labour's main theme.

Likewise the Tories. The 'One Nation' group of back-bench Tories had, as early as 1954, produced a pamphlet entitled *Change*

330 The Politics of Harold Wilson

is our Ally, and in Edward Heath's first speech as leader to a Tory
Party Conference in 1965, he proclaimed that technological and
industrial change was the mainspring of modern Conservatism.

As the classically reformist policies of the Labour Party were
systematically scrapped, so the consensus between the two parties
grew. Genuine arguments between Labour and the Tories became
sporadic and rare. The Conservatives were opposed to socialism,
but as no socialism was being enacted their opposition degenerated into Parliamentary filibuster or racialist opportunism.

Wilson's reaction, as in 1945 to 1951, was to place his faith still
more firmly in the consensus. In April 1967, for instance, he
outlined in a long BBC interview his views on the machinery of
Government:

> I would like to see defence, as far as possible, taken out of politics
> (*Listener*, 13 April 1967).

In 1951, Harold Wilson had resigned from the Labour Government because of excessive defence spending. In 1963 and 1964 as
Leader of the Opposition he had maintained a steady attack on the
'independent nuclear deterrent'. His desire as Prime Minister to
take defence out of politics demonstrated that he had nothing to
offer. So weary was he of failure only two and a half years after
taking power that he would have preferred to take not just defence
but all political issues 'out of politics' and continue with an
administrative Government permanently supported by the
Opposition. As in 1950 and 1951 the refusal of the Opposition to
support even his mildest measures perplexed but did not deflect
him. His keen delight in Parliamentary controversy, demonstrated with such sparkle in the first eighteen months of Labour
Government, was replaced by a silent, sullen introspective
inertia.

The reason for this collapse can be summed up in the two
words with which Wilson sold himself to the Labour Party before
1964: 'pragmatic socialism'. Again and again Wilson explained to
his biographers and his interviewers that he does not hold an
overall view of society. As a pragmatist, he accepts society for what
it is, and as a pragmatic socialist he seeks to work within its
industrial, nationalist and political structure in order 'to end
poverty and advance far beyond the 1945–51 reforms to a much

more real equality'. But because he works within the industrial structure, the reformist demands – for better houses, better schools, better welfare facilities and so on – are made pragmatically, without any overall view of how they can be achieved or who might seek to hinder them. If they can be achieved without jeopardizing growth or exports, they will be. If not, they will be scrapped. For the true pragmatist, that is the end of the argument.

Not surprisingly, therefore, on the rare occasions when Harold Wilson did venture into political theory, demands for ending poverty and assisting welfare played little part in his vision of socialism. In one astonishing passage in a speech which he himself, and most of his erstwhile supporters, regarded as one of his best, Wilson launched himself into a comprehensive definition of socialism.

> Socialism, as I understand it, means applying a sense of purpose to our national life: economic purpose, social purpose and moral purpose. Purpose means technical skill – be it the skill of a manager, a designer, a craftsman, an engineer, a transport worker, a miner, an architect, a nuclear physicist, a doctor, a nurse, a social worker. If you fly the Atlantic in a jet, you want to be sure the pilot knows his job, that he's been trained for it. If you're in hospital, you feel more confident if you know that the surgeon has given his lifetime to fitting himself for his work. Pilot or surgeon: it matters not who his father was, or what school he went to, or who his friends are, yet in Government and in business we are still too often content to accept social qualifications rather than technical ability as the criterion (Speech at Birmingham Town Hall, 19 January 1964, in *The New Britain* (Penguin Books, 1964), pp. 14, 15).

And, in the same vein, three years later:

> In a recent interview, I was asked what, above all, I associated with socialism in this modern age: I answered if there was one word I would use to identify modern socialism it was 'science' (Speech at Daresbury, Cheshire, 17 June 1967).

The sense of purpose, which, in Wilson's dictionary, defines socialism '*means* technical skill' and the proper application of it. Pragmatic socialism is identified *above all* 'with science'. As such it is not in any detail different from pragmatic capitalism. Pragmatic socialists, pragmatic Tories and pragmatic Liberals can, on

Harold Wilson's definition, unite to present a common front to the ideologues of the Left.

And only to the ideologues of the *Left*. For the ideologues on the Right – those of them that understand the system and its changing nature – are concerned, as are the pragmatists, with the most efficient working of the capitalist system. They may on occasions, with Enoch Powell, launch into ideological offensives against planning and the Welfare State. Yet, like Enoch Powell, when they join a Conservative or Labour Cabinet they will not object to the foundation and strengthening of planning councils like NEDC or Incomes Boards like the National Incomes Commission or the Prices and Incomes Board. *Pragmatism is not neutral.* It accepts the existing structure and values of society. Social reforms offered pragmatically, which seek to alter that structure, can, when they conflict with that structure and those values, be pragmatically abandoned. Thus the Wilsonite reforms, offered in a spirit of Yorkshire socialism and in the enthusiasm of a moral crusade, could, because of his pragmatism, be abandoned. Wilson's sentimentality, with which he hypnotized the Left; his emphasis on overseas aid and racial equality and his Donald Soper prayers for a more just, free and equal society were, as he quickly found out, irrelevant, if not hostile, to the need to improve technology and increase productivity. Pragmatism, fortunately, enabled him to abandon sentiment and concentrate on 'efficiency' – that is, efficiency for growth and profit. Before 1964, it enabled him and the Labour Party to overlook the possibility that Labour's meagre reforms would not be permitted in an atmosphere of intensifying capitalist competition, and, after 1964, when the reforms did become impossible, his pragmatism enabled him to abandon them.

The other aspect of Wilson's politics which destroyed his moral crusade was his nationalism. Throughout his life, Wilson has talked about politics in the crudest nationalist terms, and has provided for posterity volumes of Disraelian prose which can be classified under the general heading of 'making Britain great' or 'the spirit of Dunkirk'. Whether he is railing against the Americans, the Germans, the Japanese or the French; whether he is justifying a high tariff on cotton or an export subsidy; whether he is explaining deflation or devaluation or the technological revolution, the supreme justification is that of 'discovering a new greatness for Britain' of 'standing alone as we did in 1940' of 'recapturing the spirit of the merchant venturers of former years'. Harold Wilson's nationalism is an extension of his pragmatism. The world is divided into nations, competing against each other to the detriment of all. The pragmatist does not seek to solve this problem by ending the international competition, but by working within it and utilizing stale patriotic rhetoric to justify it. Naturally, perhaps, he finds himself, as his political opponents were before him, trapped in the rhetoric and the competition until he is aping his political opponents.

To place the responsibility for the collapse of the reformist policies of the Labour Party solely on the shoulders of Harold Wilson is frivolously to dabble in personalities. The suggestion that some other member of the Labour Cabinet would, as Prime Minister, have transformed the political history of the 1964–8 Labour Government is frantic absurdity. Wilson's 'mistakes' – that is errors of judgement brought on in his personal case by an obsession with public relations, a coterie of mediocrities, paralysing indecision and personal sentimentality – have been only marginal in dictating the course of events during this period, and his personal faults, errors and idiosyncrasies would only have been replaced by others, even more grotesque, from Brown, Callaghan, Jenkins, Crosland or Gunter. The casualty of the 1964–8 experiences is not the personality of Harold Wilson, nor even, necessarily, his personal reputation, but the pragmatic, nationalist politics which he represented and which won such widespread support in the Labour Party before 1966. The lack of a comprehensive social purpose in *Industry and Society*, and *Signposts for the Sixties*, both written by Wilson, is the real cause of the developments since 1966 and the resulting despair in the Labour movement.

This despair is not only psychological. It has resulted in the collapse of the traditional political institutions of the Labour Movement, which was sharply demonstrated in late April 1968, when Enoch Powell made a speech in Birmingham, calling, in flamboyantly racialist language, for further restrictions on immigration. The speech had the immediate effect of inspiring large sections of workers to strike in its support. Several thousand

London dockers, for instance, voted for a day's unofficial strike and a 'Back Enoch' march to the House of Commons. In this situation, the traditional Labour movement and its institutions were impotent. The Labour Party itself did not utter. Trade-union executives contented themselves with passing resolutions. The Communist Party reprinted *Moring Star* editorials as leaflets. *Tribune* shouted emptily. Only the Young Liberals, student organizations and 'sectarians' succeeded in mounting counter-demonstrations to the Powellite menace. The organizational bankruptcy of the Labour institutions could be contrasted with the Suez crisis eleven years previously when, with the working class split on the issue, the Labour Party succeeded in organizing massive 'Law not War' rallies all over the country.

Harold Wilson's pragmatism, and its failure, had left a theo-retical and organizational vacuum in the Labour movement, and it is upon the ability to fill that vacuum that the future of British socialism depends. A new socialist theory was never more essential. Crucial questions, allowed to languish in the hope that Parlia-mentary power would erase them, must now be asked and answered as urgently as ever. Do we live in a class society? If so, how is it to be altered? Are Parliamentary institutions sufficiently democratic to establish socialism and preserve it? Is the State necessarily an instrument of socialism? If not, are Russia, China, Eastern Europe in any sense socialist? Is the struggle for socialism in the industrial countries futile, and can socialists afford to con-centrate their efforts on the nationalist 'socialism' of the Third World?

Let us start with the simplest one: is our modern industrial society in any genuine sense, a class society? Is its dominant feature the exploitation and control of the many by the few, of the vesting of economic, social and cultural control in the hands of a small, wealthy minority?

Even in terms of wealth distribution the essential inequality of modern British society has not altered greatly in the past hundred years. Two per cent of Britain's population own more than half the nation's private wealth. The myth that incomes are growing more and more equally has been destroyed: 'The tendency towards the reduction of inequality in the distribution of personal income seems to have come to an end by 1957,' wrote Mr R. J.

Nicholson, in an article which demonstrated that the 'wealth gap' was widening, and that the rate of growth of rent, dividend and interest since 1957 has been higher than similar growth rates in wages and salaries.[1]

While the situation in wealth distribution has not greatly changed, the control of society has passed into the hands of fewer and fewer men. Half capital spending in manufacturing industry – and a third of the labour force – is controlled by 180 companies. Four years ago the same companies controlled only a third of capital expenditure. In ten years' time, their share of the market and the labour force may well have increased to two-thirds. All over the industrial world, the trend is towards monopoly and merger, and an increasingly tight control over the lives of workers. In the crucial field of propaganda, more than 90 per cent of our national daily and Sunday newspapers are in the hands of five men, all of them in ideology and investment wedded to the industrial Establishment; all of them in varying degrees anxious to propagate capitalist views and capitalist aspirations. The founding of Independent Television in 1954 has established a new form of British Television monopoly, where power is vested almost entirely in rich businessmen and in advertising. All over industry, commerce, propaganda, entertainment, publishing, banking, education and even religion the trend is towards monopoly, increasingly uncontrolled by representative or democratic organizations. The society in which we live is not only still a class society. The gap in wealth and control between the classes is widening with each economic development. The meritocracy of Harold Wilson makes no difference to these developments. The decline of the tenacious aristocratic element within the ruling class, and its replacement by rich meritocrats, equally, if not more, dedicated to preserving inequality, class divisions and 'business ethics' merely updates class society, and prolongs it.

The socialist who accepts that class society exists must seek to change it: to break up the divisions not only by redistributing

1. *Lloyds Bank Review*, January 1967, pp. 11–22. John Saville, in *Socialist Register*, 1965, argued that the post-war movement towards equality ended in 1948. A comprehensive account of the class inequalities in every aspect of British social life is given by Robin Blackburn in the opening essay of *The Incompatibles: Trade Union Militancy and the Consensus*, Penguin Books, 1967.

wealth but by placing the control of society into the hands of the majority. But how?

The Labour pragmatist has his answer pat. Elect a Labour Government, staff the civil service with men and women trained in economics, preferably at Oxford or Cambridge, 'manipulate demand' and insure growth by raising and lowering taxation, and, internationally, insure against periodic balance of payments deficits by offsetting deficits on balance of payments and moderating surpluses. Thus each economy grows permanently, balancing respective surpluses and deficits, and, by redistributive taxation, ensuring better prosperity and equality for the masses.

Almost all post-war experience is set against this model. Despite the huge concentration of 'state-owned' industries and the proliferation of 'state planning' organizations like Neddy and the little Neddies, the Prices and Incomes Board and the Industrial Reorganization Corporation, business has not been planned. During the two post-war Labour administrations, Attlee's in 1945–51 and Wilson's in 1964–8, the pretensions and promises of planning were abandoned for the free market. If anything, the degree of planning has been less under Labour than under the Conservatives, though planning has been the *sine qua non* of Labour's economic policy in Opposition. In both administrations the Labour promises of direct, purposive State intervention in private industry were diluted into state representation on some Boards, into finance to lubricate mergers and into wage restraint. The development corporations and regional planning councils have provided much-needed coordination in research, training and problems of geographic location. In no sense have they planned or intervened against the general will of private industry. Only very rarely has industry felt it necessary to intervene in politics, as it did in 1950 and 1951, when, with a skilfully timed flight of capital and a mammoth propaganda campaign, it helped to hound Labour from office.

Internationally, the economic and financial scene has been even less influenced by the dedicated Keynesians in the Central Banks. Conference after conference to discuss international liquidity and to coordinate balance of payments deficits have been thwarted by the conflicting pulls of national policies and national aspirations. The United Nations Conference on Trade and Development, established with high hopes in 1964 in an attempt to force international action to assist underdeveloped countries with international price agreements, has been effectively nullified by the stubborn selfishness of the rich countries' 'national interest'. As I write (April 1968) the Central Bank leaders have just finished meetings in Washington and Stockholm in a desperate attempt to stave off assaults on the stability of the dollar and the pound from France, South Africa, Eastern Europe and other financial enemies of the Anglo-Saxon world. They may succeed for a time in stemming the flood of speculation. But they are hardly nearer agreement on the delicate Keynesian model described above than they were at the end of the last world war.

And why? Because the pragmatist's answer to the problems posed by capitalist society, though mathematically unimpeachable and logically sound, overlook the realities of class society. Faced with ten men, one with £91 the other nine with £1 each, the Labour pragmatist quickly arrives at a solution: share the money out, £10 per man. When the man with £91 baulks at the suggestion, when he refuses to give up his money, when he buys newspapers to propagate his 'right' to the money and hires gunmen to defend it, the pragmatist is shocked, perplexed and impotent.

Parliament, he argues, will enforce the transfer. Given a good Labour majority, committed to gradual reform, its Parliamentary power will, if necessary, clobber the businessmen and the 'speculators' into line. Harold Wilson summed up this attitude in an interview with Anthony Sampson, in January 1965, only three months after becoming Prime Minister:

The Establishment can make noises, drinking gins and tonics at their New Year's Eve parties, but that doesn't have much effect on politics. Politics is a question of power, and power has been transferred. Whatever people say, at an election, the old Establishment only have one vote each at the end of the day. So has each engineer and miner in my constituency (*Anatomy of Britain Today*, Anthony Sampson, Hodder, 1965).

According to this argument, universal suffrage to a regular parliament is equivalent to the power of the people. This has been the assumption of reformers ever since universal suffrage was achieved. It is the essence of all Labour Party policies since the

Party came to power, and only occasionally, as with Sir Stafford Cripps in the 1930s, has it even been questioned.

Yet Parliament represents only one form of representation: by geography. In Parliamentary democracy, the people are represented solely as inhabitants of areas. They are not represented, as Wilson implied, as miners or engineers or housewives; but as Smethwickians or Huytonians or citizens of West Fife. The Labour Member of Parliament, therefore, does not, in Parliament, represent labour in any form. He represents his constituency: all the people of his constituency – employers, workers, Catholics, Protestants, Rotarians, trade unionists, restaurateurs, and dustmen. The more marginal his seat, the more devoted his attention towards each sectional interest in his constituency. If he does his representative job properly, he must represent everyone and no one at the same time.

Again, Parliamentary elections are well spaced apart. If things go according to plan, an average man votes eight or nine times in his lifetime. In the long periods in between, the levers of industrial power and the organs of propaganda are left entirely in the hands of proprietors and executives who have not been elected by anyone. They are unrepresentative, yet their function is wholly concerned with issues upon which, even in conventional political language, people should be represented. The employer who sacks 5,000 men cannot be removed or called to account for his decision by anyone except his own Board of Directors. The newspaper proprietor who prints unashamed racialist propaganda, dressed up with pornography to make his paper sell, is equally unaccountable. One man, one vote is, apparently, the be-all and end-all of democracy. One man may own six newspapers, two television stations, six factories. Another may earn £20 a week, £7 of which goes in rent and £13 of which has to make do for his family. Each has one vote. But are they equally represented in society?

The ruthlessness of class society, the weakness of Parliamentary democracy and the ease with which its democratic arteries can be blocked means that Labour Governments have found it increasingly difficult, if not impossible, to ensure meaningful reforms for the working people who elect them to power. Yet even in the cases when social democratic regimes *have* threatened to enact reforms which could seriously tip the class balance, the men in charge of industry and finance have not been slow to support entirely un-democratic, extra-Parliamentary parties and groups in order to vitiate the reforms.

The 1930s are rich with examples: in Vienna, in 1934, a social-democratic local authority shuffled uncertainly towards reforms. The reply from capital was instant, violent and unparliamentary, and elections were postponed in Austria for more than a decade. In Spain in 1936, a Liberal Parliament was assaulted and defeated by a Fascist revolution, financed by Spanish capital. As a result, there have been no genuine elections or trade unions in Spain for thirty years and probably more.

All this, of course, to commit the unforgivable crime (in Fabian eyes) of 'harking back to the thirties', when every issue was, in hindsight, clear cut and obvious (although of course the arguments between Left and Right in the Labour movement raged as fiercely then as ever). But the experience in the later 1960s has been even more sinister than in the 1930s. In France, for instance, President De Gaulle, having established himself in an almost impregnable position with a basically anti-Parliamentary constitution, cheerfully announced that if the Parliamentary elections did not go his way, he would ignore Parliament. More seriously, in Greece in April 1967, a band of colonels seized political power, indefinitely postponed elections, broke the trade unions and disbanded all left-wing political organizations, imprisoning and torturing their leaders. The reasons for their actions were clearly stated by the colonels. The forthcoming Parliamentary elections, they feared, would be won by a social-democratic/liberal Government, which could pave the way for 'intolerable' social reform. Accordingly, after a week or two of peevish doubt, the leaders of the Greek industries and banks registered their support for the new regime.

In contrast to what it would have been in the thirties, the reaction to these two developments has been almost total apathy through-out the so-called 'free world' (and throughout the Communist world for that matter). The new regime has been aided and fêted by the American Government, recognized by Britain, France and Russia. Sustained protest has been confined, once more, to the 'sectarians'. The less people care about Parliament, the less they care about its abolition.

Indeed the irrelevance and impotence of Parliament are the dominating political features of the post-war industrial world. Poll after poll in Europe and America demonstrates that the majority of voters do not see any real difference between the contesting parties, nor do they see any connexion between their vote and their daily lives.

And small wonder. For the most popular form of Government in Western Europe is the coalition. In Germany, there is a 'Grand' Coalition between Christian Democrats and a totally desiccated Social Democrat Party. Italy, Holland, Belgium are all ruled by coalitions in which 'socialists' participate. In America, the two big political parties have long since agreed to confine their differences to personalities. According to a standard pollster's joke, which had the ring of authenticity, J. F. Kennedy beat Richard Nixon in the American Presidential Election of 1960 because the shade of his suit showed up better against the television background. Thus the crucial floating vote was swayed. The personalization of American politics has swept through Europe, engulfing all but the most extreme. The contradictions and hypocrisies of capitalism have been adopted wholesale by Parliamentary politicians of all parties.

The bankruptcy of Parliamentary politics is not merely the result of the alienation and personal corruption of Members of Parliament. It is the inevitable result of the growth of national industrial monopoly, of vast industrial concerns which, within a nation, can act independently of political pressure groups and forces. No longer is it necessary to fight competitors within a national Parliament. Competitors today are more likely to be international, and the competition within a nation is likely to have been abolished by monopoly.

Intelligible socialist theory today is impossible without the recognition of class society and of the impotence of Parliamentary institutions to change it. The recognition of both leads inevitably to a clash with another area of the accepted dogma of British Labour: the role of the State.

As is shown in the preceding chapters, one of Harold Wilson's most consistent political themes has been the importance of the State in directing or assisting the economy. The emphasis switched from direction to assistance as Wilson moved from Opposition to office. Yet his stressing of the State won him allies in the Keynesian Right and in the Tribunite Left, even when it became apparent that the state 'interference' envisaged was not in the remotest sense interventionist. It was this obsession with the State which enabled coal, railways and other service industries in 1945 to 1951 to be placed under the bureaucratic control of state boards almost without protest. The miners, indeed, celebrated coal nationalization with the cry: 'The Mines Belong to Us' – a proposition from which they were soon disenchanted. So powerful was the call to nationalization and state activity in industry that all wings of the Labour Party could be fobbed off with vague promises of 'state control of the commanding heights' without even opening discussions as to the democratic nature of that control.

State ownership and state control became identified with socialism. 'The *socialist remedy*,' wrote a young crusader in the late 1930s, 'should be accepted in regard to industries and services where it is obvious that private enterprise has exhausted its social usefulness or where the general welfare of the economy requires that certain basic industries and services need now to be conducted in the light of broader social considerations than the profit motive provides'.

The young crusader was Harold Macmillan, writing in his book *The Middle Way*.[1] This theme – that the state should nationalize unprofitable industries – was eagerly pursued by Macmillan's admirer, Harold Wilson, whose clever rhetoric about state ownership and control before 1964 convinced *Tribune* that 'revisionism had left the agenda'.

The truth, however, is that for the workers in the industry concerned and for socialists in general the fact of state ownership, state control or state surveillance makes little if any difference. In many instances, in fact, the bureaucratic controls make life even more intolerable. Certainly, nationalization of this or that industry in itself, as has been manifestly displayed in every one of the nationalized industries, makes no difference to the overall direction and power-structure of society.

1. In the 1945 General Election *The Middle Way* was re-published in full by the Westminster Conservative Association, and distributed among the electorate in order to prove that Labour's nationalization proposals had been stolen from the Tories!

The 'state-hypnosis' of socialists has not been confined to Britain. The notion that socialism and state ownership of industry were synonymous was primarily responsible for the widespread, if not universal, attraction for socialists over the last forty years of the existence of state-owned industry throughout Russia, and later throughout Eastern Europe and China.

It is in this instance that the power of state hypnosis is most apparent. In Russia since 1928 – the first year of the first of Stalin's five-year plans – in China and Eastern Europe since 1948, there has been no vestige, not even a pretence, of democratic structure nor of popular representation either by geography or occupation. The countries have been ruled by unelected bureaucracies, loose and fragmented in China, ruthlessly centralized and controlled in Russia and Eastern Europe. Industry and production have been regimented on military lines, leaving no scope for genuine trade-union activity let alone workers' control. The Soviets established by the revolution in 1917, the 'workers' control' proclaimed by Lenin as the 'main aim' of the revolution, have vanished. In their place are bureaucracy, militarization, rigged elections, and, perhaps most significantly, a widening of the gap both in wealth, property and inheritance between the controllers and the controlled.

Yet the *forms* of state property, the vesting in the state of legal titles to the ownership of production and distribution, have strangled socialist theory for fifty years and more. The Communist Parties of Western Europe, particularly in France, and an assorted, numerous band of fellow-travellers everywhere have defined the bureaucratic horrors of the East as 'socialist'. Less disastrously, some of the finest socialist theoreticians of the age have succumbed to the statist disease. Isaac Deutscher, one of the greatest, if not the greatest Marxist theoretician of our time, though he bitterly attacked the Russian bureaucracy and its Stalinist heritage, refused to accept that the state managers of Russian and Eastern European industry performed the same function as the ruling class in confessedly capitalist countries:

The privileged groups of Soviet society are not united by any comparable ties. They are in command of industry as our business managers are; and they exercise command in an absolute manner. But behind our business managers there are the shareholders, especially the big ones.

Soviet managers have not only to acknowledge that all shares belong to the nation, but to profess that they act on the nation's behalf, and especially on behalf of the working class (*The Unfinished Revolution*, Isaac Deutscher, OUP, 1957, p. 56).

Precisely the same justification of capitalism is given in the Western capitalist countries by big shareholders, managers and the rest. The owners of wealth argue that their wealth is that 'of the nation'. National language and national unity have always been used in hypocritical justification of inequality in the West, as in the East. Similarly, the argument of capital in the West, and in Russia before 1917, was always that class society benefits the workers. Factory owners and big shareholders in the West have always argued that capitalism is in the best interests of the workers. Moreover, as Crosland showed in *The Future of Socialism*, the relevance of shareholders to the decisions and directions of capital is decreasing rapidly.

Yet the signs are that even this ultimate justification of the view that Russia and Eastern Europe are in some sense more socialist than the West – state control and direction of industry – is vanishing with the progress of the Comecon economies. Crude, Stalinist 'planning', that is the central provision of 'targets' upon which industry sets its sights, is appropriate only to a primeval industrial economy where success depends first upon the growth of massive basic industries: coal, iron and steel, heavy engineering, shipbuilding, armaments. The simple, if strenuous business of achieving 'norms' laid down at the centre meets the immediate needs of this sort of economy more effectively than any other. And the greater the centralization, the militarization of labour and the lack of political protest from workers, writers and intellectuals, the greater the economic growth.

Yet as the 'heavy industry' economies develop, as they become increasingly dependent on advanced technology and the production of consumer goods, where quality is at least as important as quantity, crude, centralized state 'target' planning becomes less and less effective. Other criteria apart from meeting the target have to be used to assess industrial and economic success. 'Return on capital' from an individual factory or group of factories becomes more important than meeting the target. 'Initiative' at manager level becomes more important than accuracy from the central state planning authority. A whole host of complexities involving skilled labour, accurate draughtsmanship and consumer choice arise where before they could be suppressed in the demand for more and more uncomplicated production.

One by one, the Russian and Eastern European economies have been plagued by these new problems, and professional economists have emerged from the universities clamouring for different industrial and economic criteria. Professor Liberman, of Kharkov University, Russia, for instance argued that his country will commit economic suicide unless she harnesses her economic bureaucracy and concentrates more on 'return on capital' (the word 'profit', for obvious reasons, is skilfully avoided). Requirement for a more diverse economy was the main reason for the hiving-off of Yugoslavia from the Soviet bloc in 1948. The generous American aid received since by that country proves that the American Government at least is delighted with its progress and its methods of achieving it. In Hungary and Poland in 1956 the rigidity of the economy provoked a reaction which involved masses of workers and whose implications were too dangerously revolutionary. The revolution in Hungary was smashed with Russian tanks, but the economic changes demanded by 'moderate' academics were hastily put into effect. More recently, and perhaps more importantly, the upheaval in Czechoslovakia, which came to a climax in April 1968, involving the deposing of the old-guard Stalinist leadership, was specifically created by middle-class, intellectual dissatisfaction with Stalinist, centralized techniques.

The distinguished Professor Sik, a Thomas Balogh of Czechoslovakia, argued at packed middle-class meetings that the economy had to be loosened from the state strait-jacket to permit a freer 'redeployment' (Sik uses the actual word again and again) and a flow of capital. Without involving any of the working-class rank and file, the Czech Government moved towards the new managerial capitalism of the West.

East and West of the 'Iron Curtain', doctrinaire state and private-enterprise orthodoxy is giving way more and more to modern managerial techniques. Common to both sides are increasing chauvinism, increasing pragmatism, increasing bureaucracy and increasing exploitation of the many by the few. For socialists, the similarities are infinitely more crucial than the differences. What matters are not the legal titles to property and forms of ownership but the actual relationship between human beings.

The futility of Stalinism has a similar root as the futility of Wilsonian pragmatism – 'state-obsession'. The failure of both calls for a new approach and new demands: for democracy, not bureaucracy; for workers' control and workers' power, not workers' regimentation by and absorption into the state machine.

Obsession with 'socialism' in the East distorted socialist theory for three decades. In the 1950s and 1960s it was replaced by another obsession, equally distorting. Many socialists, sickened by the sterility of social-democratic politics in Western Europe and America, turned their eyes outwards to what is now known as the Third World. If Western capitalism had to some extent solved its internal crises, there was no disputing the 'increasing pauperization' of the 'underdeveloped countries' and the growing gap between the world's rich and poor countries. These socialists began to place their hope for revolutionary ferment and upheaval in the Third World. The Bandung Conference in 1955 of so-called 'neutralist' nations filled them with the hope that a new force arising out of the underdeveloped countries would begin to re-shape the ugly pattern of the Cold War. The phrase 'positive neutralism' became fashionable. The five main leaders at Bandung – Sukarno of Indonesia, Nehru of India, Tito of Yugoslavia, Nkrumah of Ghana and Nasser of Egypt – became the standard-bearers of a new non-aligned, non-nuclear force which, with its power at the United Nations, would bludgeon the Great Powers into progressive policies. For a short time Ben Bella, leader of the new independent Algeria, compelled the attention of Western socialists. The Cuban revolution in 1959 provided them with an even more romantic leadership in Fidel Castro and his lieutenant, Che Guevara. The war in Vietnam elevated the President of North Vietnam, Ho Chi Minh, to a position not just as leader of the defensive, national movement against American imperialism but as standard-bearer of revolution throughout the world. Similarly, ancient Marxists, disgruntled with 'revisionism' in Russia, turned their attention even further East – to the more familiar Stalinism of Mao Tse Tung.

The attractions for Western socialists of these new heroes were innumerable. To start with, they were in power, and, for however brief a period, could shape events. They were far removed from the sterile politics of Western social democracy. Their problems were refreshingly new, intellectually invigorating. The argument about nationalization in Britain could be replaced by the task of constructing cooperative farms, and the sordid manoeuvrings at the TUC could be forgotten at a Cultural Congress in Havana. The Third World opened up opportunities for vicarious revolutionary fervour which occupied many Western socialists in the 1950s and 1960s to the exclusion of developments nearer home.

Yet, one by one, the Gods failed. Sukarno sank in personal corruption and a military coup. Likewise, Nkrumah, Ben Bella and countless other African political leaders. An ugly combination of the American Central Intelligence Agency and the Bolivian Communist Party quickly annihilated Che Guevara's guerilla movement in Bolivia and murdered Guevara. It is hard to imagine that an isolated Cuba or an independent Vietnam will be able to survive economic suffocation by the industrial countries on both sides of the 'Iron Curtain', and Mao's China is now paralysed by civil war and class conflict, her schools and universities drained for months on end in a grotesque charade entitled 'Cultural Revolution'.

'Positive neutralism' is a non-existent force. With the Sino-Soviet dispute, and the rapid changes in Cold War alignment, 'non-alignment' is no longer relevant. Even the banning of Communist China from United Nations membership gets more support each year from former advocates of positive neutralism.

The Third World is hopelessly imprisoned in its own impoverishment. One hundred and fifty years of plunder and the new imperialism of 'aid and trade' cannot be gainsaid by mere political independence or by romantic rhetoric. 'Increasing pauperization' in the Third World will not lead to socialist or even neutralist revolution. It will lead in a downward spiral to still further disillusionment and apathy. The hopes for the Third World, and for world socialism, must be placed on change and revolution in the industrial world.

Nor is the situation there as hopeless as many of the more pessimistic Fidelistas imagine. If the traditional political institutions have pragmatically deteriorated, the will to resist the onslaughts of capitalism has increased. Twenty years of full employment and economic growth have produced not only an impatience with the sterility and meaninglessness of traditional politics, but also a confidence and a refusal to be pushed around which never existed in the 1930s. With the trade-union leaders divorced from their members, 'unofficial' activity, under the more direct democracy of the shop steward, has increased in militancy tenfold. Tenants' committees have proved themselves infinitely more prepared to do battle with landlords and local authorities than before the war. Students' organizations, particularly in the United States and in Germany, have developed a militancy and a campaigning fervour which is rooted for the most part in a libertarian and egalitarian socialism. Finally, perhaps most important, the American Negroes will no longer tolerate the degradation of modern capitalism, and they are fighting against it. The resistance overall is fragmented, unattached to the traditional political or trade-union institutions. But its militancy and its potential if linked by a common socialist purpose is beyond question.[1]

A hundred years ago, Karl Marx baldly stated the alternative for humanity: socialism or barbarism. In an age where two-thirds of the world's people grow increasingly poorer and where the other third spends as much as the 'poor world' produces in the manufacture of increasingly refined and devastating means of destruction, the barbarism is always imminent. The urgency of creating a new, unsentimental, libertarian socialism out of the ashes of Harold Wilson's pragmatism cannot be overstated.

1. The fact that the paragraph was written before the events in France in the second half of May 1968 speaks for itself.

More about Penguins

Penguin Book News, which appears every month, contains details of all the new books issued by Penguins as they are published. From time to time it is supplemented by *Penguins in Print*, which is a complete list of all books published by Penguins which are in print. (There are nearly three thousand of these.)

A specimen copy of *Penguin Book News* will be sent to you free on request, and you can become a subscriber for the price of the postage – 3s for a year's issues (including the complete lists). Just write to Dept EP, Penguin Books Ltd, Harmondsworth, Middlesex, enclosing a cheque or postal order, and your name will be added to the mailing list.

Some other books published by Penguins are described on the following pages.

Note: *Penguin Book News* and *Penguins in Print* are not available in the U.S.A. or Canada

Matters of Principle
Labour's Last Chance

Tyrrell Burgess, Peter Calvocoressi, John Grieve Smith,
Michael Lipton, John Rex, Dudley Seers, John White

A vital factor in the Labour victories of 1964 and 1966 was
the votes of millions of men and women who believed that
a Labour government could and would alter British society
according to certain principles in which they believed.

Over the last four years the government has disenchanted
this vital section of the electorate by trimming principles
to conventional expediencies.

The authors of this book are academics (or on the edge of
the academic world), but they have set out to represent the
disappointment of the many disaffected Labour voters like
themselves. Their chapters deal with the general record of
the Labour government, Britain's international role, aid
and the developing countries, education, race, and the
economy. Each author – in his own subject – has posed
and tried to answer the same questions: What has been the
Labour Government's record? Where has it failed? What
ought it to do, and what could it realistically do, in the
remaining two years to make constructive change and
banish some of the deep scepticism it has generated in the
minds of thinking people?

These questions will be crucial to the health of British
Socialism between now and the next General Election.
The next two years will indeed be Labour's last chance.
All the contributors to this Penguin Special are agreed in
their conclusion: solutions can only be found by a return
to certain basic principles.

Another Penguin Special by Paul Foot

Immigration and Race in British Politics

Since 'the colour problem' crashed into British politics
with the Smethwick result in 1964's General Election, race
relations in Britain have steadily deteriorated.

Although colour is a new problem in British politics, this
book shows that racial differences arising from large-scale
immigration have in the past been exploited for party
advantage but with disastrous results. Paul Foot deals in
detail with the long campaign at Smethwick which gave
rise to the present explosive situation. He examines what
he calls 'the chauvinism, cynicism, and neglect' of the
Conservative Party's attitude to immigration from the
Commonwealth, and exposes the strange somersaults of
Labour Party policy. Written with passion and scepticism
Immigration and Race in British Politics calls for an end to
sloppy thinking and vicious propaganda which could well
present Britain with a racial heritage of American
proportions.